Wissenschaftliche Untersuchungen
zum Neuen Testament · 2. Reihe

Begründet von Joachim Jeremias und Otto Michel
Herausgegeben von
Martin Hengel und Otfried Hofius

19

Suffering and the Spirit

An Exegetical Study of II Cor. 2:14–3:3 within the
Context of the Corinthian Correspondence

by

Scott J. Hafemann

J. C. B. Mohr (Paul Siebeck) Tübingen 1986

CIP-Kurztitelaufnahme der Deutschen Bibliothek

Hafemann, Scott J.:
Suffering and the spirit: an exeget. study of II Cor. 2:14 – 3:3 within the context
of the Corinthian correspondence /
by Scott J. Hafemann.
– Tübingen: Mohr, 1986.
   (Wissenschaftliche Untersuchungen zum Neuen Testament: Reihe 2; 19)
   ISBN 3-16-144973-8
   ISSN 0340-9570

NE: Wissenschaftliche Untersuchungen zum Neuen Testament / 02

© 1986 by J. C. B. Mohr (Paul Siebeck), P. O. Box 2040, D-7400 Tübingen.

Printed by Gulde-Druck GmbH in Tübingen; bound by Heinrich Koch KG in Tübingen.

Printed in Germany.

To Debara
my partner in everything

ACKNOWLEDGEMENTS

In its present form this work is an abridged version of my doctoral
dissertation, which was accepted in January, 1985 by the protestant faculty of theology of Eberhard-Karls-Universität Tübingen. In the course
of my graduate studies in Tübingen I have incurred a deep debt of gratitude to so many people whom God used in various ways to make it possible for my family and me to undertake and complete this venture. Among
them I would like to thank especially my parents, Jack and Gin Hafemann,
and my in-laws, Harley and Nancy Jones, for their constant support and
"care-packages" which met so many needs; our friends Eric Tanquist, Tom
Varno, Tom and Julie Steller, John and Nöel Piper and Charlie and Debbie
Cosgrove, all of whom played vital roles in our lives during this time
with their friendship and support (at times even financial); the
Hausens, who helped us in many practical ways during our stay in
Tübingen; Frau Kienle, for her friendliness and assistance in the office, and Frau Stuhlmacher, who together with the entire Stuhlmacher
family, opened their home to us and made our last year in Tübingen un-
forgettable by their warmth and kindness to us.

I would also like to express my sincere appreciation to Rotary International for the fellowship which enabled us to spend a year of study
in Jerusalem, to Freundeskreis des Goethe-Instituts Blaubeuren for the
scholarship which helped pay for language school and to Professor
Otfried Hofius (Dekan at that time) and the protestant faculty of the
University of Tübingen for the scholarship they granted me which made
it possible to remain in Tübingen until I was finished.

Five of my teachers also deserve my special thanks: Dr. John Piper,
for his initial encouragement and personal interest in me as an under-
graduate student, not to mention all I have learned from him academi-
cally and personally; Professor Daniel Fuller, for his passion in pursuit of the truth, which has been a role model for me; Dr. Robert
Guelich, for his support and confidence in me and for recommending me
to the faculty in Tübingen and Professor Otto Betz for the many times he
encouraged me with his questions and interest in my work. I owe my
deepest debt of gratitude to Professor Peter Stuhlmacher, who not only
gave me the opportunity to study under his guidance as my "Doctor-
Father", but also gave of himself continually to help me in more ways

than I can list here by taking a genuine interest in my work and family far beyond what a graduate student expects and allowing me to work as his assistant while writing my thesis. His professional, scholarly, and personal life have all been a great example to me of what scholarship is all about. Moreover, whatever strengths this work might have are due to my awareness that it would be read by him.

The publication of this work at this time is only possible because of the support I have received from Dr. Richard Stanislaw, Dean of Taylor University. His help in defraying the typing costs and in hiring students to assist me in the arduous tasks of proofreading and indexing have made an otherwise unbearable load for a new teacher bearable. Thanks go to Amy Smith, Melissa Resch, Lorne Mook, Mark Brown and Shari Ehresman in this regard. A special word of thanks is also due Kurt Symanzik, my teaching assistant, for his careful work in checking the Greek texts and help in compiling the index of passages cited. I also wish to thank Tammie Byrnes and Mrs. Julia Hill, our department secretaries, for the extra work they have done. Frau Susanne Fottner also deserves my heartfelt thanks for her fine work in typing and correcting the manuscript.

Finally, I wish to thank Professors Martin Hengel and Otfried Hofius for accepting the work in their series, WUNT.

The book is dedicated to my wife, Debara. Everyone who knows me knows how much she has supported me in this project and how much I owe to her and her commitment to our life together.

January 2nd, 1986   Scott Hafemann
Upland, Indiana
U.S.A.

CONTENTS

Introduction
THE PURPOSE AND METHOD OF THE STUDY

> All historical writing and research
> must begin with first a sense of wonder
> and then a clearly formulated question.[1]

It was never my intention when I began this project to devote a full-
length study to the seven verses which now form the heart of this investigation into Paul's self-understanding as an apostle of Jesus Christ.
Rather, my original focus was on the letter/Spirit contrast found and
developed in II Cor. 3:6ff., to which II Cor. 2:14-3:3 seemed merely to
give an introduction of lesser significance. Like most commentators,
therefore, I planned simply to write an obligatory chapter on this text
in anticipation of the more weighty passage beginning with 3:6. But in
time I came to realize that because the questions raised by Paul's argument in 2:14-3:3 were themselves of such magnitude and importance for
our understanding of Paul's view of his apostolic ministry, the letter/
Spirit contrast itself could only be properly understood once this wider
context had been thoroughly mapped out. More specifically, the need to
devote a full-length study to an investigation of Paul's thought in
2:14-3:3 became apparent when a preliminary look at the meaning of
θριαμβεύειν in 2:14a and the point of Paul's argument in 2:17 led to
a new understanding of the subject under discussion in this passage. For
it soon became clear that II Cor. 2:14-3:3, being part of the "theological heart" of II Corinthians, is both a thesis-like compendium of
Paul's self-conception as an apostle, as well as a classic presentation
of his corresponding apologetic for the authority and validity of his
apostolic ministry. Hence, this study attempts to investigate this self-
understanding and apologetic as the important first step toward understanding the theological and hermeneutical issues raised by Paul's subsequent discussion in II Cor. 3:4-18. For it is imperative that Paul's
reflections concerning the letter and the Spirit be understood within
the larger context in which they are found. Thus, having investigated
II Cor. 2:14-3:3, I am now writing a second work which takes up where
this study ends by investigating II Cor. 3:4-4:6. In it, besides exe-

---

1 Norman F. Cantor, *Medieval History, The Life and Death of a Civilization*,
1969[2], p.1.

geting II Cor. 3:4ff. against its relevant Old Testament backdrop, I
will also provide the *Traditionsgeschichte* necessary to substantiate
the thesis here set forth in chapter three concerning the allusion to
Moses in II Cor. 2:17. Finally, I also hope to draw out the implications of these two studies for our understanding of the historical situation in Corinth at the time of the writing of I and II Corinthians,
especially the age-old problem of the identity of Paul's opponents and
the nature of their teaching.

The study now before us, however, is an *exegetical* one. I emphasize
"exegetical" because the questions asked and pursued in this work, despite their diverse nature, all seek to understand the meaning and significance of Paul's argument as unfolded in the various texts analyzed.
The "method" employed, therefore, consists of asking the simple questions of interpretation necessary to follow the train of thought of an
author, ancient or modern. This study is not an attempt to apply a new
method to a familiar text in order to discover something novel. Rather,
it is an attempt to start with the text itself without the assumption
that its meaning has already been ascertained and thus only needs to be
reformulated or put within a new framework of interpretation (e.g. literary, sociological, psychological, polemical, theological, etc.)[2]. My
experience has been that the Pauline texts themselves still remain to
a great degree a foreign territory in need of discovery. Hence, the
approach taken here is summarized well by Sean E. McEvenue, who when
attempting to describe his own "method" concluded that

> The fact is that method is nothing more than a description and systematiza-
> tion of acts of understanding ... ultimately the researcher must simply stare
> at his text, or fumble with it, until acts of understanding begin to take
> place.[3]

I also emphasize "exegetical" because, as a matter of methodology,
I have consciously resisted the temptation to follow the vast majority
of recent scholars in using certain aspects of the Corinthian correspondence to reconstruct a detailed picture of Paul's opponents in Corinth and their theology *from which* Paul's letters to the Corinthians

---

2 To give just one example of the opposing assumption, which is so prevalent in recent NT studies, see Bengt Holmberg, *Paul and Power, The Structure of Authority in
  the Primitive Church as Reflected in the Pauline Epistles, Coniectanea Biblica, NT
  Series 11,* 1978, pp.2,5. He concludes concerning the state of affairs in Pauline
  exegesis that "It is also apparent that there exists a considerable degree of consensus among scholars on the vast majority of details concerning philological and
  historical fact" (p.2). The problem, therefore, according to Holmberg, is that
  "... this is not accompanied by a corresponding degree of consensus as to how the
  facts are to be interpreted and fitted together into syntheses of historical reconstruction". Hence, he has "... not found it necessary to continue in the usual
  way of exegeting in detail every cited text ... There is no point in presenting a
  detailed, painstaking analysis of the relevant texts when this would only amount
  to a repetition of well-known facts".
3 *The Narrative Style of the Priestly Writer, AB 50,* 1971, p.11.

are then subsequently interpreted. I have done so not because I consider the question of the identity and theology of Paul's opponents
unimportant for understanding Paul's epistles or for tracing the history of the early Church in general. Quite the contrary! But the absence of direct evidence from their hands renders all attempts to *begin* with such a reconstruction as the interpretive key to Paul's writings uncontrollably circular at best[4], and at its worst simply a matter
of historical phantasy. It will no doubt strike readers who are familiar with the history of the interpretation of I and II Corinthians in
our century as surprising and strange, therefore, to discover that no
attempt has been made in this work to identify who Paul's opponents in
Corinth were or to outline what they taught. Instead, I have tried to
bring to the text concerning Paul's opponents only what Paul himself
reports about their criticism of him, whether accurate or not, since
it is Paul's response to this criticism as he perceived it which we
have before us. Thus, many important historical questions are intentionally left unanswered. My hope, however, is that these questions
can be better approached once Paul's own thinking has been clarified
as much as possible internally.

For this same reason I have also been very cautious in my use of the
other Pauline epistles, not to mention the rest of the New Testament,
in my interpretation of II Cor. 2:14-3:3. My procedure has been to adduce interpretive parallels primarily from the Corinthian correspondence itself, since we can be sure that Paul's comments in our passage
would be compared to the rest of his writings received by the Corinthians and were intended by Paul to be so compared. When I do point to
another Pauline writing, my purpose in doing so is to highlight the
common structure and themes in Paul's respective arguments as a confirmation of my exegesis of the text under consideration. If a parallel
in thought between our passage and another Pauline text can be demonstrated, then we can be encouraged that our exegesis is on the right
track. The only other occasion for leaving the Corinthian correspondence
is when it becomes necessary to acquire some additional historical or
traditionsgeschichtliche knowledge in order to determine the wider meaning of a word or implication of an idiom, etc. But again, the determination of the meaning of Paul's use of such idioms and traditions is
based, in the final analysis, on internal considerations. Hence, I have
also intentionally left open the question of developing a Pauline the-

---

4 For the danger of circularity inherent in this predominant approach, see E. Güttgemanns' review of Georgi's work (see below, n.6) in *Zeitschrift für Kirchengeschichte*
77(1966)126-131, pp.127f., 130; and specifically in regard to II Cor. 3, see C.J.A.
Hickling, "The Sequence of Thought in II Corinthians, Chapter Three", *NTS* 21(1975)
380-395, p.380.

ology of the various issues raised in this study. The methodology
followed in this work thus follows the basic principle outlined earlier
by Nils A. Dahl in regard to I Cor. 1-4:

> In so far as they do not directly serve the purpose of philological exegesis,
> but provide materials for a more general, historical and theological under-
> standing, information from other Pauline epistles, Acts, and other early Chris-
> tian, Jewish, Greek or Gnostic documents should not be brought in until the
> epistolary situation has been clarified as far as possible on the basis of in-
> ternal evidence".[5]

As a result, the respective strengths of this work are also its weaknesses. But inasmuch as the safest route historically is to begin with
what one has in its specificity before drawing conclusions about the
darker corners of history which surround it or its broader intellectual,
theological and literary context, it seems most appropriate to start the
unavoidable hermeneutical circle which exists between a text and its context with the particular text, rather than with a reconstruction of its
broader context. For only then will we be able to establish criteria for
distinguishing between the plethora of opinions already confronting us
concerning the nature of Paul's opposition in Corinth[6], not to mention
the myriad of interpretations of Paul's own theology, its place within
the development of the early Church and its relationship to the biblical traditions from which it sprang. The task is a formidable one. But
it is a task which is best carried out with a historical humility which
is willing to admit what can and cannot be known given the evidence a-
vailable. The results of such a "humility" will naturally be much more
modest than often found in recent literature on the Corinthian epistles,
but in turn, their modesty will carry with it a higher degree of certainty.

---

5 "Paul and the Church at Corinth According to 1 Corinthians 1:10-4:21", in *Christian History and Interpretation: Studies Presented to John Knox*, ed. W.R. Farmer,
C.F.D. Moule and R.R. Niebuhr, 1967, pp.313-335, p.318.

6 The key texts for developing a picture of Paul's opponents in Corinth have been I
Cor. 1:12; 3:22; 9:2-5 and II Cor. 11:22f. Moreover, ever since the classic work
of F.C. Baur, scholars have seen in these passages the basis for the supposition
that at the time of the writing of I Cor. Paul found himself in a conflict with
various "parties" within the church itself which had rallied around the theology
and/or special perspective of their respective namesake. For the most recent and
a balanced presentation of this view, cf. Friedrich Lang, "Die Gruppen in Korinth
nach 1. Korinther 1-4", *ThB* 14(1983)68-79. But there has been no consensus in the
last 150 years whatsoever concerning either 1) the nature of Paul's opposition in
I Cor. 9:1ff. (assuming that this opposition was already being directed against
Paul within the church); 2) the contours of the ἔριδες in I Cor. 1:11 itself; 3)
whether Paul's contrasts in I Cor. 9:2 and 5 ought to be related to his discussion
in I Cor. 1:10ff. in the first place; and 4) the problem of the relationship between Paul's opponents in I Cor. and those mentioned in II Cor. The answers to
these questions range from 1) Judaizers; an undogmatic, general enthusiasm; gnosti-
cism, protognosticism; Hellenistic pneumatics; representatives of the theology proposed by the Stephen-circle (whatever that is conceived to be); esoteric Palestinian
Judaism; to a "divine-man" Christology, and various combinations of these alternatives; 2) full-blown parties (splits and factions within the church) to merely
a "strife" between members which could develop into factions if not abated; 3)
yes (i.e. the Corinthians themselves were questioning Paul's authority and the

---

contrast between Paul/Peter etc. reflects the parties of ch. 1) to no (the Corinthians themselves were not at this time questioning Paul's authority and the contrast between Paul/Peter, etc. does not reflect tension) to a mixture of these alternatives; 4) the same opponents throughout I and II Cor., two different groups, to
no outside opponents in the church in I Cor. at all. For the best surveys of this
complicated set of problems, listing not only the various representatives of the
various positions, but also their basic arguments, cf. Christian Machalet, "Paulus
und seine Gegner. Eine Untersuchung zu den Korintherbriefen", in *Theokratia, Jahrbuch des Institutum Judaicum, II, FS K.H. Rengstorf zum 70. Geburtstag*, ed. W. Dietrich, et.al., 1973, pp.183-203, esp. pp.183-190 and E.E. Ellis, "Paul and His Opponents. Trends in Research", in his *Prophecy and Hermeneutic in Early Christianity,
NT Essays*, 1978, pp.80-115. For a simple listing of the various positions in catalog
form, see John J. Gunther, *St. Paul's Opponents and their Background, A Study of
Apocalyptic and Jewish Sectarian Teaching, Supplements Novum Testamentum XXX*, 1973,
pp.1-6. For a survey of the problem of the relationship between I and II Cor., see
D. Georgi, *Die Gegner des Paulus im 2. Korintherbrief, Studien zur Religiösen Propaganda in der Spätantike, WMANT 11*, 1964, pp.7-16 and for a helpful treatment of
the references to Peter in I Cor. see C.K. Barrett, "Cephas and Corinth", *Abraham
unser Vater, Juden und Christen im Gespräch über die Bibel, FS Otto Michel*, ed. Otto
Betz, et.al., 1963, pp.1-12. Finally, this entire discussion has been placed on a
much firmer methodological footing since Klaus Berger's important study, "Die impliziten Gegner, Zur Methode des Erschließens von 'Gegnern' in neutestamentlichen
Texten", in *Kirche, FS Günther Bornkam zum 75. Geburtstag*, ed. D. Lührmann and G.
Strecker, 1980, pp.373-400; see esp. his conclusion concerning procedure on p.390:
"Vorrang gebührt der immanenten Exegese von Text und Kontext; der nächste Schritt
sollte zunächst versuchen, die Position im Rahmen der Geschichte des Urchristentums
zu erklären; erst danach kommen außerchristliche Zeugnisse in Betracht, mit Vorrang
dabei zunächst die jüdischen" (emphasis mine). Given the confusion which presently
surrounds the entire question of the nature of Paul's opposition in Corinth, it is
the purpose of our study to map out this first and most important, but surprisingly
neglected step.

Chapter One

"LED UNTO DEATH": THE MEANING AND FUNCTION
OF PAUL'S THANKSGIVING IN II CORINTHIANS 2:14a

Paul's "second"[1] letter to the Corinthians is, without a doubt, one
of the strongest witnesses to the fact that

> Alles, was Paulus sagt, schreibt und lehrt, entfaltet sich nicht im neutralen
> Raum der allgemeinen Betrachtung, sondern ist ein Teil seines Wirkens und
> Wollens, seines dramatischen Lebenskampfes selbst.[2]

Indeed, even if Second Corinthians was not "ohne Zweifel der persön-
lichste unter den erhaltenen Paulusbriefen"[3], the subject matter of the
letter itself would force us to anchor Paul's theology in Second Corinthians within the context of his apostolic ministry. For even a cursory
reading of Second Corinthians makes it clear that the nature of Paul's
apostolic ministry provides both the input and occasion for the epistle[4].
The recognition of this fact is especially pertinent for any investigation of Paul's theological maxim "the letter kills, but the Spirit makes
alive", which, at first glance, seems so abstract and proverbial[5]. For

---

1 Regardless of the myriad of opinions concerning the literary unity of II Corinthians itself and its relationship to I Corinthians, all are agreed that on the
basis of I Cor. 5:9 the canonical II Cor. is at least the third letter which Paul
sent to the church in Corinth. On the question of the literary unity of II Cor.,
see note 11 below.
2 H. von Campenhausen, *Kirchliches Amt und geistliche Vollmacht in den ersten drei
Jahrhunderten, Beiträge zur Historischen Theologie, Bd. 14*, 1963², p.32.
3 Erich Dinkler, Art.: Korintherbriefe, *RGG³, Bd. 4*, 1960, p.21. He goes on to add
the very important warning, however, that "... die eingestreuten biographischen
Angaben (dürfen) nicht dazu verleiten, ihn als autobiographisches Dokument zu inter-
pretieren; er will zunächst und vor allem ein apostolisches Schreiben sein und
kommt auf die Person des Paulus nur als Träger des apostolischen Amtes zu sprechen".
4 One need only look at the multitude of monographs, essays, introductions and commentaries on II Cor. to substantiate this fact. At a much more fundamental level,
however, the question still remains unanswered. See P. Stuhlmacher, "Theologische
Probleme des Römerbriefpräskripts", *EvTh 27*(1967)374-389, p.375: "... die Frage
nach dem Verhältnis von apostolischen Selbstverständnis und dem Phänomen sowie der
Form der paulinischen Briefstellerei überhaupt scheint mir bisher keineswegs theo-
logisch befriedigend bedacht worden zu sein".
5 For example, it was this gnomic character of II Cor. 3:6 which led Jacob Kremer,
"'Denn der Buchstabe Tötet, Der Geist aber macht lebendig', Methodologische und
hermeneutische Erwägungen zu 2 Kor. 3:6b", in *Begegnung mit dem Wort, FS Heinrich
Zimmermann, Bonner Biblische Beiträge 53*, ed. J. Zmijewski and E. Nellessen, 1980,
pp.219-250, pp.219, 231-233, 243-246, to detach 3:6 from its moorings in order to
give it an interpretation not possible in its present context. But if we are to
understand Paul, then this is precisely what cannot be done.

once we attempt to interpret II Cor. 3:6 within its *own* context, we are confronted with the surprising[6] fact that it is embedded in "the most intricate and profound exposition of St. Paul's apostolic ministry to be found anywhere in his letters"[7]. Our task, therefore, is to understand the meaning and function of the letter/Spirit contrast in II Cor. 3:6 within the context in which it is found.

A. DELIMITING THE PRIMARY CONTEXT

It has long been recognized, even by those who argue most strongly for the literary integrity of II Corinthians, that the unmistakable transitions at 2:14 and 7:5 and the internally coherent thought structure of the passage itself serve as clear indications that II Cor. 2:14-7:4 comprises a self-enclosed literary unit[8]. As such, this is the larger literary context within which 3:6 is to be understood[9]. But within 2:14-7:4 the close parallels in thought between 2:14-3:18 and 4:1-6, combined with the introduction of the extended discussion of Paul's suffering in 4:7ff., provide a further demarcation. It thus becomes necessary to focus our attention in interpreting 3:6 on 2:14-4:6 as the *primary context* for our study. For as T. Provence has recently indicated,

> Paul answers the question of 2:16b throughout chapter 3 ... But even more importantly, 4:1-6 summarizes Paul's answer by picking up the themes of 2:16-17 *and* chapter three ... Thus the section introduced by the question in 2:16b is

---

6 It is surprising only because Paul's statement in 3:6 has usually been lifted from the context of Paul's apostolic ministry in order to relate it directly to Paul's view of the law. This is a result of the fact that 3:6 is most often related only to what immediately follows in 3:7-18 without paying close attention either to what precedes (2:14-3:6a) or to the continuation of Paul's argument in 4:1ff.

7 W.H. Bates, commenting on II Cor. 3-6 in "The Integrity of II Corinthians", *NTS 12* (1965/1966)56-69, p.59.

8 For a classic example, cf. H.A.W. Meyer, *Critical and Exegetical Handbook of the Epistles to the Corinthians, Meyer's Commentary on the New Testament, Vol. VI*, 1979 (ET and reprint of the 1870 German edition *KEK, Vol. VI)*, pp.451 and 564, who, in spite of his very strong emphasis on the unity of II Cor. (he even refuses to allow 2:14-7:4 to be called a "digression"), nevertheless points out that 7:5 refers back to 2:12f.

9 This has been confirmed most recently by the structural analysis of 2:14-7:4 by K.Th. Kleinknecht, *Der leidende Gerechtfertigte. Die alttestamentlich-jüdische Tradition vom 'leidenden Gerechten' und ihre Rezeption bei Paulus*, WUNT 2. Reihe 13, 1984, pp.250-254. Kleinknecht points to the "Leitmotiven" which run throughout the section (e.g. ἱκανός in 2:16b, 3:6; διακονία in 3:7,8,9; 4:1; 5:18; 6:3; συνιστάναι in 3:1; 4:2; 5:12; 6:4; φανεροῦν in 2:14; 3:3; 4:2,10,11; 5:10,11; οὐκ ἐγκακοῦμεν in 4:1,16 and the contrasts between death/life in 2:16; 3:6; 4:10-13; 5:5; 5:1ff.; 6:9 and old/new in 3:6,15 and 5:17, cf. also the creation motif in 4:6 and 5:17) as well as the interplay between what he calls the "monologische" (3:4-5:10 and 5:14-6:10) and "dialogische Ebene" (3:1-3; 5:11-13 and 6:11ff.) of the text as the two decisive structural arguments for the unity of 2:14-7:4.

not completed until its conclusion in 4:1-6. Indeed, the close connection between chapter three and 4:1-6 prompted Plummer to comment that 'the division
of the chapters is unintelligently made' because in the first part of chapter
four 'the Apostle is still urging the claims of his office'.[10]

The limitation of the primary context of our study to II Cor. 2:14-
4:6 is also necessary, however, in the light of the complex literary
problems surrounding II Corinthians as a whole. For the apparently
abrupt transitions at 2:14 and 7:5 constitute only one of four interrelated literary problems encountered in the canonical text of II Corinthians. Hence, the place of 2:14-7:4 within the larger development of
Paul's thought in the epistle as we have it is also dependent upon 1)
whether or not 6:14-7:1 is an interpolation, and if it is, whether its
origin is Pauline; 2) whether or not 2:14-7:4 is of a piece with 1:1-
2:13 and 7:5-16; 3) the internal relationship between chapters 8 and 9
and their respective places within the overall context of the epistle;
and 4) the relationship between chapters 1-9 and the literary unit of
chapters 10-13[11]. Thus, because of the uncertainty concerning the unity
of II Corinthians, the safest path to take methodologically is to begin with an investigation of the smallest meaningful context possible.
In our case this is 2:14-4:6. For as C.K. Barret has emphasized, "all
attempts to analyse 2 Corinthians and to trace out the record of Paul's
dealings with the Church stand or fall by the exegesis of the relevant
parts of the epistle"[12]. This does not mean that the larger questions
of literary and historical reconstruction can be ignored. The question
is simply one of methodology. For if any progress is to be made on the
complex literary and historical problems raised by II Corinthians,
Barrett is again correct in pointing out that

---

10 "'Who is Sufficient for these Things?' An Exegesis of 2 Corinthians 2:15-3:18",
   NovT 24(1982)54-81, p.57. He quotes Plummer, *A Critical and Exegetical Commentary
   on the Second Epistle of St. Paul to the Corinthians*, ICC, 1915, p.109 and offers
   a helpful chart of parallels between chapters two, three and four to illustrate
   his point. This same point has also been made by C.J.A. Hickling, "The Sequence of
   Thought in II Corinthians, Chapter Three", *NTS* 21(1975)380-395, p.393n.2.

11 For a discussion of the problems as well as the relevant literature cf. W.G. Kümmel,
   Introduction (ET of the 17th German ed.), 1975, pp.287-293; Barrett, *Commentary on
   Second Corinthians*, 1973, pp.12-20 and D. Georgi, *IDB*, *Supplementary Volume*, 1976,
   pp.183-186, each representing one of the three main approaches to the literary
   problems of II Cor. On the one extreme, Kümmel argues for the literary unity of
   the entire epistle. On the other extreme, Georgi understands II Cor. to be a compi-
   lation of no less than six different literary fragments, including a non-Pauline
   interpolation in 6:14-7:1. Barrett, representing a mediating position, contends
   that chapters 1-9 and 10-13 are two independent, but complete literary units. For
   a concise history of the debate, see Richard Batey, "Paul's Interaction with the
   Corinthians", *JBL* 84(1965)139-146, pp.139-140.

12 *Commentary on Second Corinthians*, p.18. Concerning the literary structure of II
   Cor. he also points out that "the truth or falsehood of the hypothesis (concerning
   the literary structure of II Cor.) must be determined by the possibility or impossibility of understanding the transitions ... the issue therefore is fundamentally one of exegesis" (p.97).

we are unlikely to make much advance towards their solution by surveying them
as a whole and trying to think out a comprehensive hypothesis capable of explaining everything at once. If advance is to be made at all it will be made by
the pursuit, and eventual integration, of a number of details.[13]

The limitation of our study to II Cor. 2:14-4:6 as the primary context for an investigation of the letter/Spirit contrast in II Cor. 3:6
is therefore not only justified contextually, but is also the surest and
most fruitful starting point methodologically.

B. THE FUNCTION OF PAUL'S THANKSGIVING IN II COR. 2:14-16a

Paul begins his discussion of the nature and function of the apostolic ministry in 2:14-4:6 with a characteristic *thanksgiving formula*
in praise of God. The classification of the phrase τῷ δὲ θεῷ χάρις plus
substantival participle(s) as a stylized praise-thanksgiving formula,
found not only here, but also in I Cor. 15:57 and II Cor. 8:16[14], is
based on Peter Thomas Obrien's extensive examination of the thanksgiving
(εὐχαριστέω)- and *berakah* (εὐλογητὸς ὁ θεὸς)- formulas in his important
work, *Introductory Thanksgivings in the Letters of Paul*[15]. For although
the formula in II Cor. 2:14-16a falls beyond the scope of Obrien's work,
a comparison of its form with the εὐχαριστέω- and εὐλογητός- formulas
found elsewhere in Paul's writings makes it clear that τῷ δὲ θεῷ χάρις
plus substantival participle also belongs to the *Gattung* of the "praise-
thanksgiving"[16].

The significance of this observation is twofold. First, Obrien's study
has demonstrated that the "thanksgiving periods" perform a very definite
threefold function within Paul's letters. As he summarizes it,

---

13 This was his rationale for devoting an entire paper to the "career" of Titus, cf.
   "Titus" in *Neotestamentica et Semitica, FS Matthew Black*, ed. by E.E. Ellis and
   Max Wilcox, 1969, pp.1-14, p.1.
14 This formula also occurs in modified forms in Rom. 7:25; II Cor. 9:15; I Tim.
   1:12ff. and II Tim. 1:3ff.
15 *Supplements to Novum Testamentum, Vol. XLIX*, 1977, pp.233-240. For the εὐχαριστέω-
   formulas cf. Rom. 1:8; I Cor. 1:4; Phil. 1:3ff.; Col. 1:3f.,12; I Thess. 1:2-5,
   2:13; II Thess. 1:3, 2:13ff.; for εὐλογητός cf. Rom. 1:25; II Cor. 1:3ff.; Eph.
   1:3ff.; Rom. 9:5 and II Cor. 11:31.
16 There is no need to detail the parallels, which become obvious when the various
   texts are brought together, cf. Obrien, pp.100f. for his conclusion concerning
   the "thanksgiving-period". Since this chapter was first written 2:14 has also
   been recognized to be a "thanksgiving period" by Margaret E. Thrall "A Second
   Thanksgiving Period in II Corinthians", *JSNT* 16(1982)101-124, cf. esp. pp.112-115.
   Thrall based her analysis on the introductory thanksgivings delineated in the
   earlier work of Paul Schubert, *Form and Function of the Pauline Thanksgivings*,
   1939, pp.54-55; cf. her chart and discussion on pp.114-115. Her conclusion at this
   point is nevertheless the same as mine: 2:14 is "intended to function as an introductory thanksgiving period" (p.112).

Paul's introductory thanksgivings have a varied function: *epistolary, didactic and paraenetic*, and they provide evidence of his pastoral and/or apostolic concern for the addressees. In some cases one purpose may predominate while others recede into the background. But whatever the particular thrust of any passage, it is clear that Paul's introductory thanksgivings were not meaningless devices. Instead, they were integral parts of their letters, *setting the tone and themes of what to follow.*[17]

Hence, rather than being merely an unexpected explosion of gratitude which found its expression in a Christian hymn of praise[18], Obrien's study forces us to reexamine II Cor. 2:14f. as a carefully crafted, thesis-like statement which not only encapsulates the main theme(s) of its section (i.e. 2:14-4:6(7:4)), but also contains an implicit paraenetic appeal to his readers[19].

Second, Obrien observed that although the *berakah*-formula, which he characterized as "a short Christianized form of the Jewish praise-thanksgiving or eulogy", is quite distinct from Paul's more common εὐχαριστέω-formula thanksgivings in both terminology and structure, nevertheless the two forms are essentially synonymous in their basic meaning. In his words,

---

17 Obrien, p.263. Thrall, p.113 also emphasizes this point, referring once again to the work of Schubert, p.180, who had also concluded that the purpose of the thanksgiving in Paul's writings was to introduce the main themes of the letter.
18 Plummer, *Commentary*, p.67, offers a typical understanding of 2:14: "He is so overwhelmed with thankfulness at the thought of the ultimate result, that, without going on with his narrative, he bursts out into a hymn of praise ... the gratitude here is evoked by the thought of the intense revulsion of feeling from anxiety to joy when he met Titus and heard that all was well in Corinth". H. Windisch, *Der Zweite Brief an die Korinther*, KEK, Bd. 6, 1970[9], p.96, postulates on the basis of this phrase alone that 2:14-16a was, in reality, an early Christian hymn which has been incorporated by Paul into his argument; so similarly, R. Bultmann, *Korintherbrief*, p.70. I find it doubtful, however, that the description in 2:14ff. of the twofold effect of the apostolic office would form the backbone of an early Christian hymn. Moreover, the fact that Paul is describing his own ministry (see below and cf. 3:1ff. where Paul guards against the possibility that 2:14-17 be taken as a personal self-recommendation) also seems to oppose Windisch's supposition. But, in any case, it is apparent that 2:14-17 is now wedded into the present context whatever its original origin may have been. On the meaning of χάρις as an expression of gratitude cf. Conzelmann, art. χάρις κτλ., *TDNT*, Vol IX, 1974, pp.372-415, pp. 374, 393.
19 This also holds true for II Cor. 8:16 and I Cor. 15:57, though in the former the formula occurs in the middle of the section to which it relates (i.e. 7:5-8:29), while in the latter case this thesis-like statement comes at the end of its section (15:2-57) and hence functions more like a conclusion than an introduction. This flexibility in position results from the fact that the χάρις τῷ θεῷ-formula, unlike the other thanksgiving formulas, does not function as the actual beginning of an epistle, but in every case finds its place within the argument of the epistle itself. This flexibility in position, then, is the main distinction between the χάρις τῷ θεῷ and εὐλογητός/εὐχαριστέω formulas. For Obrien's summary of the implicit paraenetic purpose of the thanksgiving periods, see *Introductory Thanksgivings*, p.263. In I Cor. 15:57 this paraenetic appeal is made explicit in v.58, while in II Cor. 8:16 Paul's thanksgiving functions as an implicit appeal for the Corinthians to accept and trust Titus and his assignment in regard to the collection (cf. II Cor. 8:24; 12:17f.).

> What we are concerned to point out is that the use of εὐχαριστέω does *not ne-cessarily exclude* the idea of praise ... while the appearance of the εὐλογητός-formula does not rule out any thought of personal gratitude.[20]

In the light of this overlap in meaning between praise and personal gratitude within the two basic types of thanksgivings found in Paul's writings, it is therefore somewhat surprising to discover that for Paul the two forms were *not* simply interchangeable. For as Obrien goes on to emphasize,

> Of far greater significance is the fact -- unnoticed by almost all scholars -- that although either the εὐχαριστέω- or εὐλογητός-formulas could have been used of thanksgiving or praise to God for blessings *either* to others *or* for oneself, Paul in the introductions of his letters, uses εὐχαριστέω consistent-ly of *Fürdank* for God's work in the lives of the addressees, and εὐλογητός for blessings in which *he himself* participated" (last emphasis mine).[21]

Similarly, when we examine the three occurrences of the formula τῷ δὲ θεῷ χάρις plus substantival participle in I Cor. 15:57, II Cor. 2:14 and 8:16 we are struck with the fact that here too it is this latter emphasis that Paul clearly has in mind. In all three instances Paul's doxology is for something he himself has experienced[22], although in I Cor. 15:57 Paul's focus is on an experience he shares with all Christians (see I Cor. 15:58). As the key to Paul's concern, the thanksgiving-formula of II Cor. 2:14-16a thus alerts us to the fact that from the beginning the focus of our attention in 2:14-4:6 is to be directed towards Paul himself.

C. THE NATURE AND PURPOSE OF THE APOSTOLIC MINISTRY IN 2:14-16a

1. The Apostle Paul as the Subject and Object of 2:14-16a

The conclusion that the thanksgiving-formula found in II Cor. 2:14ff. functions not only to signal the tone and theme of the section, but also to call our attention specifically to Paul himself can only be maintained, however, if the *plural* objects and subject of the thanksgiving itself[23] can be construed to be "literary" or "epistolary" conventions

---

20 Obrien, *Introductory Thanksgivings*, p.239.
21 Obrien, p.239. Obrien's distinction holds true in general, though it is difficult to see how Paul's praise to the Creator in Rom. 1:25 or his eulogy of God as his witness in II Cor. 11:31 could be described as relating to blessings in which Paul has participated. For clearer examples, cf. II Cor. 1:3ff.; Eph. 1:3ff. and Rom. 9:5.
22 II Cor. 8:16 can be included in this basic distinction once we realize that Paul is reflecting on his relief in knowing that Titus has been accepted by the Corinthians and has himself grown in affection for them (cf. the parallel to 8:16 in 7:15f.). This distinction is also carried through in the modified forms of the formula in Rom. 7:25 and I Tim. 1:12ff.; though it breaks down in II Cor. 9:15.
23 See 2:14: ἡμᾶς; ἡμῶν; 2:15: ἐσμέν. This holds true, naturally, for the rest of the plurals throughout 2:14-4:6 as well; cf. 2:17; 3:1,2,3,4, etc.

which actually refer to Paul alone and not to some larger circle of co-
workers (e.g. Paul and Timothy, 1:1; Silvanus, 1:19; and/or Titus, 2:13;
etc.)[24].

The vast majority of commentators in the past have in fact assumed
that the first person plurals of 2:14-16a are literary devices meant to
refer to Paul himself and therefore, usually without further comment,
have construed the entire passage of 2:14-4:6 to be part of Paul's *self-
defense*[25]. Yet there has been some significant opposition to this assumption, the most extreme of which is Lightfoot's judgment that "there
is no reason to think that St. Paul ever uses an 'epistolary' plural
referring to himself solely"[26]. Moreover, Lightfoot's judgment seems
to be born out in our context by the contrast between the consistent
use of the plurals in 2:14ff. and the emphasis on the first person
singular in 1:15-2:13 on the one hand, and the parallel statement to
2:14 in 1:19 in which δι' ἡμῶν is explicitly defined to include Silvanus and Timothy as well as Paul on the other hand.

Nevertheless, the decision of the majority to make Paul himself the
subject and object of 2:14-16a (and indeed, of 2:14-4:6 as a whole, except for 3:18) is in keeping with Paul's use of language elsewhere. For
even if we assume for the moment that 2:14ff. is of a piece with
1:15-2:13, the sudden switch from the first person singular to the plural in 2:14 does not necessarily indicate a change of subject, since

---

24 On the basis of 3:18 it is clear that the other plurals in 2:14-4:6 do not refer
to Paul and the church at Corinth. For in 3:18, when Paul wishes to include his
readers unmistakably indicates his intention to do so by modifying the subject
to read ἡμεῖς πάντες.

25 Cf., for example, Barrett, *Commentary*, p.98; Lietzmann, *An die Korinther I-II*, 1923,
p.108; Kümmel, additions to Lietzmann, 1969, p.198; A. Schlatter, *Paulus, Der Bote
Jesus*, 1962³, pp.494ff.; Windisch, *Zweite Brief*, p.97 and Isaac I. Friesen, in his
1971 diss. at the Univ. of Basel, now published as *The Glory of the Ministry of
Jesus Christ, Illustrated by a Study of 2 Cor. 2:14-3:18*, 1971, p.25.

26 *Colossians and Philemon*, 1890, p.229. Cf. also Blass-Debrunner-Funk, *A Greek
Grammar of the New Testament*, 1961, §280, where it is asserted that Paul usually
writes in the name of two or more persons and that where this is not the case,
he avoids the use of the plural. At the same time, however, it is admitted that
"it is not always possible in letters written in the name of two or more persons
to refer a plural to that plurality without some compelling reason" (II Cor. 10:
11ff. is cited as evidence for this observation). For one of the most detailed
attempts to take the interplay between "I" and "we" in II Cor. literally, see
Theodor Zahn, *Introduction to the New Testament, Vol. I* (ET of the 3rd German
ed.), 1977(1909), pp.316-317, and for further references to those who have taken
the first person plurals in Paul's writings as always referring to an actual
plurality, see N. Baumert, *Täglich Sterben und Auferstehen. Der Literalsinn von
2Kor 4:12-5:10*, 1973, pp.25-36. Most recently see J. Lambrecht, "Structure and
Line of Thought in 2 Cor. 2,14-4,6", *Biblica* 64(1983)344-380, p.350, who interprets 2:14-16b to refer to Paul and his co-workers (without substantiation); and
James I.H. McDonald, "Paul and the Preaching Ministry, A reconsideration of 2 Cor.
2:14-17 in its context", *JSNT* 17(1983)35-50, p.42, who suggests that the plural
of 2:15 refers either to those who preach in general or to the community offered
to God (pointing to Micah 4:2), though he prefers the former alternative.

there are clear examples elsewhere in II Corinthians of Paul's ability
to switch from the singular to the plural in referring to his *own* ministry[27].

For example, in I Cor. 4:15 Paul had reminded the church at Corinth that although they had "a myriad of guides" (μυρίους παιδαγωγοὺς), he alone had become their father through the gospel. Later, in II Cor. 11, Paul again reaf-
firms the fact that he was their "spiritual father" by evoking the image of
the betrothal tradition to describe his own relationship to the Corinthian
Church. Like the father of the would-be bride, who pledged his daughter to her
future husband as a guarantee of her fidelity and purity, Paul had betrothed
the Corinthians to Christ. Hence, it was only fitting and natural that he feel
a "divine jealousy" (θεοῦ ζηλῷ) over their readiness to submit to "a different
gospel" (ἢ εὐαγγελίον ἕτερον) (cf. 11:1-6). Thus when Paul defends the fact
that he had not boasted beyond limit in the assertion of his authority over
the Corinthians on the basis of this same spiritual fatherhood in II Cor. 10:14,
it can hardly be doubted that what Paul has in view is his *own* ministry,
even though he speaks in the plural! Similarly, although Paul quotes one
of the charges that has been registered against him *personally* in II Cor.
10:9f., he nevertheless responds to the charge *in the plural!* (10:11; cf.
10:1,3ff.). Finally, the fact that Paul can describe the very same set of
circumstances in either the first person singular or the first person plural indicates that the distinction between "I" and "we" cannot be strictly
maintained in Paul's letters. For in II Cor. 2:12f. Paul describes his anxiety over Titus, which eventually forced him to leave Troas in hopes of
meeting Titus in Macedonia, in the first person singular, only to continue
this report in the first person plural in II Cor. 7:5ff. Apparently then,
even in the most personal contexts, Paul is able to move from the real singular to the literary plural with ease. As C.E.B. Cranfield concluded most
recently, "that Paul did sometimes use the first person plural with reference
simply to himself we regard as almost certain."[28] Hence, it is by all means
possible that the plurals in 2:14-4:6 can be construed to refer to Paul himself.

Having come this far, our results are still, however, largely negative. In other words, we have seen that there is no compelling reason
to think that Paul could *not* have used the literary plural in II Cor.

27 A.T. Robertson, *A Grammar of the Greek New Testament in the Light of Historical
Research*, 1934, p.407, concludes on the basis of the evidence for the use of the
literary plural from the papyri and late Greek sources that there is no grammati-
cal reason why Paul could not have used this device. As examples of the literary
plural elsewhere in the NT he lists I John 1:4; Heb. 6:1,3,9,11; 13:18f. with
13:22f.; while for Paul he cites Rom. 1:5; Col. 4:3; I Thess. 2:18 and II Cor.
10:1-11:6, which he says "really settles the whole matter". M. Zerwick, *Biblical
Greek*, 1963, p.8 concurs with Robertson's judgment, having arrived at it independently, and also cites II Cor. 10:1-11:6 as the clearest example. He therefore concludes that although this use of the plural seems to be rare in the Pauline letters,
it is however "rash to regard Paul's 'we' as always referring to the apostle along
with his associates".
28 "Changes of Person and Number in Paul's Epistles", in *Paul and Paulinism, FS C.K.
Barrett*, ed. M.D. Hooker and S.G. Wilson, 1982, pp.280-289, p.286. D.W.B. Robinson,
"The Priesthood of Paul in the Gospel of Hope", in *Reconciliation and Hope, New
Testament Essays on Atonement and Eschatology presented to L.L. Morris on his
60th Birthday*, ed. R. Banks, 1974, pp.231-245, has made a similar argument for the
"we" passages throughout Romans, concluding that "while Paul is not easily confined to strict consistency, we think that the majority of his 'we's' etc. refer
to himself ... If he wishes to include his readers, or Christians generally, with
himself, he makes this clear by the argument, often with the addition of 'all'"
(p.237).

2:14ff. to refer to himself as he does elsewhere in his writings in general and in II Corinthians in particular. But are there any *positive* indications that Paul was, in fact, referring specifically to himself in 2:14ff. and not to some larger group of co-workers as in 1:19?

In II Cor. 1:19f. Paul refers to the message of Jesus Christ, which was preached to the Corinthians by Silvanus, Timothy and Paul, using the plural δι' ἡμῶν κηρυχθείς. In 4:5 Paul then describes this message preached to the Corinthians, again using the plural:

οὐ γὰρ ἑαυτοὺς κηρύσσομεν ἀλλὰ 'Ιησοῦν
Χριστὸν κύριον, ἑαυτοὺς δὲ δούλους ὑμῶν
διὰ 'Ιησοῦν.

But the ground or reason that Paul offers in 4:6 to support his statement that "they" do not preach themselves as lord, but, in contrast, are to be considered "slaves for Jesus' sake" is a clear allusion to Paul's own conversion-call[29] experience on the road to Damascus[30]. Thus, although II Cor. 1:19 might lead one to broaden the plural references throughout II Cor. 2:14-4:6 to include Paul's co-workers, 4:6 itself makes it clear that it is Paul's *own* ministry, based on his conversion-call on the road to Damascus, that he has in mind in 4:1-6[31].

Second, the fact that Paul is also referring to himself in 2:14-3:18 is made evident by his statement in 3:2f., where Paul supports his assertion that in "their" case letters of recommendation are not necessary by pointing to the Corinthians themselves as "their" letter of recommendation. The fact that this is a reference to the founding of the Corinthian church is clear[32]. Thus, Paul's argument is simply that the very existence of the church in Corinth itself serves as the recommendation

---

29 For the reason behind my choice of the awkward designation "conversion-call" to describe Paul's Damascus road experience, see below, ch.4, n.134, pp.139-140.

30 See too K. Stendahl, *Paul among Jews and Gentiles*, 1976, p.45, who takes 4:6 to be a reference by Paul "speaking about his own revelation in Jesus Christ". He therefore concludes concerning II Cor. 4:5-12 that "this is a long passage in which Paul uses first person plurals quite clearly to mean 'I, myself, Paul', i.e. simply first person singular" (p.45). The fact that 4:6 refers to Paul's conversion-call experience has also been stressed most recently by P. Stuhlmacher, "Das paulinische Evangelium", in *Das Evangelium und die Evangelien*, ed. P. Stuhlmacher, 1983, pp.157-182, pp.162f. Of special significance in this respect is the work of Seyoon Kim, *The Origin of Paul's Gospel*, WUNT, 2. *Reihe, Bd. 4*, 1981, for whom II Cor. 4:6 occupies a central role in his development of Paul's Damascus road experience as the basis not only for Paul's call, but also for his theology as a whole, see pp.6-11 and 137-268. There have been those, of course, who deny that 4:6 is a reference to Paul's call-conversion; see Windisch, *Zweiter Korintherbrief*, p.131; J. Hering, *Second Corinthians*, p.31 and 31n.11 and J. Munck, *Paul and the Salvation of Mankind*, 1959, p.34, who concludes, "there is hardly any reason to relate these words to the Damascus experience".

31 Contra, e.g. J. Lambrecht, "Structure and Thought", p.363, who distinguishes between the subjects of 4:1 and 4:2: "In 4:1 Paul states that he (and his co-workers = *we*) does not lose heart. 4:2 positively explains the content of this statement: he defends himself ("us") against every disgraceful hiddenness".

32 See below, chapter 5, for an exegesis of this passage.

of "their" ministry. But in the light of I Cor. 1:17; 2:1-5; 3:6,10;
4:14-16; 9:1-2; 15:1-3 and II Cor. 7:14; 10:13f.; 11:2-4 it is also
evident that Paul considered himself *alone* to be the founder of the
Corinthian community. Hence, Paul's argument in II Cor. 3:2f. holds true
only if the lack of the need for a letter of recommendation relates specifically to Paul and not to Paul and his co-workers, since Paul alone
was the "father" of the church. This becomes even more evident when we
consider that Paul himself had to write a letter of recommendation for
those he was sending to Corinth to settle the affairs concerning the
collection for Jerusalem (cf. II Cor. 8:18-24 and 9:3). Therefore, although written in the plural, the point of the argument in II Cor. 3:2f.
is that Paul, *unlike* other Christian emisaries (even his own co-workers!), does not need the customary letter of recommendation from other
congregations, since he alone is responsible for the very existence of
the Corinthian church. Consequently, the trustworthiness and quality of
his ministry should be beyond question to the Corinthians. This means,
however, that not only the plurals of 4:1-6, but also those of 3:1-6
and 12 must refer to Paul himself.

Finally, the close parallels already mentioned between 2:14-17,
3:1-6 and 4:1-6 make it unlikely that in 2:14ff. Paul is referring to
a wider circle of co-workers, rather than to himself alone[33]. For nowhere throughout 2:14-4:6 is there any indication of a switch in subject, except in 3:18 when Paul momentarily includes the Corinthians in
the general Christian experience of being conformed to Christ[34]. But
even then, as Baumert has pointed out, "eine solche Ausweitung (ist) von
ihm selbst her konzipiert; das bedeutet, der Akzent auch der erweiter-
ten wir-Aussagen liegt -- abgesehen von den paränetischen Stellen 5:21
und 6:16-7:1 -- immer darauf, daß *Paulus selbst* dazu gehört"[35].

---

33 See above, pp.8-9 and nn.9 and 10. Provence, "'Who is Sufficient ...", p.56 also
  observes concerning the parallel between 2:15-16 and 3:1-6 that "one of the most
  important keys to understanding 2 Cor. 3 lies in grasping its connection with
  2:15-16. Verse 16b is linked to 3:5-6 by virtue of the adjective ἱκανός and its
  cognates ... Thus Paul intends 3:5-6 to be an answer to the question raised in
  2:16: 'Who is sufficient for these things?'".
34 So also A. Schlatter, *Bote*, pp.519 and 522; Plummer, *Second Corinthians*, pp.104f.
  and 109; C.K. Barrett, *Second Corinthians*, pp.124 and 127f. and R. Bultmann,
  Zweiter Korintherbrief, pp.93 and 101.
35 *Täglich Sterben und Auferstehen*, pp.29-30. Half of Baumert's massive work is
  aimed at supporting the thesis that the first person plural in II Cor., especially
  in 4:16-5:10, does not necessarily mean an actual plurality. Concerning 2:14-3:6
  he concludes that "strenggenommen kann man nur ausschließen, daß Paulus hier all-
  gemein von den Aposteln rede, da er ja konkrete Situationen im Auge hat" (pp.30-
  31), while on 4:2ff. he writes, "wenn Paulus freilich in 4:2 seine Scheu und un-
  angebrachte Scham überwindet und *sich* vor dem Gewissen aller Menschen öffnet,
  klingt das so persönlich daß man sagen muß, Paulus spreche *praktisch* wieder nur
  von sich" (p.31). Baumert leaves the question open, however, concerning whether
  or not "am Rande der Gedanke an seine engsten Mitarbeiter mitschwingen mag"
  (cf. p.31).

But if Paul himself is the subject and object of 2:14-4:6, the question that naturally arises is why Paul chose to employ the literary plural in the first place? The answer to this question, I think, lies in
Paul's conception of himself as "an apostle of Christ Jesus by the will
of God" (II Cor. 1:1). For as Wendland has already emphasized, ἡμᾶς in
II Cor. 2:14 refers not merely to Paul as such, but to Paul *as an
apostle*[36], so that the emphasis in 2:14ff. is on the nature of the apostolic ministry. This emphasis is then made explicit in Paul's use of the
διακονέω/διάκονος motif in 3:3 and 6. Consequently, 2:14ff. becomes
"eine Hauptquelle für das Selbstverständnis des Paulus als Apostel"[36].
In other words, the use of the literary plural is best attributed to
the fact that Paul was conscious that he represented the apostolic
"office"[37]. Paul realized that his ministry carried a significance far
beyond his own personal position[38]. In fact, the man Paul becomes inseparable from his office, and indeed, is even swallowed up by it[39].
As a result, the issue at stake for Paul in Corinth was much greater
than merely the Corinthians' disenchantment with a particular person
and his ministry. In Paul's mind, if the Corinthians were to reject Paul,
they would not only be turning their backs on their own "spiritual

---

36 H.D. Wendland, *Die Briefe an die Korinther*, *NTD Bd. 7*, 1972, p.175. This point is
   also made in connection with the use of the literary plural in Romans by Robinson,
   "Priesthood of Paul", p.236. For the five different uses of "we" in Paul, all
   illustrated with examples from II Corinthians, cf. Karl Dick, *Der Schriftstellerische Plural bei Paulus*, 1900, pp.2ff.; also listed by Baumert, *Täglich Sterben*,
   p.25.

37 This is not to suggest, of course, that the role of an apostle had crystallized
   into a formal, universally recognized, church position by the time of Paul's
   writings. On the nature of the apostolic office at the time of Paul, cf. H. von
   Campenhausen, *Kirchliches Amt*, pp.56-58 and the very helpful article by R.
   Schnackenburg, "Apostles Before and During Paul's Time", in *Apostolic History and
   the Gospel, FS F.F. Bruce on his 60th Birthday*, ed. W.W. Gasque and R.P. Martin,
   1970, pp.287-303.

38 More than any other single person it has been Johannes Munck, *Paul and the Salvation of Mankind*, 1959, who has called our attention to this fact. Munck's
   central thesis is that Paul perceived himself as called to be the eschatological
   messenger, who by preaching to the Gentiles removed the last barrier to the coming
   of the Messiah in glory, i.e. the conversion of the Jews (since the conversion of
   the Gentiles moves the Jews to jealousy and then to repentance), thus preparing
   the way for the coming of the anti-Christ and then of Christ for judgment and
   salvation. His key texts are II Thess. 2:6f.; Rom. 11:13-26; 15:14ff.; Gal. 2:1-10
   and II Cor. 3. For statements of his thesis, cf. pp.33,36,41,43,49,55,61,66,68.
   The key to Munck's thesis is that for him, Paul's call put him "on the same plane
   as the experiences that made the great Old Testament figures connecting links in
   God's plan of salvation" (p.33). Moreover, because in Munck's view Paul's ministry
   plays the decisive eschatological role, Paul becomes the central figure in the
   Heilsgeschichte (cf.pp.48-49). But one must wonder if it is not pushing his valu-
   able insight too far when Paul, rather than Jesus, comes to occupy the decisive
   role within salvation history.

39 For Paul's representation of himself to the Corinthians as an apostle, see I Cor.
   1:1,17; 2:2ff.; 3:5-10; 4:1,9; 9:1f.; 9:15-18; 15:8-11; II Cor. 1:1; 2:14-17;
   3:4-6; 4:1-5:21; 6:3-10 and chapters 10-13.

father", but would, at the same time, be rejecting the very gospel itself! For as we shall come to see, Paul views himself in his apostolic
calling not only as one who *preaches* the message of good news to the
world, but equally important, as one ordained by God to be an *embodiment*
of that gospel, called to reveal the knowledge of God by and through
his very life. It is the identification of the message with its messenger, first seen in Christ and then carried on in his apostles, that
Paul develops in 2:14-16a.

2. The Roman Institution of the Triumphal Procession as the *Crux Interpretum* to II Corinthians 2:14a

a. The Problem Presented by θριαμβεύειν

The reason for Paul's praise in 2:14a is expressed in the two substantival participles θριαμβεύοντι and φανεροῦντι of 2:14a and b, i.e.
Paul praises God *because* of what God is presently doing in and through
the life of the apostle[40]. But when we turn to investigate more closely
the nature of this divine activity we are confronted with what has appeared to commentators to be an insurmountable problem. For the usual
meaning of θριαμβεύειν, which occurs elsewhere in the NT only in Colossians 2:15 and not at all in the LXX, seems to be impossible *theologically* in the present context. For as John Calvin pointed out over
four centuries ago, if the verb is taken literally to refer to the Roman
institution of the triumphal procession, one is faced with the uncomfort-
able realization that in the Roman triumph, "prisoners are said to be
led in triumph when to disgrace them they are bound in chains and
dragged before the chariot of the conqueror"[41]. But inasmuch as Paul could
hardly be praising God for being led as a prisoner in disgrace, Calvin
felt compelled to conclude, for theological reasons, that "Paul means
something different from the common meaning of this phrase ..."[42]
Calvin's solution to this problem was to ascribe to θριαμβεύειν a *factitive* sense. Instead of meaning "to lead in triumph", Calvin thus interpreted θριαμβεύειν to mean "to cause to triumph". As a result, Paul
could be understood to be praising God in II Cor. 2:14 because he shared,

---

40 The construing of these substantival participles to be causal in function is supported by Obrien's detailed study of the other two types of introductory thanksgiving forms found in Paul, the εὐχαριστέω and εὐλογητός. His study illustrates
that it is Paul's consistent pattern to follow the expression of praise with one
or more reasons for his gratitude, cf. *Introductory Thanksgivings in the Letters
of Paul*, 1977, pp.22-24, 51-54, 79-81, 109-112, 146-153, 172-177, 186-188 and
207-209.
41 John Calvin, *The Second Epistle of Paul the Apostle to the Corinthians and the
Epistles to Timothy, Titus and Philemon, Calvin's New Testament Commentaries, Vol
10*, trans. T.A. Smail, 1964, pp.33.
42 *Second Epistle*, p.33.

in one way or another, in God's victory[43]. But by the end of the nine-
teenth century this attempt to give θριαμβεύειν a factitive meaning was
recognized and "pronounced on high authority" to be "'philologically
impossible'"[44]. For those verbs which do carry a secondary factitive
sense are almost always *intransitive* (e.g. βασιλεύω, μαθητεύω)[45], while
θριαμβεύειν in 2:14 is clearly *transitive*[46]. Furthermore, no evidence
for such a factitive meaning could be found anywhere else in Greek literature. In 1879 George Findlay could therefore observe that II Cor.
2:14a was consistently being translated "triumph over us" "by nearly all
the more recent critics"[47]. As Meyer put it in 1870, θριαμβεύειν means
"to conduct, present anyone in triumph", since "the accusative is never
the triumphing subject, but always the object of the triumph"[48]. However, rather than solving the problem, the recognition that Paul must
be seen to be the object of the triumph in 2:14 only made matters worse
theologically. Since θριαμβεύειν invoked the image of a triumphal procession in which the vanquished foes were led through the streets of
the city as a public display, the idea that Paul could portray himself
as such a prisoner, and then praise God for being the one who leads the
procession, seemed quite out of place, to say the least. This image
simply did not conform to the popular understanding of Paul's view of
his apostolic ministry as one of "triumph in Christ". As Findlay himself
put it so well over 100 years ago, the metaphor appears to be

> intolerably harsh and incongruous. For it would make the Apostle *the victim
> of defeat*. And when the nature of a Roman triumph is considered - then it
> must be remembered, existing in its grim reality - with the ignominious po-
> sition of the captive, and the miserable death in which the exhibition usu-
> ally ended for him, the figure appears most unsuitable to express the re-

---

43 Besides Calvin, H.A.W. Meyer, *Epistles to the Corinthians*, 1884[6], p.451 lists
   Chrysostom, Theophylact, Jerome, Luther, Bengel, Beza, Estius, Grotius, Emmerling,
   Flatt, Rückert, Olshausen and Osiander as all representing the attempt to give
   θριαμβεύειν a factitive sense, though Meyer himself recognized that "actual usage
   is against this view". The factitive sense is still preserved today in the English
   Authorized Version.
44 George G. Findlay, "St. Paul's use of ΘΡΙΑΜΒΕΥΩ", *The Expositor* 10(1879)403-421,
   p.404.
45 A.T. Robertson, *A Grammar of the Greek New Testament*, 1934, p.801 points out that
   "there was indeed a remarkable increase in the LXX in the number of verbs used in
   the causative sense, many of which had been usually intransitive", but he gives
   no exceptions to this rule.
46 The discussion in Blass - Debrunner - Funk, *A Greek Grammar of the New Testament*,
   1961, §148 and §309 is therefore misleading. In §148 θριαμβεύειν is listed as an
   example of the transitive use of an originally intransitive verb, although to my
   knowledge there is no evidence of such an intransitive meaning of the verb. Then
   in §309 θριαμβεύειν is given as an example of the fact that "factitives (causatives)
   sometimes arise from intransitive verbs" and translated "cause to triumph", although
   in §148 it is translated, "to lead in triumphal procession ..." and said to be
   "only transitive"! Neither discussion is correct, see below.
47 "St. Paul's Use of ΘΡΙΑΜΒΕΥΕΙΝ", p.404.
48 *Epistles to the Corinthians*, p.451.

lation between the Apostle and the gracious God to whom he renders thanks.
Not *so*, surely, did God 'always triumph over' his faithful servant; nor
could such a triumph 'manifest the savour of his knowledge in every place!'[49]

Faced with such a problem, and with recourse to the factitive sense
no longer possible, almost all commentators since Findlay have simply
chosen either to ignore the significance of θριαμβεύειν altogether "by
vague generalizations which rob the metaphor of all precision and viv-
idness"[50], or to modify the meaning of θριαμβεύειν itself in order to
bring it in line with their theological convictions[51]. But against all
such attempts it must be observed that the need felt to ignore or modify the image of Paul as conquered, so that Paul becomes the conqueror
(either alone or with Christ; either his own victory or sharing in the
victory of God/Christ) finds its basis not in the immediate context[52],
but in *a-priori* judgments concerning Paul's view of the nature of the
apostolic ministry[53]. As a result, no less than ten different possibilities have already been suggested for the meaning of θριαμβεύειν in II
Cor. 2:14:

---

49 "St. Paul's Use ...", pp.404-405.
50 "St. Paul's Use ...", p.405.
51 Cf. for example, Victor Bartling, "God's Triumphant Captive, Christ's Aroma for God
   (2 Cor. 2:12-17)", *Concordia Theological Monthly* 22(1951)883-894, esp. pp.884, 886-
   888; H. Windisch, *Zweiter Korintherbrief*, pp.97-98; R. Bultmann, *Zweiter Korintherbrief*, pp.66-67; C.K. Barrett, *Second Corinthians*, pp.95, 98; Lietzmann (Kümmel),
   An die Korinther, p.108; R.V.G. Tasker, *The Second Epistle of Paul to the Corinthians*, 1958, p.57; R.H. Strachan, *The Second Epistle of Paul to the Corinthians*,
   1948[5], p.73; R. Martin Pope, "Studies in Pauline Vocabulary: 1. of the Triumph-Joy",
   The Expository Times 21 (1909/1910)19-21; J. Héring, *The Second Epistle of St. Paul
   to the Corinthians*, 1967, p.18; H.A. Kent, Jr., "The Glory of Christian Ministry. An
   Analysis of 2 Corinthians 2:14-4:18", *Grace Theological Journal* 2(1981)171-189,
   p.172 and most recently, James I.H. McDonald, "Paul and the Preaching Ministry, A
   Reconsideration of 2 Cor. 2:14-17 in its context", *JSNT* 17(1983)35-50, pp.37-40.
52 Those who have tried to argue from the context usually point to 7:5ff. as support
   for the view that it is, in fact, Paul's triumph as an apostle which is the dominating motif. But not only is 7:5ff. outside our primary context, it is also not
   clear whether Paul's "comfort" in 7:5ff. can be construed to be a "triumph", nor
   whether the two contexts are close enough to be compared, since 7:5ff. is written
   in response to news from Titus, which cannot be assumed for 2:14ff. See M. Thrall,
   "Second Thanksgiving". pp.103,106,112. As she points out, following Windisch,
   "there is an obvious objection to the view that it was the thought of Titus's
   good news which evoked the thanksgiving: it is precisely Paul's actual meeting
   with Titus which at this point in his letter he completely fails to mention"
   (p.103). Thrall then adds her own argument, i.e. that when Paul does express
   his feelings upon receipt of news of Corinth from Titus in 7:6ff. "it is the
   vocabulary of consolation that he employs" (see v.6,7,13) (p.103). But this
   word-group is entirely missing in 2:14-17! Thrall therefore concludes, "In view
   of its prevalence in 7:6-13, one would have expected some trace of it in the
   earlier paragraph, if this, too, refers to Paul's state of mind consequent upon
   hearing the good news of the improved state of affairs in the Corinthian Church"
   (p.103). Moreover, rather than a triumph of some sort, it must be kept in mind that
   2:12f. speaks of a situation in which Paul did not, in fact, triumph! (cf. pp.106,
   112).
53 To give the most recent example, cf. James I.H. McDonald, "Paul and the Preaching
   Ministry", pp.36f., who first responds to the translation "who always triumphs

1) to cause to triumph; 2) to present or lead a conquered and captive one in triumph; 3) to lead a captive criminal through the streets; 4) to lead about publicly (with no negative connotations implied); 5) to disgrace or shame someone; 6) to parade or make a show or spectacle of someone/something; 7) to triumph over one in the sense of having a victory over someone; 8) to lead one in triumph as partners or co-victors in the triumph; 9) to lead one in a festal or choral procession as in the dithyrambic procession and dance associated with the cultic processions of Dionysos; and 10) to lead one in triumph as a metaphor of social shame and humiliation.[54]

In view of this ever growing number of possible interpretations being suggested in order to bring the meaning of θριαμβεύειν in II Cor. 2:14 into harmony with Paul's apostolic conception, the question raised by Paul's use of θριαμβεύειν may be formulated as follows: Can Paul's use of θριαμβεύειν be understood in such a way that it provides a suitable backdrop against which verse 14 can be interpreted, while at the same time making sense within the larger context of Paul's apostolic self-conception as presented in the Corinthian correspondence as a whole (rather than starting with some general and abstract notion of how Paul viewed himself)? Or must we agree that the only way to make sense out of Paul's thought is to modify the image of the triumphal procession itself, under the assumption that Paul used θριαμβεύειν in his own idiosyncratic manner? In order to answer this question we must begin by re-examining the role of the conquered in the triumphal procession. For in spite of the fact that this important Roman institution has long been recognized to be the backdrop to II Cor. 2:14 and Col. 2:15, the precise significance of the fact that Paul portrays himself as led in this procession has not been clearly applied to our text.

---

over us ..." by pointing out that "Lexically, this is normal usage", only to go on to assert that "Contextually, it is hardly admissible. But what is significant for our point here is the fact that McDonald concludes his critique of this view by going beyond the context to a theological judgment of its appropriateness: "... it remains doubtful whether Paul would have grounded what appears to be an important and characteristic aspect of God's activity in the triumph of a pagan general ..." (p.36). Why not, if this serves to illustrate his point in a graphic and memorable way? In a similar fashion, McDonald criticizes the translation, "who always leads us in triumph (sc. as defeated enemies) ..." by stressing the "notion of humiliation" which is contained in this view in order to emphasize, on the one hand, that "this is not comparable with the Pauline paradox, the slave of Christ", while on the other hand, that "it is surely stretching paradox too far to suggest that Paul was using this image of the God and Father of the Lord Jesus Christ", since "the *triumphator* is necessarily conqueror and oppressor". But Paul's own use of this image shows that this is not the aspect of the triumphal procession that he wishes to stress, since, as we saw above, the focus of the entire section is on Paul himself. Hence it is his role as the one led in the triumph that is of primary concern. Note too that both Windisch, *Zweiter Korintherbrief*, p.96 and Barrett, *Second Corinthians*, p.95 concede that their respective modifications of the meaning of θριαμβεύειν are asserted in spite of a lack of evidence. For yet another classic example of this, see Kümmel, additions to Lietzmann, *An die Korinther*, p.198.

54 Taken from the summaries of Windisch, *Zweiter Korintherbrief*, pp.96f., who listed six possible interpretations, and McDonald, "Paul and the Preaching Ministry", pp.35-39, who also lists six, but three overlap with those given by Windisch; with the tenth possibility being that suggested by Peter Marshall, "A Metaphor of Social Shame: ΘΡΙΑΜΒΕΥΕΙΝ in 2 Cor. 2:14", *NovT* 25(1983)302-317.

b. *The Role of the Conquered in the Triumphal Procession and its*
   Implications for Understanding II Cor. 2:14-16a

The institution of the Roman triumphal procession (θρίαμβος/*triumphus*)
as practiced in Paul's day was the result of a long and complex development, extending back into the pre-Roman period of the Etruscan dynasties[55]. In fact, according to Orosius, 320 triumphs were celebrated between the founding of Rome and the reign of Vespasian[56]. Fortunately,
the contours of the θρίαμβος/*triumphus* have been thoroughly investigated by scholars, so that the structure and content of the procession
itself are well known[57]. In addition, H.S. Versnel's recent work, *Tri-*
umphus, An Inquiry into the Origin, Development and Meaning of the Ro-
man Triumph, provides us with a massive and methodologically sound study
of the more controversial issues surrounding the origin and early development of the Roman triumph[58].

> Versnel's theory is that the Roman triumph we encounter in our literary sources
> was not originally a Roman institution, nor a direct adaptation of the Hellenis-
> tic processions carried out in honor of Dionysos, but instead owes its origin
> to the triumphal procession practiced in Etruria in the pre-Roman period; which
> in turn was an adaptation of an originally sacral ceremony performed as part of
> a New Year's Festival in which the king represented the deity in his yearly
> arrival and/or renewal[59]. This explains why in the Roman triumphal procession
> the triumphator was portrayed to be a personification and epiphany of the god
> Jupiter[60], as well as a representative of the ancient *rex*, even though the idea
> of a human being representing, let alone embodying the presence of a deity was
> offensive to the Roman religious consciousness during the period of the repub-
> lic[61]. In his words, "By wearing the *ornatus Iovis*, the *corona Etrusca*, the

---

55 The last Etruscan kings were expelled by a revolution at the end of the sixth
   century BCE; see Donald R. Dudley, *The Civilization of Rome*, 1962², p.23.
56 *Hist.*, 7.9.8.
57 The literature on the nature and significance of the triumphal procession is extensive. For an orientation, see the standard and lengthy article "Triumphus", in
   Paulys Real-Encyclopädie der Classischen Altertumswissenschaft, II. Reihe, Bd. 7,1,
   ed. Georg Wissowa, W. Kroll and K. Mittelhaus, 1939, pp.493-511.
58 Published in 1970, 409pp.! For the important literature see Versnel's work, which
   is not only thorough, but also interacts extensively with all of the major works
   on the subject to date.
59 cf. *Triumphus*, pp.7, 34ff.; 38,47,55,72,89-91,164,196f.,293 and 396.
60 This identification is based on the fact that in the procession the triumphator
   wore a triumphal garb referred to as the *ornatus Iovis*, painted his face red as
   also reported of Jupiter's statue, was crowned with the *corona Etrusca*, carried
   the eagle-crowned staff associated with Jupiter and the *quadriga*, the counter part
   of Jupiter's "four-in-hand", as well as on the fact that the destination of the
   procession itself was Jupiter's temple on the Capitol, where the triumphator
   offered sacrifices to the deity. The key texts are Livy, 10.7.10; 5.23.5; Juvenal,
   Sat., 10.36ff.; Suetonius, *Aug.* 94; Pliny, *n.h.*,33.111, 35.157; Tertullian, *coron.*,
   13.1; Isidorus, *Orig.*, 18.2.6 and Plutarch, *Camillus*, 7. See Versnel, *Triumphus*,
   pp.58-63, 83-87. Versnel supports this conclusion with his own etymological study
   of θρίαμβε-θρίαμβος // *triumphe-triumpus-triumphus*, in which he argues that originally θρίαμβε/*triumpe* were both exclamations designed to summon the epiphany of
   the deity during the procession (see pp.11-55 and 83-87,92). Versnel also argues
   against those who suggest that the triumphator represented only the king, rather
   than Jupiter, suggesting instead that the triumphator performed a dual role, representing both (cf. pp.83ff.).
61 Cf. *Triumphus*, pp.48,83,90f.,164 and 305.

red lead, the triumphator is characterized as the representative of Iuppiter. The exclamation *triumpe* proves that he was looked upon as the god manifesting himself. This idea, however, was no longer alive during the time of the Roman republic. It had its origin in Etruscan kingship and can be explained only against the background of Etruscan religion"[62]. Thus, "... there is no doubt that the Etruscan triumph, once it had been introduced into Rome and was kept up by the republic, underwent a fundamental change of meaning ... the scene of a man acting the part of a god, a deification, is incompatible with the truly Roman religion as we know it from the republican period"[63]. As a result, the customs remained, though their meaning was reinterpreted in the Roman period. The triumphator's former role as an epiphany of the deity is now replaced by his identity as the bearer of good fortune, i.e. the magical power of *felicitas*, who returns to bring welfare and blessing to the city[64]. Nevertheless, although the triumphator himself is no longer to be identified with Jupiter in the Roman triumph, the religious significance of the procession was never lost. As Livy tell us, the triumph was intended to honor the gods as well as the valour of the victor[65]. It was a special act of worship to Jupiter[66] and the highest honor a Roman citizen could receive[67]. As Versnel summarized it so well in the beginning of his study, "The entire history of Rome has thus been marked by a ceremony which testified to the power of Rome, its mission of conquest and domination, and to the courage of its soldiers. Primarily, however, the triumph characterized the greatness of Rome as being due, on the one hand, to the excellence of the victorious general, and, on the other, to the favour of the supreme god, who, *optimus maximus*, ensured the continuance and the prosperity of the Roman empire. *In no other Roman ceremony do god and man approach each other as closely as they do in the triumph.* Not only is the triumphal procession directed towards the Capitolium, where the triumphator presents a solemn offering to Iuppiter O.M., but the triumphator himself has a status which appears to raise him to the rank of the gods. Amidst the cheers of *io triumphe* he enters the city via the Porta Triumphalis, standing on a triumphal chariot, which is drawn by four horses. He is clothed in a purple *toga* and a *tunic* stitched with palm-motifs, together called *ornatus Iovis*, and in his hand he carries a scepter crowned by an eagle. His face has been red-leaded. It seems as if Iuppiter himself, incarnated in the triumphator, makes his solemn entry into Rome"[68]. (emphasis mine).

Our purpose is not to provide another examination of the meaning or significance of the triumphal procession as such, but merely to present the role of the captives who were led in these processions. Our aim in doing so is to highlight what it meant, in Paul's day, to be led in a triumphal procession, since, as we shall see, Paul pictured himself in II Cor. 2:14a as the object (ἡμᾶς) of θριαμβεύειν, that is to say, as one led in a triumphal procession. Moreover, since this aspect of the triumphal procession has been largely neglected in studies dealing with II Cor. 2:14a[69], it will be necessary to provide a number of represen-

---

62 *Triumphus*, p.92.
63 *Triumphus*, p.305. The key texts to support this conclusion are Diodorus of Sicily, 14.117.6; Livy, 5.23.5; 5.28.1; Plutarch, *Camillus*, 7.1; Cassius Dio, 52.13.3 in which Camillus' act of putting grey horses before his chariot was met with great protest, since only Jupiter was entitled to this honor, whereas this identification was precisely the point in the earlier form of the procession.
64 For Versnel's reconstruction of the meaning of the triumph in its Roman adaptation, cf. *Triumphus*, pp.304ff., esp. pp.388-396.
65 45.39.10.
66 Cf. Tacitus, *History*, 4.58.6
67 Cf. Livy, 30.15.12 and Versnel, *Triumphus*, p.304.
68 *Triumphus*, p.1.
69 See below, p.27 n.77

tative descriptions of the fate of those led in the triumph in order to
make clear what has already been recognized outside the realm of biblical studies, namely, that the captives "led in triumph" were, in reality, being led to their death[70]. Finally, since the focus of our attention is on Paul's use of this imagery, our discussion will be limited
to the relevant Greek sources from the first century BCE through the
first century CE.

Our first significant glimpse from this period into the nature and
purpose of the Roman triumph is found in *The Roman Antiquities* of
Dionysius of Halicarnassus, whose literary activity stretched from 30/29
BCE to 2 BCE[71]. According to Dionysius, the Roman custom of the θρίαμβος
began as a spontaneous response by the people to the return of Romulus
after his victory over the Caeninenses and Antemnates (cf. Book II.33.2-
34.2)[72]. But Dionysius is quick to point out that since its early be-
ginnings the nature of the triumph had significantly changed, if not,
in his opinion, always for the better.

> Such was the victorious procession, marked by the carrying of the trophies and
> concluding with a sacrifice, which the Romans call a triumph (ἣν καλοῦσι 'Ρωμαῖοι
> θρίαμβον), as it was first instituted by Romulus. But in our day the triumph has
> become a very costly and ostentatious pageant, being attended with a theatrical
> pomp that is designed rather as a display of wealth than as the approbation of
> valour, and it has departed in every respect from its ancient simplicity (Book
> II.3)[73].

In fact, the institution of the Roman triumphal procession had become so
well established that within the more general category of the "triumph"

---

70 Cf. e.g. "Triumphus", *R.E.*, *Bd. 7.1*, 1939, p.510, where it is emphasized that at
   the end of the procession "wenn der Zug vom Forum auf das Capitol einbog, wurden
   die Gefangenen in den Carcer abgeführt und - wenigstens nach strengem Brauch - ge-
   tötet ... ursprünglich mit dem Beil ... später durch Erdrosselung ... Die Feier-
   lichkeiten auf dem Capitol begannen erst in dem Augenblick, da die Nachricht von
   der vollzogenen Hinrichtung eintraf". See too Versnel, *Triumphus*, p.95, though
   this aspect of the triumphal procession lies outside the scope of his purpose and
   is thus not treated in detail in his work.
71 The Roman triumph was, of course, known earlier; cf. Polybius, *The Histories*, Book
   VI.15.8; VI.53-7 and I.7.10-12 and Diodorus of Sicily, Book XII.64.3. The English
   translations and Greek text of Dionysius are those of Earnest Cary, *The Roman Antiquities of Dionysius of Halicarnassus*, in the *Loeb Classical Library, 7 Volumes*
   (hereafter *LCL*), ed. T.E. Page et.al., 1947-1956.
72 This is, of course, legend. Versnel, *Triumphus*, p.89 points out that the archaeo-
   logical data we now have confirms the view presented by Livy, 1.38.3 that the
   triumphal procession actually began in Etruria in connection with the reign of
   Tarquinius Priscus. For such a triumph presupposes the use of the Jupiter statue
   in the procession, but there is no evidence of such statues in Rome prior to the
   Tarquinii dynasties. "There is, therefore, every indication that the triumph is
   an Etruscan ceremony, which was introduced into Rome by the dynasty of the Etruscan
   kings" (p.91).
73 For the second and third triumphs celebrated by Romulus, cf. Book II.54.2 and
   55.5; as an example of a triumph that was lavish and yet acceptable to the people,
   cf. Plutarch, *Lucullus*, XXXVII.1-4, though Plutarch is disposed to view them positively when others are not, cf. *Publicola*, IX.5-6. On the other extreme, cf. Plutarch, *Caesar*, LVI.7-9 for an example of one triumph that "vexed the Romans as
   nothing else had done".

(θρίαμβος), there had even developed a clear distinction between a
"greater" and a "lesser" triumph, each with its own distinct set of
rituals (see Book V.47.2-3)[74]. Hence, in conjunction with the victories
of Siccius and Aquilius over the Volscians, Dionysius records that

> When the couriers sent by the consuls arrived in Rome, the people were filled
> with the greatest joy, and they immediately voted sacrifices of thanksgiving
> for the gods and decreed the honour of a triumph (τῶν θριάμβων) to the con-
> suls, though not the same to both. For as Siccius was thought to have freed the
> state from the greater fear by destroying the insolent army of the Volscians
> and killing their general, they granted to him the greater triumph. He accord-
> ingly drove into the city with the spoils, the prisoners, and the army that had
> fought under him (ὁ ἀνὴρ ἄγων τὰ λάφυρα καὶ τοὺς αἰχμαλώτους καὶ τὴν συναγωνισα-
> μένην δύναμιν), he himself riding in a chariot drawn by horses with golden
> bridles and being arrayed in the royal robes, as is the custom in the greater
> triumphs (ὡς περὶ τοὺς μείζονας θριάμβους νόμος). To Aquilius they decreed the
> lesser triumph, which they call an ovation (I have earlier shown the difference
> between this and the greater triumph); and he entered the city on foot, bring-
> ing up the remainder of the procession. (Book VIII.67.9-10, cf. also Book IX.
> 36.3, 71.4).

The striking aspect of this account is that unlike the reports referred
to above, in which only the spoils and the victorious armies were mentioned as being led through the city in the triumphal procession, we now
learn that there was also an important third component in the march,
namely, the prisoners of war (τοὺς αἰχμαλώτους). For although in Dionysius' earlier accounts he had specifically mentioned the taking of
prisoners as part of the final stages of the victory itself (cf. Book
II.33.2-34.1) and had told us that these prisoners were "carried off"
(Book V.47.1), or in one case even "carried down the river to Rome"
(Book II.55.4), he had, until now, remained silent regarding their fate.
It is nevertheless clear that they too played an important role in the
triumphal procession, though the exact nature of their role only becomes
clear when we examine the next significant source of information con-
cerning the nature of the triumphal procession, that of Plutarch's
Lives[75].

Like Dionysius, Plutarch also knows the tradition that the Roman
triumph had its origin in Romulus himself (cf. *Romulus*, XVI.5-7). But

---

74 Further indications of how well established the institution actually was can be
   seen for example in Book VI.30.2-3, in which not only is there a controversy over
   whether or not one is worthy of such a honour, having broken some of the stipula-
   tions involved in qualifying for a triumphal procession (for some of these stipu-
   lations, cf. Book IX.17.4; XVII.5.3-4; XI.49.1-50.1), but even the clothes to be
   worn in the march receive a technical designation, i.e. τὴν θριαμβικὴν ἐσθῆτα (see
   also, Plutarch, *Caius Marius*, XII.5). In the same way, the music also had its own
   satirical genre appropriate to the "triumphal entrances", cf. Book VII.72.11.
   Finally, for this same distinction between a major and minor triumph in Plutarch,
   cf. *Marcellus*, XXII.1-4 and *Crassus*, XI.8 - though Plutarch offers a different explanation for the distinction.
75 Citations and English translations are from the edition, *Plutarch's Lives*, by
   Bernadotte Perrin, LCL, Vols. 1-11, 1961-1971.

unlike Dionysius, Plutarch reports that even in the time of Romulus the
prisoners of war played a decisive part in the pageant, now in the form
of "captives" (αἰχμαλωτίδες). For in commenting on Romulus' last triumphal procession, in response to his victory over the Tuscans, Plutarch
singles out the fact that

> Romulus also celebrated a triumph for this victory (ἐθριάμβευσε ... ἀπο τούτων)
> on the Ides of October, having in his train, besides many other captives
> (ἄλλους τε πολλοὺς αἰχμαλώτους), the leader of the Veientes, an elderly man,
> who seems to have conducted the campaign unwisely, and without the experience
> to be expected of his years. Wherefore to this very day, in offering a sacri-
> fice for victory, they lead an old man through the forum to the Capitol, wearing
> a boy's toga with a bulla attached to it, while the herald cries: "Sardians for
> sale!" For the Tuscans are said to be colonists from Sardis, and Veii is a
> Tuscan city. (*Romulus*, XXV.4).

Here we encounter the use of the verb θριαμβεύειν for the first time in
our sources. Its reference is clearly to the performing of the triumphal
procession. It thus functions as the verbal equivalent of the noun
θρίαμβος[76].

Hence, although it appears that in speaking of the glories of Romulus
in *Theseus and Romulus*, IV.2 Plutarch uses θριαμβεύειν to mean "triumph
over" in the sense of "to have a victory in a battle", in the light of
the technical nature of θρίαμβος/θριαμβεύειν throughout Plutarch's
writings it is more appropriate to read this text as a reference to
three separate accomplishments rather than as a list of three synonyms.
In other words, "to subdue nations in war" must be distinguished from
"to triumph over kings and commanders". The text reads:

> ἀλλ' ἔθνη προσηγάγετο πολέμῳ καὶ πόλεις
> κατεστρέψατο καὶ βασιλεῖς ἐθριάμβευσε
> καὶ ἡγεμόνας.

We are afforded an even better look into the nature and purpose of
the triumph by Plutarch's long description of Pompey's third triumphal
procession, which took place in 61 BCE after his campaign in Asia. In
fact, Plutarch even lists some of the more illustrious prisoners "led
in triumph" in that celebration, including "Aristobulus, King of the
Jews" (see *Pompey*, XLV.1-5). But it is only in Plutarch's extensive report concerning the lavish triumph celebrated by Aemilius Paulus in 167
BCE as a result of his victory over Perseus that we learn what the role
of the captives being led in the procession actually was. For after a

---

76 For this technical sense of θριαμβεύειν in Plutarch, cf. *Publicola*, IX.5; *Camillus*,
   I.1; VII.1; for θρίαμβος, cf. *Publicola*, XX.2; XXIII.2; *Camillus*, XXXVI.1; for the
   adjective θριαμβικός, cf. *Marcus Cato*, XXIV.4; *Pompey*, XXIV.6; and for the parallel use of θριαμβεύειν and θρίαμβος cf. *Lucullus*, XXXVII.1; *Marcus Cato*, XI.3;
   Crassus, XI.8; *Pompey*, XIV.1; *Aemilius Paulus*, XXXVI.2 and *Antony*, XXXIV.4-5.
   Moreover, the close connection between θριαμβεύειν/θρίαμβος is illustrated in
   Fabius Maximus, XXIII.2, where Plutarch remarks that "Fabius celebrated a second
   triumph more splendid than his first ..." (τοῦτον δεύτερον θρίαμβον ἐθριάμβευσε
   λαμπρότερον τοῦ προτέρου Φάβιος ...).

very long and detailed description of the first two days of the three day triumphal procession (see *Aemilius Paulus*, XXXII.1-5), and following his mention of the 120 oxen being led to sacrifice and the 77 vessels of gold which were carried through the streets (XXXIII.1-2), Plutarch continues his report by telling us that

> then, at a little interval, came the children of the king, led along as slaves (δοῦλα), and with them a throng of fosterparents, teachers, and tutors, all in tears, stretching out their own hands to the spectators and teaching the children to beg and supplicate. There were two boys, and one girl, and they were not very conscious of the magnitude of their evils because of their tender age; wherefore they evoked even more pity in view of the time when *their uncon-sciousness would cease*, so that Perseus walked along almost unheeded, while the Romans, moved by compassion, kept their eyes upon the children, and many of them shed tears, and for all of them the pleasure of the spectacle was mingled with pain, until the children had passed by. Behind the children and their train of attendants walked Perseus himself, clad in a dark robe and wearing the high boots of his country, but the magnitude of his evils made him resemble one who is utterly dumbfounded and bewildered. He, too, was followed by a company of friends and intimates, whose faces were heavy with grief, and whose tearful gaze continually fixed upon Perseus gave the spectators to understand that it was his misfortune which they bewailed, and their own *fate* least of all concerned them. And yet Perseus had sent to Aemilius begging not to be led in the procession and asking to be left out of the triumph (τὸν θρίαμβον). But Aemilius, in mockery, as it would seem, of the king's cowardice and *love of live*, had said: "But this at least was in his power before, and is so now, if he should wish it, *"signifying death in preference to disgrace"*; for this, however, the coward had not the heart, but was made weak by no one knows what hopes, and became a part of his own spoils. (*Aemilius Paulus*, XXXIII.3-XXXIV.2).

Thus, the "grim reality" of the triumphal procession was even more harsh than usually recognized by biblical scholars[77]. For as Plutarch's account makes clear, the king, his family, their friends and personal attendants were led through the streets as representatives of the vanquished in prelude to their execution[78]. Even the children were led as "slaves" (δοῦλα), unaware of the fate which awaited them at the end of the parade, while the king himself, as a result of his "cowardice", begged "to be left out of the triumph". It seems, however, that Perseus did, in fact, receive mercy at the hand of Aemilius. For in commenting on the fact that the deity Fortune had, as always, balanced his suc-

---

77 To my knowledge, only Findlay, Bartling, Pope and Windisch, in our century, have even pointed out that the triumphal procession resulted in the death of those led in it; though none of them take this aspect of the procession (if the procession itself is accepted as the meaning of the verb at all) seriously as the background to II Cor. 2:14ff. Thus, the idea of being "led to death" as an essential aspect of the triumphal procession has found no acknowledgement in any of the ten views that have been previously propounded for II Cor. 2:14ff. (see above, p.21).

78 Although Polybius does not use the θρίαμβος/θριαμβεύειν terminology in his *Histories*, Book I.10-12, it is no doubt the same institution he has in mind when he writes, projecting a later custom into an earlier epoch: "When Rhegium fell, most of the besieged were slain in the actual assault, having defended themselves desperately, as they knew what awaited them, but more than three hundred were captured. When they were sent to Rome and the Consuls had them all conducted to the forum and there, according to the Roman custom, scourged and beheaded ..."

cesses with the counterweight of a painful loss, i.e. the fact that he
had lost one of his sons just prior to the celebration of his triumph
and the other one just after it, Aemilius is said to conclude that

> that deity has sufficiently used me and my afflictions to satisfy the divine
> displeasure at our successes and she makes the hero of the triumph (τὸν θριαμβεύον-
> τα) as clear an example of human weakness as the victim of the triumph (τοῦ
> θριαμβευομένου); except that Perseus, even though conquered, has his children,
> while Aemilius, though conqueror, has lost his (XXXVI.6).[79]

The fact that the prisoners in the triumphal procession were being
led to their death thus explains the cryptic saying in Plutarch's eulogy of Pompey, namely, that

> when it was in his power to lead Tigranes the king of Armenia in his triumphal
> procession (γενόμενον ἐφ' ἑαυτῷ θριαμβεῦσαι), (he) made him an ally instead,
> saying that he thought more of future time than of a single day (*Agesilaus and
> Pompey*, III.2);

or the dilemma faced by Volumnia as she contemplated the fact that her
own son Marcius was about to march against Rome, his native city, and
her ensuing decision to commit suicide if he persisted in his plan,
since in her dramatic words,

> it does not behoove me to await that day on which I shall behold my son either
> led in triumph (θριαμβευόμενον) by his fellow citizens or triumphing over
> (θριαμβεύοντα) his country. (*Coriolanus*, XXXV.3).

The significance of the Roman triumph is also graphically portrayed
in Cleopatra's speech over the tomb of Antony, after hearing that Caesar
was about to send her off to Rome to be displayed in his triumphal procession:

> After Cleopatra had heard this, in the first place, she begged Caesar that
> she might be permitted to pour libations for Antony; and when the request
> was granted, she had herself carried to the tomb, and embracing the urn which
> held his ashes, in company with the women usually about her, she said: "Dear
> Antony, I buried thee but lately with hands still free; now, however, I pour
> libations for thee as a captive, and so carefully guarded that I cannot either
> with blows or tears disfigure this body of mine, which is a slave's body (τὸ
> δοῦλον τοῦτο σῶμα), and closely watched that it may grace the triumph over thee
> (κατὰ σοῦ θριάμβους). Do not expect other honours or libations; these are the
> last from Cleopatra the captive. For though in life nothing could part us from
> each other, in death we are likely to change places; thou, the Roman, lying
> buried here, while I, the hapless woman, lie in Italy, and get only so much
> of thy country as my portion. But if indeed there is any might or power in the
> gods of that country (for the gods of this country have betrayed us), do not
> abandon thine own wife while she lives, nor permit a triumph to be celebrated
> over thyself in my person (ἐν ἐμοὶ ... θριαμβευόμενον σεαυτόν), but hide and
> bury me here with thyself, since out of all my innumerable ills not one is so
> great and dreadful as this short time that I have lived apart from thee.
> (*Antony*, LXXXIV.2-4).

But the prospect of being put to death in the triumph and buried in Italy
away from Antony was too much for Cleopatra to bear. She decides to commit suicide with an asp, her last request being that she be buried at

---

[79] For another example of clemency being shown to a captive in the triumph, this time
to an infant, cf. Plutarch's *Caesar*, LV.1-3.

Antony's side. (cf. *Antony*, LXXXV.1-3). Thus deprived of his captive, Caesar nevertheless compensates. For as Plutarch reports,

> in his triumph an image of Cleopatra herself with the asp clinging to her was carried in the procession. (*Antony*, LXXXVI.3).

The fact that the Roman triumph often meant death for the conquered prisoners who were led as slaves in the procession, or at least for a representative number of them (e.g. the defeated royalty and/or the mightiest of the captured warriors), and that their being led to death was an integral part of the institution as a whole is confirmed by Appian's (CE 95-165)[80] parallel account of Pompey's third triumph in 61 BCE, which we saw earlier was also described in Plutarch's *Life of Pompey*, XLV.1-5. As part of Appian's account we read:

> in the triumphal procession were two-horse carriages and litters laden with gold or with other ornaments of various kinds, also the son of Hystaspes, the throne and scepter of Mithridates Eupator himself, and his image, eight cubits high, made of solid gold, and 75,100,000 drachmas of silver coin; also an infinite number of wagons carrying arms and beaks of ships, and a multitude of captives and pirates, none of them bound, but all arrayed in their native costumes. (Then follows a long list of the various kings, satraps and generals, etc. who were also led in the procession) ... (But when Pompey) *arrived at the Capitol he did not put any of the prisoners to death, as had been the custom of other triumphs, but sent them all home at the public expense, except the kings. Of these Aristobulus alone was at once put to death and Tigranes somewhat later.* (*The Mithridatic Wars*, XII.116-117).[81]

The last important witness for our purposes to the nature and intent of the Roman triumph is found in the writings of Josephus (CE 37-100)[82]. In the *Jewish War* VI.414-419, Josephus describes the fate of those who had held out against the Romans within Jerusalem, but had subsequently been taken prisoner when Titus entered the city in 70 CE. According to Josephus, Titus "issued orders to kill only those who were found in arms and offered resistance, and to make prisoners of the rest" (*J.W.*, VI.414). Josephus goes on to recount, however, that "the troops, in addition to those specified in their instructions, slew the old and the feeble; while those in the prime of life and serviceable they drove into the temple and shut them up in the court of the women" (VI.415). The task was then given to Fronto, one of Caesar's friends, to determine what to do with these slightly more fortunate prisoners. As Josephus narrates it,

> Fronto put to death all the seditious and brigands, information being given by them against each other; *he selected the tallest and most handsome of the youth*

---

80 English translation and Greek text from *Appian's Roman History*, LCL Vols. 1-4, ed. Horace White, 1955.

81 For Appian's other two major descriptions of a triumphal procession, cf. *Roman History*, Book VIII, IX.66 and Book II, XV.101-102.

82 English translations and Greek text from, *Josephus, Jewish Antiquities, Vol. VIII*, LCL, ed. Ralph Marcus and Allen Wikgren, 1963; and *The Jewish War, Vols. II and III*, LCL, ed. H.St.J. Thackeray, 1961.

and reserved them for the triumph; of the rest, those over seventeen years of
age he sent in chains to the works in Egypt, while multitudes were presented by
Titus to the various provinces to be destroyed in the theatres by the sword or
by wild beasts; those under seventeen were sold. (*J.W.*, VI.417-419).

Our first indication of what it meant to be "selected" and "reserved
for the triumph"[83] is not given, however, until some time later in Josephus' narrative, when in describing the final search for those who
were still hiding in the "mines"[84] within the city after the fall of
Jerusalem (VI.429ff.), Josephus reports that

John, perishing of hunger with his brethren in the mines, implored from the
Romans that protection which he had so often spurned, and Simon, after a long
struggle with necessity ... surrendered; the latter was *reserved for execution
at the triumph,* while John was sentenced to perpetual imprisonment (ἐφυλάχθη
δ' ὁ μὲν τῷ θριάμβῳ σφάγιον, ὁ δ' Ἰωάννης δεσμοῖς αἰωνίοις). (*J.W.*, VI.433-
434).[85]

Chapter VII, sections 119-157 of the *Jewish War* are then devoted to a
description of Titus' actual return to Rome and the "triumphal ceremonies" (cf. θριάμβους in VII.158) which accompanied it[86]. Unfortunately,
Josephus' description of the triumphal procession itself, the most extensive and detailed that we have, is much too long to reproduce here
(cf. *J.W.*, VII.123-157). Like those we have already read, Josephus' account also focuses on the wealth of the spoils which were paraded
through the city and the procession of the prisoners who had been selected for their strong statures and were now beautifully adorned for
the march to their death (see *J.W.*, VII.138). Of interest to us is Josephus' narrative of the execution which took place at the culmination
of the procession[87]. As he describes it:

the triumphal procession (here the synonym πομπή is used) ended at the temple
of Jupiter Capitolinus, on reaching which they halted; for it was a time-hon-
oured custom to wait there until the *execution* (θάνατον) of the enemy's gen-

---

83 The idea of being "kept for the triumph" also occurs in *The Jewish Antiquities*,
   XV.8, where it is reported that "Antony, on taking Antigonus captive, decided to
   keep him until his triumph". But Antony's plans are dashed by the rebellious condition in Judea and he is forced to execute Antigonus prematurely (cf. XV.8-9).
84 They were actually secret passage ways, cf. *J.W.*, VII.26.
85 The actual capture of Simon is described in *J.W.*, VII.26-36, in which once again
   we read that "on the return of Caesar to Caesarea-on-Sea Simon was brought to him
   in chains, and he ordered the prisoner to be kept for the triumph (θρίαμβον) which
   he was preparing to celebrate in Rome" (VII.36).
86 For the meaning of θρίαμβος in Josephus, see the parallel between its use in *J.W.*,
   VII.121 and πομπή in VII.122: "pageant of victory" (ἡ πομπὴ ... τῶν ἐπινικίων).
87 The well established and prescribed nature of the institution also becomes evident
   in Josephus' narrative. For among other things, we once again read of "αἱ θριαμβικαὶ
   ἐσθῆτες" (*J.W.*, VII.131, see above, p.25n, 74), and of the "porta Triumphalis",
   "the gate which, in consequence of the triumphal processions always passing through
   it has thence derived its name" (VII.130). For a summary of the parade route followed in the procession, see the art. "Triumph", *The Oxford Classical Dictionary*,
   1970², p.1095. See too Versnel, *Triumphus*, pp.132-163 for a survey and analysis of
   the various positions concerning the meaning of the Porta Triumphalis and his own
   view that it signaled an "entry rite" which formed the heart of the meaning of the
   procession as such.

eral was announced. This was Simon, son of Gioras, who had just figured in the
pageant among the prisoners, and then, with a halter thrown over him and scourged
meanwhile by his conductors, had been haled to the spot abutting on the Forum,
where Roman law requires that malefactors condemned to death should be execut-
ed. After the announcement that Simon was no more and the shouts of universal
applause which greeted it, the princes began the sacrifices, which having been
duly offered with the customary prayers, they withdrew to the palace. (*J.W.*,
VII.153-155).

Having thus reproduced a representative sample of the relevant evidence from both the early Greek historians and from Josephus, it is now
possible to draw a fourfold conclusion concerning the nature and purpose
of the Roman triumphal procession (θρίαμβος) in relationship to the fate
of those "led in triumph" and to draw out the implications of this study
for our further investigation of II Cor. 2:14-16a.

1. The *explicit*[88] purpose or goal of the triumphal procession, from
beginning to end, was twofold: First, to render thanks to the deity who
had granted the victory in battle (in Rome, Jupiter and in Egypt, Dionysus, see below), and second, to glorify the general or consul who had
achieved it. These goals were by no means independent of one another,
but inextricably interwoven so that the political and religious aspects
of the triumphal procession combined to form an indistinguishable unity.
In the texts we investigated, this unity was evident in the emphasis on
the songs of praise to the deity which formed an integral part of the
procession itself[89], as well as in the fact that the Roman triumph culminated at the temple of Jupiter, where sacrificial offerings and prayers
provided the concluding climax to the parade[90]. Thus, although the focus
of the procession itself was on the triumphator, with its display of the
spoils of war, the recounting of the high points of the decisive battles
through dramatic presentations and paintings, the army's praise for its
general and the parade of the vanquished foes, the procession *itself, as
a whole*, was intended to be an act of worship to the god who had granted
the victory. Furthermore, as both Versnel and Wallisch have emphasized,
this "Vereinigung des Religiösen mit dem Politischen"[91], was not a late
adaption of an earlier, purely secular institution, but a continuation

---

88 Of course, the institution of the triumphal procession also performed an *implicit*
   sociological and politico-religious function which, though important for understanding the significance of the institution in Roman and Hellenistic society,
   need not concern us, since our purpose is merely to highlight one particular aspect
   of the procession, and that only formally. In addition to the analysis of the significance of the triumph for Roman society by Versnel (see above, p.23n.64), see
   the work of E. Wallisch, "Name und Herkunft des römischen Triumphes", *Philologus*
   99(1954-1955)245-258, esp. pp.249f.,257.
89 Cf. Dionysius, Book II.34.1-2
90 Cf. Dionysius, Book II.3; Book VIII.67.9-10; Plutarch, *Romulus*, XXV.4; Josephus,
   J.W., VII.155.
91 This phrase is Wallisch's, cf. "Name und Herkunft", p.252.

of the function which the triumph had always had[92]. Moreover, Wallisch
has pointed out that the corresponding Hellenistic triumphs, as celebrated among the Ptolemies and the Seleucids, also preserved this religious dimension. Unlike the Roman triumphs, however, these celebrations
were interpreted in terms of the legend of the god Dionysus' triumphal
procession after his successful military campaign in India, which Alexander is said to have imitated in his march through Carmania, portraying *himself* as the successor of Dionysus[93]. But regardless of whether
or not one accepts Wallisch's theory that the Roman triumph owes its
origin directly to the Hellenistic institution of the Dionysian θρίαμβος
rather than tracing it back to an intermediate Etruscan development,
the sources nevertheless make it clear that by the second century CE,
the legend of Dionysus' "discovery" or establishment of the triumphal
procession as the basis of the institution was widespread[94]. As a result, "Dionysos war das große Vorbild des triumphierenden Eroberers von
Asien geworden"[95]. Thus, whereas in Rome Jupiter became the deity of the
triumph, in Egypt it was Dionysus[96]. At this point it is therefore once
again appropriate to recall what Versnel has said concerning this dual
aspect of the Roman, and by extension also the Hellenistic, triumph,
namely, that "In no other Roman ceremony do god and man approach each
other as closely as they do in the triumph"[97].

2. The fact that the triumphal procession was a well-known and well
established Roman institution is evidenced both by the various stereo-
typical rituals which were involved (e.g. the manner of clothing, the
order of the procession itself, the prescribed activities of the triumphator, the fixed parade route), the detailed conditions which had to
be met before such a triumph could be celebrated and its relationship
to the other Roman ceremonies of the *pompa circensis* and the *pompa*

---

92 Versnel, as we saw above, pp.22-23, argues that this religious aspect is modified
   in the Roman version in regard to the figure of the triumphator himself; but for
   the opposing view that the triumphator continued to represent the epiphany of
   Jupiter even in its Roman form, cf. Wallisch, "Name", pp.249f.
93 Cf. Arrian, *Anabasis*, VI.28.1-3; Diodorus of Sicily, Book III.65.8 and Wallisch,
   "Name", p.251. Versnel objects to the conclusions which Wallisch draws from this
   fact, i.e. that the Roman triumph was a direct imitation of these Hellenistic processions, cf. *Triumphus*, p.90n.3. The question of the historical origin of the Roman
   custom is not important for our study, though it should be noted that Versnel, contra Wallisch, traces both the Roman triumph and the Dionysiac ceremony to a common
   origin in the New Year Festival celebrated in Asia Minor, cf. p.299.
94 See e.g. Arrian, *Anabasis of Alexander*, VI.28.2, Diodorus of Sicily, Book III.65.8
   and the literature cited by Wallisch, "Name", pp.250f.
95 Wallisch, "Name", p.251.
96 Cf. Wallisch, "Name", p.252. On pp.253f. and 257f. Wallisch investigates the essential differences between the conceptions of the triumph in Egypt and Rome
   and how these differences were represented and embodied in the respective deities.
   For our purposes it is enough to note that in both instances this connection between the triumph and the deity was integral to the triumph itself.
97 *Triumphus*, p.1.

funebris[98], and the corresponding *terminus technicus* nature of the θρίαμβος-word group itself. For although the verb and adjective forms occur less frequently than the noun, it is clear that all three refer specifically to the institution of the triumphal procession, and not to the more general idea of a triumph in battle, for which the word group νικάω(νικέω)-νίκη was most often used[99].

3. The use of θριαμβεύειν with prepositional phrases to indicate its object[100] or with a direct object alone[101], *always* refers to the one having been conquered and subsequently led in the procession, and never to the one having conquered, or to those who shared in his victory (e.g. his army, fellow officers, etc.).

4. Finally, the role of those thus "led in triumph" was to reveal the glory and might of the victor by illustrating the *strength* of those conquered. In other words, the function of the captive led in triumph was to provide an *a-fortiori* argument for the military strength of the victor: the greater the stature of those conquered, the greater the stature of the conqueror. And, as we have seen, this illustration often, *or even normally* culminated, as did the procession as a whole, with the execution of these prisoners (or a representative selection of them). *To be led in triumph, i.e. to be the object of* θριαμβεύειν, *could thus mean, in a word, to be led to one's death in the ceremony of the triumphal procession as a display of the victor's glory and, by implication, of the benevolence of the deity in granting this victory.*

In conclusion, therefore, there is, to my knowledge, no external evidence for the suggestion that θριαμβεύειν in Colossians 2:15 and II Cor. 2:14 could refer either to Christ's act of victory in triumphing over the principalities and powers in a battle (Col. 2:15), or to God's triumph over Paul at his conversion (II Cor. 2:14), since θριαμβεύειν refers *only* to the specific Roman ceremony of the triumphal procession, which *presupposes* this prior conquest, but is by no means to be identified with it. Rather, the θρίαμβος, which took place in Rome, was the result and expression of the νίκη which had *already* taken place on the battle field. This temporal relationship and semantic distinction between the victory or triumph and the triumphal procession is explicitly

---

98 For a discussion of both of these points, cf. Versnel, *Triumphus*, pp.164-195 and 94-131 respectively.
99 For a good example of the clear semantic distinction between νίκη and θρίαμβος/θριαμβεύειν cf. Herodian, Book III.9.1.
100 E.g. with ἐπί in Plutarch, *Agesilaus and Pompey*, III.2 and Appian, *Civil War*, Book IV.31; with ὑπό and κατά in Plutarch, *Coriolanus*, XXXV.3; and ἀπό in Plutarch, *Romulus*, XXV.4.
101 Cf. Plutarch, *Theseus and Romulus*, IV.4 and Lamar Williamson, Jr., "Led in Triumph, Paul's Use of Thriambeuō", *Interpretation* 22(1968)317-332, p.319.

indicated in Colossians 2:15. The rulers and authorities are disarmed
and then led in a triumphal procession, the result of which is God's
public display of their defeat and destruction (death). The two participles ἀπεκδυσάμενος and θριαμβεύσας are not to be taken as synonymus,
but as the two, sequentially related events which together support the
finite clause ἐδειγμάτισεν ἐν παρρησία. In II Cor. 2:14, Paul's prior
defeat, i.e. his conversion-call on the road to Damascus, although not
explicitly referred to, is thus also presupposed, even though the verb
θριαμβεύειν *itself* does not refer to Paul's conversion. For a triumphal
procession, without a prior triumph, is inconceivable[102]. In addition,
there is also no lexical evidence that to be led in triumph, i.e. to be
the object of the verb θριαμβεύειν, could refer either to the idea of
somehow sharing as a co-victor in the triumphator's victory[103], or for
the factitive meaning of being "caused to triumph". Rather, the evidence demands that we first attempt to understand both Col. 2:15 and
II Cor. 2:14 in the light of the one, common meaning of θριαμβεύειν
which is attested for the time of Paul before we conclude, as C.K.
Barrett did concerning II Cor. 2:14 that

> *notwithstanding the lack of supporting lexical evidence* it is right to follow
> Liddell and Scott, Allo and Kümmel in taking Paul to represent himself as one
> of the victorious general's soldiers sharing in the glory of his triumph[104]
> (emphasis mine).

Nor should we assume that Paul employed this verb in any other, non-at-
tested, idiosyncratic manner. Instead, the starting point for understanding Paul's view of his apostolic ministry in II Cor. 2:14-16a is
the supposition that Paul pictured himself as one of God's *previously*

---

102 One of Rory B. Egan's central criticisms of the attempt to understand 2:14a to
be a reference to the triumphal procession is based on his correct observation
that "a 'leading in triumph', since it is defeated enemies who are so led, presupposes a defeat", "Lexical Evidence on Two Pauline Passages", *NovT* 19(1977)
34-62, p.37. For in Egan's view, since there is nothing in the context that would
make an allusion to Paul's conversion appropriate, the necessary prerequisite for
taking θριαμβεύειν to refer to the triumphal procession is missing (cf.p.37).
However, as we shall see below in chapter four, there is an allusion to Paul's
conversion in the καπηλεύω-motif introduced in 2:17. But even without this contextual evidence, the θρίαμβος imagery in 2:14 is itself enough to justify positing the underlying presupposition of Paul's defeat, since the two aspects are
inextricably woven together.
103 Besides the representatives of this common idea listed by Windisch and McDonald
(see above, p.21, n.54) and those given by Barrett, along with himself (see n.104),
cf. also T.W. Manson, "2 Cor. 2:14-17: Suggestions Towards an Exegesis", *Studia
Paulina, FS Johannis de Zwaan Septuagenarii*, ed. J.N. Sevenster and W.C. van Unnik,
1953, pp.153-162, p.161.
104 *Second Corinthians*, p.98.

conquered enemies[105], who, as a "slave of Christ" (δοῦλος Χριστοῦ)[106],
was now, to take the image in its most specific meaning, *being led by*
God to death in order that he might display or reveal the majesty, power
and glory of his conqueror[107]. Or, as Paul put it, "thanks be to God
who always leads us in his triumphal procession". Only if this meaning
can be shown to be inappropriate, may we look for another! In other
words, as startling as this may sound at first, our exegetical hypothesis is that in II Cor. 2:14 Paul is rejoicing precisely because God,
like a victorious general after his victory, is leading him as a *slave*
to death!

Unfortunately, commentators have been aided in their attempt to
avoid the meaning of θριαμβεύειν by the ambiguity concerning its meaning
which exists in the two major Greek lexicons available today. For

---

105 It has been objected that the attempt to take θριαμβεύειν in its normal sense is
impossible because Paul could not have pictured himself as conquered by God as
if he had been one of God's enemies prior to his conversion-call. See e.g. Windisch,
Zweiter Korintherbrief, pp.97-98 and most recently, Egan, "Lexical Evidence", p.37,
who rejects this meaning "since it involves the scarcely tenable concept of God
defeating his apostle as if he were an enemy". But in the light of Paul's conception of all Christians as "enemies" (ἐχθροί) before their reconciliation διὰ
τοῦ θανάτου τοῦ υἱοῦ αὐτοῦ (Rom. 5:10, cf. Col. 1:21), his ability to picture
those Jews who were rejecting the gospel (his own position before the Damascus
road experience, cf. Gal. 1:13f.) as κατὰ τὸ εὐαγγέλιον ἐχθροί (Rom. 11:28) and
his judgment that those who reject his example and gospel are τοὺς ἐχθροὺς τοῦ
σταυροῦ τοῦ Χριστοῦ (Phil. 3:18) it seems very natural to find this same predicate
applied by Paul, by implication, to himself as he was prior to his Damascus road
experience via his use of θριαμβεύειν in 2:14 (cf. Gal. 1:13f. and Rom. 8:7). But
again, θριαμβεύειν in itself does not refer to Paul's conversion-call, but rather
presupposes it. Cf. Victor Bartling, "God's Triumphant Captive, Christ's Aroma for
God (2 Cor. 2:12-17)", *Concordia Theological Monthly* 22(1951)883-894 who also argues that we should not abandon the "military metaphor" in 2:14 since it is based
on the fact that "God vanquished (Paul) at Damascus" (p.887).
106 See too L. Williamson, Jr., "Led in Triumph, Paul's Use of Thriambeuo", *Inter-*
pretation 22(1968)317-328, p.324, who correctly argues that Paul's reference to
himself as the "slave of Christ" is "thoroughly consistent with the image of a
slave in Christ's triumphal procession"; and V. Bartling, "God's Triumphant Captive", p.887: "Indeed, Paul's characteristic phrase 'slave of Christ' is a parallel to the concept of 'captive' involved in our passage". It is beyond the scope
of this work to investigate Paul's more general self-conception as reflected in
terms such as δοῦλος and ἀπόστολος, both of which have been the subject of intense investigation. All that can be said at this point is that once θριαμβεύειν
is understood to refer to the triumphal procession in which the conquered enemies
were led to their death as slaves, an inner connection is established between
Paul's self-conception in II Cor. 2:14 and his other understandings of himself
as the "slave" and "apostle" of Christ, since θριαμβεύειν implies Paul's conversion-call to be an apostle of Christ in which he was compelled as a slave to
preach the gospel (cf. I Cor. 9:16 and my discussion of this text below in chapter four).
107 Although they too fail to point out the significance of what it usually meant
to be "led in triumph", i.e. that one was, in reality, being led to death, the
description of the meaning of θριαμβεύειν and its implications for understanding
II Cor. 2:14 found in K. Dahn and H.-G. Link, art. θριαμβεύω, *The New Internation-*
al Dictionary of New Testament Theology, Vol. 1, ed. Colin Brown (trans. with
additions and revisions of *Theologisches Begriffslexicon zum Neuen Testament)*,
1975, pp.649-650 corresponds more closely to the evidence than most of the studies

Liddell-Scott-Jones, *A Greek-English Lexicon*[108], list no less than four
possible meanings for θριαμβεύειν, three of which are asserted to be
current in the NT period. Moreover, they suggest the meaning "to lead
in triumph as a general does his army" for II Cor. 2:14 - a meaning which
is unattested in the literature. On the other hand, Baur (Arndt-Ging-
rich), *A Greek-English Lexicon of the New Testament and other Early
Christian Literature*[109], is even more misleading, suggesting three different possibilities for II Cor. 2:14 alone! The inadequacies of both
treatments have already been shown in detail by Lamar Williamson, Jr.
and need not be repeated here[110]. What must be emphasized, however, is
that all the evidence points to the conclusion that there is only *one*
basic and common meaning for θριαμβεύειν available in the time of Paul,
namely, that of the triumphal procession in which the conquered enemies
were usually led as slaves to death, being spared this death only by an
act of grace on the part of the one celebrating the triumph.

This conclusion seems to be called into question, however, by Rory B.
Egan's study, "Lexical Evidence on Two Pauline Passages"[111]. Egan attempts to offer a completely different and independent meaning for
θριαμβεύειν in the time of Paul (i.e. "display", "reveal", "noise

----

currently in circulation and deserves to be quoted at length: "thriambeuō first
attested in Polybius (2nd cent. B.C.), is the Gk. neologism based on Lat. *trium-
phare* and means (a) intrans: to celebrate a triumph, (b) trans: to lead someone
in a triumphal procession ... In the Hel. enviornment of the NT thriambeuo meant
the triumphal procession of a ruler which his defeated enemies had to follow"
(p.649). Concerning 2:14 they rightly conclude (except for the death motif):
"Here Paul himself is led to triumph as one whom God had defeated, who as the
slave (doulos) of Jesus Christ is at all times and in all places a part of God's
triumphal procession. The apostle understands his missionary task as the work of
a slave who puts the power of the divine victor on show and by his proclamation
spreads the perfume of the knowledge of God, the one for life, the other for
death ..." (p.650). Nevertheless, since the death motif is not incorporated into
their understanding of the meaning of θριαμβεύειν, the crucial question concerning
how Paul actually reveals this knowledge of God remains unanswered. This is also
the weakness in Peter Marshall's otherwise important analysis, "Social Shame",
esp. pp.321ff. For while the idea of "shame" is certainly present in the metaphor,
it is the concept of being led to one's death in the triumph that functions for
Paul as the key to the adaptation of his imagery for his own purposes as a picture
of his apostolic suffering (see below, ch. two). Thus both attempts fail to make
the crucial link between "death" in the imagery and the theme of Paul's suffering
in I and II Corinthians, though Marshall rightly notes a connection between this
"shame" and Paul's weakness (see p.315) and even points out that "the social metaphor of strength and weakness" is the "theological equivalent of dying and
rising" (p.316).
108 1968, p.806.
109 1957, p.364. The situation has not been improved in the new English update of
Bauer's fifth ed. of 1958, *A Greek-English Lexicon of the New Testament and Other
Early Christian Literature*, revised and augmented by F.W. Gingrich and F.W.
Danker, 1979, p.363.
110 See his study, "Led in Triumph", pp.318-323.
111 *NovT* 19(1977)34-62.

abroad", "show", "manifest", "divulge", "publicize") on the basis of the
fragmentary 14 BCE papyrus from Roman Egypt listed as Nr. 1061 in the
collection *Ägyptische Urkunden aus den königlichen Museen zu Berlin*[112].
Although F. Field first called attention to this document in 1899 in his
short notice in *Notes on the Translation of the New Testament*[113], Egan's
goal is to adduce "new arguments and additional evidence in support of
Field's suggestion with the hope of lending it the scholarly credence
which it has never won ..."[114]. But Egan's plea is unconvincing for the
same reason that Field's original article failed: *BGU* 1061 does not refer to θριαμβεύειν at all, but to ἐκθριαμβίζω. The text reads:

περὶ ὧν καὶ ἐν αὐτῆι τῆι Σιναρὺ παρεδόθησαν
καὶ πρὸς τὸ μὴ ἐκθριαμβισθῆναι τὸ πραγμα
ἀπε (λύθησαν).[115]

In addition, since ἐκθριαμβίζω is a hapax legomenon in the literature
currently available, whose semantic relationship to θριαμβεύω is by no
means clear (though it seems to be a derivative extension of the verb,
whose meaning is taken from the function of the triumphal procession),
we have no justification for assuming, as Egan does, that ἐκθριαμβίζω
and θριαμβεύω are synonyms. And finally, Egan's "new evidence" turns
out merely to be two second century witnesses (Tatian and the *Acts of
Paul and Thecla*), a series of references to the much later development
of θριαμβεύειν to mean "display" or "make known", the history of its
translation in the various Coptic, Ethiopic, Slavonic, Armenian and Old
Georgian versions and, lastly, the understanding of θριαμβεύειν found
in the commentaries of the Greek fathers on this passage, extending into
the 12th century[116]. But it is not at all surprising that the later
Church fathers would speak of II Cor. 2:14 in terms of Paul being made
known or displayed, when, as we shall see below, this is precisely how
the use of θριαμβεύειν *functions* in the context, though it is not what
the verb *means*. This does not necessarily indicate, however, that the
fathers thought that θριαμβεύειν *itself* was no longer linked to the tri-

---

112 *Teil I, Bd. 4; Griechische Urkunden*, 1912.
113 pp.181-182.
114 "Lexical Evidence", pp.181-182.
115 Egan, "Lexical Evidence", p.41, translates it: "For which crimes they were de-
    livered up in Sinary itself and they were released in order that the matter not
    be noised abroad".
116 See "Lexical Evidence", pp.42ff. Marshall, "Social Shame", pp.302-311, has now
    provided a detailed response to Egan's arguments from later sources and versions,
    rightly concluding that "Our reliance on these early interpreters of first-century
    Christian literature should be tempered with caution ... As we reconstruct the
    world of Paul, we may be in a sounder position, in many instances, as his inter-
    preters than those in the centuries immediately following" (p.308). Marshall has
    also strongly countered Egan's attempt to argue against the possibility of taking
    θριαμβεύειν metaphorically in II Cor. 2:14 (see esp. pp.303-306, 309-311).

umphal procession[117]. Instead, the tendency is to read the meaning of
φανεροῦντι in 2:14b back into θριαμβεύοντι in 2:14a, the same tendency
found in most modern commentaries and studies of the passage (see below,
chapter two). Finally, Egan himself offers no detailed exegesis of II
Cor. 2:14 in its context, or within the Corinthian correspondence as a
whole, in order to demonstrate how his suggestion would better solve the
problems he has raised against the attempt to take the triumphal procession imagery seriously, especially the problem of the logical relationship between θριαμβεύοντι and φανεροῦντι in 2:14, which if his
view is correct simply become redundant.

But Egan's study is helpful in pointing out that the only possibility
for interpreting θριαμβεύειν with any lexical support at all in the
Pauline period (discounting his own suggestion) is its attestation as a
reference to leading the previously defeated enemies in a triumphal procession[118]. Hence, Egan's study, like the studies of those who have rejected this meaning before and after him, leaves us with a clear mandate,
namely, to demonstrate that this meaning for θριαμβεύειν can be reconciled with its context and with Paul's apostolic conception in general[119]. Indeed, at first glance it appears that my study has made the
attempt to take the triumphal procession background seriously even more
problematic, since it hardly seems possible to picture Paul as actually
intending to say that he praises God for leading him to death! What must
be demonstrated, therefore, is that the common understanding of θριαμβεύειν as outlined above, with its emphasis on being led to *death*, makes
sense in this context, rather than being "scarcely tenable" as Egan be-
lieves[120], or an example of an inappropriate attempt "(to press) the
full extent of the triumph relationship" as Marshall cautions[121]. Indeed, it is my contention that once the introductory thanksgiving in
II Cor. 2:14ff. is understood against the backdrop of the "triumphal
procession", with its emphasis in our context on Paul as the con-

---

117 For a clear example of this, cf. Chrysostom, Hom.V in Epist. II Cor., *MPG*, *Vol.*
    LXI, p.429, which Egan himself points out shows that while Chrysostom "states ex-
    plicitly and repeatedly that the word means something like 'make known, make con-
    spicuous, publicize, display'", it is nevertheless "quite evident that Chrysostom
    thought that the idea of a triumph or a victory celebration influenced Paul's
    choice of words" ("Lexical Evidence", pp.48 and 47).
118 See "Lexical Evidence", pp.36ff.
119 See "Lexical Evidence", pp.37f.
120 "Lexical Evidence", p.37. That this is the issue has also been emphasized by
    Marshall, "Social Shame", p.311.
121 "Social Shame", p.312. Marshall is thus content to speak of the more general
    nuance of the shame Paul felt because of his weakness and the humiliation he
    experienced in his relations with the Corinthians (cf. pp.315f.).

quered slave of Christ who is led to death, that this meaning not only
fits the context, helping to solve the other exegetical and theological
problems of II Cor. 2:14-16a, but that it also corresponds to Paul's
apostolic self-conception as developed throughout the Corinthian correspondence as a whole. The goal of chapter two is to provide the necessary exegetical support for this assertion. As a result, it will become
clear that the key to understanding Paul's thought in II Cor. 2:14-16a,
as well as its place within the Corinthian correspondence as a whole,
is the realization that to be "led in triumph" means, in fact, to be
"led to death".

Chapter Two

THE APOSTLE PAUL AS THE SACRIFICIAL AROMA

OF CHRIST (II COR. 2:14-16a)

In the past, the problem of understanding II Corinthians 2:14-16a
has been compounded by the sudden switch in metaphors in verses 14b-
16a. For it has often been assumed that if Paul intended the two terms
ὀσμή (vv. 14b, 16a) and εὐωδία (v.15) to evoke the Old Testament cultic
image of the sacrificial aroma which arises to God from the acceptable
offering (see below), then the connection with verse 14a, understood to
be a reference to the triumphal procession, becomes tenuous at best. In
fact, though it did not effect their interpretations of v.14a, most
commentators in the past confessed that the switch in metaphors from
the imagery of the triumphal procession to that of the cultic sacrificial offering was impossible. Faced with this difficulty, the only way
out seemed to be to posit a drastic discontinuity within the thought
of Paul, or to assign a completely different meaning either to θριαμβεύειν[1], or to ὀσμή and εὐωδία[2]. The first indication that our exegeti-

---

1 So e.g. Rory B. Egan, "Lexical Evidence on Two Pauline Passages", *NovT* 19 (1977)
34-62, p.38, who rejects the idea of the triumphal procession partly because
"any attempt to construe the image of the military triumph here is not really
corroborated *by the second part of the verse*" (emphasis mine).

2 Because of their modifications of θριαμβεύειν and Paul's invocation of the cultic
imagery in vv.14b-16a, Barrett, *Second Corinthians*, p.98; Lietzmann, *An die Korinther*, p.108 and Wendland, *NTD, Vol. 7*, p.176 all see no connection in thought
between 14a and 14b. Barrett calls v.14c "an abrupt turn", while Wendland describes
the use of the new image in v.14b not only as a shift, but also as "höchst
eigenartige". Windisch, *Zweiter Korintherbrief*, p.97, attempts to overcome this
problem by interpreting the two images of ὀσμή and εὐωδία as the incense burned
at triumphal processions, thus maintaining a consistent use of the θριαμβεύειν
imagery throughout the passage. Following Lietzmann and Windisch, I. Friesen, *The
Glory of the Ministry of Jesus Christ*, 1971, p.26 also opts for the view that
ὀσμή refers to the incense burned at triumphal processions. Although this recognition of the need to find a coherent image in vv. 14-16a must be applauded, the
attempt to relate the imagery of the incense to the triumphal procession is problematic in the light of the *terminus technicus* nature of the two terms as references to the cultic OT sacrifice (see below). For the same reason, James I.H.
McDonald's recent attempt to broaden the image to refer to "religious processions
in general rather than Roman triumphs in particular" also fails, see his "Paul and
the Preaching Ministry, A reconsideration of 2 Cor. 2:14-17 in its context", *JSNT*
17(1983)35-50, pp.39f. In fact, since the terminology ὀσμή/εὐωδία does not occur
in conjunction with the triumphal procession (though there is mention of the
burning of incense), Egan seems justified in his judgment that this suggestion
is "nothing more than exegetical gingerbread, an accretion to the image seen in

cal hypothesis from chapter one is correct, therefore, is the fact that
once the θριαμβεύειν-imagery is seen to involve the idea of Paul being
led to *death*, the inner connection between the imagery of 2:14a and 14b
becomes apparent, if not less abrupt.

A. THE MEANING OF II CORINTHIANS 2:14-16a

1. The Logical Structure of 2:14-16a

Paul's explanation for his burst of praise in v.14a continues with a
second substantival participial phrase joined to what precedes by the
simple conjunction καί:

> καὶ τὴν ὀσμὴν τῆς γνώσεως αὐτοῦ φανεροῦντι
> δι' ἡμῶν ἐν παντὶ τόπῳ.

But there are two reasons for regarding Paul's thought in v.14b to be a
logical progression from v.14a. First, the *internal relationship* between verses 14a and 14b makes the need for a progression in thought
from the participle θριαμβεύοντι to φανεροῦντι evident. For if the two
ideas represented by these participles are conceived to be logically
co-ordinate, then Paul's reason for rendering praise to God ought to be
clear on the basis of v.14a alone. But the thought of v.14a, "thanks be
to God because he always leads us to death in Christ!", remains incom-
plete and unintelligible in and of itself. It thus becomes necessary
to construe v.14b to be a continuation of Paul's argument in order to
complete the sense of v.14a. Second, the *external relationship* between
v.14b and v.15 also demands that we interpret v.14b to be a logical progression in Paul's thought. For the clause introduced by ὅτι in v.15
makes sense only as a ground for v.14b, and not as a support for both
vv.14a and 14b, which would be expected if the two statements were intended to be read as separate co-ordinate ideas:

> ὅτι Χριστοῦ εὐωδία ἐσμὲν τῷ θεῷ ἐν
> τοῖς σῳζομένοις καὶ ἐν τοῖς ἀπολλυ-
> μένοις.

θριαμβεύοντι", "Lexical Evidence", p.38. For a similar rejection of this attempt,
see R.H. Strachan, *Second Corinthians*, pp.74f. and V. Bartling, "God's Triumphant
Captive, Christ's Aroma for God (2 Cor. 2:12-17)", *CThM* 22(1951)883-894, p.888.
Bartling himself decides to accept Delling's suggestion, art. ὀσμή, *TDNT, Vol. V*,
pp. 493-495, p.495 that "Paul uses the traditional physiological idea of ὀσμή to
symbolize the power of God which gives life to the believer and creates the new
man in him", based on the ancient notion concerning animal and plant physiology
in which "Odours are thought of in such material terms that the idea of their
power to give life (or death) is self-explanatory" (p.494). But Delling himself
recognizes the development of the image in the OT and intertestamental literature
to refer to the odours of the sacrifice so that he too states, "ὀσμή εὐωδίας
simply becomes another term for sacrifice" (p.495, following Behm, *TDNT, Vol.III*,
pp.184ff.). Furthermore, Delling also recognizes that "the naturalistic metaphor
is completely forgotten ...".

Paul then completes his description of the apostolic ministry with a
statement of its twofold effect among those whom he encounters, linked
to the statement in v.15 by two relative pronouns:

οἷς μὲν ὀσμὴ ἐκ θανάτου εἰς θάνατον,
οἷς δὲ ὀσμὴ ἐκ ζωῆς εἰς ζωήν.

The flow of Paul's logic in II Cor. 2:14-16a may thus be reconstructed
in the following manner:

> v.14a Thanks be to God
> because he always leads me as his conquered
> slave to death
> v.14b and in so doing reveals through me as an
> apostle the fragrance (ὀσμή) of the knowledge
> of him in every place.
> v.15 The fact that God reveals himself through me
> is evident because as an apostle I am the
> aroma (εὐωδία) of Christ to God among those
> who are being saved and among those who are
> perishing.
> v.16a As a result, my ministry as an apostle is a
> fragrance (ὀσμή) from death to death among
> those who are perishing and a fragrance (ὀσμή)
> from life to life among those who are being saved[3].

In order to understand the meaning of Paul's argument, however, the nature of the imagery evoked by Paul in his use of ὀσμή and εὐωδία in
verses 14b-16a, through which he not only completes the thought of v.
14a, but also supports his contention that as an apostle he functions
as God's revelatory agent, must now be determined.

2. The Sacrificial Imagery of 2:14b-16a

The problem of understanding the imagery suggested by the terms ὀσμή
and εὐωδία is twofold. First, there is the difficulty of determining the
precise meaning of the two terms themselves, which are usually translated "fragrance" and "aroma" respectively. Second, there is the problem of determining what relationship, if any, exists between the ideas
which they represent, i.e. whether or not the meaning of εὐωδία can, or
should be extended to ὀσμή in our present context. In response to this
twofold problem three solutions have been suggested, which can be summarized as follows:

> 1) v.14b: Hellenistic reference to incense
> v.15a: Jewish reference to sacrifice
> Therefore discontinuity between vv.14b/15a,
> but continuity between 14a/14b[4].

---

3 The underlining indicates my attempts to make Paul's logical connections explicit.
4 For example, Windisch, *Zweiter Korintherbrief*, pp.97-98, calls the relationship
between vv.14 and 15 a "Häufung der Assoziationen" which work together "unschön".
Since for Windisch ὀσμή refers to the incense carried in the triumphal procession
(see above, n.2), and since he recognizes that τῷ θεῷ (not εὐωδία!) in v.15 brings
in the association from the LXX of an offering to God, he therefore views the

2) v.14b: Jewish reference to sacrifice
   v.15a: Jewish reference to sacrifice
   Therefore continuity between vv.14b/15a,
   but a discontinuity between vv.14a/14b-15a[5].

3) v.14b: non-sacrificial reference to fragrance
   v.15a: non-sacrificial reference to fragrance
   Therefore continuity throughout vv.14-15, but [6]
   only at the expense of the sacrificial imagery.

At first glance it does appear as if Paul intends to evoke two distinct images by his use of ὀσμή and εὐωδία. For the referents with which
the two terms are associated appear to be quite different. In v.14b
ὀσμή is associated with the knowledge of God, whereas in v.15 εὐωδία is
associated with Christ. For although grammatically αὐτοῦ in v.14b could
also refer to Christ[7], the fact that the praise is directed to God for
what he does "in Christ" (ἐν τῷ Χριστῷ) indicates that the referent for
αὐτοῦ is, indeed, God[8]. This is confirmed by the parallels to 2:14b in
II Cor. 2:17 and 4:6. For in 2:17 Paul describes a second[9] characteristic of the genuine apostles, i.e. that they are not engaged in
καπηλεύοντες τὸν λόγον τοῦ θεοῦ, but speak ἐν Χριστῷ. The δι' ἡμῶν of
v.14b is thus further explicated by the apostolic activity of v.17: God
reveals the knowledge of himself *through the apostle* (v.14b) who speaks

---

introduction of an offering motif in v.15 to be such an interruption in Paul's
thought that it must either be removed as a gloss (!) or retranslated as "Gott
zu Ehren" or "Gott zu Dienst".

5 So Lietzmann, *An die Korinther*, p.108, who on the other extreme sees no difference
in meaning between the two expressions and hence observes no discontinuity. Instead he sees a break in the imagery between 14a and 14b and thus feels no need
to relate either term to the triumphal procession. Consequently, against Windisch,
he doesn't think that the meaning of ὀσμή arises from the "Vorstellung der Weih-
rauchdüfte, welche den Triumphzug begleiten", but rather, is a totally new image:
    E. Lohmeyer, Heidelb. Sitz.-Ber. 1919,9, s.26ff. hat in Sir. 24:15, 39:13
    die spät-jüdische Wendung vom 'Wohlgeruch der Weisheit' als eine Vergeisti-
    gung der vielfach in antiken Religionen begegnenden Vorstellung vom "gött -
    lichen Wohlgeruch' nachgewiesen, der mit dem Gott wohlgefälligen Opfer und
    mit dem Paradies verbunden ist: hier ist Paulus der ἱερουργῶν τὸ εὐαγγέλιον
    τοῦ θεοῦ Rm. 15:16, der den Opferduft der γνῶσις θεοῦ zu Gott aufsteigen
    läßt (p.108).
As a result, following a suggestion by Lohmeyer, Lietzmann sees a Jewish sacrificial meaning, albeit spiritualized, in ὀσμή itself. Εὐωδία then refers to the
"odor" associated by Judaism with the life- and death-working power of the Torah
(for a further development of this idea, see below).
6 E.g. Wendland, *An die Korinther*, p.176, interprets not only ὀσμή, but εὐωδία as
well to refer to the ancient conception of divine fragrance which belongs to the
heavenly world, also comparing it to the use of the terms in Sir. 24:15 and 39:13.
Hence, Wendland extends a non-sacrifical meaning to both ὀσμή and εὐωδία.
7 See for example, P.E. Hughes, *Second Corinthians*, p.79n.11, who argues for this
reading.
8 This was the main point made earlier by T.W. Manson in his article, "2 Cor. 2:14-
17: Suggestions Towards an Exegesis", in *Studia Paulina, FS Johannis de Zwaan
Septuagenarii*, ed. J.N. Sevenster and W.C. van Unnik, 1953, pp.155-162, see esp.
pp.157 and 159f., though for very different reasons.
9 For the point that 2:14 ought not to be read in the light of 2:17, so that 2:14
also becomes a statement primarily concerning Paul's ministry of preaching, see
below.

his word ἐξ εἰλικρινείας (v.17, for the meaning of this statement, see below, chapter four). Hence, the subject of both v.14b and v.17 is the revelation of the knowledge of *God*; in the former by means of the display of the apostle in the triumphal procession as one led to death, and in the latter by means of his preaching. Similarly, in 4:6 the content of the revelation which is made known by God is described as the φωτισμὸν τῆς γνώσεως τῆς δόξης τοῦ θεοῦ ἐν προσώπῳ Χριστοῦ, so that the γνῶσις portrayed in 2:14 "unter dem Bild des Duftes" is now pictured in 4:6 "unter dem Bild des Lichtglanzes"[10]. But in both cases it is the knowledge of *God* which is in view.

Nevertheless, in spite of this difference, the unity of the two images becomes clear in view of the fact that in v.15 the support for Paul's assertion that he reveals the knowledge of God is precisely that he is the aroma of *Christ*! Thus, the "fragance of the knowledge of God" in v.14b must be equated with the "aroma of Christ" in v.15 in order for the logic indicated by the ὅτι to make sense. The reason why Paul is confident that God is revealing the knowledge of himself δι' ἡμῶν is because (ὅτι) *he* is the aroma of Christ who, in the light of II Cor. 4:6, is the manifestation of the knowledge of the glory of God. In other words, since it is Paul who reveals the knowledge of God in v.14b and Paul who, at the same time, is the fragrance of Christ, the fact that this latter statement functions to support or ground the former one demands that the two be equated, the latter functioning to define the former, and in so doing, to provide the reason for Paul's confidence in v.14b. T.W. Manson was right, therefore, in observing over thirty years ago that the *entire* phrase τὴν ὀσμὴν τῆς γνώσεως αὐτοῦ must refer to Christ, although αὐτοῦ itself refers to God (see τῷ θεῷ in v.14a)[11]. But even more importantly, the fact that ἐν τοῖς σῳζομένοις καὶ ἐν τοῖς ἀπολλυμένοις modifies the predicate ἐσμὲν εὐωδία Χριστοῦ in v.15, while its corresponding relative pronouns οἷς ... οἷς provide the link to the *parallel* phrases ὀσμὴ ... ὀσμὴ ... in v.16a demonstrates, without a doubt, that the two concepts must be equivalent in meaning in II Cor. 2:14-16a[12].

This conclusion is confirmed by the use of the world-pair ὀσμή-εὐωδία elsewhere in the New Testament. For it can be no mere coincidence that

---

10 The quotation as well as this last insight are from R. Bultmann, *Zweiter Korintherbrief*, p.67.
11 "2 Cor. 2:14-17", p.157. Manson missed the point of the imagery in v.14 as a whole, however, concluding that what Paul intended to express was that, in spite of his anxiety over the Corinthian church (2:12f.), "we must be thankful to God, who does not leave us a prey to our cares and anxieties but carries us along in the victorious progress of the Messianic triumph, which is sweeping through the world" (p.161).
12 So too Lietzmann, *An die Korinther*, p.108.

in the other two instances in which εὐωδία occurs in the NT it also
appears in conjunction with ὀσμή (see Phil. 4:18 and Eph. 5:2). In addition, in both cases the terminology is exactly the same. In Philip-
pians 4:18 Paul describes the gifts he has received from the Philip-
pians at the hand of Epaphroditus as "ὀσμὴν εὐωδίας, θυσίαν δεκτήν,
εὐάρεστον τῷ θεῷ", while Ephesians 5:2 refers to the fact that Christ
gave himself up for us, a προσφορὰν καὶ θυσίαν τῷ θεῷ εἰς ὀσμὴν εὐωδίας.
Thus, the two terms appear to have merged in meaning and in both contexts function together as a metonymy for the idea of sacrifice, as
evidenced by their use as a parallel to θυσία[13].

Finally, this merging of ὀσμή and εὐωδία to produce a metonymy, witnessed to in the NT, finds its origin in the Old Testament[14]. For the
terms ὀσμή and εὐωδία are the standard LXX renderings of the Hebrew
terms ריח and ניחח respectively[15]. ריח is a derivative from the very

---

13 The only other occurrence of either term is in John 12:3, where ὀσμή occurs alone
and retains its literal meaning. Stumpff, in his article on εὐωδία, *TDNT, Vol. II*,
p.809 also notices that this terminology "is both linguistically and materially
connected with the sacrificial context well known from the O.T.".

14 Cf. Delling, *TDNT, Vol. V*, p.494, though he himself rejects this as the background
to II Cor. 2:14f. (see above, p.42, n.2): "Esp. in the sacrificial regulations
of the Pentateuch we constantly find the statement that the offering serves as a
sweet savour to God, εἰς ὀσμὴν εὐωδίας κυρίῳ (e.g. Lv. 2:12; Da. 4:37a), that it
is an ὀσμὴ εὐωδίας τῷ κυρίῳ (e.g. Lv. 1:9,13,17)". For an opposing view, cf.
Windisch, *Zweiter Korintherbrief*, p.98, who postulates the possibility of seeing
the background to ὀσμή in v.16 in the fact that incense worked fatally on several
different kinds of animals as attested to by Aristotle and Aelian (see p.98 for
his list of sources). He proposes that this idea was then taken up by the Rabbis
of later times and applied to the twofold effect of the law "womit eine vollkom-
mene Analogie zu den Gedanken des Paulus gegeben ist". This same rabbinic background was already suggested by G.F. Moore, "Conjectanea Talmudica: Notes on Rev.
13:18; Mtt. 23:35f.; 28:1; 2 Cor. 2:14-16; Jubilees 34:4,7; 7:4", *Journal of the
American Oriental Society* 26(1905) 315-333 and then once again taken up by Manson,
"2 Cor. 2:14-17", pp.157-161 on the basis of the rabbinic parallels assembled by
J.J. Wettstein's *Novum Testamentum Graecum, Tomus II*, 1752, p.182 and Strack-
Billerbeck, Vol.III, 498f. The contention is that 2 Cor. 2:14-16a parallels the
rabbinic conception of the Torah as a drug which brought either benefit or harm,
i.e. that it was either a סם חיים or a סם מות (cf. e.g. Dt. Rabbah 1.6; b.Shab.
88b; b.Yoma 72b, etc.). But this parallel in *function* between the law and the
gospel in these texts ought not to be taken as an indication that ὀσμή itself in
v.16a is intended to be equivalent in *meaning* to this סם חיים. For there is no
evidence that ὀσμή was ever used either as an equivalent to the idea of a medicine
(סם) or linked directly with the Torah. On the other hand, it is questionable if
the Hebrew term סם ever meant "odor", cf. Kümmel's addition to Lietzmann, *An die
Korinther*, p.198, though Barrett, *Second Corinthians*, p.102 points to Exod. 25:6
and 30:7, where it is associated with anointing oil and incense respectively "and
this might have helped Paul to form the connection". In this regard, cf. too II
Baruch 67:6 where we read of "the vapour of the smoke of the incense of the righteousness which is by the law" (trans. Charles, *Apocrypha, Vol.II*, p.516). It is
entirely possible, therefore, that Paul was associating the twofold effect of his
own gospel with the twofold function of the law in order to build a parallel between the effect of his own ministry and the ministry of Moses! We will return
to this point in volume two.

15 Ὀσμή also renders באש in Isaiah 34:3 and בשם in Isaiah 3:24, but both lie beyond
the scope of our study. As a translation of ריח, ὀσμή occurs 55 times within the
Hebrew canon and εὐωδία, which always renders ניחח, 47 times. ריח is otherwise
translated by ὀσφρασία in Hosea 14:7 and ניחח by θυσία only in Lev. 26:31.

common root רוח ("breath", "wind", "spirit") and normally means "scent"
or "odor". As such, it can be used concretely of plants and fields (Gen.
27:27; Song Sol. 1:12, 2:3, 4:11, 7:14; Hosea 14:7), ointments (Song
Sol. 1:13, 4:10), persons and/or their garments (Song Sol. 4:11, 7:9)
and water (Job 14:9); or figuratively of one's influence or reputation
(Ex. 5:21; Jer. 48:11). In a similar manner, when ניחח is used alone as
a derivative of the verb נוח ("to rest"), it usually means a "quiet",
a "soothing" or a "tranquilizing" (cf. Job 36:16; Num. 28:2; Lev. 26:31
and Ezek. 20:28).

But when the two terms are combined in the construct phrase ריח ניחח
both lose their usual meanings and take on instead the nature of a
terminus technicus meaning "a soothing, tranquilizing odor of sacrifices
acceptable to YHWH"[16]. It is this new meaning which is then rendered in
the LXX with the phrase ὀσμὴ εὐωδίας, exactly as it is found in Phil.
4:18 and Eph. 5:2[17]. Genesis 8:21 is a classic example of this phenomenon. Here the covenant promise of YHWH, which was given in response to
Noah's burnt offerings, is introduced by the phrase

וירח יהוה את ריח הניחח ויאמר
יהוה אל לבו

which is then translated in the LXX tradition[18] as

καὶ ὠσφράνθη κύριος ὁ θεὸς ὀσμὴν εὐωδίας
καὶ εἶπεν κύριος ὁ θεὸς διανοηθείς.

On the other hand, Ezekiel 20:40-41 is a good example of the fact that
the *terminus technicus* ריח ניחח could also be used figuratively: Israel
is portrayed as a pleasing sacrifice which YHWH will one day accept as
his own, despite their present wickedness. The beginning of v.41 reads
according to the MT

בריח ניחח ארצה אתבם בהוציאי
אתבם מן הצמים

which is paralleled in the LXX by

---

16 Cf. Brown-Driver-Briggs, *Hebrew and English Lexicon*, pp.629 and 926. Barrett,
   Second Corinthians, p.99 translates εὐωδία "sweet savour of sacrifice" and lists
   Gen. 8:21; Ex. 29:18; Lev. 1:9; Num. 15:3; Ezek. 6:13 and Dan. 4:34 as examples
   of its use as a technical term for sacrifice. But he does not notice that it is
   only the use of the two terms *together* which constitutes this *terminus technicus*.
17 This observation is confirmed by John 12:3 where ὀσμή occurs outside of the *terminus technicus* ὀσμὴ εὐωδίας. Here it reverts back to its usual meaning of "fragrance" in reference to the smell of the ointment which Mary used to anoint the
   feet of Jesus.
18 All quotations from the LXX follow Alfred Rahlfs' edition. In the case of the
   Apocrypha, both the LXX and its English translation according to the edition by
   Charles are cited (unless otherwise noted), but the numeration is given according
   to Ralphs' ed. in order to avoid the confusion caused by the periodic discrepan-
   cies between the two editions.

$$\dot{\epsilon}\nu \; \dot{o}\sigma\mu\tilde{\eta} \; \epsilon\dot{\upsilon}\omega\delta\acute{\iota}\alpha\varsigma \; \pi\rho\sigma\sigma\delta\acute{\epsilon}\xi\omega\mu\alpha\iota \; \dot{\upsilon}\mu\tilde{\alpha}\varsigma$$
$$\dot{\epsilon}\nu \; \tau\tilde{\omega} \; \dot{\epsilon}\xi\alpha\gamma\alpha\gamma\epsilon\tilde{\iota}\nu \; \mu\epsilon \; \dot{\upsilon}\mu\tilde{\alpha}\varsigma \; \dot{\epsilon}\varkappa \; \tau\tilde{\omega}\nu \; \lambda\alpha\tilde{\omega}\nu.$$

It thus becomes clear that the phrase ὀσμὴ εὐωδίας is a rendering of
the Hebrew *terminus technicus* נחח ריה[19].

But of most significance for our study is the fact that the technical
term ὀσμὴ εὐωδίας as a metonymy for sacrifice seems to have been so well
established by the post-exilic period that not only could the term
εὐωδία be used alone to dignify the odor of the acceptable sacrifice,
but when used in the same context, the two terms could also be *separated* and used as *synonyms*. In contrast, when ὀσμή was used alone it
retained its usual meaning "scent"[20]. The fact that εὐωδία had itself
taken on a sacrificial meaning is demonstrated by its use in the synonymous parallelisms of the following wisdom sayings of Sirach:

$$\pi\rho\sigma\sigma\varphi\sigma\rho\grave{\alpha} \; \delta\iota\varkappa\alpha\acute{\iota}\sigma\upsilon \; \lambda\iota\pi\alpha\acute{\iota}\nu\epsilon\iota \; \vartheta\upsilon\sigma\iota\alpha\sigma\tau\acute{\eta}\rho\iota\sigma\nu,$$
$$\varkappa\alpha\grave{\iota} \; \dot{\eta} \; \underline{\epsilon\dot{\upsilon}\omega\delta\acute{\iota}\alpha} \; \alpha\dot{\upsilon}\tau\tilde{\eta}\varsigma \; \ddot{\epsilon}\nu\alpha\nu\tau\iota \; \dot{\upsilon}\psi\acute{\iota}\sigma\tau\sigma\upsilon.$$

"The offering of the righteous maketh
the altar fat,
and its sweet savour (cometh) before
the most high" (35:5).

$$\delta\grave{\sigma}\varsigma \; \underline{\epsilon\dot{\upsilon}\omega\delta\acute{\iota}\alpha\nu} \; \varkappa\alpha\grave{\iota} \; \mu\nu\eta\mu\acute{\sigma}\sigma\upsilon\nu\sigma\nu \; \sigma\epsilon\mu\iota\delta\acute{\alpha}\lambda\epsilon\omega\varsigma$$
$$\varkappa\alpha\grave{\iota} \; \lambda\acute{\iota}\pi\alpha\nu\sigma\nu \; \underline{\pi\rho\sigma\sigma\varphi\sigma\rho\grave{\alpha}\nu} \; \dot{\omega}\varsigma \; \mu\grave{\eta} \; \dot{\upsilon}\pi\acute{\alpha}\rho\chi\omega\nu.$$

"Give the aroma of sacrifice and a
memorial of the finest grain,
and make fat an offering as if you no
longer existed" (38:11)[21].

However, it is Sirach 24:15 which provides the crucial link for understanding Paul's use of this terminology in II Cor. 2:14ff. For here, as
in 2:14ff., the *terminus technicus* has been split up, but the two terms
have nevertheless retained their sacrificial meaning:[22]

---

19 Besides those texts listed by Barrett (see above, p.47n.16) this same phenomenon
   can be seen in Ex. 29:25,41; Lev. 1:13,17; 2:2,9,12; 3:5,11,16; 4:31; 6:15,21;
   8:20,27; 17:4,6; Num. 15:5,7,10,13,14,24; 28:2,6,8,13,24,27 and Ezek. 6:13; 16:19;
   20:28.
20 See above, p.47n.17 and below, n.24.
21 This translation is my own since Box and Oesterly, *Apocrypha, Vol. 1*, ed. Charles,
   p.450, attempt to represent the Hebrew original at this point in their translation.
   This unusual idea is explained in note K to Sir. 38:11 in the translation found in
   E. Kautzsch, *Die Apokryphen und Pseudepigraphen des Alten Testaments, Bd. 1*, 1900,
   p.418 as being based on the conception that "Wer sich so schon für verloren hält,
   wird ja wohl das Beste, was er vermag, Gott darbringen". See too Sir. 45:16 and
   I Esdras 1:13 for further examples of the use of εὐωδία in a sacrificial context.
22 Stumpff, *TDNT, Vol. II*, p.809n.5 points out that the speaker in Sir. 24:15 is a
   personified wisdom, and from this draws the conclusion that ὀσμὴν and εὐωδίαν in
   this context are simply recalling "a figurative intermingling of the old idea
   that Paradise ... is full of fragrance with the association of sweet fragrance
   with the self-declaration of the Godhead". this is also the interpretation of Sir.
   24:15 suggested by Lietzmann, Lohmeyer and Wendland (see above, p.44nn.5f.). But
   the last line of the stanza makes this interpretation highly unlikely, since the
   reference there is clearly to offerings in the temple/tabernacle.

ὡς κιννάμωμον καὶ ἀσπάλαθος ἀρωμάτων δέδωκα <u>ὀσμὴν</u>
καὶ ὡς σμύρνα ἐκλεκτὴ διέδωκα <u>εὐωδίαν</u>,

ὡς χαλβάνη καὶ ὄνυξ καὶ στακτὴ
καὶ ὡς λιβάνου ἀτμὶς ἐν σκηνῇ.

"As cinnamon and aspalathus have I given ὀσμὴν
and as choice myrrh I spread abroad εὐωδίαν.

As galbanum and onyx and stacte
and as the smoke of incense in the tabernacle"[23].

This then is precisely the same pattern found in 2:14-16a[24]. For here
Paul also splits the *terminus technicus*, using the two terms ὀσμή and
εὐωδία as synonyms. Objections such as the one raised by Plummer[25] that
"it is worth noting that the sacrificial phrase ὀσμὴ εὐωδίας, so fre-
quent in LXX, is not used here, and this makes any allusion to sacrifice
doubtful" thus lose all their force. Moreover, although it is certainly
true that in the mystery religions and later gnostic Christianity the
idea of fragrance came to denote "ein Zeichen göttlicher Gegenwart und
ein Zeichen göttlichen Lebens"[26], there is no evidence that this meaning is at play in II Cor. 2:14-16a -- but even if it were somehow implied, G. Barth[27] is correct in emphasizing that this more general
meaning does not exclude a connection with the "Opfergedanken". The
burden of proof thus rests on those who want to deny the sacrificial
backdrop to 2:14-16a. For there is no compelling reason to interpret
the meaning of ὀσμή and εὐωδία against any other background than that
of the cultic sacrifice of the Old Testament.

Moreover, it is not without significance for understanding II Cor.
2:14-16a that this terminological development takes place in conjunction with the wisdom tradition found in Sirach 24:15. For on the one
hand, in Sir. 24:15 the wisdom which offers the sacrificial fragrance
is *itself* identified with this fragrance (see καὶ ὡς λιβάνου <u>ἀτμὶς</u> ἐν
σκηνῇ[28]). On the other hand, in the Wisdom of Solomon wisdom is not

---

23 Box and Oesterly, Charles, *Apocrypha, Vol.I*, p.398 render this line: "(I was) as
   the smoke of incense in the Tabernacle".
24 Of course, the regular form of the *terminus technicus* ὀσμὴ εὐωδίας still occurs,
   cf. for example Judith 16:16. Hatch-Redpath also list Sir. 20:9; 38:13 and 43:26
   as possible examples of the occurrence of εὐωδία, but in each case the textual
   variant εὐοδία seems more probable. Thus, the only other example is Sir. 50:15.
   When ὀσμή occurs alone it always carries its usual meaning "scent", cf. Tobit
   8:3; Sir. 39:14 and II Macc. 9:9,10,12. As an exception, in Baruch 5:8 εὐωδία also
   seems to carry this meaning.
25 *Second Corinthians*, ICC, p.71.
26 R. Bultmann, *Zweiter Korintherbrief*, p.68. Cf. G. Bornkamm, *Paul*, 1971, p.114.
27 "Die Eignung des Verkündigers in 2 Kor 2:14-3:6", in *Kirche, FS Günther Bornkamm
   zum 75. Geburtstag*, ed. D. Lührmann and G. Strecker, 1980, pp.257-270, p.261n.17.
28 Cf. Lev. 16:13 LXX where ἀτμίς is used of the smoke of the incense used to cover
   the mercy seat to protect Aaron in his offering. For an examination of a similar
   spiritualization of the sacrificial cult found in Qumran and in the NT view of
   the Christian(s) as the temple of God, see Georg Klinzing, *Die Umdeutung des
   Kultus in der Qumrangemeinde und im Neuen Testament*, SUNT 7, 1971, and the earlier
   work of Hans Wenschkewitz, "Die Spiritualisierung der Kultusbegriffe Tempel,

only equated with the power and glory of God (see especially Wisd.Sol.
7:25: ἀτμὶς ἐστιν τῆς τοῦ θεοῦ δυνάμεως), but can also be said to be filled with a πνεῦμα νοερόν, ἅγιον (Wisd. 7:22), or even equated with the
πνεῦμα ἅγιον itself (see Wisd. 9:17b in comparison with 9:17a and 9:10).
In addition, one of the primary functions of wisdom's power or the Holy
Spirit in this context is to enable one to understand God's ways and in
so doing to make one a friend of God (cf. Wisd. 7:22,27; 9:2,5,9-18,
especially vv.15-18), something which remains impossible otherwise (cf.
Wisd. 9:14-17). It is precisely this threefold constellation of ideas,
i.e. wisdom as the personified giver and substance of the sacrificial
odor before God who is at the same time the power, glory and Holy Spirit
of God whose function it is to enable one to understand the ways and
revelation of God, which provides the background to Paul's understanding
in I Cor. 1:18-2:16 of his own role in relationship to the sacrificial
death of Christ on the cross, now itself identified in I Cor. 1:18-2:16
with the power, glory and wisdom of God (see 1:18,23,30; 2:7f.)[29]. For
in the light of this tradition concerning the revelatory function of
wisdom = Holy Spirit, Paul's emphasis that only those who have received
the Spirit are able to understand = accept (cf. I Cor. 2:14) the wisdom
of God in the cross of Christ (see I Cor. 2:10-12) and his corresponding
emphasis that his own ministry in Corinth therefore consisted in preaching the gospel of this divine wisdom *in the power of the Spirit and in
words taught by the Spirit* (cf. 2:4,13) become understandable, since it
is the Spirit alone which can reveal the wisdom of God in the cross.
Furthermore, the inner connection between Paul as a bearer of the Spirit
and the Corinthians' own reception of the cross/death of Christ as the
wisdom of God becomes manifest: the Corinthians have come to know the
crucified Christ as the wisdom and power of God precisely *because* Paul
came to Corinth as the bearer of the Spirit whose preaching was carried
out ἐν ἀποδείξει πνεύματος καὶ δυνάμεως (I Cor. 2:4). Hence, they owe

---

Priester und Opfer im Neuen Testament", ΑΓΓΕΛΟΣ, *Archiv für neutestamentliche Zeitgeschichte und Kulturkunde 4*, 1932, pp.70-230. Wenschkewitz observed that the basis
of the NT perception and the "rote Faden" which runs through the NT "ist die Deutung des Todes Jesu als Opfer" (p.226) and "daß diesem als Opfer angesehenen Tode
eine solche Bedeutung beigemessen wird, daß er als Gegenbild zur Stiftung der
alten διαθήκη durch Gott erscheint" (p.227).

29 I owe this insight to a seminar and colloquium discussion led by Prof. Stuhlmacher
and to personal conversations with him. For a detailed development of the wisdom
tradition as the backdrop to Paul's argument in I Cor. 1:18-2:16 and his contrast
between the σοφία τοῦ θεοῦ/σοφία τοῦ κόσμου τούτου; πνευματικοί/ψυχικοί etc. now
see Gerd Theißen, *Psychologische Aspekte paulinischer Theologie*, *FRLANT 131*, 1983,
pp.341-363. The classic example of the distinction between these two types of knowledge can be seen in Paul himself in his attitude toward Christ before and after
his Damascus road experience as formulated in II Cor. 5:16f. On the meaning of this
often misunderstood text, see most recently Otto Betz, "Fleischliche und 'geistliche' Christuserkenntnis nach 2. Korinther 5:16", *ThB* 14(1983)167-179 and below,
p.166n.200.

their very existence as Christians to the fact that Paul preached the
wisdom of God in the power of the Spirit, a power which was manifest
even though he himself came to them ἐν ἀσθενείᾳ καὶ ἐν φόβῳ καὶ ἐν
τρόμῳ πολλῷ (I Cor. 2:3)! With this contrast between Paul's personal
weakness and his role as the bearer of the Spirit firmly in mind, we
can now turn our attention to the meaning of II Cor. 2:14-16a itself.

3. The Meaning of II Cor. 2:14-16a

Having come this far, our exegetical hypothesis from chapter one,
i.e. that by his use of θριαμβεύειν in 2:14a Paul is picturing himself
as a conquered slave who is led to his death in the triumphal procession,
can now be brought together with our conclusion that in 2:14b-16a Paul
completes his thought by picturing himself in terms of the sacrificial
imagery of the Old Testament, especially as this culminated in the post-
exilic wisdom tradition. For although the origin of the imagery in vv.
14b-16a has certainly shifted from the Roman-Hellenistic backdrop of
the "triumphal procession" to the OT cultic backdrop of the "sacrificial aroma", the two images nevertheless form a coherent picture of Paul
as the medium of the revelation of the knowledge of God manifested in
Christ: Paul is always being led to death as an apostolic slave of
Christ and, through the display of Paul as the bearer of God's Spirit
in this triumphal procession (δι' ἡμῶν, v.14b), God is revealing
(φανεροῦντι) the knowledge of himself in every place (2:14). Moreover,
rather than presenting a problem for the appropriation of the imagery
of the triumphal procession[30], Paul's emphasis that God is leading him
to death πάντοτε underscores that this revelation is something which is
to be identified with his very being and continual experience as an
apostle. In other words, Paul's use of πάντοτε in II Cor. 2:14 indicates
that Paul views his entire life as one long triumphal procession. This
is confirmed by the parallel passage found in II Cor. 4:10, where Paul
again emphasizes that his call to "carry in (his) body the death of
Jesus" is something which constantly characterizes his life as an apostle
(for the parallels between the two texts, see below pp.69ff.). For
here too he does so by stressing that this process of carrying in his
body the *death* of Jesus goes on πάντοτε. It is not surprising, therefore, that the "knowledge of God" thus revealed through Paul in II Cor.
2:14 is then further defined and made concrete as that revelation of
God which took place in the cross and is now made known in Paul's ministry of the Spirit carried out in and through his own weakness = "death"
(2:15-16a). In other words, in II Cor. 2:14-16a Paul asserts that the

---

30 For the most recent example of this objection, see McDonald, "Preaching Ministry",
   pp.36f.

sacrificial aroma of the crucified Christ, which is itself the knowledge and wisdom of God, is being made known to all in every place
through Paul's own experience of being led to death, since *Paul himself*, as an apostle entrusted with the Spirit of the crucified Christ
(= the wisdom of God), *is* the sacrificial aroma of Christ to God
(Χριστοῦ εὐωδία ἐσμὲν τῷ θεῷ, v.15). Hence, the continuity between the
triumphal procession and the cultic sacrifice is established by Paul's
conception of his *own* "being led to *death*" as the *revelatory vehicle*
through which the Spirit makes known to all the significance of Christ's
death on the cross. There is, of course, no explicit mention of the
Spirit in 2:14-16a, but the parallels between II Cor. 2:14f. and I Cor.
1:17f.; 4:8-13; II Cor. 4:7ff.; 12:9f., etc. which will be investigated
below, as well as Paul's argument in 3:3 (see chapter five), make this
connection manifest. Paul's revelatory function is grounded in the fact
that *in his suffering* he preaches and acts *in the Spirit*, and that in
the midst of his being led to *death* the Spirit is poured out on others
to bring them to *life* in Christ. The thread that ties the two images in
2:14f. together, which at first seem so disparate, is therefore Paul
himself (cf. ἡμᾶς, v.14a; δι' ἡμῶν, v.14b; ἐσμέν, v.15). For from start
to finish the focus of attention in 2:14ff. is on Paul's revelatory role
as the apostolic slave of Christ who in his being led to death is
spreading the knowledge of God by means of the Spirit[31]. As a result,
the attempt to posit a distinction between v.14b, taken to refer to
Paul's ministry of preaching the word, and v.15, taken to be a reference
to Paul himself, is unjustified[32].

But in the light of the continuation of Paul's thought in 2:17, it
must also be emphasized that Paul's apostolic role of *"being led to
death"* ἐν τῷ Χριστῷ in order to reveal the knowledge of God in 2:14-16a
cannot be separated from his call to *preach the word of God* ἐν Χριστῷ
in 2:17. For although the two aspects are distinct and ought not to be

---

[31] It is difficult to decide whether the imagery of II Cor. 2:15 implies that Christ
himself is to be pictured as a (burnt offering) sacrifice as C.K. Barrett, *Second
Corinthians*, p.99 has suggested when he interprets the meaning of Paul's imagery
to be that "the apostles are the smoke that arises from the sacrifice of Christ
to God ...". For on the one hand, although Lev. 4:31 does speak of such an atoning
burnt offering (cf. Lev. 1:4; 16:24), the sin atonement was usually performed outside the camp and was distinguished from such a burnt offering, see Lev. 4:12,21
and Heb. 13:13. Moreover, the Passover lamb was not presented as a burnt offering,
so that the identification of Christ as the paschal lamb who was sacrificed in I
Cor. 5:7 (see Mk. 14:12; Lk. 22:7; John 1:29,36; Heb. 9:13f.,23-28) does not seem
to provide a suitable background to II Cor. 2:14f. On the other hand, Eph. 5:2
speaks explicitly of Christ as having παρέδωκεν ἑαυτὸν ὑπὲρ ἡμῶν προσφορὰν καὶ
θυσίαν τῷ θεῷ εἰς ὀσμὴν εὐωδίας! We can, however, leave this question open for
our purposes.

[32] The classic example of this attempt is R. Bultmann's treatment of this passage in
his commentary on II Corinthians, see his *Zweiter Korintherbrief*, pp.67, 70, 97f.

collapsed into one another, they nevertheless do interpenetrate and
confirm each other as the essential hallmarks of the genuine apostolic
calling. For the apostolic message is embodied in the life of the
apostle itself, and in both cases this twofold apostolic activity takes
place "in Christ". Paul's emphasis in 2:14-17 that his role of suffering and call to preach as an apostle are anchored "in Christ" is merely
an extension of his fundamental conviction that he has been called to
be an apostle Χριστοῦ Ἰησοῦ (I Cor. 1:1; II Cor. 1:1) and as such ought
to be regarded as a servant of Christ and steward of the mysteries of
God (I Cor. 4:1). Being called by Christ to be his apostolic servant,
Paul's life and message can naturally be said to take place "in Christ".
Moreover, given the nature of this apostolic calling and its fruits,
Paul's relationship to the Corinthians as *their* apostle can also appropriately be described in the same manner: he became their father
through the gospel ἐν Χριστῷ Ἰησοῦ (I Cor. 4:15); he has a boast or
pride in them ἐν Χριστῷ Ἰησοῦ (I Cor. 15:31) and extends his love to
them ἐν Χριστῷ Ἰησοῦ (I Cor. 16:24). Conversely, since the church in
Corinth came into existence as a result of Paul's apostolic life and
message "ἐν Χριστῷ", it too can be described in the same terms: the Corinthians have been set apart ἐν Χριστῷ Ἰησοῦ (I Cor. 1:2), given specific gifts of grace ἐν Χριστῷ Ἰησοῦ (I. Cor. 1:4f.) and thus find
their life ἐν Χριστῷ Ἰησοῦ (I Cor. 1:30; cf. I Cor. 15:19, 22 and II
Cor. 5:17). In short, the church is the σῶμα Χριστοῦ (I Cor. 12:27),
even though certain members of it are still babes "in Christ" (I Cor.
3:1), since the status of being "in Christ" is based on the work of
God ἐν Χριστῷ as described in II Cor. 5:19. Fourthly, Paul's awareness
of the fact that as an apostle of Christ he speaks "in Christ" (II Cor.
2:17; 12:19) is the foundation for his confidence that Christ is speaking "in him" (see II Cor. 13:3), just as the Corinthians' new existence
"in Christ" (II Cor. 5:17) is the foundation for their confidence that
Christ is in them if they maintain their faith (see II Cor. 13:5). For
Paul to emphasize that as an apostle he is being led to death "in
Christ" in II Cor. 2:14, or that he speaks "in Christ" in 2:17, is thus
another example of his essential self-understanding that his very existence as such is part and parcel of God's continuing self-revelation "in
Christ". As J.H. Schütz has pointed out,

> taking ἐν Χριστῷ in its adverbial sense, with θριαμβεύειν, we see that Paul
> is describing God's activity in Christ by making the focus of that activity
> the life of the apostle himself. In the apostle is the manifestation of God's
> activity[33].

---

33 *Paul and the Anatomy of Apostolic Authority, SNTS Monograph Series 26,* 1975, pp.
210-211.

For it is Christ whom Paul imitates (I Cor. 11:1), the suffering of
Christ which Paul shares (II Cor. 1:5) and the power of Christ which
rests upon him in that weakness (II Cor. 12:9).

Finally, although Paul himself does not highlight them, the coherence
between the two images in 2:14 and 15 is supported by the inner connections which exist between the two motifs themselves. For as we saw in
chapter one, the triumphal procession was itself an act of worship
through which the benevolence of the deity was glorified and revealed.
Moreover, the captives who are led to death in the procession were in-
tricately linked to the sacrifices which played such an integral role
in the celebration. Hence, the thoroughly religious nature of the triumphal procession provided a conceptual basis for an association of the
two motifs. And, as we will see below, the act of being rescued from
this death in the triumphal procession as an act of grace by the emperor
also seems to picture an essential aspect of Paul's own understanding of
how God's glory and power are manifested through his suffering. Furthermore, Paul's understanding of himself as the conquered slave of Christ
implicit in the θριαμβεύειν-imagery in 2:14 is surely the counterpart
to his understanding of himself as one who now labors and lives only
by God's grace or the life of Christ in him (cf. I Cor. 15:10; Gal.
2:20). Hence, in his life as an apostle he becomes the "fragrance of
Christ", i.e. what he accomplishes *and suffers (!)* (see Phil. 3:10) is
an outworking of the grace of God on his behalf. Unfortunately, it is
not possible to go beyond these general observations in determining the
implicit link which Paul had in mind and which led him to wed these two
images together. For as we have already seen, the only explicit point
of contact is the *revelatory function* which Paul himself performs as
both the captive and the sacrificial aroma in the two metaphors[34].

---

34 Paul's ability to employ an OT cultic image in II Cor. 2:15f. in order to picture
himself as the sacrifical aroma of Christ to God is further confirmed by his corresponding ability to describe his apostolic ministry in terms of the cultic
service of the priest in Romans 15:16, although the two texts are not identical.
In II Cor. 2:15f. Paul pictures himself as the sacrificial aroma of Christ, while
in Rom. 15:16 Paul is the priest who offers up the Gentiles, or their obedience
and glorifying of God (see Rom. 15:9, 18), in the priestly service of the gospel.
For helpful discussions of this important Pauline self-understanding, see K. Weiß,
"Paulus - Priester der Christlichen Kultgemeinde", *ThLZ* 79(1954)355-364 and D.W.B.
Robinson, "The Priesthood of Paul in the Gospel of Hope", in *Reconciliation and
Hope, FS L.L. Morris on his 60th Birthday*, ed. R. Banks, 1974, pp.231-245. Both
Weiß, p.357 and Robinson, p.231n.1, point out the connection between Paul's self-
conception as a δοῦλος 'Ιησοῦ Χριστοῦ and λειτουργὸς Χριστοῦ 'Ιησοῦ. It is not
going too far, therefore, to suggest that II Cor. 2:14-16a is implicitly built
upon these other two important aspects of Paul's self-understanding as an apostle,
especially when in the wisdom tradition the priest serves because of and in the
wisdom = Spirit given to him (see Sir. 24:10f.), just as Paul serves in the Spirit
(Rom. 15:19) and because of God's grace (Rom. 15:15). This relationship between
Paul's role as priest and his description of himself as the aroma of the crucified
Christ has also been explained on the basis of the sacrificial component in this

4. The Significance of the Parallel between II Cor. 2:14-16a and
   I Cor. 1:17-18

The interrelationship between Paul's experience as an apostle *under
the cross* and his apostolic message *of the cross*, which, as we saw
above, comes to light in the transition from 2:14-16a to 2:17, is also
made evident by the "offenkundige(r) Parallele" which exist between I
Cor. 1:17f. and II Cor. 2:14-16a[35]. For in I Cor. 1:17 Paul explains
the goal of his having been sent by Christ to preach the gospel οὐκ ἐν
σοφίᾳ λόγου in terms of a negative purpose, namely, ἵνα μὴ κενωθῇ ὁ
σταυρὸς τοῦ Χριστοῦ. He then proceeds in v.18 to support this purpose
by providing the rationale behind his mandate from Christ to conform
the mode of his message to the content of the message itself (cf. I Cor.
2:1-5): Even Paul's manner of preaching must conform to the cross since
it is specifically the *cross* of Christ which is the power of God. Thus,
when we compare I Cor. 1:17f. to II Cor. 2:15-16a three important results follow. First, it becomes clear that Paul considered both the
style of his proclamation, as well as that of his life, to be determined by the cross (I Cor. 1:17 and II Cor. 2:14, cf. I Cor. 2:1,4)[36].
Second, Paul's rationale for this, in *both* cases, resided in the fact
that it was the cross which provided the foundation and content of his
apostolic preaching and existence (cf. the γὰρ in I Cor. 1:18a and the
ὅτι in II Cor. 2:15a). Finally, the "horrifying truth"[37], which for Paul
undergirded both the message and existence of the apostle was the function his ministry played in furthering the process either of one's salvation (life), or of one's damnation (death) (I Cor. 1:18bc and II Cor.

---

analogy by H. Schürmann, "Die Apostolische Existenz im Bilde; Meditation über 2
Kor 2:14-16a", in *Ursprung und Gestalt, Erörterungen und Besinnungen zum Neuen
Testament*, 1970, pp.229-235, pp.233-234.

35 So G. Eichholz, *Theologie des Paulus im Umriss*, 1977², p.58, though he takes both
   passages to refer to the preaching of the gospel. Cf. also A.Schlatter, *Bote*,
   p.497 and Windisch, *Zweiter Korintherbrief*, p.99. But although all notice the
   parallel between the ἀπολλυμένοις ... σωζομένοις complex, they do not mention
   the parallels between I Cor. 1:17-18a and II Cor. 2:14-15a.

36 So too U. Luz, "Theologia crucis als Mitte der Theologie im Neuen Testament", *EvTh*
   34(1974)116-141, p.122: "Für Paulus besteht Kreuzes-theologie nicht darin, daß er
   das Kreuz interpretiert, sondern daß er vom Kreuz her die Welt, die Gemeinde, den
   Menschen interpretiert". Speaking of the word of the cross as power he goes on to
   say, "Wie diese Macht des Wortes vom Kreuz sich am Menschen auswirkt, zeigt Paulus
   an den Korinthern (I Kor 1:26ff.) und noch deutlicher an sich selbst: Das Wort
   vom Kreuz macht den Apostel selbst kreuzförmig (I Kor 2:1ff.; II Kor 4:7ff. und
   passim; Gal 6:14) und weist ihm so eine bestimmte Rolle zu, die ihm überhaupt vom
   Kreuz legitim zu reden allererst erlaubt" (p.122). From these perspectives he thus
   concludes that, *"Paulinische Kreuzestheologie ist somit nicht zu trennen von der
   eigenen Existenz des Apostels, dem über ihn selbst fortwährend ergehenden Gericht*.
   Eine negative Feststellung ist noch wichtig: Es gibt bei Paulus keinerlei Anzeichen
   dafür, daß seine Kreuzestheologie ein Produkt, gleichsam eine Projektion seines
   Leidens gewesen wäre" (p.128).

37 C.K. Barrett's appropriate response to 2:16, *Second Corinthians*, p.102.

2:15b-16a). For whether one thinks that the ἐκ ... εἰς structure in 2:16 refers to the Pauline concept of predestination or not[38], what is clear in *both* contexts is that for Paul one's eschatological fate was already being realized (note the present tense participles!). To reject Paul's message of the cross as foolishness, or to be offended by his personal "sacrificial aroma of Christ" was, for Paul, a confirmation that one was already perishing. Conversely, to accept Paul and his message was a demonstration that the power of God (I Cor. 1:18c) was already at work within (and without, cf. Rom. 8:28-39) to save[39]. Finally, and most significant for our study, is the fact that a comparison of II Cor. 2:14-16a with I Cor. 1:17f. makes particularly clear that everything Paul could say about the message of the cross which he preached, he could also say about his *experience or way of life* as the apostolic slave of Christ who was "being led to death"[40]. For as Heinz Schürmann observed on the basis of this same comparison,

> Die gleiche widerspruchsvolle Erfahrung deutet Paulus an unserer Stelle (i.e.
> II Cor. 2:15-16) noch grundsätzlicher aus: Er selbst, die apostolische Verleib-
> lichung des Wortes Christi, wirkt auf die einen wie ein Todesgeruch, auf die

---

38 For examples of those who do see a reference to predestination in 2:15-16a, cf. Schlatter, *Bote*, p.497, who attributes a "kausale Kraft" to the ἐκ-εἰς construction; Windisch, *Zweiter Korintherbrief*, p.99, who speaks of its "prädestinatianischen Klang" and Wendland, *Korinther*, *NTD*, p.176, who translates it, "Für die dem Tode Bestimmten ist dieser 'Duft' todbringend, die zum Leben Bestimmten aber führt er zum Leben". Against this view, see V. Bartling, "God's Triumphant Captive", pp. 890-891, who calls this attempt simply "un-Biblical"; Lietzmann, *An die Korinther*, p.109 and Hughes, *Second Corinthians*, p.81n.18, who both take it to be merely an idiom of some sort which is not to be pressed too far; cf. also Kümmel's additions to Lietzmann, p.198 for this point. Bultmann, *Zweiter Korintherbrief*, p.71, takes a mediating position, denying the sense of predestination to the construction itself, but granting it to the participles. In my opinion this text does not address the question of predestination at all, but rather simply assumes the already existing states as such. The fact that predestination is, nevertheless, a Pauline concept (contra Bartling) seems clear (cf. Rom. 8:29; 9:11f.,16.f.). Yet the difficulty of understanding the ἐκ ... εἰς structure in 2:16 has long been recognized, as evidenced by the textual tradition which eliminated the two occurrences of ἐκ (i.e. D F G Ψ latt sy); though with the vast majority of commentators I regard the ἐκ to be the preferred reading since it is better attested (p[46], A B C etc.), it is in accordance with Paul's thought elsewhere (cf. 3:18; Rom. 1:17) and is the more difficult reading.
39 Moreover, as V. Bartling has correctly pointed out, the chiastic structure of 2:15-16a (ABBA) places the emphasis on *life* as that result of Paul's ministry which was intended to be stressed.
40 Unfortunately, this point is often missed by commentators because they make the subtle shift of substituting Paul's proclamation of the gospel, which is not introduced until 2:17, for Paul himself as the subject and object of 2:14-16a. E.g. cf. K. Schelkle, *Der Zweite Brief an die Korinther*, *Geistliche Schriftlesung, Bd.8*, 1964, p.59; Eichholz, *Theologie*, p.58; Wendland, *Korinther*, *NTD*, p.176; E. Käsemann, "Die Heilsbedeutung des Todes Jesu bei Paulus", *Paulinische Perspektiven*, 1972[2], p.91, who, as a classic example of this move, points to II Cor. 2:15f. as his proof text as part of his extensive polemic against grounding faith on "facts of redemption" rather than solely on the proclamation of the word; and most recently, James I.H. McDonald, "Paul and the Preaching Ministry, A reconsideration of 2 Cor. 2:14-17 in its context", *JSNT* 17(1983)35-50, pp.42ff., whose false equation of the "apos-

anderen wie ein solcher zum Leben ... Es ist nicht nur das verkündete Wort, das die Geister in dieser Welt scheidet, sondern die Sichtbarwerdung Christi in Paulus selbst ..., was so in die Entscheidung führt.[41]

The parallels between I Cor. 1:17-18 and II Cor. 2:14-16a may thus be represented as follows:

I Cor. 1:17f.	II. Cor. 2:14-16a
1. Paul is sent to preach in a mode which corresponds to the cross of Christ (1:17, cf. 2:1,4)	1. Paul is "being led to death", which is a mode of existence that reveals the cross of Christ (2:14)
2. γὰρ (18a)	2. ὅτι (15a)
3. ὁ λόγος ὁ τοῦ σταυροῦ	3. Χριστοῦ εὐωδία ἐσμὲν τῷ θεῷ (15a)
4. τοῖς ἀπολλυμένοις μωρία ἐστίν (18b)	4. ἐν τοῖς ἀπολλυμένοις ... οἷς ὀσμὴ ἐκ θανάτου εἰς θάνατον (15c, 16a)
5. τοῖς σῳζομένοις ἡμιν δύναμις θεοῦ ἐστιν (18c)	5. ἐν τοῖς σῳζομένοις ... οἷς ὀσμὴ ἐκ ζωῆς εἰς ζωήν (15b, 16a)

A study of II Cor. 2:14-16a has thus led to the conclusion that Paul understood his own experience of being "led to death" as an apostle to be the "flip side" of his apostolic mandate to preach the word of the cross[42]. The question that remains to be answered, however, is *how* Paul's "being led to death" actually functioned, in his view, to reveal the knowledge of God[43]. In order to answer this question we must place II Cor. 2:14-16a within the context of the Corinthian correspondence as a whole. By doing so, we will, at the same time, further confirm our

---

tolic spectacle (θρίαμβος)" with the "eschatological preaching" leads him to suggest as his central thesis that "2 Cor. 2:14-17 is a theme statement for a discourse or sermon, the gist of which is given in 3:1-7:1" (p.43). But, as we shall see below, Paul's life as an apostle itself does function as evidence for the truth of the gospel on the one hand (contra Käsemann), while the focus of Paul's attention throughout this section is on his own apostolic lifestyle as an essential aspect of his ministry of the gospel (cf. Phil. 1:20).

41 "Die Apostolische Existenz im Bilde", pp.234-235.

42 This conclusion corresponds to the central point of E. Güttgemanns' study, *Der leidende Apostel und sein Herr, Studien zur paulinischen Christologie*, FRLANT 90, 1966, p.195 that "Das die bisherige Exegese der Leiden des Apostels weithin beherrschende Stichwort der 'Analogie' ist unsachgemäß und muß durch das Stichwort der 'christologischen Epiphanie' ersetzt werden ... Die Leiden des Apostels sind lediglich eine *Form* der Offenbarung des Christus", but is not an endorsement of his entire program. For example, Güttgemann links Paul's view of his suffering to a reconstruction of Paul's opponents as Jewish-Christian Gnostics, which need not be the case (cf. pp.97ff.). For Güttgemann's main point, however, with which I am in basic agreement, i.e. that Paul's suffering is an "epiphanie of the Lord", cf. pp.111n.100; 112-124, esp. 116-119, 123-124; 134; 140f.; 153; 195f. As he puts it, "Der Kyrios dokumentiert und qualifiziert sich selbst am Soma des Apostels als der gekreuzigte Jesus" (p.117).

43 Although many commentators have seen the close connection between Paul and his message, the subsequent question of *how* Paul actually understood his life to function in revealing the knowledge of God is seldom asked, cf. A. Schlatter, *Bote*, p.496; Plummer, *Second Corinthians*, p.70 and most recently, G. Barth, "Die Eignung", p.262, who for the most part captures the general sense of 2:14, but fails to ask how Paul's "Aufgabe und Amt des Apostels" to be a "Werkzeug" actually, in fact, reveals the knowledge of God.

exegetical hypothesis concerning the meaning of θριαμβεύειν in II Cor.
2:14 and our interpretation of 2:14-16a in general.

B. THE APOSTOLIC "SENTENCE OF DEATH" IN THE CORINTHIAN
   CORRESPONDENCE

Once II Cor. 2:14-16a is recognized to be a statement of Paul's apostolic role in the salvific plan of God as the one who is "led to death",
its place within the Corinthian correspondence as a whole becomes clear.
For as such, II Cor. 2:14a functions as one of four thesis-like summaries of Paul's understanding of the significance of his suffering as
an apostle, a significance which is otherwise expressed in the so-called
"*Peristasenkataloge*", i.e. I Cor. 4:8-13, II Cor. 4:7-15, 6:1-10 and
11:16-12:10[44].

1. I Cor. 4:8-13

As has long been recognized, I Cor. 1:10-4:21 is the *locus classicus*
for the development of the Pauline theology of the cross. But as Nils
Dahl has so clearly pointed out, Paul's *theologia crucis* actually serves
a penultimate purpose within I Cor. 1-4. For as Dahl observed, it is
rather the nature of Paul's apostleship and his relationship to the
church at Corinth, and not the meaning and significance of the cross in
and of itself, which occupies all the important points of transition in
1:10-4:21 (i.e. 1:13-17; 2:1-5; 3:1-2; 3:10-11; 4:3-4) and which serves,
therefore, as the focal point and key for understanding the structure of
the entire argument[45].

a. *The Purpose of I Cor. 1-4*

Given Dahl's insight, the primary purpose of I Cor. 1:10-4:21 is not
to provide a theological reflection on the meaning and significance of

---

44 Paul's view of his suffering as expressed in these catalogs has been the subject
   of intensive study in the last twenty years. Cf. E. Güttgemanns, *Der leidende
   Apostel*, esp. pp.94-198, 304-328; W. Schrage, "Leid, Kreuz und Eschaton. Die Pe-
   ristasenkataloge als Merkmale paulinischer theologia crucis und Eschatologie",
   EvTh 34(1974)141-175; J.H. Schütz, *Paul and the Anatomy of Apostolic Authority*,
   SNTS Monograph Series 26, 1975, pp.165-248: Robert Hodgson, "Paul the Apostle and
   First Century Tribulation Lists", *ZNW* 74(1983)59-80 and now K. Th. Kleinknecht,
   *Der leidende Gerechtfertigte, Die alttestamentlich-jüdische Tradition vom 'leidenden
   Gerechten' und ihre Rezeption bei Paulus*, WUNT 2. Reihe 13, 1984, pp.208-304.
45 Nils A. Dahl, "Paul and the Church at Corinth According to I Corinthians 1:10-4:21",
   in *Christian History and Interpretation: FS John Knox*, ed. by W.R. Farmer, C.F.D.
   Moule and R.R. Niebuhr, 1967, pp.313-335, pp.320-321.

the crucifixion, but to reassert the authority of Paul as the founder
and spiritual father of the *entire* church at Corinth (cf. 4:14-17);
while at the same time preparing for the answers to be given to the
Corinthians' questions in the rest of the letter by indicating the
theological criterion which determines both the nature of Paul's
apostleship (cf. 1:17-19) and his evaluation of the church's problems
(cf. 3:1-4)[46]. In other words, I Cor. 1-4 is best understood as an
"Apologie des paulinischen Apostolates"[47], which finds its focal point
in Paul's own theological understanding of the significance of the
cross, first for his own ministry, and then, by extension, for the
life of the Corinthian church in general (cf. 4:16). The point of the
apology in I Cor. 1-4, however, is *not* to reestablish Paul's authority
per se, but rather to reassert that the authority of Paul, which is
still recognized by some, or perhaps even by most of the Corinthians
(cf. 1:12; 3:4f.), ought to be maintained as the *foundation* for the
entire church. Hence, the work of the other "guides" (4:15) must be
measured by the character and message of Paul and not vice versa (cf.
3:10-15) -- i.e. by the cross. For the problem in Corinth was not that
Paul's authority was no longer being accepted, but that the Corinthians
had forgotten that his was the *primary* authority to be followed. Hence,
the focus of the argument in I Cor. 1-4 is not to justify Paul's
apostleship, but to correct the Corinthians' attitudes and behavior.
This can be seen in the fact that the contrast between wisdom (σοφία)
and the cross first introduced in 1:18-19 to support the nature of
Paul's apostolic preaching (cf. γάρ of v.18) is then reintroduced in
2:1f., together with a description of Paul's appearance in Corinth in
2:3f., to support Paul's intention for the *Corinthians*, namely, ἵνα ἡ
πίστις ὑμῶν μὴ ᾖ ἐν σοφίᾳ ἀνθρώπων ἀλλ᾽ ἐν δυνάμει θεοῦ (2:5). Conversely, the contrast between wisdom and the cross first "verified
empirically" "an der soziologischen Struktur der Gemeinde" itself in

---

46 This is my own expansion and reworking of the main point of Dahl's article (see
   n.43), pp.333-334, which I take to be sound. For if "Christ crucified" was the
   heart of Paul's Christology, then it is only natural that this would become the
   criterion for Paul's own apostleship and the basis for his evaluation of the problems he encountered. For the idea of the cross of Christ as that which "(markiert)
   das Zentrum des paulinischen Denkens", cf. P. Stuhlmacher, "'Das Ende des Gesetzes'.
   Über Ursprung und Ansatz der paulinischen Theologie", ZThK 67(1970)14-39, p.16
   (now in his *Versöhnung, Gesetz und Gerechtigkeit, Aufsätze zur biblischen Theologie*,
   1981, p.168); while for an outline of Paul's theology of the cross as such, cf.
   his "Achtzehn Thesen zur paulinischen Kreuzestheologie", in *Rechtfertigung, FS
   Ernst Käsemann zum 70. Geburtstag*, ed. J. Friedrich, W. Pöhlmann and P. Stuhlmacher,
   1976, pp.509-525 (now too in *Versöhnung*, pp.192-208).
47 So Philipp Vielhauer, "Paulus und die Kephaspartei in Korinth", in *Oikodome, Aufsätze zum Neuen Testament, Bd. 2*, 1979, pp.169-182, p.171. Dahl, "Paul and the
   Church at Corinth", p.317 makes this same point.

1:26-31[48], is then verified on the basis of the *apostolic* experience in
4:8-13, the "summierende(n) Höhepunkt(s) der ersten vier Kapitel des I
Kor"[49]. As a result, the interplay between Paul's theology of the cross
and its significance for his ministry and the life of the Corinthian
church is expressed in a chiastic structure (ABBA) which once again
serves to emphasize the foundational and paradigmatic role of Paul's
apostleship (cf. I Cor. 1:23f.; 2:1f.; 3:6,10f.; 4:1,16):

(A) The Nature of Paul's Ministry (1:17, 2:3f.)	SUPPORTED BY	The Theology of the Cross (1:18-19)
(B) The Life of the Church (1:26-31)	SUPPORTED BY	The Theology of the Cross (1:21-25)
(B) The Life of the Church (2:5-4:5)	SUPPORTED BY	The Theology of the Cross (2:1f.)
(A) The Nature of Paul's Ministry (4:8-13)	SUPPORTED BY	The Theology of the Cross (4:6a)[50]

Having thus determined the overall structure of Paul's argument in
chapters 1-4, we can now turn our attention to the meaning of I Cor.
4:8-13 and its relationship to II Cor. 2:14-16a.

*b. The Meaning of I Cor. 4:8-13 and its Relationship to II Cor.
2:14-16a*

As Kleinknecht has already argued, I Cor. 4:8-13 is the "high point"
or climax of chapters 1-4. More specifically, the description of the
apostolic experience in 4:8-13 functions as the final step in Paul's
argument against the Corinthians' propensity to boast "in men" (3:21;
cf. 1:29,31; 3:18-20; 4:6f.), which Paul saw to be the basic problem
lying behind the dissensions (σχίσματα, 1:10), quarreling (ἔριδες, 1:11,
cf. ἔρις, 3:3) and jealousy (ζῆλος, 3:3) which were threatening to split
the church[51]. This boasting had recently manifested itself in the form
of a party-spirit (1:12f.; 3:4) which was based on the Corinthians' in-
flated view of their own spiritual wisdom (3:1-4,18; 4:18f.) as a result of their over-realized eschatology (4:8). To counter this trend,

---

48 The idea that 1:26-31 is an empirical verification of 1:18-25 I owe to Kleinknecht,
   Leidende, p.210, who observes that "an der soziologischen Struktur der Gemeinde ist
   abzulesen, daß Gottes κλῆσις nicht den Wertmaßstäben der Welt entsprechend er-
   folgt (wobei wieder genau dieselben Gegensatzpaare wie zuvor gebraucht werden)..."
   Kleinknecht does not make the connection, however, between 1:26-31 and 4:8-13.
49 Kleinknecht, *Leidende*, p.222.
50 For an explanation of 4:6a as a reference to the theology of the cross, see below,
   p.64n.63.
51 Cf. E.E. Ellis, "Christ Crucified", in *Reconciliation and Hope*, FS L.L. Morris on
   his 60th Birthday, ed. R. Banks, 1974, pp.69-75, pp.74-75, who also emphasizes
   that the central problems in Corinth were boasting, envy, strife, etc., i.e. of
   an ethical nature and not simply a mistaken eschatological perspective. As he put
   it, the Corinthians' problem was that they boasted in their gifts as if they were
   their own attainment and engaged therefore in a "competitive wrangling (I Cor.
   1:5; 4:7)". There is no doubt, however, that the Corinthians' mistaken eschatology
   played a crucial supportive role in aggravating their problems. See below, pp.62f.

Paul had already pointed to the message of the cross (1:17-19; 2:1-5) and to the nature of the Corinthians themselves (2:26-31) as a demonstration of the fact that "God chose what is foolish in the world to shame the wise and what is weak in the world to shame the strong; i.e. God chose what is low and despised in the world, even things that are not, to bring to nothing things that are, so that no human being might boast in the presence of God" (1:27-29), neither in one's own particular spiritual gifts (1:7; 3:18; 4:7), nor in one's own particular spiritual leaders (3:7,21f.; 4:1). That the problem of the party-spirit in Corinth was closely related to their boasting in their spiritual gifts and/or spiritual leaders is also evident when the thesis statements of 1:7 and 4:7 are brought to bear on Paul's discussion in chapters 12-14. For if, on the one hand, the opposite of boasting in one's own particular leaders is to be "united in the *same* mind and the *same* judgment" (1:10), the opposite of boasting in one's own particular gifts is the recognition that "to each is given the manifestation of the spirit for the *common good* (12:7, cf. 12:21-26). This ability to use one's gifts as a member of the *one* body of Christ for the *other's* good is then, in a word, love, which *by definition* is οὐ ζηλοῖ, οὐ περπερεύεται, οὐ φυσιοῦται ... οὐ ζητεῖ τὰ ἑαυτῆς (13:4f.)[52].

Finally, in support of his disavowal of the Corinthians' attitudes and in direct opposition to their mistaken eschatology, Paul then concludes his argument by comparing the Corinthians to the "apostles" themselves in I Cor. 4:8-13. The point of Paul's comparison is clear. In contrast to the Corinthians, who consider themselves to be filled, rich and reigning with Christ already (4:8), stands the apostle "sentenced to death" (4:9): if they are φρόνιμοι, Paul is μωρός; if they are ἰσχυροί, Paul is ἀσθενής; while they are "held in honor" (ἔνδοξοι), Paul is "despised" (ἄτιμος) (4:10).

But the significance of Paul's comparison in I Cor. 4 only becomes clear in the light of Paul's earlier statements in 2:1-5. For there Paul had called attention to the fact that his decision to preach only "Jesus Christ and him crucified" was confirmed and supported not only by the way he preached (cf. vv. 1,4), but also by his very *mode of appearance* in Corinth itself (v.3)[53]. As "the corollary of his knowing

---

52 Cf. K. Stendahl, *Paul among Jews and Gentiles*, 1976, p.111, who sees in Paul's handling of glossolalia in I Cor. 12-14 another example of "Paul's consistent argument against any piety or theology marked by triumphalism, i.e. by an overstatement of spiritual superiority ...".

53 I.e. by the fact that he had come to Corinth ἐν ἀσθενείᾳ καὶ ἐν φόβῳ καὶ ἐν τρόμῳ πολλῷ. J.H. Schütz, *Anatomy of Apostolic Authority*, p.201, makes this point well: " ... Paul couples together in 2:1-5 the two ideas of what he does and how he does it. Insofar as he decides to know only one thing, Jesus Christ and him crucified, his responsibility is exercised toward the 'what' of the kerygma, over against which stands σοφία. Insofar as he comes 'in weakness, and in fear and much trem-

only Christ crucified"[54], Paul's weakness in appearance, together with
his refusal to preach ἐν πειθοῖς σοφίας λόγοις, had worked to ensure
that the faith of the Corinthians μὴ ᾖ ἐν σοφίᾳ ἀνθρώπων ἀλλ' ἐν δυνάμει
θεοῦ (v.5). Against this background, I Cor. 4:8-13 functions as the
needed explanation of *how* it is that Paul's "weakness", in its various
expressions, actually functions to support his message of the cross, and
in so doing not only completes the thought of I Cor. 2:1-5, but of II
Cor. 2:14-16 as well.

Paul's answer to this question is twofold. First, the very fact itself that the apostolic life is characterized by weakness is an indication that the eschaton has *not yet* arrived in its fullness, but that
the power of God, once displayed in the cross, is still to be found *in
the midst* of the suffering of this world[55]. At the same time, however,
the kingdom of God *has* come "in power" (cf. I Cor. 2:4; 4:20). Hence
Paul's own "sentence to death" (4:9) not only corresponds to his preaching of the cross as its verification, but also, through Paul's *positive responses and acceptance* of the suffering which he must undergo
ὡς περικάθαρμα τοῦ κοσμοῦ and the περίψημα πάντων[56], functions to affirm, and in this way, proclaim his message of the cross. For since the
call to suffer in this way implies a corresponding rejection of the
"wisdom of men" (2:5), the fact that Paul responds *positively* to this
suffering thus testifies to the power and wisdom of God which have been
displayed in the cross (1:18, 24). In this way, God has made the wisdom
of the world foolish (ἐμώρανεν, 1:20) both through the cross itself and
through the life of his apostle, who not only proclaims the message of
the cross (1:18,21,23,25) and experiences the corresponding suffering
of this world (4:9), but who also becomes himself "a fool for Christ's
sake" (ἡμεῖς μωροὶ διὰ Χριστόν, 4:10) in his acceptance of that suf-

---

bling', his responsibility is exercised toward the 'how' of the proclamation, over
against which stands the ὑπεροχὴ λόγου ἢ σοφίας. Ultimately both are an obedience
to one and the same thing, the δύναμις θεοῦ...".

54 Schütz, *Anatomy*, p.202. Cf. also E.E. Ellis, "Christ Crucified", pp.70-71, who
argues that "Christ crucified" "refers primarily to the exalted Lord who, in his
exaltation, remains the crucified one". As a result, the cross of Christ can be
equated with God's power so that the weakness of Paul becomes "the ethical corollary, and indeed the proof, of the wisdom 'that is from God'".

55 So also G. Bornkamm, *Paul*, p.161, who in commenting on I Cor. 4:9-13 writes, "For
Paul apostleship meant being branded by the 'word of the cross' and *not yet* being
delivered from the hardships of daily life and death".

56 Recently A. Hanson, "I Cor. 4:13b and Lamentations 3:45", *Expository Times* 93
(1982)214-215, has made the "probable conjecture" that I Cor. 4:13b recalls Lam.
3:45; though since the parallel is not attested in the LXX itself, he concludes
that no firm conclusion can be drawn. What is interesting, however, is that in
Lam. 3:45 the suffering referred to has been inflicted by God himself, who then
also responds to the cry for help in the midst of that suffering (cf. 3:55-57).
Moreover, if the suffering referred to in 3:45 is a reference to the unjust treatment of the righteous mentioned in 3:58-66, and not to the punishment of sins mentioned in 3:39-44, then the probability of Hanson's conjecture is increased, especially in the light of Kleinknecht's study, see below.

fering in the positive endurance of faith (4:11-13a; 2:5). For Paul,
therefore, his suffering is not mere circumstance, nor simply fate[57],
but an integral part of God's plan to "destroy the wisdom of the wise"
(1:19) on the one hand, and to exhibit the power of God in the cross on
the other. It is this divine intention which is then expressed in I Cor.
4:8-13, specifically in 4:9, which, as the central assertion of the passage, functions to support Paul's critique of the Corinthians' attitudes
in 4:8. Verses 10-13 then provide a further explication of 4:9 by spell-
ing out *what* Paul's "sentence to death" consists of (namely, his suffering as an apostle) and *how* God's power is actually made known through
it (i.e. through Paul's acceptance and positive response to his suffering). It is thus especially instructive for our study, and by no means
coincidental, that Paul's *central point* in I Cor. 4:9 forms an exact
parallel to Paul's statement in II Cor. 2:14:[58]

I Cor. 4:9	II Cor. 2:14
1. ὁ θεὸς	1. τῷ δὲ θεῷ χάρις
2. ἡμᾶς τοὺς ἀποστόλους	2. ἡμᾶς ἐν τῷ Χριστῷ
3. ἀπέδειξεν ἐσχάτους ὡς ἐπιθανατίους	3. τῷ θριαμβεύοντι
4. ὅτι θέατρον ἐγενήθημεν	4. καὶ τὴν ὀσμὴν τῆς γνώσεως αὐτοῦ φανεροῦντι δι' ἡμῶν
5. τῷ κόσμῳ καὶ ἀγγέλοις καὶ ἀνθρώποισ.	5. ἐν παντὶ τόπῳ

In both passages God is the author of the "death sentence". And in
both contexts the apostles are the objects of God's activity. In I Cor.
4:9 God exhibits/displays[59] the apostles last of all like men sentenced
to death in the arena[60], while in II Cor. 2:14 God leads the apostle

---

57 As H. Conzelmann, *Der erste Brief an die Korinther, KEK Bd. V,* 1981², p.116, has
   correctly emphasized: "Dieses Schicksal ist nicht 'notwendig' im Sinne eines Fa-
   tum. Es ist von Gott zu einem bestimmten Zweck - der außerhalb des Betroffenen
   liegt - verfügt".
58 To my knowledge, the similarity between I Cor. 4:9 and II Cor. 2:14 has been noticed
   in the past only by Hughes, *Second Corinthians*, p.78n.10 and Schütz, *Anatomy*, p.247.
   But because both scholars have not seen the full implication of the θριαμβεύειν-
   imagery in 2:14, the parallel itself has not been noticed, though Schütz's comment
   is especially insightful: "This parallelism of Paul's 'making manifest' what the
   gospel also makes manifest is hinted at in II Cor. 2:14 and made explicit by the
   unusual language in I Cor. 4:8ff". As we have seen, however, this idea is much more
   than hinted at in 2:14!
59 Bauer-Arndt-Gingrich, *A Greek-English Lexicon of the New Testament*, p.89 even
   translate ἀπέδειξεν in I Cor. 4:9, "he has made, or exhibited us (as) the last
   ones perh. in a triumphal procession".
60 On the phrase ὡς ἐπιθανατίους as a reference to those "wretches" brought on to die
   at the close of a display in the arena, cf. C.K. Barrett, *A Commentary on the First
   Epistle to the Corinthians*, 1968, pp.110-111; P.E. Hughes, *Second Corinthians*, p.
   143 and H. Conzelmann, *Der erste Brief*, p.115, 116n.39, who interpretes ἐπιθανατίους
   to mean, "zum Tode verurteilt" so that the image is that of "die römische Theater-
   aufführung mit zum Tode Verurteilten". N. Baumert, *Täglich Sterben und Auferstehen.
   Der Literalsinn von 2 Kor 4:12-5:10, SANT 34,* 1973, p.196 connects this imagery

like one sentenced to death by his captors. Finally, the reason for
Paul's vivid imagery in I Cor. 4:9 is to illustrate the fact that the
apostles have become a "spectacle" to the whole world, to angels and
to men[61]. Similarly, God's purpose in leading the apostle to death in
II Cor. 2:14 is to reveal himself in every place! Thus, in both passages, the role of the apostle is characterized by "death", a death
which reveals the knowledge of God.

The parallels between II Cor. 2:14-16a and I Cor. 1:10-4:13, especially 1:17f. and 4:8-13, make it clear, therefore, that for Paul
the "knowledge of God" to be revealed in the apostolic ministry is the
power and wisdom of God found in the cross, while the way in which it
is revealed is not limited to the apostolic preaching, but also includes
the apostles' own "sentence of death". Finally, I Cor. 4:8-13 also
makes it clear that Paul's "sentence of death" (I Cor. 4:9; II Cor.
2:14) refers specifically to the *suffering* which he is called to endure (cf. 4:12) as an apostle of the crucified Christ[62]. And Kleinknecht's recent study[63] has demonstrated that in Paul's conception,
the experience of the apostle, pictured in terms of the suffering
righteous of the bible, functioned as a demonstration of the fact that
God's righteousness, and hence his power (cf. Rom. 1:16f.:), is displayed in the lives of those who, like God's son[64], suffer at the hands
of the world. Paul's suffering in I Cor. 1-4 is therefore both a confirmation (I Cor. 2:1-5) and display (I Cor. 4:9) of the meaning of the
cross[65].

---

with the rest of the Pauline corpus: "Er (God) hat uns ja an den letzten Platz ge-
stellt und wie zum Tod Bestimmte vor aller Welt in die Arena der wilden Tiere ge-
führt ... so daß wir Toren sind *infolge von Christus* (1 Kor 4:9f.; vgl. 15:32).
Und da wir *mit ihm* ans Kreuz geheftet sind (Gal. 2:19), leiden wir *mit ihm* (Röm.
8:17) und haben Anteil an seinen Leiden (Phil. 3:10), denn die *Leiden des Christus*
strömen auf uns über (2 Kor 1:5)".

61 For the Roman custom of using prisoners as a "spectacle" (θεωρία) to show off the
glory of the conqueror by "displaying" them in various ways in the arena, a display which usually ended in the death of the captives, cf. Josephus, *Jewish War*,
VII.23-24, 38-40,96.

62 Paul's ability to speak of his suffering as "death" is also confirmed by I Cor.
15:30-32, where in reflecting on his "peril every hour" he can exclaim, "I die
every day!" (καθ' ἡμέραν ἀποθνήσκω). For the parallel between κινδυνεύομεν
πᾶσανὥραν//καθ' ἡμέραν ἀποθνήσκω and its relationship to I Cor. 4:9 and 11f. cf.
Kleinknecht, *Leidende*, pp.238-240. Baumert, *Täglich Sterben*, p.60 is thus correct
in observing that "Er (Paul) sagt eben nicht Todes-'Not', Todes-'Leiden' oder
Todes-'Macht'. Offenbar hat für ihn 'Tod' auch dieser weiteren Bedeutungen, die
er ohne Veränderung des sprachlichen Ausdrucks aktualisiert, während wir dafür
lieber verschiedene Unterbegriffe gebrauchen".

63 See *Leidende*, pp.193ff.

64 So too M. Hengel, "Leiden in der Nachfolge Jesu", in *Der Leidende Mensch, Beiträge
zu einem unbewältigten Thema*, ed. Hans Schulze, 1974, pp.85-94, p.92, who, in
speaking of I Cor. 4:11-13 emphasizes that "der christologische Bezug, der hinter
diesen Aussagen steht, ist mit Händen zu greifen: Für Paulus bleibt der Verkündiger
des Evangeliums mit seinem Herrn durch die Solidarität des Leidens verbunden".

65 Thus Bornkamm, *Paul*, p.171: "Paul was convinced that he presented men with Christ
crucified both in the gospel he preached and in his own life".

2. II Cor. 4:7-12

a. *The New Situation Behind II Corinthians*

As we have seen, Paul's suffering as an apostle functioned in I Cor.
1-4 both as a warning to the Corinthians not to "boast" in anything
other than the cross of Christ as the source of their spiritual power
and wisdom (1:24) and as a critique of the eschatology upon which this
false boasting was based. What remains to be made explicit, however, is
that the strength of Paul's entire argument in I Cor. 1-4 rests in the
fact that although a "myriad of guides" (μυρίους παιδαγωγούς) now existed in Corinth, Paul's own authority as their "spiritual father"
nevertheless still remained basically intact, though perhaps it was now
being rejected by some as relevant for the *entire* church (cf. I Cor.
4:14-16)[66]. It is this presupposition that allows Paul to assume in I
Corinthians that his suffering and weakness as an apostle, the very
suffering and weakness that marked Paul's ministry when the church was
founded (cf. 2:1-5), could also be appealed to as that characteristic
of an apostle which was accepted as genuine and true by both Paul and
the Corinthians. For without this common ground, Paul's argument, both
in structure and content, collapses. There is no indication in I Cor.
1:10-4:21 that Paul's suffering was being rejected by the Corinthians
as illegitimate *for Paul as an apostle*, though certain members of the
church may have been critical of Paul for other reasons (see I Cor.
4:3-5, 18-21). Rather, Paul seems to have been confronted with the
opposite problem. Although *Paul's* suffering had always been accepted
as legitimate, some of the Corinthians had nevertheless recently been
persuaded, most likely on the basis of a misunderstanding of Paul's
own teaching[67], that Paul's life under the cross no longer applied to
them! At the same time, on the basis of I Cor. 4:18-21 (cf. 5:3f.),
the objection was also being raised by some that although Paul was
the founder of the church at Corinth, his absence now meant that his

---

66 This point is supported not only by I Cor. 4:17, but also by the fact that Paul
   himself remains the object of one of the factions (cf. 1:12f; 3:4, 21). Moreover,
   the tone and purpose of the rest of the letter, i.e. to answer the Corinthians'
   questions and straighten out their misunderstandings, is also predicated on this
   assumption. Cf. for example, 7:12,25, which assume that Paul's commands will be
   considered authoritative without further justification.
67 Following H. Conzelmann, *Der erste Brief an die Korinther*, p.34, who, after a very
   balanced response to past attempts to pinpoint the source of the problems in Corinth
   on the basis of external *religionsgeschichtliche* reconstructions (cf. pp.31-33),
   concludes that "Sicher ist nur, was aus dem Text zu erheben ist" (p.33). Taking
   as his starting point the ways in which the Corinthians themselves, from their
   own recent pagan backgrounds, could have interpreted their new Christian faith -
   so that their new "Glauben" itself becomes a primary "Einfluß" - Conzelmann then
   offers his own persuasive reconstruction of the possible development in Corinth,
   based on the problems referred to in the text (cf. p.34).

authority was no longer valid for the entire church, but only for
those whom he personally had won to the Lord. As for the rest, they
owed their allegiance to their own particular "guides". In response,
the purpose of Paul's argument in I Cor. 1-4 is twofold: to "remind"
(ἀναμνήσει)[68] the Corinthians of "his ways in Christ" (4:17)[69], and,
in so doing, to call their attention to the fact that as their "father
in Christ Jesus through the Gospel" (4:15), it is *his* "way", i.e. the
way of the cross, that is to be imitated (4:16, cf. 11:1)[70]. The appropriateness of Paul's apostolic suffering, in and of itself, is thus
nowhere defended, but is *itself* the foundational premise for his argument, based, as it is, on his parental relationship to the Corinthian
church. For if suffering and weakness are the essential characteristics
of the apostolic ministry, upon which the Corinthians' very lives as
Christians were based, then as children of their spiritual father, their
lives also ought to be characterized by the power of the cross, and
not by boasting in their own spiritual attainments or leaders. The significance of the cross for Paul's life as an apostle was therefore not
in question -- though its significance for his church was. Hence, Paul's
response could simply be: μιμηταί μου γίνεσθε (4:16)[71].

---

68 Although in the context Timothy is the one sent to remind the Corinthians of
Paul's ways, it is clear that Timothy's task, if not to be associated with the
deliverance of the letter itself (he is not mentioned in 1:1, and in the light
of 16:10f. seems not to be associated with it, cf. Barrett, *First Corinthians*,
pp.116-117), is nonetheless to be seen as the same as Paul's in writing.

69 Schütz, *Anatomy of Apostolic Authority*, pp.209f. argues convincingly on the basis
of the transition in v.14 and the use of ὁδός in the LXX in a figurative sense
that Paul's "ways" in I Cor. 4:17 refer not to his travel plans but to his conduct
in 4:9-13: "It is not impossible that his "ways" are both taught and illustrated
by his life ... so we should probably connect ὁδοί with vv. 9-13 and assume that
his example there is also what he 'teaches'". In order to stress this unity, I
have consciously chosen to translate ὁδούς in my discussion with a collective
singular, since his teaching and his apostolic lifestyle are, in reality, one
"way", the way of the cross.

70 Again see Schütz, *Anatomy*, p.210: "His ways in Christ are to be their ways in
Christ".

71 It is beyond the scope of this study to develop this point further. Nevertheless,
it should be pointed out that Paul's apostolic experience in I Cor. 4:8ff., which
provides an essential part of Paul's "ways" in Christ and, as such, also forms the
backdrop to Paul's command in 4:16 that the Corinthians become imitators of Paul,
does not seem to be intended to be the basis for a command or call to suffering
itself. Rather, Paul's apostolic experience in I Cor. 4:8ff. is intended to support Paul's emphasis throughout chapters 1-4 on the *attitude* towards one's experience as a Christian which is appropriate this side of the parousia. The problem in Corinth was not that the Corinthians were not suffering enough (!), but
that they were using their spiritual experiences as a ground for boasting in themselves, as if everything they had were not a gift (cf. I Cor. 4:7). As a result,
it is not entirely correct to interpret the reality of the present participation
in Christ's resurrection life *only* in terms of actualizing the crucifixion (so
Ellis, "Christ Crucified", p.74), or to understand Paul's paradigmatic function
in I Cor. 4 as implying that his experience of suffering is "the *only* way (power)
can be appropriated before the end" (as Schütz, *Anatomy*, p.203, concludes), nor
does it seem appropriate to describe the glory of the Church as exclusively "veiled"

By the time of the writing of II Corinthians, however, the situation had changed. As a result of the influence of some of Paul's opponents, who had recently arrived[72], the Corinthians had now taken the additional step of rejecting the nature, and hence authority, of Paul's apostleship itself. In turn, the purpose of the *Peristasenkataloge* in II Corinthians has also changed. Rather than functioning as a warning to the Corinthians, Paul's catalogs of suffering now form an essential part of his *self-defense* as an apostle. For the meaning and necessity of Paul's suffering as an apostle are no longer common ground between Paul and his church, but are the very points of contention in the Corinthians' growing distrust of the legitimacy of Paul's apostolic claim. This becomes evident when we compare I Cor. 4:8-13 to II Cor. 4:7-12.

b. The Two Essential Differences between I Cor. 4:8-13 and II Cor. 4:7-12

The first thing that strikes one's attention in reading II Cor. 4:7-12 is its remarkable similarities to I Cor. 4:8-13. As in I Cor. 4:8ff., here too Paul's point is that the power of God (cf. I Cor. 1:18,24; 2:5 and II Cor. 4:7) is made known *through* or *by means of* the adversative relationship which is expressed in the apostolic experience of suffering in its various manifestations (compare I Cor. 4:12f. with II Cor. 4:8-9)[73]. Moreover, in both passages Paul portrays his apostolic suffering as a divinely orchestrated "death" which performs a revelatory function (compare I Cor. 4:9 and Paul's use of φανερόω in II Cor. 4:10-11)[74]. Finally, in both cases, not only the

---

(as Dahl, "Paul and the Church", p.332, posits), or to select suffering as "*die* ... notwendige Konsequenz" for both the life of the apostle and the life of the church "in gleicher Weise" (so Kleinknecht, *Leidende*, pp.196-197). For there is no "martyr-theology" hidden within Paul's application of the theology of the cross to the life of the church, such as we find a generation later in the writings of Ignatius (cf. his *Letter to the Romans*, IV-VII in which he interprets his suffering in the Pauline categories of I Cor. 15:32 and 4:4, while at the same time using them to express part of his longing for martyrdom).

72 Although Dahl's observation over 15 years ago that "no clarity has been reached with regard to the relation between the situations reflected in 1 Corinthians and in 2 Corinthians" is still true today (cf. Conzelmann, *Der erste Brief*, p.32), there is now almost universal agreement that the situation reflected in II Cor. is a result of the opponents who figure so predominantly in chs. 10-13. For the quote above from Dahl, cf. his "Paul and the Church at Corinth", pp.316-317.

73 As Schrage, "Leid, Kreuz und Eschaton", pp.145-146, has pointed out, it is the paradoxical antitheses "im radikalen Sinn, wo Gottes Kraft gerade *in* der Schwachheit und das Leben gerade *im* Tode gefunden würde ...", in contrast to the "nacheinander" character of the relationship between the negative and positive experiences in the apocalyptic tradition of the suffering of the righteous, which make Paul's catalogs distinctive.

74 So Güttgemanns, *Der Leidende Apostel*, pp.106-107: "Paulus gibt seinen Leiden in V.10f. den finalen Zweck des φανεροῦσθαι. Die Leiden des Apostels haben also *Offenbarungscharakter* ... Die Aktivität des Apostels bei diesem Geschehen ist in keiner Weise betont. Paulus beschreibt vielmehr 'objektiv' was sich in seinen Leiden und

texts themselves, but also the wider context make it clear that Paul pictures this suffering in terms of the biblical tradition of the suffering of the righteous; in the case of I Cor. 4:8-13 by the four scripture quotes in I Cor. 1:19,31; 2:9 and 3:19f., and in the present context by the reference to Psalm 116 (LXX 114-115) in II Cor. 4:13[75].

But once these parallels have been noted, it is the two essential differences between the texts which become apparent. First, the *purpose* of Paul's argument has changed, as evidenced by its corresponding switch in focus. In I Cor. 4, not only the larger context (cf. I Cor. 4:7f. and 14), but also the comparison which stood at the heart of the "catalog" itself (see I Cor. 4:10) made it clear that Paul's primary purpose was *hortatory*, since his attention was focused on the Corinthians. In contrast, the fact that Paul's attention in II Cor. 4:7ff. is focused on himself indicates that his primary purpose is now clearly *apologetic*. For instead of establishing a comparison between Paul and his readers, II Cor. 4:7-12 is an explanation of *why* the glory of Paul's ministry of the new covenant, a glory which is so exceeding in its magnitude (cf. 3:7-11), *must*, nevertheless, be contained "in earthen vessels" (ἐν ὀστρακίνοις σκεύεσιν), i.e. in "seinen schwachen gebrechlichen Leib"[76].

Second, the *context* within which Paul interprets his suffering has also significantly changed. In contrast to I Cor. 1:1-4:13, where Paul's apostolic ministry of suffering was the means by which the wisdom and power of God *in the cross* (I Cor. 1:24; 2:5 and 6-16) was both attested (I Cor. 1:17f. and 2:1-5) and made known (cf. I Cor. 4:9-13), in II Cor. 2:14-4:6 Paul's ministry of suffering now functions to attest (II Cor. 4:7) and reveal (II Cor. 4:11) "the knowledge of the *glory of God in the face of Christ*" (II Cor. 4:6; cf. 3:18; 4:4f.). Thus, instead of Paul's "sentence to death" being linked to the *death* of Christ as its "corollary", Paul now emphasizes that he is being "given up to death"

---

an seinem 'Leibe' vollzieht, oder besser: wie *Gott* an ihm handelt" (emphasis his). So too already L. Brun, "Zur Auslegung von II Cor. 5:1-10", *ZNW* 28(1929)207-229, p.213: "Das hier (i.e. in II Cor. 4:11-14) erwähnte Glaubenszeugnis der 'sterbenden' Paulus ist es eben, das den Korinthern das Leben vermittelt -- *ein neuer Ausdruck für die Offenbarung der Lebensmacht Jesu durch ihn*" (emphasis mine).

75 For the influence of Ps. 116 on II Cor. 4:13 and an analysis of the traditions behind II Cor. 4:7-18 as a whole, see Kleinknecht, *Leidende*, pp.257-263.

76 L. Brun, "Zur Auslegung von II Cor. 5:1-10", p.212. This does not mean, however, the "body" in contrast to the soul, but the man as bearer of the message, cf. Schrage, "Leid, Kreuz und Eschaton", p.151n.28 and Ch. Maurer, art. σκεῦος, *TDNT*, Vol. VII, 1971, pp.358-367, esp. p.359. For the opposing position, cf. Güttgemanns, *Der leidende Apostel*, p.115. As Kleinknecht, *Leidende*, p.272 puts it, 4:7ff. functions as the "Kontrapunkt" to the δόξα of Paul's διακονία so that the "treasure" refers to "die gerade als so 'herrlich' erwiesene διακονία selbst" (this is also the view of Bultmann, contra Lietzmann and Windisch, see p.272n.96). That 4:7 is a continuation and extension of the thought of 3:4-4:6 is also one of the central points made by Baumert, *Täglich Sterben*, pp.39-40.

(εἰς θάνατον παραδιδόμεθα) in order that the *life* of Jesus (ἡ ζωὴ τοῦ Ἰησοῦ) might be manifested or revealed (φανερωθῇ) in Paul's mortal flesh (ἐν τῇ θνητῇ σαρκὶ ἡμῶν, 4:11). In short, if Paul's suffering in I Cor. 1-4 was inextricably linked to his "theology of the cross", in II Cor. 2:14-4:12 it is of a piece with his (paradoxical) "theology of glory"[77]. As a result, the *symmetry* between Paul's message and his apostolic suffering, which we saw to be at the heart of I Cor. 1-4, has seemingly been replaced by an insoluble *contradiction*. Hence, as a matter of *self*-defense, Paul must now explain what in I Cor. 4:8-13 was taken for granted, namely, why the apostolic treasure can only genuinely be carried in "clay pots". Paul's answer to this question is contained in the three ἵνα-clauses of verses 7b, 10b and 11b.

c. The Meaning of II Cor. 4:7-12 and its Relationship to I Cor. 4:8-13 and II Cor. 2:14-16a

II Cor. 4:7-12 is therefore best interpreted as a carefully structured argument designed to ellucidate the connection between Paul's suffering and his (paradoxical) "theology of glory". It accomplishes this through an interrelated series of three statements, each of which supports a ἵνα-clause, and which together combine to support the conclusion of verse 12 (see ὥστε, v.12a).

As we have already noted, the first statement and its ἵνα-clause in vv. 7-9 repeat the themes that are familiar to us from I Cor. 4:8-13, though in an entirely different context. For as in I Corinthians, Paul's suffering in II Cor. 4:7, here pictured in terms of the ὀστράκινα σκεύη, also functions to call attention to the fact that the power evident in the gospel belongs to God and not to the apostle (cf. I Cor. 1:17 and 2:1-5). Now, however, the reference is not to the power of God in the cross, but to the power of God seen in the "face of Christ" (II Cor.4:6), i.e. to God's glory. According to 4:7, therefore, the treasure is thus carried in a simple pot, *in order that* (ἵνα) the "extraordinary quality" (ἡ ὑπερβολή) of the treasure, i.e. the "power" (ἡ δύναμις), will in no way be confused with its container, but be recognized for what it

---

77 Of course the twin emphases of Paul's theology of the cross and theology of glory are not to be seen as contradictory to one another. Paul's whole point in II Cor., in fact, is to demonstrate their unity as found in Paul's apostolic ministry. The apparent conflict is rather between Paul's suffering and his theology of glory — Paul's task is therefore to show *how* his apostolic experience of being "led to death" can support *both* his *theologia crucis* and his *theologia gloriae*. The problem of overemphasizing Paul's theology of the cross at the expense of his theology of glory was already pointed out over twenty years ago by W. Bieder, "Paulus und seine Gegner in Korinth", *ThZ* 17(1961)319-333. As he put it: "Paulus vertritt eine solche *theologia crucis*, die sich in einer ihm eigenen *theologia gloriae* entfaltet" (p.319).

is, i.e. the power "of God" (τοῦ θεοῦ)[78]. Consequently, although II Cor.
4:7 restates the same "corollary" or "attesting" function that we saw
in I Cor. 1:17f. and 2:1-5, the change in subject matter from the *cross*
of Christ to the *glory* of God has significantly altered the *way* in
which Paul's suffering attests to his message. In a word, as an earthen
vessel, Paul now confirms his message not by being its "corollary", but
by becoming its "*antithesis*".

In a similar way, the eight participles which are grouped in four
pairs, each exhibiting an adversative relationship (cf. the ἀλλά-constructions throughout), all modify the statement of 4:7, thus illustrating the *means by which* Paul's suffering confirms the fact that the
glory(treasure)-power belongs to God. Hence, in terms of function, 4:8
relates to 4:7 in much the same way as I Cor. 4:8-13, especially vv.
11-13, related to I Cor. 2:1-5. But whereas the focus in I Cor. 4:11-13
was on *Paul's* response to his suffering, in II Cor. 4:8 the focus has
switched to the ways in which *God* responds to Paul's suffering -- namely,
by rescuing him again and again from his peril[79]. This means, therefore,
that the suffering of the apostle does not serve as a disconfirmation
of his ministry, but is rather an integral part of it. For Paul's suffering not only provides the *occasion* for the manifestation of God's
power/glory as the one who rescues the apostle from his suffering, but
also ensures that the power thus displayed is recognized to be God's
alone.

The second statement[80] in verse 10 is a further interpretation of
this basic principle, which plays such a crucial role in the biblical

---

78 Hence the purpose of 4:7 is not to prevent Paul from boasting, or the Corinthians
for that matter, contra R. Tannehill, *Dying and Rising with Christ*, BZNW 32, 1967,
p.90. The problem with this view is simply that it is not Paul's faith nor his own
personal struggle not to boast which is in view -- but the gospel of the glory of
Christ in Paul's ministry. Paul need not be reminded of his weakness -- he is weak,
that is precisely the problem! Tannehill thus makes the common mistake of reading
the different emphasis of I Cor. 4 and II Cor. 12 into II Cor. 4.

79 This essential difference, attested to not only by the passive nature of the passage in general, but also by the widely recognized parallel in II Cor. 1:8-10,
has often been observed -- cf. already L. Brun, who in answer to the question "How
is the life of Jesus manifested?" writes concerning the relationship between II
Cor. 1:9; 4:7b and 12:9: "Er hätte sehr wohl wieder auf die Kraft des die Toten
erweckenden Gottes verweisen können" (p.212, "Zur Auslegung"). Cf. also W. Bieder,
"Paulus und seine Gegner", p.320; Schütz, *Anatomy*, pp.242-243 and most recently,
H. Moxnes, *Theology in Conflict, Studies in Paul's Understanding of God in Romans,
Supplements to Novum Testamentum, Vol. 53*, 1980, p.280: "The passage from 1:8-11
with its strictly theological language has a parallel in 4:7-15. With its Christo-
centric language this paragraph serves almost as an interpretation of the earlier
one ...".

80 Although syntactically v.10 is a continuation of the string of participles which
modify ἔχομεν in v.7, two factors justify taking it as its own independent statement: 1) the absence of the adversative ἀλλά-structure found in the first four
pairs; and 2) the fact that περιφέροντες also supports its own ἵνα-clause in v.10b.

and Jewish tradition of the suffering of the righteous[81], in terms of the suffering of *the* Righteous One, Jesus[82]. Using the categories of the "death of Jesus" (τὴν νέκρωσιν τοῦ 'Ιησοῦ) and the "life of Jesus" (ἡ ζωὴ τοῦ 'Ιησοῦ), Paul is thus able to interpret his own experience of being delivered from situations of suffering in terms of the death *and* resurrection of Christ. As John Schütz has observed,

> The point of contact between Christ's death and Paul's weakness is in Paul's suffering. In Phil. 3:10 Paul speaks of the 'sufferings of Christ' when he actually refers to Christ's death. The reference to suffering is unusual, for Paul never describes Christ's death as a suffering, nor does he speak of any other sufferings of Christ. Since this connection is made elsewhere only in conjunction with Paul's own sufferings, it must be his device. *In order to understand the death of Christ working in himself Paul connects his death with his sufferings* and then speaks of Christ's sufferings, by which he actually means Christ's death. This is clearly what has happened in II Cor. 1:3ff. ... παράκλησις is an eschatological - soteriological term denoting what Paul often calls 'life' ... It is noteworthy here that Paul understands his tribulation/suffering as Christ's suffering (Christ's death) and his comfort as the equivalent of the new life in Christ. *The death and resurrection of Christ inform the life of the apostle with perfect analogies.* The actual specification of tribulation/suffering is given in vv.8-11. Paul means that his physical hardships and persecutions are to be understood as the equivalent of Christ's weakness (i.e. Christ's death) in this parallelism. This identification is also made in II Cor. 4:7-12[83].

Moreover, the fact that Paul's revelatory role of "carrying around the death of Jesus in the body" in order that (ἵνα) the life of Jesus might also be revealed (φανερωθῇ) in his body (ἐν τῷ σώματι ἡμῶν) is a *continuous* one that takes place in the *present* (περιφέροντες) reflects his conviction that in the death and resurrection of Christ the new age has already begun, though, of course, not in its fulness (cf. II Cor. 4:14!)[84]. This Pauline (and early-Christian in general) "already-but-not-yet-in-its-fullness" modification of the traditional apocalyptic,

---

81 This principle is ably summarized in Ps. 116(114-115 LXX), where in verses 3f. (LXX 114:3f.) the Psalmist describes being in a situation of death, only to be rescued by the Lord (cf. vv.6 and 8). The Psalmist's response is therefore to fulfill his "vow" of praise to the Lord (116:14, LXX115:9), his "sacrifice of praise" (116:17, LXX115:8; cf. II Cor. 4:15; 1:11!) -- which is the intent of the Psalm itself (cf. 116:1, LXX114:1; 115:1)! The parallels to II Cor. 1:8-11 and 4:7-15 are both clear and instructive, see the next note.
82 Kleinknecht, *Leidende*, pp.275 and 277 has summarized this point well: "Ergibt sich von hier aus eine die Vorgänge an Jesus und Paulus in eine Linie rückende Perspektive, so bekommt diese aber durch den besonderen Charakter Jesu eine neue Ausrichtung: indem nämlich in Jesus der *Messias und Kyrios* in die Reihe der leidenden Gerechten eingetreten ist, wird für Paulus das Leiden dieses *einen*, des gerechtmachenden Gerechten zum neuen, unverwechselbaren Zentral- und Fluchtpunkt, so daß er sein eigenes Leiden in der διακονία (cf. V 11: διὰ 'Ιησοῦ) als Herumtragen der νέκρωσις τοῦ 'Ιησοῦ bezeichnen kann". "2 Kor 4:7-18 ist der Text, an dem sich bisher am deutlichsten beobachten läßt, wie Paulus die Tradition vom leidenden Gerechten christologisch zentriert ...". So also Güttgemanns, *Der leidende Apostel*, p.100, who writes concerning v.10f.: "Hier wird die theologische tiefsinnigste Deutung des apostolischen Leidens gegeben ...".
83 *Anatomy of Apostolic Authority*, pp.242-243. See Kleinknecht, p.275.
84 For a good summary of this consequence of Paul's Christology for his apostolic self-conception, see Kleinknecht, *Leidende*, pp.275, 277.

two-age conception is, of course, well-known and widely recognized[85].
But it is important to notice that it is precisely this tension between the present and the future in Paul's eschatology which enables
him to interpret his *own* suffering and deliverance in terms of the decisive eschatological events of the death and resurrection of Christ.
Thus, in Paul's view, because the kingdom is not yet present in its fullness it becomes necessary for him to continue to carry in his body the
"death of Jesus". Nevertheless, because the new age has already deci-
sively broken into the present aeon in the resurrection of Christ, it
is also possible for Paul's *present* suffering to be at the *same time* a
present revelation of God's resurrection power, i.e. ἡ ζωὴ τοῦ Ἰησοῦ.
For as II Cor. 1:8-11 illustrates, God's deliverance of Paul from his
suffering is intended to be interpreted as an expression of God's ability to raise the dead.

Paul's third statement in v.11 then provides the theological basis
(cf. the γὰρ of v.11a) for his interpretation of his apostolic suffering as a mediation of the new age in the midst of the old (v.10). It is
not surprising, therefore, that we encounter in v.11 the *same* idea that
we have already discovered in I Cor. 4:9 and II Cor. 2:14, namely, that
Paul's afflictions and persecutions, i.e. his "death", are not mere circumstance, but instead are the outworking of God's plan to spread the
gospel. For in II Cor. 4:11 Paul once again asserts, this time through
the use of the divine passive παραδιδόμεθα[86], that God himself is the
one who has delivered the apostle up to death (εἰς θάνατον) "for Jesus'
sake", in order that (ἵνα) the life of Jesus might also be revealed
(φανερωθῇ) in his mortal body (ἐν τῇ θνητῇ σαρκὶ ἡμῶν). This is confirmed by a comparison of these three texts, which reveals the following parallels:

---

85 For two classic treatments of this theme, cf. Oscar Cullmann, *Christ and Time, The
   Primitive Christian Conception of Time and History*, rev. ed., 1975 and G.E. Ladd,
   The Presence of the Future, The Eschatology of Biblical Realism, 1974.
86 For other examples of παραδίδωμι as a divine passive, cf. Lk. 4:6; Rom. 4:25 and
   possibly Rom. 6:17. It is also possible that the tradition found in Mtt. 17:22/Mk.
   9:31/Lk. 9:44 and Mtt. 20:18/Mk. 10:33/Lk. 18:32 ought to be construed as a divine
   passive, though of course Judas is clearly identified as the one who "hands Jesus
   over" throughout the synoptic tradition and John. For παραδίδωμι in the active,
   with God as the subject, cf. Acts 7:42 and its close parallel in Rom. 1:24, 26, 28.
   Especially instructive is Rom. 8:32, where God is said "to hand over Jesus", while
   in Gal. 2:20 Jesus gives himself up. Cf. also Eph. 5:2, 25.

II Cor. 4:11a	II Cor. 2:14a	I Cor. 4:9a
1. divine passive	1. τῷ δὲ θεῷ χάρις	1. ὁ θεός
2. ἀεί (cf. πάντοτε in the parallel v.10a)	2. πάντοτε	2. (cf. ἄχρι τῆς ἄρτι ὥρας, v.11 and ἕως ἄρτι, v.13)
3. ἡμεῖς οἱ ζῶντες	3. ἡμᾶς	3. ἡμᾶς τοὺς ἀποστόλους
4. εἰς θάνατον παραδιδόμεθα	4. τῷ θριαμβεύοντι	4. ἐσχάτους ἀπέδειξεν ὡς ἐπιθανατίους
5. διὰ 'Ιησοῦν	5. ἐν τῷ Χριστῷ	5. (cf. διὰ Χριστόν)

II Cor. 4:11b	II Cor. 2:14b	I Cor. 4:9b
1. ἵνα καὶ ἡ ζωὴ τοῦ 'Ιησοῦ φανερωθῇ	1. καὶ τὴν ὀσμὴν τῆς γνώσεως αὐτοῦ φανεροῦντι	1. ὅτι θέατρον ἐγενήθημεν
2. ἐν τῇ θνητῇ σαρκί ἡμῶν	2. δι' ἡμῶν	2. -----------
3. -----------	3. ἐν παντὶ τόπῳ	3. τῷ κόσμῳ καὶ ἀγγέλοις καὶ ἀνθρώποις

Hence, Paul's bold assertion that the same eschatological events that took place in the death and resurrection of Christ are now being expressed in his own apostolic ministry (v.10) is supported and legitimized by the fact that he too, like Jesus, is being "delivered over to death" (παραδιδόμεθα) (v.11a). For Paul's own suffering and being rescued, first interpreted as an expression of the "death" and "life" of Jesus in his own body in verse 10, is now given its own independent status as his *own* death and life in verse 11a. In other words, while in v.10 Paul merely "carries" the death of Jesus in his own body, in v.11a Paul *himself* is the one who is both living and delivered up to death. Yet, in *both* verses the purpose remains the same, as is clearly shown by the almost exact parallels between the two ἵνα-clauses of vv. 10b and 11b:

v.10b: ἵνα καὶ ἡ ζωὴ τοῦ 'Ιησοῦ ἐν τῷ σώματι   ἡμῶν φανερωθῇ
v.11b: ἵνα καὶ ἡ ζωὴ τοῦ 'Ιησοῦ ἐν τῇ θνητῇ σαρκὶ ἡμῶν φανερωθῇ.

Hence, the fact that Paul's own "death" also functions as a revelatory agent in v.11a does not lead Paul to the conclusion that the "life" revealed through it is also his own -- this remains, of course, the "life of Jesus"[87]. One must be careful, therefore, not to extend the identification which exists between verses 10b and 11b back into verses 10a and 11a. Verses 10a and 11a are parallel, but not identical. The

---

87 For the association of the life of Jesus with divine power, i.e. the power of the resurrection, cf. Rom. 1:4; I Cor. 6:14; II Cor. 13:4 and Phil. 3:10; especially the last two references in which Paul shares in the power of Christ's resurrection! Cf. Tannehill, *Dying and Rising*, p.85 for these parallels. This then establishes the connection between power/resurrection/life of Jesus which links vv.7 and 11 together.

γὰρ of v.11a must thus be given its more usual sense of indicating a
ground or support, rather than an interpretation[88]. Verse 11 is therefore, in this sense, better interpreted as a restatement of Paul's
first assertion in v.7. Although he is the one being delivered up to
death as an earthen vessel, the life/power revealed through his suffering belongs to God. As a result, Paul's understanding of the relationship between his apostolic experience and its result is once
again emphasized to be an antithetical one. This self-understanding of
Paul leads, then, to the conclusion of verse 12, which in the light of
Paul's earlier argument in I Cor. 4:14-17 is, at first glance, somewhat surprising.

Earlier, Paul's suffering as the *corollary* of the cross was coupled
with the conclusion in I Cor. 4:14-17 that the Corinthians, as his
spiritual children, ought to become "imitators" of Paul (see v.16). For
in their own apostle Paul, the Corinthians could see the embodiment of
the gospel of the cross and thereby be reminded that their own boast
was only in the cross of the Lord, which, in turn, would solve the
problem of the party-spirit in the church (cf. 4:6f.). Now however,
when Paul's apostolic role of suffering is pictured as the *antithesis*[89]
of "the glory of God in the face of Christ", Paul goes on to conclude
that there is an essential and valid *distinction* between himself, *in
his role as an apostle*, and the Corinthians which is different from
the illegitimate and pejorative contrast in I Cor. 4:8ff. (see above).
For now the contrast is between the "death" (θάνατος) which is at work
in Paul and the "life" (ζωή) which is at work in the Corinthians. In
other words, as a result (cf. the ὥστε of v.12a) of Paul's being led
to death in the pattern of Christ, the resurrection power, i.e. the
"life of Jesus", is revealed in such a way that those who accept his
message and apostleship (cf. I Cor. 1:18 and II Cor. 2:15f.) already
begin to experience this "life" in the present (note the present tense
of ἐνεργεῖται in 4:12 and the ἐκ ζωῆς εἰς ζωήν as a modifier of Χριστοῦ
εὐωδία ἐσμὲν, also the present tense in 2:15f.). Paul, however, *as*

---

88 Cf. for example, the statement of J.H. Bernard, *The Second Epistle to the Corinthians, The Expositor's Greek Testament, Vol. 3*, 1979(1903), p.62: "The key to the
interpretation of ver. 10 is to observe that ver. 11 is the explanation of it
(ἀεὶ γὰρ κ.τ.λ.); the two verses are strictly parallel: 'our mortal flesh' of v.11
is only a more emphatic and literal way of describing 'our body' of ver.10. *Hence*
the bearing about of the νέκρωσις of Jesus *must be identical* with the continual
deliverance to death for his sake". But this second statement does not necessarily
follow from the first.

89 The central importance of this "antithesis" in Paul's theology and apostolic self-
conception is one of the repeated and constant themes in the collected essays of
E. Käsemann, *Paulinische Perspektiven*, 1972². In fact, this is one theme that occurs in every essay of the book, cf. e.g., pp.21,70,101-106, 119-122,148-151,159-
163 and 197. As he states it: "Es hängt alles daran, daß solche Sätze nicht als
dialektische Rhetorik abgetan werden. Paulus bleibt in seinem Eigensten unbegriffen,
solange sein paradoxer Ruhm der Anfechtung nicht ernst genommen wird" (p.70).

an apostle, experiences "death" in the present. This is not to deny, of course, that Paul also experienced the "life of Jesus" -- just the opposite is asserted in II Cor. 4:7-11 and 4:16-5:5. Instead, the point to be made is that v.12 concerns the specific *apostolic* role assigned to Paul over against the Church, and not the general Christian experience. In a *derivative sense*, therefore, it is appropriate to describe Paul's conception of his suffering as being endured *for the sake of* the Corinthians: Paul is delivered over to death, a death which he interprets in terms of the death of Jesus, in order that the Corinthians might experience the "life of Jesus".

Again the parallel to II Cor. 1:3-11 is instructive. Paul had received "the sentence of death" (τὸ ἀπόκριμα τοῦ θανάτου, v.9) in order that he might trust only in God, who raises the dead (v.9). Yet, like the Psalmist (see above, n.81), Paul too was delivered and is thus filled with the hope that God will continue to deliver him in the future (v.10). God's purpose in establishing this "death" and "resurrection" pattern within Paul's life, however, is not primarily to strengthen Paul's faith, though that too is intended, but rather to provide a basis in Paul's life from which he may "comfort" the *Corinthians* (cf. vv.3-5). Thus, Paul understands *both* his "afflictions" *and* his "comfort" to be *for* (ὑπέρ) the Corinthians in order that they might be saved and comforted enough to endure the same sufferings (v.6). It is important to note, however, that in II Cor. 1:3ff. the roles are not reversed, which would be expected if Paul conceived of his suffering to be equivalent to that of the Corinthians not only in kind, but also in purpose -- especially when Paul's intent is to explain the relationship between the apostle and his church. The relationship between Paul and his church cannot be described, therefore, as reciprocal when it concerns the apostolic call to share abundantly in the sufferings of Christ (v.5). As Paul put it in II Cor. 4:15: "It is all for your sake, so that as grace extends to more and more people it may increase thanksgiving, to the glory of God" (cf. also 5:13). Yet here too, Paul's self-conception remains a derivative one, since it is Jesus' death and resurrection which provide the pattern for Paul's experience, and it is God's comfort which is made manifest[90]. Paul's conception of his suffering is

---

90 Paul thus derived his apostolic self-conception concerning his suffering from his understanding of the death and resurrection of Christ -- *not* from his understanding of the nature of general Christian experience as Ellis, "II Cor. 5:1-10", pp.215-216 and Schütz, *Anatomy*, p.245 posit. Ellis does this because he mistakenly applies II Cor. 4:11; Phil. 3:10 and II Cor. 1:5 to *all* Christians and not primarily to Paul as an apostle; while Schütz fails to see that Paul's uniqueness as an apostle includes his call to suffer as well as his commission to preach. For although Schütz is correct in concluding on p.206 that "Paul does not *repeat* what Christ has done. He *reflects* what Christ has done. In him, the account of that action is made manifest" (cf. p.230 for the same point), he nevertheless fails to recognize the unique role as *mediatory agent* that Paul does occupy (see below)!

therefore derived from his understanding of the nature of Christ's death, but is not intended to be understood as a repetition of it, even in some sort of modified form, that is, as some sort of "second atonement". For both II Cor. 1:3-11 and 4:7-12 demonstrate that Paul conceived of his own "death" as merely a *mediation* of the significance of the death and life of Jesus. Paul remains, in a word, a "minister" (διάκονος) of the new covenant (II Cor. 3:6) whose task is to reveal or mediate the "gospel of the glory of Christ" both in his preaching (II Cor. 2:17; 4:5f.) and in his suffering (II Cor. 2:14; 4:7ff.).

In conclusion, as a minister of the new covenant, Paul stands *between* the death and resurrection of Christ, i.e. the glory of God, and the "life" of his church in the apostolic role of *mediatory agent* (II Cor. 4:12; cf. 3:7-18!)[91]. Thus, in the context of the mediation of the "life of Jesus" / "glory of God in the face of Christ", Paul's apostolic suffering functions as an antitype which cannot, in the strict sense, be imitated, but only accepted or rejected. For Paul's apostolic ministry is now the means *through* which God makes his appeal to the world (cf. 5:20). It is this last point that Paul makes explicit in II Cor. 6:1-10 and chapters 10-13.

3. II Cor. 6:1-10 and 10-13

In II Cor. 5:18 Paul once again asserts that God has entrusted him with his διακονία (cf. 3:6; 4:1,6), so that as an "ambassador of Christ"

---

91 I have chosen "mediatory agent" to describe the function of Paul's apostolic ministry instead of the seemingly more appropriate term "mediator" in order to avoid confusion with Paul's own statement in Gal. 3:19f. and the Christological statements in I Tim. 2:5; Heb. 8:6; 9:15 and 12:24. Nevertheless this is precisely the function which best captures Paul's ministry as portrayed in II Cor. 2:14ff. By "agent" I thus do not mean someone who arranges something (i.e. a "travel-agent"), but I am using it in the technical sense of "means" or "instrument", i.e. "to act as an intermediary agent in bringing, effecting, or communicating"; so *Webster's Seventh New Collegiate Dictionary*, 1972, entries "agent" and "mediate", pp.17 and 526. For this point see too J. Christiaan Beker, who has referred to Paul as "mediator" in his *Paul the Apostle, The Triumph of God in Life and Thought*, 1980, p.6; i.e. in describing Paul's call he writes, "Paul is a 'called apostle' (Rom. 1:1) and thus the direct mediator of the gospel and its authoritative interpreter". But Beker does not develop this notion beyond this bare notice. Although the noun itself was not used, Paul's role as a mediator was also emphasized strongly by E. Kamlah, "Wie Beurteilt Paulus sein Leiden?", *ZNW* 54(1963)217-232, p.225, who, on the basis of I Thess. 2:14 and 3:4 wrote: "Hier hat Paulus vielmehr eine *vermittelnde Rolle*, so daß die Reihe Christus - Apostel - Gemeinde entsteht. Sicher, zunächst kennzeichnet diese Reihe nur eine zeitliche Abfolge. Über den Apostel hören ja die Thessalonicher zuerst vom Leiden des Herrn. Das zeigt sich darin, daß nun auch die Thessalonicher so Vorbild für die späten Bekehrten werden. Aber für Paulus hat das grundsätzliche Bedeutung. Ja, es ist nach meiner Auffassung *der Schlüssel zum Verständnis seines apostolischen Selbstbewußtseins*" (emphasis mine), and most recently see P. Marshall, "A Metaphor of Social Shame: ΘPIAMBEYEIN in 2 Cor. 2:14", *NovT* 25(1983)302-317, p.316, who also takes 2:14 to be "thoroughly consistent" with Paul's self-conception as "the medium of the message".

his ministry occupies the mediating role between God and the world (see
5:20)[92]. But having done so, Paul must again stress the unique nature
of his apostolic experience. For although his appearance as an apostle
is certainly not what one might expect of God's ambassador, Paul's point
is that it is precisely his weakness and suffering that "commends" him
(cf. 6:3f. and 3:1!), being both the "corollary" to the cross of Christ
and the revelatory "antithesis" to the glory of God in the face of Christ,
i.e. to the twin aspects of the gospel which he has just summarized in
the classic formulation of 5:14-21. By incorporating the themes of I
Cor. 1-4 (see 6:4-8a) *and* those of II Cor. 4:7-12 (see 6:8b-10), II Cor.
6:1-10 thus provides an appropriate capstone for Paul's self-defense as
an apostle. As K. Prümm so aptly put it, "Der Abschnitt will also ge-
lesen sein als apostolische Ausweiskarte"[93]. Moreover, Paul's self-understanding and interpretation of his weakness as an apostle are once a-
gain derived from the biblical tradition of the suffering of the righteous as confirmed and given its decisive formulation by the death of
Jesus. For the "auffallend dichte Bezugnahme zum deuterojesajanischen
Textfeld"[94], which already exists in Paul's summary of his ambassador-
ship and its message in 5:20-6:1, is then made explicit by the quotation
in 6:2 from the suffering servant tradition of Isaiah 49:8a.

Now however, since the themes of 6:1-10 are already familiar to the
Corinthians it is rather the structure of the passage which serves to
highlight Paul's point. Syntactically, the negative disclaimer of v.3
and the positive catalog of commendation in vv.4-10 are both participial
phrases intended to modify the finite verb παρακαλοῦμεν of v.1, the only
finite verb of the entire section other than the parenthesis of v.2. The
catalog itself is a long list of phrases linked to the participle of
v.4 συνιστάντες by the prepositions ἐν and διά, and the comparative
particle ὡς, so that the catalog is divided into two main sections: the
prepositional phrases of vv.4b-8a and the concessive clauses of vv.8b-
10c introduced by ὡς. As a result, the argument of 6:1-10 is very com-
pact and abbreviated, forcing the reader to fill in the important logi-

---

92 O. Hofius, "'Gott hat unter uns aufgerichtet das Wort von der Versöhnung' (2 Kor
5:19)", *ZNW* 71(1980)3-20. As Hofius himself points out on the basis of parallels
to Is. 6:8; Ex. 4:16 and Jer. 15:19 concerning v.20: "Dabei ist es Gott, der Ver-
söhner, selbst, der im Wort der Apostel das Wort ergreift (V.20b; vgl. 2 Kor.
2:14). Im gleichen Sinn will das zweimalige ὑπὲρ Χριστοῦ (V.20a; V.20c) verstanden
sein. Es besagt m.E. nicht, daß die Apostel als Stellvertreter und Repräsentanten
Christi wirken und reden, sondern daß der auferstandene und gegenwärtige Kyrios
'durch' die von ihm autorisierten Botschafter redet, daß sie der 'Mund' ihres
Herrn sind" (p.10, cf. 10n.34).
93 *Diakonia Pneumatos. Der Zweite Korintherbrief als Zugang zur apostolischen Botschaft, Bd II: Theologie des Zweiten Korintherbriefes, 1. Teil,* 1960, p.184. Cf.
Bornkamm, *Paul,* pp.169f.
94 Kleinknecht, *Leidende,* p.280. For his discussion of the tradition of the suffering
of the righteous which stands behind this passage, see pp.263-268.

cal relationships between the propositions him/herself. Moreover, the
meaning of the first section of the catalog (vv.4b-8a) further depends
upon how the punctuation of v.4 is construed:

ἀλλ' ἐν παντὶ συνιστάντες ἑαυτοὺς ὡς
θεοῦ διάκονοι ἐν ὑπομονῇ πολλῇ ἐν θλίψεσιν
ἐν ἀνάγκαις ἐν στενοχωρίαις ...

Although there have been no less than five different possibilities suggested[95], the central issue is whether the phrase ἐν ὑπομονῇ πολλῇ ought
to be considered part of the preceding clause so that the catalog which
follows would, in effect, modify ἐν ὑπομονῇ πολλῇ, or whether the phrase
ἐν ὑπομονῇ πολλῇ is simply one of the members of the catalog itself, all
of which would then directly modify συνιστάντες. In other words, there
are two possible ways to construe Paul's thought in v.4:

> 1) We commend ourselves in every way as
> servants of God by means of great
> endurance; an endurance in the midst
> of afflictions, hardships, calamities,
> etc.

or

> 2) We commend ourselves in every way as
> servants of God; namely, in great
> endurance, in afflictions, hardships,
> calamities, etc.

But the addition of the adjective πολλῇ, which distinguishes the phrase
ἐν ὑπομονῇ πολλῇ from the catalog of one-word phrases which follows; the
contrast between the positive quality of "endurance" and the list of
adverse circumstances in vv.4b-5, which parallels the concessive relationships established in 8b-10c; and the difficulty of understanding
how afflictions, hardships, calamities, etc. in and of themselves serve
to commend the apostle all combine to suggest that the first alternative
is preferable (cf. Rom. 5:3f.). Therefore, according to 6:4-10, the
true apostle commends himself[96] (and at the same time disqualifies his
opponents!) in two ways:

> 1) *by actively* exhibiting great endurance in the midst
> of the most adverse circumstances, an endurance which

---

95 The Textus Receptus, Bover (4th ed.), Nestle-Aland (26th ed.), Authorized Version,
Revised Version (1881) and the American Standard Version all place a minor stop
before and a minor stop after ἐν ὑπομονῇ πολλῇ. The Zürich ed. of Die Heilige
Schrift has no punctuation at this point at all, while Westcott and Hort (1881),
RSV and Luther's Bible place a major stop before and a minor stop after the
phrase. The Jerusalem Bible reads only a major stop before the phrase.
96 In a private conversation, Prof. Gert Jeremias suggested to me that ὡς θεοῦ
διάκονοι in 6:4 could be rendered "as appropriate for servants of God", which
would strengthen the interpretation being suggested here by placing the emphasis
even more strongly on the manner of recommendation. The only appropriate commendation is the one Paul adduces.

manifests itself in a demonstration of those qualities
befitting a servant of God (6:4-8a; i.e. Paul as the
"corollary" to his theology of the cross) and

2) *by passively* displaying the power of God as he is delivered by God from his afflictions, so that his
"sentence of death" mediates life to the church
(6:8b-10; i.e. Paul as the "antithesis" to his theology
of glory).

Consequently, in reading II Cor. 6:1-10 we are again made aware of
the fact that the problem which now faced Paul in Corinth was the
growing rejection of his authority as an apostle because his suffering
seemed to disqualify his claim to be a "διάκονος" as it was currently
being defined by his opponents and accepted by the Corinthians. For
although the exact reasons remain unclear, it is nevertheless apparent
that the criteria now being accepted in Corinth *excluded* weakness as an
appropriate sign of God's commission. This brief look at II Cor. 6:1-10
makes it evident, however, that Paul's response to this criticism is
still the same: his suffering is not an obstacle to the gospel, but in
fact is an essential part of it. For the *true* apostle verifies (i.e.
Paul as "corollary") and reveals (Paul as "antithesis") the gospel of
Christ by his suffering. Rather than being a cause for his rejection,
it is Paul's weakness *itself* which "recommends" him and, by implication,
disqualifies his opponents as genuine ministers of Christ.

The new element in 6:1-10 is the note of appeal and urgency which
accompanies Paul's description of his apostolic role (cf. 5:20b; 6:1,
11ff.). For Paul's conviction that his weakness and afflictions are
the true characteristics of the apostolic office and his assurance that
God is thus "making his appeal through him" (5:20) carry with them the
awareness that to reject his ministry is, in effect, to reject the gospel of Christ as well[97]. Consequently, in Paul's mind, the Corinthians
now stand in danger of having "accepted the grace of God in vain" (6:1).
Paul's battle for the legitimacy of his apostolic ministry is, in reality, a battle for the truth of the gospel which he bears, and the
life of the Corinthians to whom he brought it. This becomes evident in
the light of the connection between II Cor. 2:15f.; 6:1 and 13:1-10.
For Paul's conviction that a person's reaction to his ministry acts
to signify and further his/her destiny (2:15f.) leads quite naturally
to the entreaties of 6:1 and 13:1-10. As a result, the "test" of faith
becomes whether or not the Corinthians will remain loyal to Paul, not
because Paul somehow stands independent of or above the gospel, but
because he is convinced that he is its true and genuine representative
and embodiment. Hence, for Paul, it is not *his* ministry that is present-

---

97 K. Rengstorf, *Apostolat und Predigtamt*, 1954, p.20, makes this same point based
on the role of the apostle and the OT שלׁיח.

ly being called into question, but the genuineness of the faith of the
Corinthians themselves! This explains why Paul's begging (δεόμεθα) the
Corinthians to be reconciled to God in 5:20 and his entreating
(παρακαλοῦμεν) them not to accept the grace of God in vain in 6:1 can become an appeal for the Corinthians to reaffirm their loyalty to him in
chapters 10-13 (cf. παρακαλῶ in 10:1 and δέομαι in 10:2!). Paul's self-
identification with his gospel, which was the implicit presupposition
behind all three of the previous "catalogs", is now made explicit in
chapters 10-13 (cf. 11:1-6). It is a fitting conclusion, therefore, that
when forced to boast about the "signs" of his apostleship, Paul does not
take refuge in the "signs and wonders and mighty works" which he had performed in Corinth (cf. 12:12!), but in those things that show his weakness (cf. 11:30). For like his opponents, Paul too is interested in manifesting the "power of God" in his ministry. But unlike his opponents,
Paul is convinced that the same pattern displayed in the Christ who
ἐσταυρώθη ἐξ ἀσθενείας, ἀλλὰ ζῇ ἐκ δυνάμεως θεοῦ (13:4), is also to be
the distinguishing characteristic of his apostles. As he himself put it,

> Most gladly, therefore, I will rather boast about my weakness, that the power
> of Christ may dwell in me. Therefore I am well content with weakness, with in-
> sults, with distresses, with persecutions, with difficulties, for Christ's
> sake; for when I am weak, then I am strong. (12:9b-10, NASV).[98]

For as we have seen, part of the μυστήριον τοῦ θεοῦ which Paul preached
and cared for as its steward (cf. I Cor. 2:1; 4:1) was the revelation
that God was making himself known not in the outwardly flamboyant, self-
confident display of "spiritual" power so characteristic of the spirit-
uality of the Corinthian church, and of the false apostles which they
had come to accept, but through the "weakness" and "death" of his genuine apostles. The good news of the revelation of God's power in the
deliverance and vindication of those who trust in him in spite of their
suffering, first declared in the biblical and post-biblical tradition
of the suffering of the righteous, and then proclaimed and embodied in
the ministry, death and resurrection of God's own son, "the Lord of
glory" (I Cor. 2:8), was *now* being made known to the world through
Paul's διακονία καινῆς διαθήκης. Thus, as a revelatory agent of the
gospel of the power of God, Paul's "sentence to death" could become
both his "boast" (II Cor. 12:5,9) and the ground for his thanksgiving
(II Cor. 2:14).

---

98 For an outline of the various interpretive possibilities for this text, cf. Gerald
G. O'Collins, "Power Made Perfect in Weakness: 2 Cor. 12:9-10", *CBQ* 33(1971)528-
537, pp.528-530. O'Collins emphasizes that Paul's stress in 12:9f. is on the
simultaneity of the weakness and power (cf. I Cor. 2:3f.). Hence, this text also
points to the "Christological setting in which Paul sees his ministry" (p.536).
"Far more important than any moral education he undergoes is the fact that his
apostolic activity involves participation in the weakness and power of Calvary
and Easter" (p.536).

4. Summary

Paul's answer to the question of *how* his "sentence to death" as an
apostle, expressed in the parallel statements of I Cor. 4:9, II Cor.
2:14 and II Cor. 4:11, functioned to make known the knowledge of God in
Christ and its corresponding implications for the church at Corinth are
now clear. When forced in I Cor. 1-4 to respond to the boasting of the
Corinthians, Paul could point to his suffering as an apostle as the necessary *corollary* or *verification* of his gospel of the cross. Here,
Paul's acceptance of his suffering, manifested through his endurance
of faith, functioned to affirm that the power of God found in the cross
was still being made known through and in the midst of the tribulations
of this world[99]. Furthermore, by responding *positively* to the suffering
he encountered Paul became a "fool for Christ's sake", who, as the spiritual father of the Corinthian church, could urge the Corinthians to
"imitate him" in his active affirmation and acceptance of the fact that
the *cross* is the power of God. In other words, to imitate Paul was to
"boast *only* in the Lord" (1:31), thus becoming a "fool" in the eyes of
the world (3:18), since "the Lord of glory" in whom one was to boast
was the *crucified* Christ.

On the other hand, when Paul is forced to defend the very nature of
his apostolic ministry itself in II Corinthians, he is able to point to
his suffering as an apostle as the necessary *antithesis* to his "gospel
of the glory of Christ" (II Cor. 4:4). For since the knowledge of God
being revealed through the apostles, which was defined as the "*power* of
God in the cross" in I Corinthians, was now being defined in II Corinthians in terms of the "*glory* of God in the face of Christ" (4:6, cf.
the link to "power" in 4:7), this change in focus necessitated a corresponding change in Paul's depiction of how his suffering functioned
to reveal God's power. This new situation in II Corinthians, whether a
further development of the old problems or an entirely new constellation,
was no doubt instigated by the arrival of Paul's opponents and had as
its center of gravity a denial of the legitimacy of Paul's apostleship.
It is probable, therefore, that not only the διάκονος-terminology, but

---

99 The importance of this fundamental conviction for Paul's theology has been emphasized recently by C.J.A. Hickling, "Centre and Periphery in the Thought of
Paul", *Studia Biblica 1978. III. Papers on Paul and Other New Testament Authors*,
ed. E.A. Livingstone, 1980, pp.199-214, who even sees this "Aeonenwende" in the
midst of the present evil age to be at the center of Paul's thinking. Commenting
on II Cor. 12:9 he writes, "ἀσθένεια is elsewhere, with its cognates, a word frequently characteristic of the state of affairs under the old order apart from Christ,
or as it still persists temporarily alongside the new order in Christ. Here,
ἀσθένεια with all that it implies - both Christ's crucifixion (cf. 2 Cor. 13:4),
and the apostle's participation in his suffering - are seen to be the locus of
God's fullest revelation of himself" (p.209).

also the "theology of glory" motif itself was originally introduced by
Paul's opponents. Nevertheless, Paul does not reject either, but instead strives to show the genuineness of his own ministry (διακονία),
using categories supplied by his opponents. Hence, although the agenda
is set by Paul's opponents, the interpretation of the themes of the true
διάκονος/διακονία and the glory of Christ is Paul's own. Consequently,
in response to this new apologetic context, Paul's *active* role in affirming the power of the cross by accepting his suffering in faith is
now replaced by his *passive* role in revealing God's glorious power
through the rescuing activity of God as manifested again and again in
Paul's situations of suffering. Moreover, as the parallels to II Cor.
1:3-11 make clear, Paul's experience in his suffering is now interpreted
in terms of the death and resurrection of Jesus himself. Paul's suffering, like the death of Christ, also becomes a platform for the display
of God's resurrection power.

Nonetheless, despite the difference in emphasis and in the role which
Paul's suffering actually plays, it is Paul's conviction that the new
age or "new covenant" has already been inaugurated which forms the foundation of his thinking in both I and II Corinthians. Thus, whether as
the "active corollary" to the cross (I Cor.) or the "passive antithesis"
to the glory of Christ (II Cor.), Paul understands his role as an
apostle to be the mediation of the *power* of the new age in the midst of
the old. Paul regards himself as the eschatological and mediatory agent
who stands between God in Christ and the Church and who, as the minister
of the new covenant (cf. 3:6), is entrusted with the task of revealing
the gospel of the glory of Christ in his preaching and suffering. As
such, Paul's role as an apostle or διάκονος of the new covenant, as this
is fulfilled in his apostolic suffering, cannot be imitated, but only
accepted or rejected. This is the point of II Cor. 6:1-10 and 10-13.

Finally, this identification of Paul with his gospel creates an
urgency in his self-defense which can only be explained by Paul's corresponding conviction that his ministry and gospel were the true and
genuine expressions of the death (cross) and resurrection (glory) of
Christ. For it is only in Paul's ministry that the cross and glory of
Christ do not stand in opposition or exclude one another, but are, in
fact, necessitated by each other. That is to say, it is precisely Paul's
suffering as an apostle which ties together these two aspects of the
proclamation of the gospel of Christ. Hence, as the affirmation of the
cross *and* the revelation of God's glory, Paul's suffering, rather than
calling into question the legitimacy of his apostolic calling, becomes
an essential aspect of his apostolic ministry. It is only natural,
therefore, that from Paul's perspective, to reject the nature of his

apostolic ministry is to reject the true and only gospel itself and to give indication of the fact that one's own eschatological fate has already been determined (cf. 2:15f.)[100].

C. CONCLUSION: THE APOSTLE PAUL AS THE MEDIATORY AGENT
OF THE GLORY OF GOD

The implications of our study thus far for an understanding of the letter/Spirit contrast in II Cor. 3:6 can now be drawn.

1. The Letter/Spirit Contrast as an Expression of Paul's Apostolic Self-Understanding

As we have seen, II Cor. 2:14-16a is of a piece with the theme of Paul's weakness as an apostle which runs throughout the Corinthian correspondence. As one of the three thesis-like statements within I and II Corinthians which express the role of Paul's apostolic "sentence to death" in the salvific plan of God (cf. I Cor. 4:9; II Cor. 4:11), II Cor. 2:14-16a makes it clear that the context within which the letter/Spirit contrast is to be understood is Paul's apostolic *self-conception* as the one who is called to reveal the knowledge of God by means of his suffering. More specifically, the use of the θριαμβεύειν-imagery in 2:14 not only serves as a preparation for Paul's thought in 4:7ff. by highlighting the *passive* role of Paul's apostolic agency, inasmuch as the captive "led to death" in the triumphal procession was at times rescued from his fate of death by the grace and power of the conqueror (see above, chapter one, pp.27f.). It also anchors Paul's statement in II Cor. 3:6 within a very specific thematic context within the Corinthian correspondence as a whole. Hence, the introduction of the theme of Paul's suffering in II Cor. 2.14-16a necessitates that we also understand the letter/Spirit contrast as an essential aspect of Paul's apologetic, rather than as a detached and dogmatic theological maxim.

2. The Relationship Between 2:12f. and 2:14-16a

Moreover, once II Cor. 2:14-16a is understood to be an assertion of the legitimacy of Paul's suffering as an apostle, its function within

---

100 This same urgency is also reflected in Gal. 1:6-24, where Paul's need to defend his gospel cannot be separated from his need to defend the genuine nature of his apostleship. Hence, Paul's *first* response to the Galatians' rejection of the gospel (see 1:6-9) is not to defend his message *per se*, but to defend himself! (see 1:10ff.).

II Cor. 1-7 also becomes evident. The fact that Paul bursts into praise
in 2:14 in the midst of a description of his trials and tribulations as
they culminated in his experience of anxiety over Titus in Troas has
led many recent commentators to posit a literary break between 2:12f.
and 2:14, with the original train of thought being picked up in what
is now 7:5. II Cor. 2:14-7:4 thus becomes a fragment of a lost letter
which was later introduced into this strange new environment. However,
once the *cause* of Paul's praise in 2:14-16a is recognized to be precisely these trials and tribulations, i.e. his being "led to death",
of which his "sentence of death" in 1:3-11, his prior "affliction and
anguish of heart" in 2:4 and his anxiety in 2:12f. (cf. 11:28!) are
certainly a part; and once 2:14 is anchored firmly within the polemical
situation behind II Corinthians as a whole, the logical relationship
between 2:12f. and 2:14ff. is manifest. For inasmuch as Paul's legitimacy as an apostle was now being called into question precisely *because*
of his sufferings, Paul's reference to yet another change in his plans
as a result of his anxiety over Titus (cf. 1:15-22) makes it necessary
to remind the Corinthians immediately of the essential role his suffering plays in his apostolic ministry[101]. Not to do so would simply supply
more ammunition for his opponents' attack. Thus, Paul counters this possibility by praising God for the very thing which the Corinthians are
being led to believe disqualifies Paul as an apostle, namely, his suffering. The burst of praise in II Cor. 2:14 is therefore not a pre-
mature response to his recollection of the joy and relief he felt at
meeting Titus in Macedonia as reflected in 7:5ff.[102], nor the beginning

---

101 C.J.A. Hickling, "The Sequence of Thought in II Corinthians, Chapter Three", *NTS*
21(1975)380-395, p.383 has also stressed the unity between 2:12f. and 2:14-17 by
taking 2:14-17 to be a response to the reproach that Paul's sudden change of plans
in 2:12f., as in ch.1, indicates instability or a wanderlust. In Hickling's view,
2:14 counters this charge by emphasizing that as part of the triumphal procession
Paul is led and does not decide himself the route he is to take - i.e. he travels
"dictated by the needs of that gospel or by supervening pastoral necessity". But
Hickling's view does not take into account the full force of the θριαμβεύειν
metaphor, nor the problem of Paul's anxiety, which is clearly the focus of 2:12f.
The problem is not just that Paul changed his plans, but rather *why* he was forced
.to do so.

102 This has been the most common explanation among those who try to link 2:14 to
something other than 2:12f. For only a few typical examples, cf. Schelkle,
Korinther, p.57; Bartling, "God's Triumphant Captive", p.886; Barrett, *Second
Corinthians*, p.97 (Barrett sees 2:12f. itself as already reflecting relief!) and
Plummer, *Second Corinthians*, p.67, who is so certain of this position that he
can conclude, "to seek for any other explanation is an unintelligent waste of
time"! It is also interesting that although Bultmann, *Zweiter Korintherbrief*,
p.66 realized that the formula τῷ δὲ θεῷ χάρις was a fixed one and that "sie hat
ihren Bezug sonst auf das unmittelbar Vorhergehende, indem sie einen Gegensatz
oder ein neues Moment, das an das Vorangehende organisch anschließt (8:16), ein-
führt", he was nevertheless content simply to say that "Hier ist ein solcher Bezug nicht vorhanden. Der Zusammenhang ist verloren". The inappropriateness of
reading 2:14 in the light of 7:5ff. has been strongly argued by M. Thrall, "A

of a lost letter now retained only in the fragment 2:14-7:4, but rather
the necessary and logical response to the suffering of Paul reintroduced in 2:12f.[103]. There is thus no compelling reason to split II Cor.
1-7 into one or more fragments, except perhaps for the notoriously
difficult text of 6:14-7:1[104].

The importance of a proper understanding of θριαμβεύειν for this
conclusion is illustrated by the recent article by M. Thrall[105]. For
despite her emphasis on the unity of II Cor. 1-7[106], she nevertheless
fails to understand the connection between 2:12f. and 2:14ff. because
she was not aware of the precise meaning of θριαμβεύειν. She is forced
to conclude, therefore, that "the state of anxiety described in verses
12-13 could scarcely be said to provide grounds for the expression of
thanksgiving in verse 14"[107], since she assumes that πάντοτε and ἐν

Second Thanksgiving Period in II Corinthians", *JSNT* 16(1982)101-124. For a good
critique of those who try to split 2:13/14 and 7:4/5, cf. Thrall's article, pp.
107-111 and above, p.20n.52

103 Πάντοτε and ἐν παντὶ τόπῳ in II Cor. 2:14, as the parallels to I Cor. 4:9 and
II Cor. 4:11 confirm, are thus best interpreted as relating back to the anxiety
Paul felt in Troas. Cf. II Cor. 11:28 in which Paul asserts that part of his
suffering and weakness as an apostle includes "the daily pressure upon me of
anxiety for all the churches". Although he did not realize the precise nature
of the θριαμβεύειν metaphor, Th. Zahn, *Introduction to the New Testament, Vol.1*,
1977 (reprint of the 1909 ET of the 3rd. German ed.), p.343n.1 has been one of
the few exegetes who has seen that 2:14-16 is intended to be a response to Paul's
weakness in 2:12f. In his words, "When in 2:14-16, in contrast to the confession
of the weakness which prevented him from making use of the opportunities to
preach in Troas, Paul expresses his gratitude to God ... this statement, like
1:18-22, is intended to prevent a false generalization and interpretation of
his weakness. It also furnishes a natural transition to the detailed contrast
between the genuine preachers of the gospel, of whom he is one, and the wandering
Jewish Christian teachers, who peddle the word of God (2:17-5:21 ...)". M. Rissi,
Studien zum Zweiten Korintherbrief: Der alte Bund - Der Prediger - Der Tod,
AThANT, Bd. 56, 1969, pp.15-17 also argues for the unity between 2:12f. and 2:14,
though he views 2:12f. as an example of Paul's love for the Corinthians, with
2:14 functioning in the same way as 1:18 - i.e. Paul separates himself from the
past "mit einem Aufblick zu Gott ... Beide Sätze mit ihrem betonten δὲ trennen
den glaubenden Apostel von den schweren Gedanken an die Vergangenheit ...".
Even apart from the missing connection in content in this view, it is questionable whether δὲ can bear the weight of this interpretation. Rather, the importance
of the past is precisely what Paul wants to affirm!

104 In a very important, but often overlooked article, James L. Price has argued
that the key to the unity of the sections 1:1-2:13 and 2:14ff. is to be found
in an understanding of the role of affliction in Paul's thinking. He emphasizes
in particular the link between 1:6f. and 4:8-11 on the one hand, and 3:1-3 on
the other hand. He also relates 3:5f. and 3:1ff. to 1:21 and 4:14f. to 1:13f.,
while at the same time stressing the connection between the theme of suffering
in 1-7 and the "weakness" theme of 10-13, concluding that it is the theme of
Paul's suffering that ties the various sections of the letter together. Cf. his
"Aspects of Paul's Theology and their Bearing on Literary Problems of Second
Corinthians", in *Studies in the History of the Text of the New Testament, FS
Kenneth Willis Clark*, ed. B.L. Daniels and M. Jack Suggs, 1967, pp.95-106, esp.
pp.96-99,103 and 104f.

105 See above, n.102.

106 "Thanksgiving Period", p.101.

107 "Thanksgiving Period", p.101.

παντὶ τόπῳ in 2:14 could not refer to Troas, where Christ did not triumph in Paul[108]. Consequently, she must also conclude that there still
exists some sort of "break" between 2:13/14, though her arguments for
the unity between 7:4 and 5, are strong[109]. Hence, in her final analysis, Thrall is forced to admit that 2:14-17 "seems to be almost contradicted" by 2:12f.[110]. Moreover, because of its form as an introductory
thanksgiving, 2:14-17 can only be related to chapters 3-5! In her words,
2:14-17

> essentially ... looks forward, not back. The general theme of evangelization
> provides *some sort of a* link with 2:12, but because *Paul is primarily looking
> ahead*, he is not greatly concerned about providing a strictly logical connex-
> ion with what he has just written in 2:12-13. The possible conflict between
> his admission of having abandoned his missionary opportunities in Troas and
> his claim that he is used by God as a medium of revelation πάντοτε and ἐν
> παντὶ τόπῳ may not have presented itself to his mind.[111]

Once the meaning of θριαμβεύειν becomes clear, however, so that II Cor.
2:14-17 can be located within Paul's statements concerning his suffering as an apostle, the connection between 2:12f. and 2:14 is patent.
Rather than not occurring to him, as Thrall argues, the contrast between his suffering as an apostle as reflected in 2:12f. and his being
used by God to reveal the knowledge of God becomes the very heart of
his apostolic self-understanding. Hence, when θριαμβεύειν is understood
to refer to Paul as the prisoner who is being led to death by God, it
becomes the *crux interpretum* of 2:14-16a by solving the three interpretive problems encountered in this text:

> 1) it makes the "abrupt" transition between
>   2:13 and 14 understandable;
>
> 2) it allows θριαμβεύειν itself to be under-
>   stood against the backdrop of the "triumphal
>   procession", without having to do damage
>   either to the image itself, or to the con-
>   text; and
>
> 3) it provides the missing link conceptually
>   between the images of v.14b and vv.14c-16a.

3. The Relationship Between 2:14-16a and 2:16b-4:6

On the other hand, as the necessary apologetic response to Paul's
suffering in 2:12f., II Cor. 2:14-16a also exercises a specific and
important threefold function in relationship to what follows[112]. First,

---

108 "Thanksgiving", pp.106,112.
109 "Thanksgiving", pp.109,111.
110 "Thanksgiving", p.112.
111 "Thanksgiving Period", pp.118-119.
112 On the threefold function of introductory thanksgivings, see above, chapter one,
    p.11.

Paul's use of the introductory-thanksgiving formula in 2:14 signals
literarily his intention to introduce the significant train of thought
which runs from 2:14-4:6, and then to the end of chapter seven. In
addition to this *epistolary* purpose[113], the other two functions commonly performed by introductory thanksgivings can also be detected here
as well. For as the parallels to I Cor. 4:9 and II Cor. 4:11 make clear,
II Cor. 2:14-16a also performs a clear *didactic function* in reminding
the Corinthians that the suffering Paul endures is an inextricable
part of the divine intention for his apostleship. And finally, in the
light of the new polemical situation which existed in Corinth, II Cor.
2:14-16a also performs a *paraenetic function* as an implicit appeal not
to reject, but to accept Paul's interpretation of his apostolic role
as the aroma of Christ. It is apparent, therefore, that the "tone and
themes"[114] of 2:14-4:6 are already clearly outlined in II Cor. 2:14-16a.
The tone is apologetic. The thesis to be defended is the genuine nature
of Paul's apostolic role as the mediatory agent between God and his
new people. Moreover, Paul's first point has already been established:
Paul's suffering as an apostle is an essential part of God's plan,
functioning as it does to affirm the cross and reveal God's glory.
Therefore, rather than calling into question his legitimacy as an a-
postle, Paul's suffering is *itself* evidence of his authenticity. But
it is not the only evidence to support the integrity of Paul's apostolic calling. A second, and even more compelling proof is the spiritual
existence of the Corinthian church itself. This becomes the main point
of II Cor. 2:16b-3:6 and the bridge between Paul's self-defense and his
paradigmatic statement that "the letter kills, but the Spirit makes
alive"[115]. But, as we shall see below, *both* Paul's description of his
apostolic ministry of suffering in II Cor. 2:14-16a *and* his emphasis
on his ministry of the Spirit in II Cor. 3:1-3 are anchored in his
understanding of his *sufficiency* (ἱκανός) to be an apostle -- a sufficiency which is derived from his call and modeled after the sufficiency of Moses himself. This, then, is the subject of chapter three.

---

113 As in I Cor. 15:57 and II Cor. 8:16, the introductory-thanksgiving formula in
   II Cor. 2:14 differs from its normal usage as an introduction to an epistle in
   that here the thanksgiving relates equally well both to what follows and to
   what precedes. Thus, II Cor. 2:14 might just as well be described as a transitional thanksgiving formula because of its location within Paul's train of
   thought.
114 This is the twofold purpose of the introductory thanksgivings as summarized by
   Obrien, see above, chapter one, p.11.
115 In A.D. Nock's classic work, *St. Paul*, 1938, p.202 he observed concerning II Cor.
   1-9 that it was here that "Paul sets forth his deepest reflection on the Christian
   ministry in its relation to those who hear its message and to those whose minds
   are closed, in relation again to the ministry of the law. Suffering is of the
   essence of this vocation".

Chapter Three

THE QUESTION OF PAUL'S SUFFICIENCY AND A WORKING

HYPOTHESIS CONCERNING ITS *TRADITIONSGESCHICHTLICHE*

BACKGROUND (II COR. 2:16b)

As we have seen in chapter two, Paul's contention in II Cor. 2:14-
16a that his suffering was the vehicle through which the knowledge and
glory of the crucified Christ was now effecting salvation and judgment
in the world was a tightly knit apologetic intended to *commend* Paul's
apostolic ministry to the Corinthians within the church, as well as to
defend it from the onslaught of his opponents, who had recently arrived
from without[1]. In order to accomplish this goal Paul painted a picture
of his apostolic ministry which could hardly be more profound in its
theological meaning, nor more important in its practical significance.
For in 2:14-16a, Paul portrayed himself as an eschatological mediatory
agent in the salvation/damnation of the world (see 2:15+16)[2]. As G.
Barth expressed it, "mit dem Verkündiger ist die leben- und todbringende
Kraft des Evangeliums selbst präsent"[3].

Having reminded the Corinthians of the meaning and significance of
his apostleship, Paul now continues his apologetic by posing the question: καὶ πρὸς ταῦτα τίς ἱκανός; (2:16b). It is to this question and
its "answer" that we now turn our attention.

---

1 Since this study was originally completed, this point has also been made by J.
  Lambrecht, "Structure and Line of Thought in 2 Cor. 2:14-4:6", *Biblica* 64(1983)
  344-380, p.347. In commenting on all of 2:14-3:6 Lambrecht writes, "the tone of the
  passage is at the same time apologetic (an apology directed towards the Corinthian
  Christians) and polemic (a counter-attack against the intruders and opponents)".
2 For the classic development of Paul's understanding of his eschatological role as
  the apostle to the Gentiles, see J. Munck, *Paul and the Salvation of Mankind*, 1959,
  pp.11-68. For a summary of his central point, see above, chapter one, n.38. For a
  presentation of this point which is close to my own, see Peter Marshall, "A Metaphor
  of Social Shame: ΘΡΙΑΜΒΕΥΕΙΝ in 2 Cor. 2:14", *NovT* 25(1983)302-317, pp.315f. (see
  above, chapter one, n.107 and pp.38f., n.121; chapter two, n.91).
3 "Die Eignung des Verkündigers in 2 Kor 2:14-3:6", in *Kirche, FS Günther Bornkamm*,
  1980, pp.257-270, p.262. See too Peter Jones, *Second Moses*, pp.17-20 (for biblio-
  graphical information, see below, p.99 and p.99n.43), who emphasizes that in 2:14-
  16 the gospel is expressed in Paul's lifestyle, with the apostle and the gospel being identified. In his words, "Paul is aware of having been made the human vehicle
  or medium of the gospel" (p.20).

A. THE UNRESOLVED PROBLEM CONCERNING THE 'UNANSWERED'
   QUESTION OF 2:16b

The first and most important observation to be made concerning Paul's
question in II Cor. 2:16b is that Paul nowhere directly answers it. It
is not surprising, therefore, that scholars have understood Paul's question and its implied answer in various, and often contradictory ways.
For example, the "sudden" polemical tone of 2:16b created for Windisch
an irresolvable tension in Paul's logic[4]. As a result, this tension led
Windisch to posit the existence of a lacuna between 16a and 16b due to
a pause in Paul's dictation, or even to suggest, following Völker, that
2:16b-4:5 be eliminated as a post-Pauline gloss! Moreover, since Paul
had already assumed that he was in God's service in 2:14-16a, and had
even praised God for it, in Windisch's opinion the question of 2:16b
was moot. The real question ought to have been, "Wer gehört zu uns?".
Nevertheless, when confronted with the text as it now stands, Windisch
viewed verse 17 to *imply* that Paul and his co-workers were to be understood as the only legitimate answer to the question of 2:16b[5]. He emphasized, however, that this answer could only be implied, since the
normally expected enumeration of the qualities demanded for the acceptance of the apostolic office, or a direct indication of its appoint-
ments are not given in response to the question. As it stands, therefore,
the question can be perceived as a question of *resignation*, as in Joel
2:11, Revelation 6:17, Mark 10:26, Romans 11:34, etc. Hence, Windisch
also posited the possibility of a second answer to Paul's question,
namely, οὐδεὶς εἰ μὴ ὃν ὁ κύριος συνίστησιν[6].

On the other extreme, C.K. Barrett's emphasis on the unity between
2:16a and b, believing that "Verse 16a makes the question of 16b readily
intelligible", led him to posit a *negative* answer to Paul's question[7].
For in Barrett's view, the question of 2:16b was to be seen as the logical response to the overwhelming responsibility outlined in 2:14-16a.
Hence, again taking verse 17 as his clue to the answer of 16b, Barrett's
logic ran as follows: Since "those who handle the word of God in its
purity know how inadequate they are for the task" (i.e. as outlined in
2:14-16a), the unanswered question of 16b must be understood to mean

> I make no claims to *self*-sufficiency
> for we are not, like the majority,
> watering down the word of God (emphasis
> mine).[8]

---

4 *Zweiter Korintherbrief*, 1924, pp.99-100.
5 *Zweiter Korintherbrief*, p.100.
6 *Zweiter Korintherbrief*, p.100. We will return to these possibilities below.
7 *Second Corinthians*, 1973, pp.102-103.
8 *Second Corinthians*, pp.102-103.

In a similar way, R.V.G. Tasker argued that if the unexpressed answer were, in fact, "we apostles", then

> such a note of *self*-satisfaction would seem ill-fitted to the context. The logic of the passage seems to demand the answer that *no one* is sufficient for such a high calling in his own unaided strength, for it does not mean carrying the gospel about like a hawker, who adulterates his goods and gives bad measure for the sake of his own personal gain.[9]

In yet a third solution, Dieter Georgi employs his understanding of Paul's opponents as θεῖοι ἄνδρες to forge a middle position between the views of Windisch and Barrett[10]. For like Windisch, Georgi also sees the introduction of the question in 2:16b to be abrupt and unexpected. But unlike Windisch, Georgi does not see in this "Gedankensprünge" a lacuna of some sort, but rather an indication that Paul is now switching to discuss the position of his opponents, who must have said, "ἱκανοί ἐσμεν"[11]. Hence, although for Georgi Paul has already asserted his sufficiency in 2:14-16a, his failure to give a *direct* answer to the question of 2:16b is to be taken as a sign that Paul is comparing himself to his opponents in their self-affirmation of ἱκανότης. As a result, like Barrett, but for different reasons, Georgi takes Paul's refusal to answer the question of 2:16b to be, in reality, a *negative* answer in opposition to the position of his opponents[12]:

> Paulus sagt demnach in 2 K. 2:16ff zu-
> nächst dies, daß er sich keine göttlichen
> Fähigkeiten anmaßen mag, sondern alles von
> dem Urteil Gottes erwartet.[13]

But Georgi also wishes to emphasize that the key to Paul's thought is to be found precisely in the fact that the question in 2:16b remains unanswered. For Georgi's exegesis of 2:16ff. is not only derived from his view of the opponents' claim of "sufficiency", but also from his understanding of the *eschatological* context of Paul's question itself.

---

9 *The Second Epistle of Paul to the Corinthians, An Introduction and Commentary*, 1958, p.58.
10 *Die Gegner des Paulus im 2. Korintherbrief*, 1964, pp.220-225.
11 Georgi, *Gegner*, p.224.
12 *Gegner*, p.224.
13 *Gegner*, p.223. This is actually Georgi's summary of the meaning of 3:5, but is seen by him to be the main point of Paul's entire argument in 2:16-3:5. Georgi's exact position on Paul's implied answer to 2:16b is difficult to pin down. On p. 221 he points out that Paul has already said "wir" in answer to 2:16b, and that the question is referring, with reservation, to himself. Moreover, on pp.221-222 he argues that in v.17b Paul gives grounds for his own "sufficiency", although not as we would expect. But then in discussing 3:5 he points to I Cor. 15:9 as evidence that Paul denied his own sufficiency (cf. p.222). Finally, he then goes on to argue, in the light of Joel 2:11, that Paul's *Resignationsfrage* in 2:16 demands a negative answer (cf. p.224). This confusion arises perhaps from Georgi's insistence on the abrupt nature of 2:16, together with his attempt to view the "sufficiency" being talked about as one of the opponents' self-characteristics, i.e. a "Stichwort der Gegner", which then, by definition, makes it a negative term (cf. pp.220-221). For my critique of Georgi's position, see below.

Georgi sees a parallel between II Cor. 3:4ff. and I Cor. 4:1-5 (cf. λογίζεσθαι in 3:5 and I Cor. 4:1), with I Cor. 4:3 understood to be a paraphrase of what Paul intends in 2:16f. and 3:4ff. This leads him to suggest that, for Paul, the question of his own sufficiency as an a-postle can only be decided by God's eschatological judgment. II Cor. 2:16f. thus becomes a statement of Paul's *present resignation* as he awaits the final eschatological evaluation of his apostolic ministry, as well as a statement of his confidence in the future judgment of God itself (cf. I Cor. 4:4//II Cor. 3:4f.)[14]. The fact that this is the point cf Paul's argument in 2:16b, i.e. that Paul "alles von dem Urteil Gottes erwartet", is then further confirmed for Georgi by the alleged parallel between II Cor. 2:16b and the LXX version of Joel 2:11. For when faced with the reality of having to pass before the eschatological judgment of God, Joel too responds with the unanswered question: καὶ τίς ἔσται ἱκανὸς αὐτῇ;. In Georgi's words,

> Wenn wir die Joel 2:11 vertretene Anschauung ergänzend zu 2.K. 2:16 heran-ziehen, so würde Paulus dadurch, daß er diese Frage stellt, aber keine un-mittelbare Antwort gibt, sagen: Wenn vor dem göttlichen Gericht keiner be-stehen kann, wie kann dann überhaupt ein Mensch Mittler eben dieses Gerichtes sein? Ich verstehe also die Frage ebenso wie die in Joel 2:11 als *Resigna-tionsfrage*. Die Antwort ist *nicht* ausgefallen (emphasis mine)[15].

For Georgi, therefore, the unanswered question in 2:16b is meant to be Paul's critique of his opponents confidence that they are already suf-ficient, a confidence which no one can claim before the just God! In posing this question, Paul is rejecting the attempt of his opponents to appropriate for themselves the characteristics of God, which they are only able to do because of their self-conception as θεῖοι ἄνδρες on the one hand, and their lack of an eschatological perspective on the other hand[16].

Finally, as a fourth alternative, Hans Lietzmann and Rudolf Bultmann are examples of those who not only assume the *unity* between 2:14-16a and 16bff., but who, at the same time, also stress the fact that Paul's question is to be answered *positively*[17]. Again, both scholars also

---

14 *Gegner*, p.223.
15 *Gegner*, p.224.
16 For a slight variation of this position, see G. Barth, "Die Eignung des Verkündi-gers", pp.262-263. Like Georgi, Barth also sees 2:16b to be Paul's response to his opponents, though unlike Georgi, Barth recognizes that 2:16b follows directly from 2:16a as the natural response to the contrast between the lowliness of the apostle as "Besiegter" and the greatness of his office (cf. p.263).
17 Lietzmann, *An die Korinther*, 1969⁵, p.109 and R. Bultmann, *Zweiter Korintherbrief*, 1976, pp.72-73.

point to verse 17 for a confirmation of their view. Thus for
Lietzmann the question is, in reality,

> Und wie muß der Mann beschaffen sein, welcher Träger einer so hohen Aufgabe
> sein will? Antwort: so wie ich! Das sagt Pls nicht selbst, er überläßt die
> Ergänzung dem Leser und setzt sie im Fortgang οὐ γάρ etc. voraus.[18]

Or as Bultmann put it,

> Die Frage hat doch den Sinn: wer kann ein solcher Träger des Wortes sein, bzw.
> wie kann ich ein solcher Träger sein? Deshalb auch die Antwort V.17, die ...
> nicht die erforderlichen Eigenschaften aufzählt, sondern ein Selbstbekenntnis
> ist ... V.17 ist an V.16 durch γάρ angeschlossen, das ein unausgesprochenes
> ἐγώ begründet. Die Antwort auf die Frage V.16 ... lautet also: Ich! und sagt
> zugleich indirekt: wer selbstlos das Wort verkündigt.[19]

From this survey of the interpretive possibilities usually represented in the literature four observations may be made. First, the relative
strengths and weaknesses of the four basic positions become clear in
their mutual critique of one another. Hence, on the one hand, those
who stress the unity between 2:16a and b (e.g. Barrett, Tasker, Lietzmann, Bultmann) have, in my opinion, shown that it is unnessessary to
posit additional external hypotheses in order to explain the logical
transition between Paul's elevated description of his apostolic ministry in 2:14-16a and the natural response of raising the question of
sufficiency for this ministry in 2:16b. Moreover, my own study in
chapters one and two has shown that the polemical tone of 2:16b is
neither new, nor in tension with 2:14-16a. Thus, the need to posit an
abrupt break in Paul's thought between 2:16a and b, which must then be
explained by some external hypothesis (à la Windisch, Georgi), does not
exist. This point has recently been emphasized by T. Provence, who also
sees v.16b to be occasioned by the bold statement of vv.15-16a[20]. Nevertheless, Provence too must bring to the text the assumption of a certain reader-response in order to explain v.16b:

> Were Paul not to ask the question of 2:16b, those who opposed him would have
> had grounds to accuse him (as some may have done) of the most repugnant sort
> of arrogance. Paul had no choice but to raise and answer the question of his
> qualification to preach a message which may bring about salvation for some,
> but which may, on the other hand, 'prove fatal to those who come in contact
> with it'".[21]

---

18 *An die Korinther*, p.109. Lietzmann also combines with this a very cautious approach
to determining the background to Paul's apology: "Soviel nur können wir sagen, daß
er seine persönliche Vollwertigkeit zu verteidigen Ursache gehabt hat: vgl. bereits
1:12 und vollends zu c.11:7-12:11", p.109.
19 *Zweiter Korintherbrief*, pp.72-73. Bultmann hesitates to couple his interpretation
with a reconstruction of Paul's opponents, offering only the observation that
"Veranlaßt aber ist die Frage offenbar dadurch, daß in Korinth die ἱκανότης des
Paulus bestritten wurde, wie 3:1ff. und besonders 3:5f. zeigen, ja, wie schon der
polemische V.17 zeigt" (p.72).
20 "'Who is sufficient for these things?' An Exegesis of 2 Corinthians 2:15-3:18",
NovT 24(1982)54-81, pp.56f.
21 "'Who is sufficient", pp.56-57.

But it is not necessary to assume that 2:15-16a would lead Paul's readers to react in a certain way in order to explain v.16b, especially when in v. 16b, in contrast to 3:1, Paul gives no indication that he is anticipating a certain response. As we shall see below, it is rather Paul's *answer* to v.16b which provides his adversaries with grounds for their accusation. Furthermore, once the *traditionsgeschicht-liche* background to Paul's question is clarified, additional evidence can be adduced to support the contention of those who have argued that the occasion for the question of 2:16b is Paul's understanding of his apostolic ministry in 2:14-16a[22].

On the other hand, Windisch, Bultmann and Lietzmann have pointed out that the logical relationship between v.16b and 17 (γάρ!) only makes sense when Paul's question in 2:16b is understood to imply a *positive* answer[23]. The weakness of the alternative position is further confirmed by the fact that both Barrett and Tasker must import into 2:16b the pejorative theological construct of "*self*-sufficiency" or from Paul's statements in 3:4f. in order to construe v.17 to mean that Paul, unlike the οἱ πολλοί, is disavowing all claims to self-sufficiency or adequacy. But ἱκανός, in and of itself, carries no such pejorative connotations[24], and v.16b simply does not pose the question καὶ πρὸς ταῦτα τίς ἱκανός ἀφ' ἑαυτοῦ;. Moreover, Paul's statements in 3:1 and 3:5 ought not to be read back into 2:16b since they make sense *only* if the question of 2:16b has *already* been answered positively. In other words, Paul's assertion in 3:5 that his sufficiency (cf. ἡ ἱκανότης ἡμῶν) is not ἀφ' ἑαυτοῦ or ἐξ ἑαυτοῦ, makes sense only if this sufficiency has already been implied. For in 3:5 Paul does not assert his sufficiency, he *assumes* it. That is to say, 3:5 does not answer the question of 2:16b, it clarifies the answer which has alredy been given, albeit indirectly[25].

---

22 E.g. K.H. Schelkle, *Der zweite Brief an die Korinther*, 1964, p.60: "Die Predigt des Evangeliums beduetet für die Welt eine Entscheidung zwischen Leben und Tod. Angesichts dessen entsteht die Frage: Wer ist geeignet und fähig, diesen höchst Verantwortungsvollen Dienst der Predigt zu tun?" We have seen, however, that the focus of 2:14-16a is primarily directed toward his apostolic ministry of suffering.

23 So too already Charles Hodge, *An Exposition of the Second Epistle to the Corinthians*, 1980(1859), p.47 and the classic work of H.A.W. Meyer, *Critical and Exegetical Hand-Book to the Epistles to the Corinthians*, 1979 (ET from German 5th ed. 1883) on 2:17.

24 One need only check the 48 times ἱκανός appears in the LXX, or its widespread use in Josephus (over 80 times) and Philo (over 150 times) to see that ἱκανός, when used alone, connotes a purely neutral sense of "sufficiency", "adequacy" or "capability". This is also true for the New Testament, where ἱκανός appears 39 times (or 40 depending on the reading of Rom. 15:23) but, as K.H. Rengstorf, art. ἱκανός κ.τ.λ., *TDNT*, *Vol. III*, 1965, p.293, has emphasized, carries no particular moral connotation.

25 Barrett himself seems to recognize this fact inasmuch as he contradicts his view of 2:16b in commenting on the meaning of 3:5. For in noting the link with 2:16, Barrett remarks that "It is true that Paul is here in effect answering the ques-

Similarly, if Paul had answered the question of 2:16b negatively, then the implied criticism of Paul reflected in 3:1 would lose its force. No one would accuse someone of commending himself who had just disavowed all claims to sufficiency! Therefore, although Provence is again right in emphasizing that "one of the most important keys to understanding 2 Cor 3 lies in grasping its connection with 2:15-16 ...", it is not entirely accurate to say that "Paul intends 3:5-6 to be an answer to the question raised in 2:16 ...", though in a broader sense it is true that "Paul answers the question of 2:16b throughout chapter 3"[26]. Those who argue for the internal coherence of the text as well as for an implied positive answer to the question of 2:16b on the basis of verse 17 (e.g. Lietzmann and Bultmann) do the most justice, therefore, to the text on *internal* grounds.

This brings us to our third observation, an observation occasioned by the work of Dieter Georgi, inasmuch as Georgi's attempt to develop the significance of the parallels between our text and I Cor. 4 and Joel 2:11 points to a weakness in the other positions. For only Georgi has felt the need not only to explain the internal function of 2:16b, but also to take the important additional step of attempting to clarify the *traditionsgeschichtliche* background necessary to understand the broader theological significance of the text. Thus, although Georgi's own internal analysis of the text, which necessitates that he posit the theology of Paul's opponents in order to explain the "abrupt" introduction of Paul's question in 2:16b and its "negative" answer, is inadequate, his observation that Paul's question cannot sufficiently be understood merely on the basis of its internal function in Paul's argument is correct. For even when the question is seen to be a natural response to Paul's description of his apostolic ministry in 2:14-16a and to imply a positive answer on the basis of 2:17, 3:1 and 3:4-5, one is still left exegetically troubled by Paul's *form* of argumentation itself. The fact that Paul introduces the theme of his adequacy for the apostolic ministry in the form of an indefinite question which is never directly answered, but whose answer is intended to be so unmistakably clear that Paul can later assume it in his argument (cf. 3:5!), raises not just the question of *what* Paul said, but also forces us to ask *why* he said it in the particular way he did[27]. In other words, what is the

---

tion of 2:16, 'we are!'", *Second Corinthians*, p.111. But although he notes the link between 3:5 and 2:16, he makes nothing of it for the structure of the argument (cf. pp.110-111).

26 "'Who is sufficient", pp.56 and 57.

27 This is not meant, however, to be an exercise in reading Paul's mind, thus falling prey to the so-called "intentional fallacy", but is simply to pose the question of form to the text itself as a clue to a further aspect of Paul's *expressed* intention.

reason for this seemingly circuitous mode of argumentation, if Paul's point is simply to stress that he is sufficient for the apostolic task outlined in 2:14-16a (cf. I Cor. 15:9f.)? To answer this question, we must, like Georgi, look outside our immediate context for a parallel Pauline or non-Pauline tradition which might shed some light on Paul's argument.

The fourth and final observation to be made, therefore, is that although Georgi has indeed raised an important question, his own attempt to answer it on the basis of the alleged parallels between II Cor. 2:16b and I Cor. 4:1-5 and Joel 2:11 is nevertheless not compelling for several reasons. First, the link between I Cor. 4 and II Cor. 2:16ff. cannot be maintained. For in contrast to I Cor. 4:1-5, the context of II Cor. 2:16b-3:6 nowhere indicates that Paul is thinking of God's *future* eschatological evaluation of his ministry *as* an apostle. Instead, the consistent emphasis in this text is on Paul's past and present sufficiency *to be* an apostle[28]. For while in I Cor. 4:1-4 the issue is whether or not Paul has faithfully exercised his office as a servant and steward, in II Cor. 2:16ff. the issue at stake is now whether or not Paul even has a right to occupy the office at all! In I Cor. 4 Paul is *primarily* on the offense, while in II Cor. 2:16ff. he is on the defense. In I Cor. 4 Paul's purpose is *primarily* hortatory, in II Cor. 2:16ff., apologetic. I emphasize *primarily*, however, because I do not want to deny, of course, that already in I Corinthians Paul's role as an apostle was being questioned in relationship to the other "guides" in Corinth (cf. I Cor. 4:15). But the debate in Corinth has taken a significant turn by the time II Corinthians 2:16ff. was written. For while in I Corinthians Paul must merely reestablish his role as the Corinthians' "father" among the "guides", in II Corinthians he must fight for his right even to be considered an apostle at all[29]! This basic distinction between I Cor. 4:1-6 and II Cor. 2:16ff., which we have already seen in chapter two to be characteristic of I and II Corinthians elsewhere[30], together with Paul's emphasis on the present in 2:16ff., make it difficult to use I Cor. 4 as an interpretive key to II Cor. 2:16ff., except by way of *contrast*. Georgi's attempt to build a case for a parallel between I Cor. 4:1ff. and II Cor. 2:16ff. on the basis

---

28 Cf. 2:17: ἐσμεν; 3:3: διακονηθεῖσα; 3:4: ἔχομεν; 3:5: ἐσμεν; 3:6: ἱκάνωσεν.
29 K. Bailey, "The Structure of I Corinthians and Paul's Theological Method with Special Reference to 4:17", *NovT* 25(1983) 152-181, p.160, comes to this same conclusion based on his study of the structure of I Cor. 1:4-4:16: " ... in this essay (i.e. 1:4-4:16) Paul is not *primarily* defending his position as an apostle" (emphasis his). He too thus concludes, "We grant that in the process Paul defends his apostleship. But his theological method (as seen here) indicates that the primary topic is the proper attitude for Christians in regard to their leaders" (p.160).
30 See above, chapter two, pp.65ff.

of the existence of λογίζομαι in the two passages (cf. I Cor. 4:1 and II Cor. 3:5) thus remains unconvincing[31].

Second, the alleged parallel between II Cor. 2:16b and Joel 2:11, which Georgi sees to be a confirmation of his eschatological interpretation of 2:16b, is also tenuous[32]. For not only is the context of eschatological judgment lacking in reference to Paul's ministry in II Cor. 2:16ff., but the link between the subject matter of the two texts is also missing. Indeed, the problem of trying to relate Joel's resignation in the face of God's judgment to Paul's sufficiency to be an apostle is, it seems, even felt by Georgi himself, who fills this gap by inserting the idea that

> Wenn vor dem göttlichen Gericht keiner bestehen kann, *wie kann dann überhaupt ein Mensch Mittler eben dieses Gerichtes sein?*[33]

Moreover, even if Joel was speaking of the insufficiency of a man to mediate God's judgment, the parallel would not be established. For the premise found in Joel needed for the argument, i.e. Joel's resignation before God's judgment, is *also* missing in Paul. Rather than resignation in the light of God's coming judgement, Paul consistently expresses an unreserved hope based on the atoning work of Christ, both for the salvation of those "in Christ", and for the effectiveness of his own apostolic ministry[34]. In this context, it is also significant that even though Paul never assumes, without question, that his converts will continue in their faith, and can even call into question the genuineness of certain members of his congregations[35], he nevertheless never seems to doubt that his own call to be an apostle and its results are from God. Thus, when faced with the prospect of God's judgment of the believer, or his eschatological evaluation of Paul's ministry (cf. I Cor. 9:24ff.), Paul's response is not one of resignation, but of confidence.

Moreover, Windisch's attempt to draw a parallel between 2:16b and other examples of *Resignationsfragen* in the NT also falls down[36]. The question in Rev. 6:17 is not posed by the faithful, but by those who are faced with "the wrath of the Lamb" (cf. 6:15f.). In contrast, the faithful do not shrink from the

---

31 Cf. *Gegner*, p.223
32 As we saw above, Georgi is following Windisch, *Zweiter Korintherbrief*, p.100 for this point, who, in turn, referred to Loesner, *Observationes ad NT e. Philone Alex.*, 1777, pp.301ff.
33 Georgi, *Gegner*, p.224, (emphasis mine).
34 One need only think of the basic principle applied to believers in Rom. 1:16f.; 5:1f.; 6:3-8, 9-11; 8:1 and 28-30; I Cor. 15:21f., 49 and 57; II Cor. 4:13-17; 5:14-21; Phil. 1:6; 3:20f.; Col. 2:9-16; 3:4 and I Thess. 3:11-13; 4:14-17; 5:9f.; and of Paul's own attitude to his work as an apostle in Romans 15:5b-19; I Cor. 3:1-10; 4:4a(!), 15f.; 7:10,12,17,25; 9:1-2, 18-27; 11:1; II Cor. 5:20; 6:1; 10:7f.; 11:5; 12:11f.; 13:4,6(!); Gal. 1:10-12; 2:8f.; 4:14 and Col. 1:24-29.
35 Cf. Rom. 11:20-22; 14:10-12; I Cor. 10:1-12; 15:2; II Cor. 1:24; 6:1f.; 13:5f.; Gal. 3:1-4; 4:11; 5:4; Phil. 2:15f.; Col. 1:21-23; I Thess. 3:6-8.
36 Cf. *Zweiter Korintherbrief*, p.100.

final judgment, but look forward to it (cf. 6:10f. and 19:1-9)! The same holds
true for Mark 10:26. In response to the disciples' question, Jesus' simple
reply is that "all things are possible with God!". Finally, the link between
the question of Rom. 11:34 and II Cor. 2:16b is difficult for me to establish. The resignation one feels when faced with God's wisdom, knowledge and
mercy, if the questions of Rom. 11:34f. are even meant to be so interpreted,
has little, if any bearing on the context of 2:16b. In II Cor. 2:14-16a Paul
may be marveling that in God's wisdom he has chosen to display his glory
through the suffering of his apostle, but this only makes the question of
2:16b more necessary; it does not change the question itself into one of resignation. For in 2:16b Paul is not asking a question about God, but about
himself.

Thus, Georgi's (and Windisch's) attempt to interpret Paul's question
in II Cor. 2:16b to be one of resignation runs aground not only on the
basis of the alleged parallels themselves, but also because it stands
in opposition to Paul's consistent confidence for the future because
of his understanding of the salvific work of the cross of Christ. We
are thus left with the unresolved problem of whether or not a *traditionsgeschichtliche* background can be found which will help explain
the significance of Paul's mode of argumentation in II Cor. 2:16b-17,
while at the same time remaining true to his apostolic self-conception
as evidenced not only in the immediate context, but elsewhere in the
Pauline corpus as well.

B. THE SUFFICIENCY OF MOSES: A WORKING HYPOTHESIS

In the light of the conscious effort in the past to determine an OT/
traditional background to Paul's question in II Cor. 2:16b, it is surprising that more attention has not been focused on the only other possible parallel besides Joel 2:11 in the LXX to the ἱκανός-theme of
2:16b, namely Exodus 4:10[37]. In fact, although it has been overlooked
by recent scholarship, this solution to the problem of the *traditionsgeschichtliche* background to II Cor. 2:16b was pointed out, but not developed, almost 40 years ago by Austin M. Farrer. Farrer observed that
when called at the burning bush, Moses responded with the confession,
"I am not sufficient" (ἱκανός), but was nevertheless "made sufficient
by the All-sufficing (El Shaddai, interpreted as *theos ho hikanos*)"[38].
Taking this as the antitype to Paul's statements in II Cor. 2:16; 3:4f.

---

37 This becomes immediately clear upon an investigation of the 48 occurrences of
  ἱκανός and 14 occurrences of ἱκανοῦσθαι in the LXX.
38 "The Ministry in the New Testament", in *The Apostolic Ministry, Essays on the
  History and the Doctrine of Episcopacy*, ed. K.E. Kirk, 1946, pp.115-182, pp.171,
  173.

and I Cor. 15:9[39], Farrer posited that Paul was casting his own question in terms of this tradition, thus paraphrasing Paul's question and
its "answer" in 2:16 to be,

> Who then, says the apostle, is sufficient (*hikanos*)
> for the second and greater ministry? We are: but
> our sufficiency also is infused by grace.[40]

Farrer then goes on to combine this insight with the contrasts between
the apostolic and Mosaic ministries in II Cor. 3:7-4:10 and concludes
that "the fulfilment of Moses, St. Paul says, is found not in Christ
but in the apostles ..."[41] and that the apostle as such can be described
as a "new Moses"[42].

   Recently, Farrer's insight concerning the parallel between II Cor.
2:16b and the call of Moses has been taken up and extended by Peter
Ronald Jones in his unpublished 1973 Princeton Theological Seminary
Ph.D. dissertation, *The Apostle Paul: A Second Moses according to II
Corinthians 2:14-4:7*[43]. As his title indicates, Jones takes the additional step of arguing that the parallels and contrasts between the call
and ministry of Paul and Moses in II Cor. 2:14-4:7 indicate that Paul
consciously understood and portrayed himself as the eschatological fulfillment of the hope for a non-messianic "second Moses" found in the OT
and developed in Jewish literature, the most distinct example being the
conception of the Teacher of Righteousness found in the Qumran writings[44]. In his words,

> in the exercise of his apostolate Paul is not only following the terms of his
> "commission" and the leading of the Spirit, but is consciously determined by
> a prior common tradition of the second Moses.[45]

More specifically, in

> II Cor. 2:14-4:7, Paul's description of his apostolic task is radically shaped
> and conditioned by an already existing second Moses tradition.[46]

But regarding II Cor. 2:16b itself, Jones is content merely to refer to
Farrer's earlier study and to observe that

---

39 The meaning of I Cor. 15:9f. and II Cor. 3:4f. will be dealt with in my forth-
   coming study of II Cor. 3:4-4:6. Cf. too the related texts of Gal. 1:11ff., Eph.
   3:8 and I Tim. 1:15f.
40 "Ministry", p.173.
41 "Ministry", p.172.
42 "Ministry", p.173.
43 For his reference to Farrer, see pp.40-41. The main points of his dissertation
   have been summarized in Jones' essay, "The Apostle Paul: Second Moses to the New
   Covenant Community, A Study in Pauline Apostolic Authority", in *God's Inerrant
   Word: An International Symposium on the Trustworthiness of Scripture*, ed. J.W.
   Montgomery, 1974, pp.219-241, pp.224-233. He again handles II Cor. 2:16b by
   pointing to Farrer, see p.226.
44 See esp. his *Second Moses*, pp.6, 33f., 40f., 59-69, 187-202, 252-255, 257, 316ff.,
   351, 374-376 and "Apostolic Authority", pp.220, 233.
45 *Second Moses*, p.109. He then outlines this tradition on pp.110-255.
46 *Second Moses*, p.255.

the terminology which is characteristic of the call of Moses is also an appropriate term for Paul, for whom the notions of grace and apostleship are
intimately tied.[47]

Or in the words of his later summary,

It is significant, and perhaps more than coincidental, that the account of
Moses' own vocation at the burning bush contains the pregnant term ἱκανός.[48]

Having accepted Farrer's assertion, Jones then incorporates it into his
overall thesis as another example of the Moses/Paul = Second Moses
parallel in II Cor. 2:14-4:7.

Without entering into a detailed critique at this point of Jones'
interpretation of II Cor. 2:14-4:7, especially 3:6b-4:7[49], his *traditionsgeschichtliche* methodology or his basic thesis that Paul conceived
of himself as the "second Moses" promised in Jewish tradition, suffice
it to say here that despite his many helpful insights[50] Jones' reca-
pitulation of Farrer's original, but likewise undeveloped observation
concerning the parallel between II Cor. 2:16b and the call of Moses, as
well as his view of II Cor. 3:4f. as a reference to Paul's call, nevertheless remain unsubstantiated. This is especially true in view of the
fact that elsewhere Paul portrays his call *not* in terms of the call of
Moses, but in reliance on the call of the prophets, especially that of
Jeremiah and/or the Isaianic "Servant of YHWH"[51]. Hence, the central
weakness of Jones' argument is that he jumps from the "implied comparison with the call of Moses"[52] found in 2:16b and 3:4f. to the history
of the tradition of the expectation for a "second Moses", *rather than
analyzing the tradition of Moses' call itself and its development in
the OT and non-canonical Jewish literature.* For only after this has
been done can the assertion that Paul is alluding to and reflecting
upon the Mosaic(-prophetic) call tradition in II Cor. 2:16b gain its
necessary support. Hence, although it is also my contention that the
solution to the unsolved problem concerning II Cor. 2:16b outlined
above is, as Farrer observed, to be found in Paul's allusion to the

---

47 *Second Moses*, pp.40f.
48 "Apostolic Authority", p.226.
49 Where relevant, his position regarding II Cor. 3:1-3 will be taken up below, while
his exegesis of 3:6-4:7 will be analyzed in my projected second volume of this
study. For his view of II Cor. 2:14-16a, see *Second Moses*, pp.14-21. His interpretation differs from mine at this point inasmuch as he takes θριαμβεύειν to be "the
implicit claim of honor and privilege ..." in reference to "Paul's commission and
resultant ministry ..." "via the image of overpowering force" (p.16) and the
ὀσμή-imagery as a parallel with the rabbinic image of law as a drug (p.19). See
above, chapter one and chapter two.
50 See especially his helpful interpretation of I Cor. 3:5-16 against the backdrop
of the OT and wisdom traditions in "Apostolic Authority", pp.220-224 and his
view of the function of Paul's "letter of recommendation" in 3:1-3 (see below,
chapter five).
51 See below, chapter four, p.138f.n.129
52 "Apostolic Authority", p.225.

LXX version of Exodus 4:10, Paul's question and the structure of his argument will become clear only when we view them within the context of the biblical and extra-biblical traditions concerning the "call" and "sufficiency" of Moses, rather than transposing II Cor. 2:16b into the, if not unrelated, then certainly more distant context of the "second Moses" expectation[53]. For our present purposes, however, it is sufficient simply to allow this contention to remain frozen as a "working hypothesis" to be substantiated later. For as Jones has also pointed out (see above), the comparison between Paul and Moses alluded to in 2:16b is then picked up and further developed in 3:4-4:6. Thus the *implicit* significance of Paul's initial allusion to the call and sufficiency of Moses in 2:16b can only adequately be understood when viewed in the light of this continuing argument. It seems best, therefore, to postpone an investigation of the *traditionsgeschichtliche* background to II Cor. 2:16b until it can be combined with a detailed exegesis of 3:4-4:6. The point now to be made is simply that II Cor. 2:16b is a rhetorical question which is intended to be answered positively and which, in doing so, introduces Paul's *explicit* support for the assertion of sufficiency in 2:17. To examine how Paul chooses to argue *explicitly* for his sufficiency is thus the next step in our study.

---

53 See *Second Moses*, p.351, where Jones himself admits that "II Cor. 3:4f. is the only place in Paul's writing where a second Moses conceptual framework arises to reasonable explicitness". And, of course, it could be questioned, even here, whether the apostle of the "new covenant" in fulfillment of Jer. 31:31ff. is to be seen as the second Moses of Jewish tradition.

Chapter Four

THE APOLOGETIC FUNCTION OF PAUL'S MINISTRY OF SUFFERING

IN THE CORINTHIAN CORRESPONDENCE (II COR. 2:17)

Paul's introduction of the ἱκανότης-motif in 2:16b and its resumption and resolution in 3:5f., together with the obvious transition in 3:7ff., make it clear that 2:16b-3:6 form the next unit of thought in Paul's ongoing apologetic for his apostolic ministry. Within 2:16b-3:6 itself, Paul's argument is further composed, however, of two distinct, but closely interrelated themes:

1) Paul's question (καὶ πρὸς ταῦτα τίς ἱκανός;)
and his response to it in 2:17 and 3:4-6; and

2) Paul's relationship to the church at Corinth in
3:1-3.

That 3:1-3 is intended to be distinguished from Paul's first answer to the question of 2:16b is indicated in two ways. First, Paul's discussion of the Corinthians as an ἐπιστολή is introduced and occasioned by its own question in 3:1. Second, the subject matter of 3:1-3 is no longer the question of Paul's sufficiency for the apostolic ministry *per se*, but rather the relationship between Paul and the church in Corinth *as it relates to the question of Paul's sufficiency* (see 3:2, ἡμῶν (2 xs) and 3:3, ὑφ' ἡμῶν). For as we shall see in chapter five, 3:1-3 is actually intended to provide further evidence in support of Paul's assertion that he is indeed sufficient to be Christ's apostle, which is first introduced as an unexpressed assumption in response to the question of 2:16b and then defended in 2:17, while at the same time responding to the criticism implied in Paul's rhetorical question of 3:1.

A. THE PROBLEM PRESENTED BY II COR. 2:17

As we have seen above, the γάρ of verse 17 necessitates that we posit an implied, positive answer (i.e. "I am" or, in keeping with the apostolic plural, "we are") to Paul's question in 2:16b[1]. Verse 17 thus functions to support Paul's assertion that he is, in fact, sufficient

---
1 So e.g. too Windisch, Lietzmann and Bultmann. See above, pp.93ff.

for the apostolic ministry of suffering which he has outlined in 2:14-
16a. It is at this point, however, that we encounter difficulties. For
the majority of commentators[2], regardless of whether or not they agree
that v.17 presupposes a positive answer to the question of 2:16b, have
nevertheless taken verse 17 to be a declaration of the genuine nature
of Paul's gospel[3]. That is to say, verse 17 is understood to mean that,
unlike the οἱ πολλοί, Paul does not "water down" or "adulterate"
(καπηλεύω) the word of God, but instead preaches the pure and unadulterated gospel, i.e. he speaks ἐξ εἰλικρινείας ("from purity, 2:17b).
As Provence summarized it in his recent study of this text,

> Paul contrasts his preaching with that of others who dilute, and so make in-
> offensive and ineffective, the Word of God. His word is pure and therefore
> powerful enough to lead both to salvation and destruction ... Thus Paul's
> point in this verse is to support his qualification to be a minister whose
> ministry leads both to salvation and destruction. His 'pure' preaching con-
> trasts with the diluted preaching of others. The 'watered down' gospel of
> the 'many' was neither offensive enough to lead to destruction nor power-
> ful enough to lead to salvation (cf. I Cor. 1:18). Paul's gospel was such a
> word, however, since it was a pure gospel from God[4].

But if verse 17 refers to the "purity" of Paul's gospel, it becomes
difficult to see how this assertion, introduced with γάρ, offers additional evidence which could be construed to support Paul's assertion
of sufficiency. For according to this view of verse 17, Paul's unexpressed assertion that he is sufficient for the apostolic ministry
would be grounded only in the fact that he then *claims* to be the one
preaching the pure gospel, with the actual support for Paul's assertion
of sufficiency not being adduced until 3:2f, when Paul points out that
the Corinthians themselves are his letter of recommendation. But the
fact that Paul's argument in 3:2f. is undoubtedly also meant to support
Paul's claim to sufficiency ought not to blind us to the fact that
Paul's *first* argument in favor of his sufficiency is *already* given in
2:17 (γαρ!). And the attempt to take καπηλεύοντες in 2:17 to mean "water
down", "corrupt" or "adulterate", etc. renders Paul's argument logically abstruse, since to move from an assertion of one's personal adequacy for a task to the quality of the task itself is a confusion of
categories. In other words, it is not immediately clear how the purity
of Paul's preaching could be used to support his own personal adequacy
as an apostle. Thus, for example, Provence must insert an additional

---

2 See e.g. the commentaries of Meyer, Heinrici, Hodge, H.C.G. Moule, Plummer,
   Windisch, Barrett, Tasker and J. Hering to II Cor. 2:17.
3 It is interesting to note in this regard that this interpretation can be used to
   support either a negative *or* a positive answer to the question of 2:16b. Cf. e.g.
   C.K. Barrett, *Second Corinthians*, p.103 for the former and Thomas E.. Provence,
   "'Who is Sufficient for these Things?' An exegesis of 2 Corinthians ii 15-iii
   18", *NovT* 24(1982)54-81, pp.58f. for the latter.
4 "Sufficient" pp.58f.

link in Paul's argument in order to facilitate the connection between
2:17 and 2:16b, namely, that the gospel of Paul's opponents, in contrast to Paul's gospel, was not effective, neither positively nor negatively. This link, however, is not only foreign to the text, but also
does not correspond to the fact that Paul's opponents seem to have
been enjoying tremendous success with their gospel, at least in Corinth,
which was precisely the problem (cf. II Cor. 11:3f.). Finally, rather
than supporting Paul's claim to be sufficient for the apostolic ministry in some way (assuming for the moment that a more suitable missing
link could be found), an emphasis on the purity of his gospel in 2:17
would merely add to Paul's problems. For although Paul's gospel itself
was under attack in Corinth at this time (see II Cor. 11:4), the *main*
issue in Corinth at the time of the writing of II Corinthians was whether or not Paul was even sufficient for the gospel he did preach, since
his suffering and weakness seemed to call that gospel into question[5].
Thus, for Paul to emphasize that he was the one who was preaching the
pure gospel would simply raise the issue of his sufficiency for that
gospel without, at the same time, positively furthering his argument.
In fact, the most common interpretation of 2:17, i.e. "I am sufficient
because I am the one who is preaching the pure and unadulterated gospel",
only leads one to conclude that the criticism reflected in 3:1 was, in
reality, warranted. Paul was simply recommending himself and doing so
in a way that, at best, was logically confuse. This is, of course, possible. But the difficulties with such an interpretation raise the question of whether Paul's statement in 2:17 has been adequately understood
in modern research. Is it possible that 2:17 can be understood in such
a way that Paul's use of γάρ is justified? That is to ask, does Paul's
statement in 2:17 *itself* offer some *external* evidence which, from Paul's
perspective, would support his assertion that he is sufficient for the
apostolic ministry? The answer to this question, as well as the key to
Paul's argument as a whole, lies in a reinvestigation of the meaning
of καπηλεύειν.

---

5 See above, pp.68f. and the discussion of the problem in Corinth by J. Christiaan
  Beker, *Paul the Apostle, The Triumph of God in Life and Thought*, 1980, pp.295-
  300, who emphasizes that in II Corinthians the issue is that Paul was simply
  weak and unimpressive and hence unfit to be a minister of the gospel of the glory
  of Christ. In response, "Paul attacks his opponents by focusing on the cruciform
  nature of Christian existence, in contrast to their view of it as empirically
  victorious and glorious" (p.299). Thus, "What is at stake is the nature of the
  victory of Christ as it embodies itself in Paul's apostolic experience in the
  world" (p.299). See below for my exegesis of II Cor. 11:4 in this regard.

B. THE MEANING OF καπηλεύειν IN THE POLEMIC AGAINST THE
SOPHISTS AND IN HELLENISTIC JUDAISM

1. The Meaning of καπηλεύειν in Recent Research

The dominance in our century of the view that καπηλεύειν ought to be
translated "to adulterate", "to corrupt", "to water down", "to falsify",
etc. in II Corinthians 2:17 can be traced back to Hans Windisch's observation in 1924, based on the parallels listed in J.J. Wettstein's
Novum Testamentum Graecum to II Cor. 2:17[6], that "der Ausdruck καπηλεύειν τὸν λόγον τοῦ θεοῦ geht wohl auf die von Plato inaugurierte Polemik gegen das Sophistenwesen zurück"[7]. For on the basis of this background, Paul's statement in II Cor. 2:17 was interpreted by Windisch to
refer to those "Vielen" who "1) Gottes Wort verschachern, d.h. für Geld
anbieten, vgl. Apg. 8:18f. *und* 2) es fälschen, d.i. mit falschen, un-
echten, selbstgemachten Zusätzen versehen, vgl. 4:2 δολοῦντες τὸν λόγον
τοῦ θεοῦ, Mt. 7:13"[8]. Nevertheless, in spite of this apparent *twofold*
meaning of the verb, Windisch himself chose to translate it "verschachern" in his commentary since, as he concluded, "Erstgenanntes Moment
kommt zunächst in Betracht"[9]. The most that Windisch was willing to concede concerning the second meaning was that

> Das Zweite Moment wird sich, *wenn Pls es*
> *mitfühlt,* auf das Einfälschen einer 'anderen'
> Lehre beziehen (11:4), vermutlich judaistischen
> Irrlehre ...[10].

But 14 years later, when Windisch expanded his position in his 1938
article on καπηλεύω in the *Theologisches Wörterbuch zum Neuen Testament*[11], three significant changes took place. First, in defining the
verb, Windisch now listed the two meanings "betrügerisch, mit Betrug,
mit Wucher, mit unerlaubtem Gewinn verkaufen, verschachern" and "die
Sache, die Ware verfälschen" as *synonymous* meanings, using "oder", thus
giving the impression that both meanings belonged to the same verb[12].

---

6 See *Tomus II*, 1962(1752), p.183. I have decided to follow the recent discussion
  in building my treatment around the evidence listed by Windisch rather than the
  16 pieces of evidence Wettstein listed. An examination of Wettstein's parallels
  makes it clear that Windisch selected the most important texts in his study.
  The issue is how these texts are to be interpreted.
7 *Zweiter Korintherbrief*, p.100.
8 ibid., p.100, emphasis mine.
9 ibid., p.100.
10 ibid., p.101, emphasis mine.
11 *Bd. 3*, 1938, pp.606-609.
12 *ThWb, Bd. 3*, p.607. In a private conversation, Dr. Stuhlmacher has pointed out
  that "oder" in this context does not carry the emphasis on "alternative" found
  in the English "or", but rather indicates a synonymous meaning and is thus best
  here translated "and"; hence my emphasis above.

Second, Windisch now incorporated the LXX into his discussion, concluding that in both Isaiah 1:22 and in Sirach 26:29 the κάπηλος in view
"steht im Verdacht, ein Warenverfälscher, Sünder und Betrüger zu sein"[13].
Hence, in the LXX as well, "das Wort hat einen üblen Nebenklang be-
kommen genau wie τελώνης"[14], corresponding to the "Nebenbedeutung des
Betrügerischen und Gewinnsüchtigen" present in classical literature[15].
And third, his investigation of Paul's own use of καπηλεύω, especially
its parallel to II Cor. 4:2, now led him to conclude, in contrast to
his previous, more cautious position, that the meaning "das Wort verfälschen", although described as a "Nebenbedeutung", is nevertheless
clearly in view in 2:17. In his words,

> Diese Nebenbedeutung wird von manchen Auslegern
> hier abgelehnt; doch spricht die Fortsetzung
> dafür, daß sie mitschwingt[16].

As a result, Windisch's programmatic article could now be used to
legitimize translating καπηλεύειν "to adulterate", "to falsify", etc.
in 2:17, even though Windisch himself continued to stress that the idea
of "selling" or "offering the Word of God for money", based on the polemic against the Sophists found in secular Greek literature, was the
primary denotation of the verb. In addition, Windisch's discussion of
the Septuagint's use of κάπηλος, and his allusion to Is. 1:22 in his
summary statement that "im Munde des Paulus" καπηλεύειν could "auch be-
deuten: 'das Wort verfälschen (*wie der* κάπηλος *den Wein mit Wasser ver-
mischt, aber als ungemischt verkauft*) ...'"[17], gave the impression that
the two ideas of selling and watering down were, in reality, inextricably linked together in the verb καπηλεύειν. Without further investigation, therefore, it became easy for subsequent commentators to assume,
on the basis of Windisch's treatment of the verb, that the Sophists
and pseudo-philosophers of the ancient world had been attacked for selling their teaching under the suspicion that just as a dishonest wine
dealer dilutes the wine to make a greater profit, so too the Sophists
diluted their teaching in order to make it more palatable to their
audiences. In this way, the two distinct meanings originally suggested
by Windisch naturally melt together into a coherent whole. Consequently,
Paul's statement in 2:17 could be read as implying either meaning, or
both meanings, depending on the emphasis detected by the interpreter[18].
The alleged parallel between II Cor. 2:17 and 4:2 (καπηλεύοντες/

---

13 *ThWb, Bd. 3*, p.607.
14 ibid., p.607.
15 ibid., p.607.
16 ibid., p.608n.7.
17 ibid., p.608, emphasis mine.
18 See e.g. J. Héring, *Second Epistle*, p.19; Barrett, *Second Corinthians*, p.103 and
   Tasker, *Commentary*, p.58.

δολοῦντες), also pointed out by Windisch, simply confirmed this conclusion[19].

It is highly significant, therefore, that also in the English-
speaking world we find this exact fusion of meaning independently
attested in Alfred Plummer's standard commentary on II Corinthians in
the ICC series, which came to occupy the same influential role in Eng-
land and America as the works of Windisch did on the continent. For
although Plummer also refers to the anti-Sophist polemic as a background to II Cor. 2:17, he disregards the emphasis of "selling" altogether in his translation and simply renders καπηλεύοντες τὸν λόγον τοῦ
θεοῦ, "'Adulterating the Word of God' (since) 'Adulterate' suggests
more clearly than 'corrupt' (AV., RV.) that the corruption is done for
the sake of some miserable personal gain"[20]. It is also significant
that Plummer referred to the two occurrences of κάπηλος ("retail dealer") in the LXX (i.e. Is. 1:22 and Sir. 26:29) as the basis for his
interpretation. Plummer even ventures to suggest that "St Paul may have
had Is. 1:22 in his mind in using καπηλεύοντες"[21]. Consequently, whether
one turned to Windisch or Plummer, the impression could not be avoided
that καπηλεύειν carried an emphasis on "adulterating" or "falsifying"
the object of one's trade. Under their influence, the only exegetical
decision was whether this idea should be considered to be secondary
(à la Windisch) or primary (à la Plummer) in II Cor. 2:17.

Within the last fifteen years, largely on the basis of the use of
κάπηλος in the LXX and the alleged parallel between II Cor. 2:17 and
4:2, it has been Plummer's emphasis and translation which have won the
day. Thus, for example, M. Rissi wrote in 1969,

> Was καπηλεύειν hier bedeutet, *kann nur aus dem Zusammenhang der ganzen Ge-
> dankenführung erklärt werden.* Es geht nicht so sehr um 'gewinnsüchtiges Ver-
> hökern' des Evangeliums, denn das Thema Geldgier spielt *im Kontext keine
> Rolle*, wohl aber um die Verfälschung des Gotteswortes (*vgl. 4:2* δολοῦντες
> τὸν λόγον τοῦ θεοῦ). Vielleicht denkt Paulus an ein *alttestamentliches* Wort,
> das er auf die Verkündigung anwendet: 'οἱ κάπηλοί σου μίσγουσι τὸν οἶνον
> ὕδατι' 'deine Krämer mischen den Wein mit Wasser' (Jes. 1:22).[22]

---

19 This received its classic formulation in the reference work by R.Ch. Trench,
   Synonyma des Neuen Testaments, 1907 (G.T. of *Synonyms of the New Testament*),
   pp.141-145. Trench argued against those who tried to assert that καπηλεύω and
   δολόω were identical, in order to maintain that the former actually included
   everything implied in the latter and more! For in his view, because καπηλεύειν
   was also related specifically to the wine trade, it combined the aspect of mixing
   and falsifying denoted by δολόω (p.142) with the idea of selling this diluted
   product for a dishonest profit. He thus followed Bently in understanding 2:17 to
   refer to those "corrupters of the Word of God for filthy lucre" (p.144).
20 *Second Corinthians*, 1915, p.73.
21 *Second Corinthians*, p.73.
22 *Studien zum Zweiten Korintherbrief*, 1969, pp.18f. The predominance of this view
   is reflected in the fact that Rissi need not even refer to the opposing positions
   of, for example, Schlatter, Lietzmann and Bultmann; see below.

Or as T. Provence recently concluded, "it appears that Paul had the
idea of adulteration primarily in mind"[23]. Moreover, like Rissi,
Provence bases his conclusion on Windisch's suggestion that 2:17 is
parallel to 4:2 (see above), which he then maintains is "confirmed by
further reference to the LXX reading of Isaiah 1:22"[24]. Unlike Rissi,
however, Provence goes on to argue that his interpretation "receives
still further confirmation" from its contrast to εἰλικρινείας in 2:17b
since

> 'sincerity' is here a sincerity which derives from purity. Since Paul is con-
> trasting his motives with those of the καπηλεύοντες, the image of the purity
> of his preaching contrasts nicely with the image of their polluting the word
> of God[25].

Thus, as Plummer suggested over 50 years ago, both Rissi and Provence
argue that the context of 2:17, together with the OT parallel from
Isaiah, demand that Windisch's "Nebenbedeutung" be regarded as the
primary and determinative meaning of 2:17[26]. Our first task, therefore,
is to reexamine, in turn, each of the three pieces of evidence usually
adduced to support the supposition that καπηλεύειν, either primarily
or secondarily, means "to water down" or "to adulterate" in II Cor.
2:17, namely, the anti-Sophist polemic in the Greek classics and Hellenistic Judaism, the LXX usage of κάπηλος in Is. 1:22 and Sir. 26:29
and the context of 2:17 itself, especially the meaning of εἰλικρινείας
on the one hand, and the parallel to II Cor. 4:2 on the other hand.

2. A Reexamination of the Relevant Evidence

In contrast to the impression gained from recent research, the
central issue in determining the meaning of II Cor. 2:17 is not whether
the idea of "falsifying", "adulterating" or "watering down", etc. ought
to be regarded as the primary or secondary meaning of καπηλεύειν; as if
both the ideas of "selling" and "adulterating" were always signified
by the verb. Rather, the question is whether the pejorative idea of
"falsifying" ought to be included as part of the wider semantic field
of the verb at all. As we have seen, the first reason given for doing
so is the assumption that the use of καπηλεύειν in the polemic against
the Sophists, inaugurated by Plato, implied that those who sold their
wisdom also fell to the temptation of compromising their message by
accomodating it to the likes and dislikes of their audiences. But a

---

23 "Sufficient", p.59.
24 "Sufficient", p.59.
25 "Sufficient", p.59. For his interpretation of εἰλικρίνεια as "a sincerity which
   derives from purity", Provence refers to F. Büchsel, *TDNT, Vol. II*, 1964, p.397.
26 Though neither Rissi nor Provence refer to Plummer.

closer look at this polemic reveals that the issue, in reality, was quite different[27].

a. Plato and Isocrates

Plato's problem with the Sophists was not that their practice of accepting money for their teaching compromised their message, but rather that the presupposition for their very existence, i.e. that they were the "wise ones" (and hence the name σοφισταί) whose wisdom (σοφία) and virtue (ἀρετή) could be taught to others, was fundamentally false[28]. Moreover, in addition to this basic philosophical disagreement concerning the nature of knowledge[29], Plato argued that the Sophist's claim to be the wise teacher was also called into question by the content of what the Sophists themeselves taught. Thus, in *Theaetetus* 161C and E, Socrates is said to object to the great Sophist Protagoras' claim to teach wisdom on the basis of Protagoras' own cardinal doctrine that "man is the measure of all things", since, for Protagoras, perception was to be equated with knowledge[30]. For in Plato's (Socrates') view, this radical empiricism implied, in effect, that no one could teach or examine another person since each person, by definition, must always be right! (cf. *Theaetetus* 152C). Hence, for Plato, Protagoras' claim to be wise and to be able to impart wisdom to others was not only philosophically impossible, but was also contradicted by his own most fundamental principal. As Plato put it,

> Why in the world, my friend, was Protagoras wise, so that he could rightly be thought worthy to be the teacher of other men and to be well paid (μετὰ

---

27 This is not to deny that the temptation among rhetoricians and Sophists to accommodate their message existed in the ancient world, since it clearly did. For Paul's era, cf. Samuel Dill's chapter on "The Philosophic Missionary", in his *Roman Society from Nero to Marcus Aurelius*, 1964(1956), pp.334-383. Dill refers to the condemnation of those philosophers who did anything for applause as reported in Seneca, Musonius, Plutarch, Epictetus and Lucian (cf. p.345), concluding that "the volume and unanimity of these criticisms of the rhetorical philosophers show that such men abounded; but they also show that there must have been a great mass of serious teachers whom they travestied" (p.346). The issue for us, however, is whether this is the critique implied in καπηλεύειν as initiated by Plato (Socrates).

28 E.R. Dodds, *Plato: Gorgias, A Revised Text with Introduction and Commentary*, 1959, p.7, refers to the Sophist "claim to be able to teach ἀρετή (cf. Plato, *Meno* 459C6-460A4)" as "perhaps their most distinctive common feature". For Plato's description of the Sophists as those who teach virtue, cf. *Gorgias* 519E; *Prot.* 349A and *Meno* 95B. This, of course, was to be contrasted with Socrates' view of himself as merely a "midwife", whose task it was to elicit the knowledge already latent within each person by a dialectical method of teaching; cf. Plato, *Theaetetus* 148E-151D, 157C and 161AB. For Socrates' main point that knowledge cannot be taught, cf. M.I. Finley, *Die Griechen, Eine Einführung in ihre Geschichte und Zivilisation*, 1976 (G.T. of *The Ancient Greeks*, 1963), p.94.

29 For an outline of Plato's critique of the Sophists' theory of knowledge, cf. Hermann Gauss, *Philosophischer Handkommentar zu den Dialogen Platos, 3. Teil, Erste Hälfte*, 1960, pp.31-34.

30 Cf. *Theaetetus* 151E-152C for this classic definition and its implications.

μεγάλων μισθῶν) and why were we ignorant creatures and obliged to go to school
to him, if each person is the measure of his own wisdom?".[31]

Thus, the fact that Protagoras was the first philosopher to demand a
regular fee for his teaching (cf. *Prot.* 349A), in and of itself, was
not the problem. Nor was it that the Sophists' teaching was correspondingly "watered down". The problem, quite simply, was that they claimed
to be able to teach what could not be taught in the first place, i.e.
wisdom and virtue[32]. Therefore, when we read in the texts from Plato
listed by Windisch that "the Sophist is really a sort of merchant or
dealer (ἔμπορός τις ἢ κάπηλος) in provisions on which a soul is nour-
ished", who is "hawking (καπηλεύοντες) his doctrine to everyone who
will buy and commending everything they sell"[33]; or that the Sophist
is "a retailer" (κάπηλος) in "articles of knowledge for the soul"[34],
we must be careful not to read into these statements more than is intended or to place the accent on the wrong element. Because of the
negative connotations which we naturally associate with "selling" or
"hawking" something in such a context (so too with the German "ver-
hökern", etc.) it is easy to read these two descriptions as a condemnation of the Sophist because he receives money for his teaching *per se*.
This is even more natural given Plato's critique of the Sophists. But
as W. Nestle has pointed out, we must keep in mind that it was common
practice for doctors, artists and poets to charge a fee for their instruction and that even the philosopher Zeno, himself a Socratic (!),
accepted payment for his lectures[35]. The practice of accepting money
for one's teaching was not, in and of itself, morally reprehensible.

Indeed, the statement from *Protagoras* 313CD quoted above is a response to Hippocrates' ignorance concerning the nature of the knowledge
he will gain from Protagoras and is intended, within its context, simply to make clear to Hippocrates that Protagoras is claiming to be able
to make one a "sophist", or at least to be able to educate one in the
Sophist tradition (cf. 311B-312B). It is not intended to criticize
Protagoras for selling his teaching as such. Moreover, in contrast to
the impression given in recent literature, when Socrates then goes on
to warn Hippocrates that he must be careful

---

31 *Theaetetus* 161DE. Text and translation from Harold North Fowler, *Plato*, LCL,
   Vol. II, 1952(1921).
32 For a good discussion of this problem and the meaning of ἀρετή itself (i.e.
   as "Glück", "Gedeihen", etc. rather than "Tugend"), cf. Wilhelm Nestle, *Platon,
   Ausgewählte Schriften IV: Protagoras*, 1931[7], pp.53f.
33 *Protagoras* 313CD; text and translation from W.R.M. Lamb, *Plato*, LCL, Vol. IV,
   1952(1924), as well as for the passages from *Prot.* cited below.
34 *Sophist* 231D; text and translation of *Soph.* are from H.N. Fowler, *Plato*, LCL,
   Vol. II, 1952(1924).
35 *Platon*, p.9 and 9n3 for the relevant literature.

that the Sophist in commending his wares does not deceive us, as both merchant
and dealer (ὁ ἔμπορός τε καὶ κάπηλος) do in the case of our bodily food
(*Prot.* 313D),

the nature of the deception in view, which is common to both the "dealer" (κάπηλος) and the "Sophist" (σοφιστής), is not that they falsify
their goods, but rather that they commend *all* of their wares indiscrim-
inately, regardless of the fact that both the dealer and the Sophist are
not able to distinguish between those things which are good or bad for
the body and soul respectively (cf. *Prot.* 313DE). Hence, somewhat surprisingly, Socrates can conclude by advising his young friend that

> if you are well informed as to what is good or bad among these wares, it will
> be safe for you to buy doctrines from Protagoras or from anyone else you
> please; but if not, take care, my dear fellow, that you do not risk your
> greatest treasure on a toss of the dice. For I tell you, there is far more
> serious risk in the purchase of doctrines than in that of eatables (*Prot.*
> 313E-314A).

In a similar way, Plato's sixfold description of the Sophist in
Sophist 231DE (cf. the entire discussion from 223D on, of which the
list in 231DE is merely the summary) is also intended to emphasize that
the Sophist, in contrast to the statesman and the philosopher (cf. *Soph.*
217A), is, by definition, the one dedicated to trading in the knowledge conveyed by words and disputation, in contrast to the other class
of "art-merchants" who deal in the kind of knowledge which is conveyed
materially (i.e. in painting, sculpture, etc.) (cf. 224C and E). Hence,
although Plato also distinguishes between those who engage in the "ex-
changing" (μεταβλητική) of goods which they have not made themselves
within a city, the practice of which he calls "retailing" (καπηλική),
and those who exchange goods from *city to city* by selling and buying,
the practice of which he calls "merchandising" (ἐμπορική) (*Soph.*
223D)[36], the Sophist can nevertheless be described as either a "merchant" (ἔμπορος) or a "retailer" (κάπηλος), or even a "seller of his
own productions" (αὐτοπώλης). The decisive characteristic of the Sophist
is simply the fact that he belongs to the class of those who are "merchandising in knowledge" (μαθηματοπωλικόν) (see *Soph.* 224E)[37]. But here

---

36 Although Plato's basic distinction between the retailer and retail selling
(κάπηλος/καπηλεύειν) and the wholesaler and wholesale trade (ἔμπορος/ἐμπορεύομαι)
holds up, the categories were by no means so well defined as they are in modern
commerce. In fact, in the fourth and fifth centuries BCE the two terms could
even be used interchangeably to denote "trader"/"trade" in a general, generic
sense. Cf. Plato, *Republic* 260CD and 525C; Aristotle, *Politics* 1256a-1258a;
1258b and Moses I. Finkelstein, "Ἔμπορος, Ναύκληρος and Κάπηλος: A Prolegomena
to the Study of Athenian Trade", *Classical Philology* 30(1935)320-336, pp.323f.,
327,329,332. What is important to keep in mind is that for Plato the essential
nature of retail dealing was its practice of trading/selling for the sake of
gain or profit; cf. *Laws*, VIII.847D. That this is also the case for Paul's day
is clear from Pliny the Elder, *Natural History* 18.225.
37 *Soph.* 224E: "that part of acquisitive art (κτητικῆς) which proceeds by exchange
(μεταβλητικόν) and by sale (ἀγοραστικόν), whether as mere retail trade (καπηλικόν)

as well, the Sophist practice of selling his teaching receives its negative connotation in Plato as a hunt after "rich and promising youths"
(223B; cf. 231D) only because of its accompanying claim to provide an
education in wisdom and virtue (223A). For to Plato, the Sophist's only
accomplishment is his ability to appear wise about everything, as a result of his mastery of the art of disputation, without actually con-
veying knowledge or wisdom about anything (235A). It is this ability to
appear wise that attracts the young and the rich (cf. *Soph.* 232B-233C)
and wins for the Sophists the negative reputation of being

> nothing else, apparently, than the money-making class of the disputatious,
> argumentative, controversial, pugnacious, combative, acquisitive art ...

It must again be emphasized, however, that for all of its negative nuances, the point of Plato's critique in his extended discussion in
Sophist 223D-235A is not that the Sophists "water down" their message,
nor indeed that they even sell it(!), but instead, that they claim to
sell, and appear to sell as a result of their rhetorical skills, what
they do not have, do not understand well enough to be able to identify
and cannot produce, namely the wisdom needed to nourish the soul[38]. For
it must be kept in mind that the basis of Plato's criticism of the
Sophists was not that they sold their wares, but that their wares, if
properly understood, could not be sold. In other words, it was Plato's
philosophical conviction that knowledge and wisdom could not be taught
that made the practice of accepting money for teaching it reprehensible -
not the fact that it was being sold *per se*[39]. For Plato, Sophistry was
a sham, and its teachers were mere entertainers (see *Soph.* 235A). What
they sold was worthless.

That the practice of accepting money for one's instruction, in and
of itself, did not necessarily imply either a negative judgment concerning the teaching being sold, nor a criticism of the motives of the
one selling it in the fourth century BCE can be further illustrated by
the writings of Plato's contemporary Isocrates (436 BCE-388 BCE), who
was not only influenced by Socrates, but also by the Sophist Gorgias[40].
For in Isocrates' own critique of the Sophists, those teachers who de-

---

or the sale of one's own productions, no matter which, so long as it is of the
class of merchandising in knowledge (μαθηματοπωλικόν), you will always, apparently, call Sophistry (σοφιστικόν)".
38 As Gauss, *Philosophischer Handkommentar* 3/I, p.192 put it, they fall prey to what
Plato called the second grade of "Unwissenheit" (ἀμαθία), or the "doppelte Unwissenheit", namely, "wenn jemand, der etwas nicht weiss, sich trotzdem ein-
bildet, darum zu wissen". Cf. *Soph.* 229C.
39 As evidenced by the fact that according to Diogenes, even a student of Socrates
himself, Artistippus (ca. 435-350 BCE), could charge fees for his teaching; cf.
Diogenes Laertius 2.65,72. Diogenes goes on to tell us that Aristippus sent
money from his earnings to his teacher as well, though this bothered Socrates.
40 Cf. George Norling, *Isocrates*, LCL, *Vol. I*, 1954(1928), pp.xi-xviii.

vote themselves to "disputation" (ἔριδας) manifest the perversity of
their proposals not in that they offer them for money, but rather in
the fact that they don't charge enough for their services, i.e. they
fail to charge what their teaching would genuinely be worth if their
claims were valid. In his words,

> Although they set themselves up as masters and dispensers of goods so pre-
> cious, they are not ashamed of asking for them a price of three or four
> minae! Why, if they were to sell any other commodity for so trifling a
> fraction of its worth they would not deny their folly; nevertheless, al-
> though they set so insignificant a price on the whole stock of virtue and
> happiness, they pretend to wisdom and assume the right to instruct the rest
> of the world.[41]

Conversely, in *Antidosis* 225-226 and 240-241, Isocrates can point to
the fact that his pupils go to great lengths to come to him, paying
him for his instruction, and that parents gladly pay him for teaching
their sons, as evidence of the integrity of the education he offered.
It is significant, moreover, that when Isocrates explicitly takes up
the criticisms usually leveled against the Sophists in *Antidosis* 197ff.,
there is no mention whatsoever of the fact that they charged a fee for
their instruction. What is to be criticized is the duplicity of those
Sophists who "speak contemptuously of wealth as 'filthy lucre', claiming not to want money", while at the same time holding "their hands
out for a trifling gain" (*Against the Sophists* 4). Thus, in Plato's
day, the mere fact that one charged a fee for teaching could be either
positive or negative, depending on the attending circumstances. Furthermore, the fact that one did so in no instance implied that one's message had been accommodated or watered down according to the interests
of the audience. Instead, rather than casting doubt on one's message,
to sell one's instruction implied that what one had to teach was valu-
able enough to warrant its purchase. To sell one's teaching was, in
effect, to make a positive claim concerning the worth of one's message[42]. This, then, is the underlying presupposition behind the anti-
Sophist polemic of both Plato and Isocrates. For in selling their teaching, the Sophists were implicitly claiming a value for that which had
none.

41 Text and translation from G. Norlin, *Isocrates*, LCL, Vol. II, 1956(1929). Cf.
   also Plato, *Apology* 20B for the same critique!
42 Socrates himself is said to take Protagoras' demand for a fee as evidence of his
   confidence in his own abilities; cf. Plato, *Prot.* 348E. Conversely, Protagoras
   boasts that he gives "full value for the fee that (he) charge(s) - nay, so much
   more than full, that the learner himself admits it" (*Prot.* 328B). In fact,
   Protagoras is said to have only charged what people thought his teaching was
   worth, while his students were required to pay what he asked only if they were
   satisfied with what they had learned (cf. *Prot.* 328B). See Diodorus Siculus
   XII.53.2 for a first cent. BCE positive evaluation of the fact that Gorgias was
   paid. As he reports, Gorgias "so far excelled all other men in the instruction
   offered by the Sophists that he received from his pupils a fee of one hundred
   minas".

The only other occurrences of the word-group κάπηλος/καπηλεύειν in
the corpus of Plato's writings of significance for our study[43] are
found in Book XI of Plato's *Laws*, which as his last work is dated between 357 and 347 BCE[44]. Here Plato takes up business dealings of all
sorts, devoting a large section to a discussion of commercial honesty
(cf. *Laws* XI. 915D-920C), within which there is an extended treatment
of the nature and limitations of retail business (XI.918A-919C). At
first glance, this discussion seems to support those who wish to translate καπηλεύειν in II Cor. 2:17 "water down", "adulterate", etc., since
Plato's reflections concerning retail business take place immediately
after his discussion of the practice of adulterating goods (cf. 916D-
918A). For in Plato's words, "Following close upon practices of adulteration (κιβδήλοις) follow practices of retail trading (καπηλείας)"
(XI.918A)[45]. But a careful reading of Plato's treatment of this theme
shows that these two ideas are so closely linked together not because
retail trading necessarily implies an adulteration of one's goods, but
because both the practice of adulteration and the corruption of retail
business lead to a similar sort of commercial injustice and are motivated by the same impulse of human greed. Hence, the lawgiver must
deal with both areas in a similar manner (cf. XI.920B). Plato's treatment of the nature of retail business itself nowhere associates selling
(καπηλεύειν) with the corrupting or adulterating (κιβδηλεύειν) of goods.
Rather, Plato's burden is to offer an apologetic for the positive and
necessary purpose of retail business, i.e. "to provide all men with
full satisfaction of their needs", in spite of the fact that it "is
reputed to be a thing not noble nor even respectable" (XI.918C). For
in Plato's view, the problem with retail trade does not lie in its
practice of selling something for a profit, for which it has even been
ordained(!) (cf. XI.918B), but in the greed of those who do the selling[46]. In his words,

---

43 Based on an investigation of the 25 occurrences of the word group listed by
   Fridrich Ast, *Lexicon Platonicum Sive Vocum Platonicarum Index*, 1959(1835-1838),
   Vol. 2, pp.139-140.
44 So R.G. Bury, *Plato*, LCL, *Vol. IX*, 1952(1926), p.vii.
45 Text and translation for Plato's treatise *Laws* from R.G. Bury, *Plato*, LCL, *Vol.
   IX*, 1952(1926).
46 The importance of Plato's position becomes clear when we compare it with Aristotle's largely negative discussion of the origin and nature of retail trade in
   Politica I.8.1256[a] 41-I.9.1257. For although he too seems to admit that retail
   trade is necessary for the state (cf. *Pol.* IV.4.1290[b] 40-1291[a]5), it nevertheless
   remains, in and of itself, something negative, since its aim, in his view, is to
   make a profit at the expense of others on the one hand (cf. *Pol.* 1258[b]1-2), and
   since it deals only in money, which for Aristotle is an "unnatural" basis for
   self-sufficiency, on the other hand. His position is ambiguous, however, since in
   Pol. 1258[a]14-18 he seems to grant that the retail business is unnecessary altogether. Cf. M.I. Finley, "Aristotle and Economic Analysis", in *Studies in Ancient
   Society*, ed. M.I. Finley. 1974, pp.26-52, esp. pp.42-44.

when they desire, they desire without limit, and when they can make moderate
gains, they prefer to gain insatiably, and it is because of this that all the
classes concerned with retail trade (πάντα τὰ περὶ τὴν καπηλείαν), commerce,
and inn-keeping are disparaged and subject to violent abuse (XI.918D).

Conversely, if someone compelled

the best men everywhere for a certain period to keep inns or to peddle (καπηλεύειν) or to carry on any such trade, - or even to compel women by some necessity
of fate to take part in such a mode of life, - then we should learn how that
each of these callings is friendly and desirable; and if all these callings
were carried on according to a rule free from corruption, they would be hon-
oured with the honour which one pays to a mother or a nurse (XI.918E).

An investigation of Plato's use of καπηλεύειν, etc. thus yields a
surprising result. For even if Windisch is correct in asserting that
Paul's use of this verb in II Cor. 2:17 "geht wohl auf die von Plato
inaugurierte Polemik gegen das Sophistenwesen zurück"[47], his corollary
that καπηλεύειν also carries the "Nebenbedeutung" of "adulterating" or
"falsifying" the object of one's trade cannot be substantiated on the
basis of Plato's writings, not to mention the attempt to consider this
its primary meaning. For nowhere in Plato's discussion does the idea
of retail selling for the purpose of making a profit, καπηλεύειν,
either in its concrete sense, or in its transferred sense as applied
to the Sophists, denote, or even connote, the idea of falsifying or
adulterating the object being sold. Rather, if that which is sold is
itself of no value, then to sell it becomes reprehensible. But even
more surprising is the fact that Plato nowhere disparages the Sophist
practice of charging a fee for their teaching in and of itself, while
on the other hand he can even defend the practice of retailing, though
he recognizes that the greed of those engaged in such an occupation can
easily lead to its corruption. As a result, it must be carefully regu-
lated (see *Laws* IX.919C-929C)[48].

It is this realization that provides the key to Plato's use of
κάπηλος-καπηλεύειν in his critique of the Sophists. For given Plato's
realization that those engaged in market-trade often fall prey to their
greed and are therefore tempted to take advantage of people's need in
order to make an undue profit (cf. *Laws* 918E), it served Plato's purpose well to use this often pejorative *technical terminology*[49] to de-

---

47 *Zweiter Korintherbrief*, p.100.
48 Though nowhere explicitly stated, one cannot help but wonder, therefore, whether
even for Plato, if one's motives were pure and if virtue could be taught, if
there would then be any reason that one could not sell it, as Plato himself
assumes in the case of doctors, poets, artists, language teachers, music teachers
and sports instructors (cf. *Prot.* 311BC; 312AB).
49 Again, it is important to keep in mind that the word-group κάπηλος/καπηλεύειν is
a technical designation referring to the type of business carried on in the
market. As Finley, "Aristotle", p.42 summarizes it: "Greek usage was not wholly
consistent in selecting among the various words for 'trader', but *kapelos* usually denoted the petty trader, the huckster, in the market place", i.e. it refers specifically to "trade for the sake of gain" or "commercial trade".

scribe those philosophers whose message he wished to call into question.
It should be emphasized that Plato did not use this motif, associated
with the problem of greed in *Laws* 918DE, in order to criticize the
Sophists for being greedy, but simply to cast doubt on their teaching
in general. For as we have seen, the function of κάπηλος/καπηλεύειν in
Plato's critique of the Sophists is not to impugn their motives, but
to cast doubt upon the value of their teaching. As such, the importance
of recognizing the negative nuances associated with market-trade in
Plato's day is *not* that it now provides a key to the *content* of a critique in which this motif is employed, but that it signals to us *that*
a critique is intended[50]. In Plato's case, the negative connotations
which were associated with the trader/retail dealer in his day[51] provided him with a linguistic vehicle by which he could cast doubt on
the legitimacy of a particular circle of Sophists who sold their teaching, *without necessarily condemning the practice of charging a fee for
one's teaching in and of itself*. In the same way, he could speak of the
negative reputation of those engaged in retail trade (see *Laws* 918C-E,
919C), while at the same time defending its legitimacy (*Laws* 918E).
But since for Socrates virtue and wisdom could not be taught to begin
with, he refused to accept payment for his "teaching" as a matter of
principle.

b. Sirach, Josephus and Philo

The widespread nature of this negative nuance associated with the
κάπηλος is evidenced by its attestation in the second century BCE
Jewish world of Jesus ben Sirach. For the statement in Sirach 26:29,

---

50 Contra Ronald F. Hock, *The Social Context of Paul's Ministry, Tentmaking and
Apostleship*, 1980, pp.52f., who writes that "the practice of charging fees, as
popular as it was, was criticized by others, most notably by Socrates. Widely
known for not charging fees, Socrates, particularly in the Platonic writings,
compared Sophists to traders and merchants (κάπηλοι), the comparison being made
to impute to Sophists the motives of deceit and avarice". Hock lists in support
of this statement, Plato, *Men.* 92a and *Euthyd.* 277B (as evidence for the motive
of deceit) and Xenophon, *Mem.* 1.2.7 (as evidence for the motive of greed) (cf.
p.95n.23). I was unable to find a reference to κάπηλος in either of the first
two references, while in the last context Socrates refuses to accept money not
because of the negative connotations associated with doing so, but because doing
so would "enslave" him, i.e. he would then be forced to converse with whoever
paid him.
51 For other clear examples of such negative views of market-place trade from this
period, cf. Herodotus 1.152-3; Xenophon, *Cyropaedia* 1.2.3. and possibly Aeschylus,
Fragments 322, though the fragment is too small to be sure. It must be pointed
out, however, that this negative perception of the retailer and of retail trade
among the philosophers and intellectuals was a reaction against what, in reality,
was the rapidly growing importance of the market in the economy and everyday
life of the Greek people, beginning in the fifth century BCE. For a good summary of the vital importance of retail dealers in the ordinary Greek city of the
Hellenistic period, cf. M. Rostovtzeff, *The Social and Economic History of the
Hellenistic World, Vol. II*, 1953(1941), pp.1271-1274.

> Hardly shall the merchant (ἔμπορος) keep himself from wrongdoing, and a huck-
> ster (κάπηλος) will not be acquitted of sin

is surely built on the premise expressed in Sirach 27:1-3 that

> Many have sinned for the sake of gain; and he that seeketh to multiply (gain)
> turneth away his eye. A nail sticketh fast between the joinings of stones,
> and sin will thrust itself in between buyer and seller. My son, if thou hold
> not diligently to the fear of the Lord, thy house will soon be overthrown.[52]

Hence, for Sirach as well, although it was not sinful to be engaged in
retail trade in and of itself (there is no admonition to leave this
sort of work altogether!)[53], it undoubtedly carried with it an undeniable note of suspicion and caution.

Moreover, the writings of Philo and Josephus illustrate that this
same negative connotation was still current among Hellenistic Jews of
Paul's day, and that it could be employed in a variety of ways. In his
treatise *De Gigantibus* 39, Philo supports his admonition not to seek
wealth or glory, which "infects philosophy with the baseness of mere
opinion", by referring to the practice of those philosophers who sell
their teaching in the market. Equally important for our study, however,
is the fact that Philo can assume that his judgment concerning these
philosophers is common ground between him and his readers, thus pre-
supposing an opinion which must have been widespread. In his words,

> For manifest surely and clear is the disgrace of those who say that they are
> wise, yet barter their wisdom (πωλούντων δὲ σοφίαν) for what they can get, as
> men say is the way of the pedlars who hawk their goods in the market. And some-
> times the price is just a trifling gain ....[54]

Thus, although like Isocrates Philo's critique of those who barter
their wisdom seems to focus on the fact that they cheapen it by selling it for so little[55], and not on the fact that it is sold *per se*, it
is nevertheless clear that he assumes that his readers would agree with
him that for a philosopher to be compared to a pedlar is no compliment.
This is confirmed by his statement in *Vita Mosis* II.212, where Philo
asserts that true wisdom

> must not be that of the systems hatched by the word-catchers and Sophists who
> sell their tenets and arguments like any bit of merchandise in the market,
> men who forever pit philosophy against philosophy without a blush ...[56]

---

52 Translations from R.H. Charles, *Apocrypha, Vol. I*, 1963(1913), p.405.
53 It is therefore misleading to relate Sir. 26:29 to the condemnations of traders
   in Zech. 14:21 and Zeph. 1:11, as Windisch, *ThWb, Bd. 3*, p.607n.2, does, inasmuch as these are not general denunciations of those engaged in trade, but rather,
   as Windisch himself points out, a specific judgment against those foreign traders
   who were selling on the Sabbath. Cf. Neh. 10:31; 13:16-22.
54 Text and translation from G.H. Whitaker, *Philo, LCL, Vol. II*, 1958(1929).
55 Philo uses the verbal form ἐπευωνίζων to describe their practice, which is
   best translated as "selling cheap"; cf. F.H. Colson and G.H. Whitaker, *Philo,
   LCL, Vol. II*, 1958(1929), p.486, §123 and *De cher.* 123.
56 Text and translation from F.H. Colson, *Philo, LCL, Vol. VI*, 1959(1935).

For here as well, the fact that the Sophists are associated with the
retail practice of the market place obviously casts a shadow of suspicion on the quality of their wisdom. But once again, the problem in
view is not the practice of selling, but rather, in this case, the fact
that the Sophists manifest the disunity of their teaching by their practice of competitively pitting one philosophy against another, in contrast to the unity of the true wisdom represented by Philo. Nevertheless,
the market-place continues to carry the negative connotations necessary
to call the Sophist into question.

In yet a third context, Josephus expands the prohibition from Levi-
ticus 21:7, which for the sake of purity forbade a priest to marry a
harlot, by adding to it those women "who gain their livelihood by hawking or innkeeping" (τάς ἐκ καπηλείας ... πανδοκεύειν)(Ant. III.276)[57].
In doing so, Josephus seems to be influenced by the targumic practice of
translating the Hebrew זונה ("harlot") with פונדקיתא (from πανδοκεύειν,
"to keep an inn"), perhaps due to the ill-fame of inns in the ancient
world[58]. It is significant, therefore, that καπηλεία, i.e. "retail
trade", is drawn into this negative association - an indication that
it too must have carried a similar negative connotation, though the
precise nature of this connotation remains unclear[59]. Hence, although
the nature of the negative connotation associated with the market-place
and those engaged in its trade could vary from the "cheapness" associated with bartering, to its competitive nature, to the morally "shady"
character of its milieu, it is nevertheless evident that to be compared
with the κάπηλοι meant to suffer guilt by association[60]. Indeed, the

---

57 Text and translation from H.St.J. Thackeray, *Josephus, LCL, Vol. IV*, 1957(1930).
58 So Thackeray, *Josephus, Vol. IV*, p.451note. He refers to the targumic rendering
of Joshua 2:1; Jud. 11:1; I Kings 3:16 as examples. M. Jastrow, *A Dictionary of
the Targumim, Vol. II*, 1950, p.1144, lists in addition the Targ. to Ezekiel 23:44
and translates the word "keeper of a public house, harlot".
59 Cf. also *c.Ap.* I.61, where Josephus uses καπηλεία together with ἐμπορία (inter-
city commerce) without any negative overtones. It is possible that Josephus is
using καπηλεία here to mean "inn-keeping" or "tavernkeeping" as found also in
Xenophon, *Anabasis* I.2.24; Plutarch, *Isis and Osiris* 369; Dio Cassius, *Roman
History* 62.14.2; 65.10.3. Cf. too M. Rostovtzeff, *The Social and Economic History
of the Hellenistic World, Vol. III*, 1959(1941), p.1628n.196, who points out that
"the meaning of the term κάπηλος in Ptolemaic Egypt appears to be, not retail
trader in general, but dealer in certain foodstuffs and caterer, keeper of an
inn, of a tavern, or of a wineshop (καπηλεῖον) ...".
60 We must be careful, however, not to assume that this was always the case. Thus,
for example, when Liddell-Scott list Demosthenes, *Against Aristogeiton* 25.46 as
an example of a metaphorical use of κάπηλος to mean a "dealer in petty roguery"
(*Greek-English Lexicon*, p.876), we should not assume that κάπηλος itself carries
this negative connotation. In the context it simply refers to Aristogeiton's
practice of dealing in wickedness, i.e. his business was πονηρία. This same thing
is true of their references to Dio Cassius, *Roman History* 60.17.8 and Herodotus
III.89. In both cases the negative judgment falls not on retail-trading, but on
the fact that those in view were selling what should not have been sold. Finally,
Liddell-Scott also list Dionysius of Halicarnassus, *Roman Antiquities* 9.25.2 to

significance of the usage of this motif by Philo and Josephus lies in the fact that the market-place can now be seen to represent a *variety* of negative attributes depending on the context in which it is employed[61]. In other words, the semantic field encompassed by the καπηλ-word-group and its synonyms has obviously been widened with time to include a broad spectrum of related, negative connotations and qualities[62].

But there is still no evidence for the supposition that the verb καπηλεύειν itself can mean "adulterate", "water down" or "falsify", etc. The variety of negative connotations which now surround καπηλεύειν have not changed its basic meaning, but are all related to the general practice of selling as it was carried on by the lower class retail traders in the market. With this in mind, we can now turn our attention to the last, and perhaps most important, uses of καπηλεύειν for our study, namely, its use by the second century writer Lucian in his essay *Hermotimus* 59 on the one hand, and in Isaiah 1:22 on the other hand. For here we encounter what appears to be the strongest evidence for the fact that καπηλεύειν could also signify the idea of "watering down" something, as a wine dealer dilutes his wine. As such, these two passages become the non-Pauline proof texts most often cited in support of the idea that Paul is accusing his opponents of adulterating the gospel in II Cor. 2:17[63].

c. Lucian, Philostratus and Isaiah

In turning to the voluminous works of Lucian (ca. 125-180 CE), the first thing to note is that the verb καπηλεύειν itself nowhere occurs

---

support the meaning of "cheating, knavish" for κάπηλος. But all we learn from this reference is that "no Roman citizen was permitted to earn a livelihood as a tradesman (κάπηλον) or artisan". (Text and translation from Earnest Cary, *The Roman Antiquities of Dionysius of Halicarnassus*, LCL, *Vol. VI*, 1963(1947).

61 Cf. e.g. Aeschylus, *Seven against Thebes* 545, where καπηλεύειν can even represent the idea of acting in a small and insignificant manner, based no doubt on the fact that most retail trading in the ancient world was done on a very small scale. For in describing the fifth chief to come up against Thebes, the poet writes, ἐλθὼν δ' ἔοικεν οὐ καπηλεύσειν μάχην, which A.W. Verrall translates "once arrived he will do no petty cozening in the trade of war, but something worthy of the long journey he hath travelled", *The 'Seven Against Thebes' of Aeschylus, with an Introduction, Commentary and Translation*, 1887, p.158 (verse 531 in his numeration).

62 This same negative connotation concerning merchants is also found later among the rabbis; cf. b.Erubin 55a and b.Kidd. 82a; though Pirke Aboth II.2 illustrates the positive value attached to the practice of those rabbis who supported themselves with an occupation.

63 Cf. for example, besides the commentaries already listed above (see n.2), the standard NT lexicon of Bauer-Arndt-Gingrich, p.404, where we read, "Because of the tricks of small tradesmen (Dio Chrys. 14 (31), 37f.; Lucian, *Hermot.* 59 ... Is. 1:22 ...) the word comes to mean almost *adulterate* (so Vulg., Syr., Goth.)", which has not been altered in the new English edition, Bauer-Gingrich-Danker, *A Greek-English Lexicon of the New Testament and other Early Christian Literature*, 1979², p.403.

in his writings, though the two related nouns, κάπηλος ("retailer")
and καπηλεῖον ("bazaar"), occur three and two times respectively[64].
Thus, in *The Wisdom of Nigrinus* 25, in the context of a description
of the disgust Nigrinus felt over those "self-styled philosophers" of
his day who frequented the dinner parties of the rich, Lucian comments
that not only did Nigrinus think this ridiculous, but he also "made
special mention of people who cultivate philosophy for hire (τῶν ἐπὶ
μισθῷ φιλοσοφούντων) and put virtue on sale over a counter, as it were:
indeed, he called the lecture-rooms of these men factories and bazaars
(καπηλεῖα)"[65]. But, as we saw in the case of Isocrates and Philo, here
too this negative reference to the practice of selling one's lectures
is not grounded in the fact that to do so is itself reprehensible, but
in the fact that by doing so these philosophers contradict their own
teaching, thus becoming hypocrites[66]. As Lucian puts it

> one who intends to teach contempt for wealth
> should first of all show that he is himself
> above gain (*Nigr.* 26).[67]

Hence, Nigrinus gave "instruction without recompense to all who desired
it ..." (*Nigr.* 26). Moreover, Lucian's essay *On Salaried Posts in Great
Houses* makes it clear that earning a living or receiving a salary for
teaching philosophy is not, as such, morally wrong. For here one of
his basic criticisms of those who attached themselves to the house-
holds of the rich was not that they were seeking money for their teaching, but that they sold their teaching (and, in effect, themselves) for
a trifling of what it was worth. Hence, although it often appeared to
be otherwise from the outside, Lucian can maintain, albeit with a great
deal of irony, that those philosophers who became the resident intellectuals for rich patrons had settled for an existence which was financially no better than poverty (cf. *Salaried Posts* 4, 5, 20-22, 30, 38-
39). In his later essay, *Apology for the 'Salaried Posts in Great
Houses'*, Lucian goes on to defend the practice of being paid as a
philosopher, as well as to remind those who would criticize him for

---

64 Acc. to Caroli Iacobitz, *Lucianus, Accedunt scholia auctiora et emendatiora,
   index et rerum et verborum*, 1966(1841), pp.551-552.
65 Text and translation from A.M. Harmon, *Lucian, LCL, Vol. I*, 1953.
66 For this same point, cf. Lucian, *Menippus* 5.
67 On the centrality of the theme of hypocrisy in Lucian's writings, which he applies to almost all of the professions alike except historians, cf. Graham
   Anderson, "Lucian: a Sophist's Sophist", in *Yale Classical Studies*, ed. John J.
   Winkler and Gordon Williams, Vol. 27: *Later Greek Literature*, 1982, pp.61-92,
   pp.66f. He calls Lucian's various uses of the critique of hypocrisy "the main
   achievement of Lucian's satirical output". He also points out that although such
   hypocritical philosophers no doubt existed, that nevertheless we must also keep
   in mind that this critique had become "a tiresome cliché since Socrates ... and
   that fact in itself was surely one of its chief attractions for sophistic rhetoricians ..." (p.80).

now being paid himself as a government employee that previously he had commanded "the highest fees for the public practice of rhetoric" and that his "fees were as high as those of any professor" - for which he was never criticized! (*Apology* 15)[68]. Finally, in Lucian's essay, *A Professor of Public Speaking* 9, the fact that the teachers of the old and arduous school of rhetoric demanded large sums of money for their education is seen as a *positive* indication of its value, in contrast to the short and easy education in oratorical methods which was becoming increasingly popular in Lucian's day and which might have been characterized by its free teaching[69]. As a result, we must be careful not to create a general maxim out of what in *The Wisdom of Nigrinus* 25 was intended merely to be a criticism of a specific instance of hypocrisy.

This same caution must be expressed concerning the reference from Philostratus (b.170CE) in his *Life of Apollonius* I, 13, where we read that Apollonius attempted to "wean" his rival Sophist Euphrates "of his love of filthy lucre and his huckstering his wisdom" (ἀπῆγε τοῦ χρηματίζεσθαί τε καὶ τὴν σοφίαν καπηλεύειν)[70]. For here too this disparaging comment owes its origin to Apollonius' own extremely ascetic life-style and not to a widespread and popular condemnation of selling one's instruction (cf. *Life*, I.13-14). In fact, as Philostratus' own biographical treatise *The Lives of the Sophists* shows, Sophists of his day enjoyed tremendous popularity and amassed huge fortunes from their teaching (cf. *Lives*, 527, 566). Indeed, the presence of a leading Sophist often brought great benefits to a city (cf. *Lives*, 530-533)[71]. Consequently, the same ambiguous attitude toward selling one's teaching, which we encountered almost five centuries earlier in Plato and Isocrates, continues to be attested in the writings of Lucian and Philostratus. Furthermore, when Lucian and Philostratus wish to criticize certain circles of philosophers for selling their teaching, though they themselves assume and even defend the right of philosophers to be paid, they too draw on the market-place/selling analogy to do so[72].

---

68 Text from K. Kilburn, *Lucian*, LCL, Vol. VI, 1959.
69 Cf. the introduction to the essay by A.M. Harmon, *Lucian*, LCL, Vol. IV, 1953 (1925), p.133.
70 Text and translation from F.C. Conybeare, *Philostratus, The Life of Apollonius of Tyrana*, LCL, Vol. I, 1948(1912).
71 For a recent discussion of this theme, cf. E.L. Bowie, "The Importance of Sophists", *Yale Classical Studies, Vol. 27: Later Greek Literature*, 1982, pp.29-59, who argues that the primary factor in the rise of the Sophists to positions of wealth and power was not their professional status and abilities, but their aristocratic family backgrounds (cf. p.53).
72 This corresponds to the negative view of the market-place current among the Roman upper class in general. Cf. the entry κάπηλος in Ramsay McMullen's "Lexicon of Snobbery", in his *Roman Social Relations, 50 B.C. to A.D. 284*, 1974, pp.138-141, p.139. Of the seven texts listed, however, only Cicero, *De off.* I.150 predates the second century CE - and there is a question about just how representative Cicero's view actually was, cf. below, pp.136f.

This becomes even clearer in Lucian's important statement in
Hermotimus 59, where we find the assertion that wine and philosophy
have one thing in common, namely, "that philosophers sell their lessons
as winemerchants (κάπηλοι) their wares - most of them adulterating and
cheating and giving false measure (κερασάμενοί γε οἱ πολλοὶ καὶ δολώσαν-
τες καὶ κακομετροῦντες)"[73]. This statement seems to be the ideal proof
text for the usual understanding of II Cor. 2:17 because of the use of
κάπηλος to mean "wine merchant" and because of the link between the
wine merchant and δολόω, which seems to support the decision to read
II Cor. 2:17 in the light of 4:2. But the use of κάπηλος to refer specifically to those who sell wine in *Herm.* 59 does not signify a new
technical use of the word, but refers back to *Herm.* 58, where the
κάπηλος in view has already been explicitly defined as those retailers,
good and bad, who deal in wine. This is confirmed by the fact that in
Herm. 61 κάπηλος is again used, in a different context, to refer to
those merchants who deal in grain, while in *Pseudologista* 9 and *Nigrinus*
25 on the one hand, and *How to Write History* 16 on the other hand,
καπηλεῖον and κάπηλος, without further specification, maintain their
general and neutral sense of "bazaar" and "pedlar" respectively[74].
Thus, *Herm.* 59 also refers to a *particular* criticism of philosophers,
i.e. that they water down their teaching, which can only be associated
with οἱ κάπηλοι in this context because the dealers in view have already been identified specifically as wine merchants. Moreover, even
though this identification has been made, the related idea of "watering
down" or "adulterating" is still not implied in the substantive ideas
of κάπηλος or καπηλεῖον, but is only expressed by the *additional* assertion in the context concerning those in the wine trade (not all!,
cf. οἱ πολλοί) who "water down" (δολόω) their wine. In a word, it is
δολόω and not καπηλεύω which signifies this idea[75].

---

73 Text and translation from K. Kilburn, *Lucian*, LCL, Vol. VI, 1959.
74 This confirms for the second century CE what Moses I. Finkelstein, "Prolegomena",
   p.334 observed for the fourth and fifth centuries BCE, namely, that κάπηλος cannot
   be linked exclusively to the wine trader, since "all the evidence clearly indicates that this commercial terminology took in every aspect of trade". Contra the
   position expressed by Trench, *Synonyma*, p.142.
75 Again, one must be careful not to read too much into κάπηλος. For example, Hock,
   The Social Context of Paul's Ministry, p.95n.24 lists Lucian's references to the
   κάπηλος in *Nig.* 25 and *Herm.* 59 as evidence for his assertion that this noun is
   applied to "greedy philosophers", although, as we have seen, the idea of greed is
   not in view in either context, though it is associated with καπηλεύειν in Philostratus, *Life* I,13, also listed by Hock. But here too, this idea is not carried
   in the verb καπηλεύειν. It its expressed by an additional assertion. So it is not at
   all certain whether καπηλεύειν itself could imply this nuance. Hock also refers
   to Philostratus, *Lives of the Sophists* 526 as evidence for the fact that Sophists
   were labeled "κάπηλοι" when they were thought to be deceitful or avaricious (cf.
   p.53, 95n.24). But I am unable to find any mention of κάπηλοι in this text. In
   fact, the Sophists in view in this context, Dionysius and Lullianus, are both
   treated very favorably.

In the same way, the use of κάπηλος in the statement from Isaiah
1:22 (LXX)

> Your silver is worthless, thy wine merchants
> mix the wine with water
>
> (τὸ ἀργύριον ὑμῶν ἀδόκιμον, οἱ κάπηλοί σου
> μίσγουσι τὸν οἶνον ὕδατι)[76]

receives its specific connotation "wine dealer" only because of the explicit reference to wine in the sentence. Furthermore, as in Lucian's
statement in *Herm.* 59, here too the idea of "watering down" or "adulteration" is not signified by κάπηλος, but by the predicate μίσγουσι
(from μίγνυμι, "to mix")[77]. In addition, it is important to note that
the point of Is. 1:22, as part of Isaiah's condemnation of Judah and
Jerusalem (cf. Is. 1:1ff.), is to illustrate the idea expressed in Is.
1:21 that the faithful city of Zion, which once was full of judgment,
has now become a harlot, i.e. that that which *once* was good, is now
corrupt. Hence, the κάπηλοι in view, like the silver, only carry negative connotations because they are now explicitly said to have been
corrupted, not because, as we saw in Sir. 26:29, to be a retailer (of
wine), in and of itself, is suspect.

d. *Conclusion*

Our investigation of the use of κάπηλος/καπηλεύειν in the polemic
against the Sophists and its attestation in Hellenistic Judaism thus
leads to two important conclusions. First, to my knowledge, there is
no evidence that this word-group ever directly signified the idea of
"watering down", "adulterating" or "falsifying"; or that these ideas
were ever present as part of the wider semantic field of the verb[78].
When the idea of "adulterating", etc. is present in association with
καπηλεύειν it is not signified by the verb itself, but by an *additional*
verbal statement (i.e. δολόω in Lucian, *Herm.* 59, κιβδηλεύειν in Plato
and μίγνυμι in Is. 1:22) on the one hand, *and* by a *contrast* with the
ideal practice, exemplified in those with whom the ones "selling"
(καπηλεύοντες) their wares/teaching are compared (e.g. the practice of
Socrates, Isocrates, Moses (!) - see Philo, *Vita Mosis* II 212 - Nigrinus,
Lucian and Apollonius). The parallel to Paul's usage is clear. Unless
Paul is deviating from normal semantic usage, for which there is no in-

---

76 Translation from *The Septuagint Version of the Old Testament, Zondervan Edition*,
  1970. Text from A. Rahlfs, *Septuaginta, Vol. II*, 1935.
77 For the derivation of the form, cf. Liddell-Scott, *Lexicon*, p.1092.
78 Cf. too J.H. Moulton and G. Milligan, *The Vocabulary of the Greek New Testament
  Illustrated from the Papyri ...*, 1920, p.321, who list no evidence of it ever
  meaning "to adulterate" and even state that "this verb is confined in Biblical
  Greek to 2 Cor. 2:17, where the meaning 'deal in for purposes of gain' rather
  than 'adulterate' may be illustrated from BGU IV.1024vii23 ...".

dication in the context of II Cor. 2:17, καπηλεύοντες τὸν λόγον τοῦ
θεοῦ ought to be rendered "selling the Word of God as a retail dealer
sells his wares in the market"[79]. The attempt to read καπηλεύειν in
2:17 as a direct synonym of δολόω in 4:2 thus finds no lexical support
in the evidence available to us. This is not to deny that 2:17 and 4:2
are related to one another, or even parallel. It is simply to suggest
that these two statements, though parallel in function, nevertheless
represent two *distinct* assertions, i.e. Paul wishes to deny that he is
selling (καπηλεύοντες) *and* watering down (δολοῦντες) God's word.

Second, on the basis of the literary evidence available it is clear
that this market motif, when used in a transferred sense in reference
to the practice of selling one's teaching, always carries an additional
negative nuance, although the precise nature of this negative connotation is by no means uniform, but can vary given the particular nature
of the critique intended by the author[80]. Hence, in II Cor. 2:17 Paul
is intending to *criticize* the "majority" (οἱ πολλοί), rather than simply
indicating that they are earning their living from the gospel. This is
confirmed by the comparative structure of 2:17 itself, in which Paul
presents *himself as the representative of the ideal practice!*

This conclusion concerning the negative metaphorical use of the
market-place imagery finds an important confirmation in the *Didache*
XII.5, where the Church is warned about those who wish to live off
her generosity without working, i.e. of one who is simply "making
traffic of Christ" (χριστέμπορός ἐστι)[81]. Once again, however, this
warning ought not to be taken as a prohibition against earning one's
living from the gospel *per se*. For as *Didache* XIII.1-6 makes clear,
genuine residential prophets *are* to be supported by the firstfruit-of-
fering of the Church, while prophets who are traveling may receive two
days lodging and food to last for the next day's journey (cf. XI.5f.).
Thus, here as well, the practice of earning one's living from the gospel is viewed positively, while those who are fraudulent in claiming
this privilege can be appropriately described in market-place imagery.

The impression left by the evidence available to us, therefore, is
that the practice of selling in the market was suspicious enough in the
ancient world to enable καπηλεύειν, etc. and its synonyms to be used

---

79 So too Wendland, *An die Korinther*, p.177, who interprets 2:17 as directed against
   those "die aus der Predigt des Evangeliums ein Handelsgeschäft machen und das
   Evangelium wie eine Ware auf dem Markt feilbieten". He correspondingly translates
   2:17: "Denn wir machen nicht wie so viele ein Gewerbe aus dem Worte Gottes ..."
   (p.175).

80 It is misleading, therefore, to limit the nuance to "betrügerisch" or "gewinn-
   süchtig", as Windisch does, *ThWb*, *Bd. 3*, p.607; or to "deceit" and "avarice" as
   done by Hock, *Social Context*, p.53.

81 Text and translation from Kirsopp Lake, *The Apostolic Fathers*, LCL, Vol. I, 1977
   (1912).

in a pejorative sense without the nature of that suspicion being so
well defined that καπηλεύειν itself came to imply a standard criticism.
It thus provided an ideal vehicle for those who wished to call someone
into question who was earning their living from teaching without calling into question the practice of being paid for teaching itself, since
it cast doubt upon the integrity of their being paid and/or their teaching, while at the same time leaving room for the individual author to
supply the content of that criticism. Hence, the question before us,
once it becomes clear that καπηλεύειν cannot be translated "to water
down" or "adulterate", etc. in II Cor. 2:17, as found not only in the
Vulgate[82], but also in the majority of modern commentaries, is twofold.
First, what is the nature of Paul's criticism of those in view, implied
by his use of this market-place imagery and the comparative structure
of 2:17, and second, how does this criticism support his own claim to
be sufficient for the apostolic office? The answers to these questions
can only be determined, of course, on the basis of II Cor. 2:17 itself
and its place within the Corinthian correspondence.

C. THE THEME OF II COR. 2:17 AND ITS PLACE WITHIN
THE CORINTHIAN CORRESPONDENCE

Once it becomes evident that καπηλεύειν refers to the practice of
selling in the market place, Paul's decision to employ this motif to
support his claim to be sufficient for the apostolic ministry, albeit
in a negative way, indicates that the issue in view in II Cor. 2:17 is
again Paul's refusal to seek his financial support from the Corinthian
church. For Paul's insistence in II Cor. 2:17 that he not be classed
with those who are "selling the Word of God" is no doubt intended to
remind the Corinthians of his prior discussion in I Cor. 9, where Paul
had explained in detail the reasons for his refusal to earn his living
from the gospel[83]. At the same time, however, Paul's use of the market-
place motif to describe those with whom he compares himself also points
forward to II Cor. 11 and 12. For the negative connotations which certainly surround καπηλεύειν in this context anticipate the intensely
polemical nature of Paul's later discussion of this theme as part of

---

82 II Cor. 2:17a: non enim sumus sicut plurimi adulterantes verbum Dei.
83 See J. Munck, *Paul and the Salvation of Mankind*, 1977(1959), p.181, who recognized
   that 2:17 referred to the fact that Paul is not a pedlar of God's word and hence
   concluded that "we see, therefore, that the question of Paul's economic indepen-
   dence is an old problem for the Corinthians ...". But as we shall see below, although II Cor. 2:17 does refer back to I Cor. 9, the issue of Paul's decision to
   support himself was an intensification of the "old problem".

his apology for his apostolic ministry in chapters 10-13[84]. As a result, not only the meaning of II Cor. 2:17 itself, but also the organic
relationship in our present context between Paul's view of his suffering, his claim to sufficiency, and his refusal to accept financial support from the Corinthians will only become clear in the light of Paul's
prior discussion of these themes in I Cor. 9 and their resumption in
II Cor. 11:7-21 and 12:12-19[85].

1. I Cor. 9

a. The Function of I Cor. 9 within Paul's Argument in I Cor. 8-10

The first observation to be made concerning I Cor. 9, as well as the
first point of significance for our study, is that Paul's discussion
of his apostolic life-style of self-support in I Cor. 9 is not accorded
an independent status. Instead, rather than being discussed for its
own sake, Paul's discussion in chapter 9 is embedded within, and intended to be an integral part of Paul's larger discussion of the problem in Corinth concerning meat offered to idols, which extends from I
Cor. 8:1 through 11:1[86]. For as the close parallels between Paul's admonitions to the Corinthians in I Cor. 8:9 and 10:24,32 and his own

---

84 Regardless of how it has been understood, the connection between II Cor. 2:17 and
   ch. 10-13 has become a commonplace in modern research. Cf. the various commentaries and the standard studies of II Cor. 10-13 by E. Käsemann, "Die Legitimität
   des Apostels, Eine Untersuchung zu II Korinther 10-13", *ZNW* 41(1942)33-71, pp.
   35f.; 38f.; D. Georgi, *Die Gegner des Paulus im 2. Korintherbrief*, WMANT, Vol. 11,
   1964, pp.110-113, 219-222, 225-227 and C.K. Barrett, "Paul's Opponents in II Corinthians", *NTS* 17(1971)233-254, p.236 and his "ΨΕΥΔΑΠΟΣΤΟΛΟΙ (2 Cor. 11:13)", in
   Mélanges Bibliques, FS R.P. Béda Rigaux, ed. A. Descamps and R.P. André de
   Halleux, 1970, pp. 377-396, pp.384f. The issue here is whether 2:17 relates to the
   polemic against the teaching of Paul's opponents in chs. 10-13 (e.g. 10:5f.; 11:4),
   i.e. if 2:17 is taken to be a contrast to those who "water down" the gospel; or
   to his discussion of his decision to support himself in 11:7-15 and 12:12-19.
85 Those commentators who render καπηλεύειν "adulterate", etc. naturally do not see
   these important parallels. But it is somewhat surprising that neither Bultmann,
   Zweiter Korintherbrief, pp.72-74; Wendland, *An die Korinther*, p.177; Schlatter,
   Bote, pp.499f. or Lietzmann-Kümmel, *An die Korinther*, pp.109, 198f.; all of whom
   correctly reject this interpretation, do not develop these parallels between
   2:17 and Paul's discussion elsewhere in the Corinthian correspondence, though
   Schlatter and Lietzmann do refer to Paul's discussion in II Cor. 11 and 12. Cf.
   too Margaret E. Thrall, "Super-Apostles, Servants of Christ, and Servants of
   Satan", *JSNT* 6(1980)42-57, p.44, who notes the general parallel between II Cor.
   11:7-11/12:13-15 and I Cor. 9, but does not include II Cor. 2:17.
86 This has also been emphasized by G. Dautzenberg in his important article, "Der
   Verzicht auf das apostolische Unterhaltsrecht. Eine exegetische Untersuchung zu
   1 Kor 9", *Biblica* 50(1969)212-232, p.212. David L. Dungan, *The Sayings of Jesus
   in the Churches of Paul*, 1971, pp.5f., points out that the similarity in structure between chs. 8 and 9, "as being integral to his effort to explain and defend the position stated in chapter 8, is not usually noticed". But he fails to
   point out the close connection between chs. 9 and 10. See too Barrett, *First
   Epistle to the Corinthians*, 1968, p.200. For the opposite position, cf. e.g. H.
   Conzelmann, *Der erste Brief an die Korinther*, 1981[2], p.187.

practice as outlined in I Cor. 9:12,18-22 and 10:33 make clear, Paul's
decision not to take advantage of his apostolic right to financial
support was intended to provide an illustration of the ethical principle of love-controlled freedom (cf. 8:1) articulated by Paul as the
solution to the Corinthians' problem (cf. esp. the parallel between I
Cor. 8:9//9:12 and 10:32//9:20-22a)[87]:

Paul's Admonition to the Corinthians	Paul's Own Apostolic Practice
I Cor. 8:9: βλέπετε δὲ μή πως ἡ ἐξουσία ὑμῶν αὕτη	9:12b: οὐκ ἐχρησάμεθα τῇ ἐξουσίᾳ ταύτῃ
I Cor. 8:9: πρόσκομμα γένηται τοῖς ἀσθενέσιν.	9:12d: ἵνα μή τινα ἐγκοπὴν δῶμεν τῷ εὐαγγελίῳ τοῦ Χριστοῦ.
I Cor. 10:32: ἀπρόσκοποι ... (//10:24) γίνεσθε	9:20- 22a: καὶ ἐγενόμην
Ἰουδαίοις	τοῖς Ἰουδαίοις ὡς Ἰουδαῖος τοῖς ὑπὸ νόμον ὡς ὑπὸ νόμον
Ἕλλησιν	τοῖς ἀνόμοις ὡς ἄνομος
τῇ ἐκκλησίᾳ τοῦ θεοῦ	τοῖς ἀσθενέσιν ἀσθενής (summarized in 9:19, 22b)

In a word, those Corinthians who were "strong" in knowledge[88] and hence
felt free to eat such meat were to join Paul in "becoming a slave"
(δουλόω, I Cor. 9:19) to the weaknesses of others in order that, by
not placing undue obstacles in the way of the gospel, as many people
as possible might be saved (cf. I Cor. 8:9, 11, 13; 9:12, 19-22; 10:29,
32). For in Paul's opinion, "the love which edifies" (8:1) does not
insist upon its own rights, but is willing "to do all things for the
sake of the gospel" (9:23)[89], whether this means giving up the right
to earn one's living from the gospel in Paul's case, or refusing to

---

87 R.F. Hock, *Social Context*, pp.60f. appropriately refers to this as the "paradigmatic function" of ch. 9, which he summarizes by saying, "just as Paul had not
exercised his right to be supported (cf. 9:6) in order not to hinder the gospel
in any way (v.12), so the Corinthians were encouraged to waive their right to
eat meat offered to idols in order not to offend any weaker brother (see esp.
8:9)". Most recently, see Gerd Lüdemann, *Paulus, der Heidenapostel, Bd II*,
FRLANT Nr. 130, 1983, p.110, who on the basis of the chiastic structure of
I Cor. 9 concludes that it is to be understood as an "Illustration des in 1Kor
8 ausgesprochenen Gedankens der Rücksicht gegenüber dem schwachen Bruder ...".
However, neither Hock nor Lüdemann stress the relationship between I Cor. 9 and
10.

88 For the content of this "knowledge", cf. the creedal statement in I Cor. 8:6 and
the implications Paul draws from it in 8:4f. and 7.

89 For the importance of this Pauline principle for other aspects of church life,
cf. I Cor. 14:3-5,12,17,19,26; Rom. 14:9; 15:2. It is significant, therefore,
that in II Cor. 10:8 and 13:10 Paul interprets his own apostolic authority as
having been given to him by God for the purpose of building up the church (εἰς
οἰκοδομήν), and that he defends his boasting in chs. 10-13, which is not an
apology(!), by asserting that, in reality, he has been speaking "ὑπὲρ τῆς ὑμῶν
οἰκοδομῆς" (II Cor. 12:19). We will return to the function and significance of
this motif within Paul's defense below.

exercise one's right to eat meat offered to idols in the case of the
Corinthians[90]. Hence, Paul can point to his own apostolic life-style
as the paradigmatic example of the embodiment of this ethic of love
since it is orientated to the spreading of the gospel and, as a result
of this orientation, is also determined by the weakness of others[91].
As Paul summarized it in I Cor. 9:22: "I have become all things to all
men, that I may by all means save some"[92].

But, in addition to illustrating the ethic Paul proposed, it is
equally important to realize that Paul also intended his apostolic
life-style to be an authoritative standard for his churches. This is
evidenced in I Corinthians not only by the parallels indicated above,
but also by the reoccurrence of the "imitate me" motif in I Cor. 10:32-
11:1. For given his authority as the father of the Corinthian church[93],
and his conviction that his life as an apostle conforms to the life of
the crucified Christ[94], Paul can thus conclude his discussion of the
important ethical principle outlined in I Cor. 8-10 with the admonition:

> Give no offense either to Jews or to Greeks or to the Church of God; *just as
> I also* (καθὼς κἀγὼ) please all men in all things, not seeking my own profit,
> but the profit of the many, that they may be saved. Be imitators of me, *just
> as I also* (καθὼς κἀγὼ) am of Christ (10:32-11:1, NASV, emphasis mine).[95]

The significance of these observations concerning the function of I
Cor. 9 and its parallels in II Thessalonians for determining the larger
context of our passage lies in the light they shed on the status of

---

90 See Dautzenberg, "Verzicht", p.220, who also concludes that "der letzte Grund für
den Verzicht liegt aber in der Hingabe an das Evangelium Jesu Christi, in dem Be-
streben, jedes mögliche Hindernis, das seinen Siegeszug durch die Welt hemmen
würde, fernzuhalten (vgl. Röm. 14:13). Die erst in 10:23, 33 genannte Kategorie
des συμφέρει bzw. des τὸ τῶν πολλῶν σύμφορον könnte sachgemäß schon hier zur Ver-
deutlichung der positiven Begründung eingeführt werden".

91 As E. Käsemann put it in his now classic article on I Cor. 9:15-18, "Eine paulinische Variation des 'amor Fati'", in *Exegetische Versuche und Besinnungen, Bd.
2*, 1970³, pp.223-239 (= *ZThK* 56(1959)138-154), p.224, the point of chapter 9 is
that "Paulus gegenüber Enthusiasten an seinem persönlichen Verzicht den Grund-
satz exemplifiziert, daß die Liebe der christlichen Freiheit Schranken zieht".

92 Although it is beyond the scope of our present study, it is important to note
that Paul's argument in I Cor. 8:1-11:1 is strikingly similar to the argument
in II Thess. 3:6-15, where Paul's work and practice of self-support is pointed
to as a "model" for the church to follow (3:7, 9b) and of the "tradition" which
the Thessalonians had received (3:6f.). It seems that Paul's practice of working
to support himself constituted an important part of his regular catechetical instruction (see 3:10).

93 Cf. I Cor. 3:10; 4:14-16 (where Paul's authority as the father of the Corinthian
church also leads to the command, "Become imitators of me"); 9:2; II Cor. 10:14
and 11:2.

94 So too Dautzenberg, "Verzicht", p.224, who concludes that Paul's refusal to be
paid and the "resultierende harte Arbeit" is to be understood "als Teil der besonderen Beziehung des Apostels zum Leiden Christi".

95 Again, see the similar way in which Paul's example to the Thessalonians in II
Thess. 3 functions to support the strong commands given in II Thess. 3:6 and 12,
which here too are related to the authority of Christ himself.

Paul's apostolic authority at the time of writing of I Corinthians. For
the very fact that Paul can enlist his practice of preaching the gospel
free of charge to support his larger hortatory purpose in chapters 8-
10 indicates that at the time of the writing of I Corinthians, as in
II Thessalonians[96], Paul's apostolic life-style of self-support was
still being held in high esteem among the Corinthians themselves[97].
In other words, rather than being seen to be in conflict with Paul's
apostolic authority, his refusal to accept financial support from his
church was still being taken to be an appropriate expression of Paul's
standing and authority as an apostle. For if this had not been the case,
Paul's larger argument in chapters 8-10, based as it is on his own example (cf. esp. 11:1), would have collapsed. This is not to suggest
that Paul intended the unusual character of his decision to support
himself to be taken for granted by the Corinthians. Paul's contrast between his own practice and that of "the rest of the apostles, and the
brothers of the Lord, and Cephas" (I Cor. 9:5), together with the theological and practical significance for his own ministry which Paul
attaches to this practice in 9:12 and 9:15-22, not to mention its "paradigmatic function" for the Corinthians, all indicate the vital importance of this aspect of his apostolic ministry - both for himself and
for his church. But it is to suggest that here too we encounter evidence that at the writing of I Corinthians Paul's authority as an a-
postle was still basically accepted in Corinth. Thus, Paul expected
the rhetorical questions of I Cor. 9:1 to be answered affirmatively
and without hesitation[98]. He could also count on the fact that his
statement in 9:2 would be accepted as adequately representing the state

---

96 E.g. Bruce, *Thessalonians*, p.xxvii, concludes from the evidence that Paul's relations to the Thessalonian and Macedonian churches "were outstandingly happy".
   If II Thess. is deutero-Pauline (which I doubt), this impression is simply
   strengthened, since one hardly writes in the name of someone whose authority is
   disputed.
97 Contra G. Dautzenberg, "Verzicht", p.213, who argues that ch. 9 is a response to
   criticism from the Corinthians, "die dem Paulus Selbstsucht bei der Missionierung
   und Leitung der Gemeinde vorwarfen, die vielleicht auch an seiner Schwachheit und
   an den Eigenheiten seiner Person und seines Schicksals Anstoss nahmen". The idea
   that in I Cor. 9 Paul must defend himself before the Corinthians is, of course,
   very widespread in recent literature. To give just one representative position,
   cf. Ch. Wolff, *Der erste Brief des Paulus an die Korinther, 2. Teil*, ThHK VII/2,
   1982, p.19, who then goes on to relate this controversy to the fact that Paul
   worked with his hands to support himself, which "war schon überhaupt für Griechen ... eines freien Bürgers unwürdig" so that "Man wird dies als Argument benutzt haben, von den Apostolat des Paulus in Frage zu stellen (vgl. auch 15,1-11)"
   (p.19). But it is by no means clear how representative this negative view of the
   craftsman in antiquity actually was, since it seems to be confined to the extremely small upper class. See below, p.137 and Sirach 38:24-34!
98 Although commentators emphasize that these rhetorical questions function to support Paul's apostolic authority, it is not often pointed out that Paul raises
   these questions precisely *because* he knows how they will be answered, not because
   he must argue for his legitimacy. Cf. Schlatter, *Bote*, p.270; Lietzmann, *An die*

of affairs in Corinth at the time the letter was received: even if
Paul's apostleship was being called into question *elsewhere*, Paul could
be sure that his apostolic authority was basically still intact in Corinth. For as we saw above in our discussion of I Cor. 4, the problems
in Corinth at the time of the writing of I Corinthians were not essentially problems between Paul and his church, but rather problems of
strife within the church. The crucial point, therefore, is to see that,
on the one hand, Paul *distinguishes* in 9:2 between how the Corinthians
will react and how the "others" respond to his claim to be an apostle,
while, on the other hand, the subject matter of 9:4ff. and 9:1 are *not*
identical. In 9:1f. the question concerns *whether or not* Paul is an a-
postle, while in 9:4ff. the question concerns the rights of those who
are apostles[99]. This means, however, that Paul's "defense" in I Cor.
9:3ff. (cf. ἀπολογία in 9:3) actually served a *double* function. For the
Corinthians who accepted the authority of Paul's apostleship and the
propriety of Paul's practice of self-support, Paul's arguments in support of the right of earning one's living from the gospel in I Cor. 9
served as the background necessary to demonstrate that Paul's own decision not to exercise this right was the perfect illustration of the
ethical principle of love Paul advocated[100]. This explains why Paul
must argue so extensively for the legitimacy of this right in I Cor.
9:7-14 even though it was not itself a point of contention between Paul
and his church. In contrast, the many commentators who see I Cor. 9:4-
14 to be a defense of Paul's apostolic authority against those who
criticized Paul for *not* being paid must explain why Paul argues so extensively for this right, when, if he was being attacked for not being
paid, it would merely add to his problems! The point of Paul's argument
in 9:4-14 is rather that apostles, as such, have this right (not Paul
alone), and that, *as a result*, Paul shares it more than anyone else in
the case of the Corinthians, since, as the one who founded the church
in Corinth, he is specifically *their* apostle (cf. 9:1f; 12). Thus,

---

Korinther, p.39; Barrett, *First Corinthians*, pp.200f.; Conzelmann, *Der erste
Brief an die Korinther*, pp.187ff.; Ch. Wolff, *Der erste Brief ... an die Korinther*, p.20, who points out that Paul expects a positive answer, but goes on to
conclude, "Paulus ist sich aber bewußt, daß sein Apostolat von Korinthern be-
zweifelt wird, und verweist deshalb auf das entscheidende Charakteristikum eines
Apostels ..."; and most recently, G. Lüdemann, *Paulus, der Heidenapostel, Bd. II*,
pp.79 and 108f., where he identifies the themes of 9:4ff. with Paul's rhetorical
questions in 9:1.

99 Contra Lüdemann, *Paulus, Bd. II*, pp.108f. and most commentators, who fail to make
this distinction.

100 As von Campenhausen, *Die Begründung kirchlicher Entscheidungen beim Apostel
Paulus*, 1957, p.11n.15 observed, Paul's purpose in 9:4-14 was to "set forth
his well-known decision not to accept support from his congregations in a new,
explicitly 'pedagogical' interpretation" (quoted from Dungan, *Sayings of Jesus*,
p.13), though von Campenhausen saw this to be the sole purpose of Paul's argument
(see Dungan, p.13).

Paul's entire argument rests on the fact that the validity of Paul's
apostleship is assumed. Paul's burden is not to argue for the legitimacy of his apostleship, but to show that this apostleship, *by definition*, meant that he had the right to be paid for his ministry.

For the "others" (cf. ἄλλοις, 9:2) who were questioning Paul's
apostleship, Paul's argument served to demonstrate that even though Paul
did not make use of his apostolic rights to financial support, that he
nevertheless included himself within the category of those who possessed
this right (cf. 9:4-6). His reason for doing so was the existence
of the Corinthian church itself (cf. 9:2b; 12a) -- sure evidence that
he too performed the work characteristic of an apostle (cf. 9:11,14)[101].
The weight of Paul's "apology" thus rests on his relationship to the
Corinthian church, not on his argument for the right to be paid. Hence,
Paul's ἀπολογία in I Cor. 9 not only provided the Corinthians with a
powerful *a-fortiori* inducement to obey Paul's injunctions in I Cor.
8-11:1 (i.e. "if our apostle, to whom we owe our very lives as Christians (cf. 9:11), has given up his "rights", how much more ought we to
give up ours!"), but it also provided his supporters with the ammunition
they needed to defend their apostle from those who might use his practice of self-support to attack his authority (cf. II Cor. 5:12 for this
same purpose). For we should not underestimate the fact that in I Cor.
9:2 the contrast is not between various groups from within the church,
but between the Corinthians as a whole and the "others" who question
Paul's authority[102].

Thus, Paul's mode of argumentation in I Cor. 8-11:1 is parallel to
and based upon the same presuppositions as his previous argument in I
Cor. 3:1-4:16 (see above, pp.65ff.). For as we have seen above, Paul
supported his prior plea that the Corinthians not become arrogant in
their relationships with one another, as reflected in the party-strife
currently existing in Corinth (cf. 3:3, 18, 21; 4:6f.), by pointing to
the theological significance of his own apostolic suffering (cf. 4:6,
14). In 8:1-11:1, Paul's response to this same underlying problem of
arrogance (cf. 8:1), now manifested in the indiscriminate eating of
meat offered to idols, is likewise supported by an aspect of his own
apostolic experience, i.e. his decision to offer the gospel without
charge, which we will see in a moment is also part of his suffering as
an apostle. Thus, in both instances, Paul's exhortations to the Corin-

---

101 Schlatter, *Bote*, p.270, summarized this point well: "Daß ... die Korinther selbst
die Bestätigung seines Apostolats sind, das ist die endgültige Abwehr aller gegen
ihn gerichteten Angriffe". We will return to this point in chapter five.

102 So too H. Conzelmann, *Der erste Brief an die Korinther*, p.188, who observes concerning I Cor. 9:3 that "Die Ausdrucksweise läßt darauf schließen, daß die
ἀνακρίνοντες (noch) außerhalb der Gemeinde von Korinth stehen".

thians can be based upon and illustrated by his own apostolic way of
life. And in both instances, Paul is able to do so because his experience as an apostle is still accepted as an appropriate expression of
his apostolic authority, which itself remains common ground between
Paul and the Corinthians[103]. It is not surprising, therefore, that
Paul can conclude *both* of these arguments with the same admonition:
"imitate me" (cf. 4:16; 11:1).

b. *The Structure of Paul's Argument in I Cor. 9*

The second point of significance to be drawn from I Cor. 9 for our
study derives from the structure of Paul's argument itself. For a closer
investigation of the reasons Paul adduces for his decision not to
avail himself of his apostolic right to financial support reveals that
Paul's refusal to earn his living from the gospel is intended to be
seen as a sign of his *love* for the Corinthians[104], as evidenced by his
voluntary decision to *suffer* for them. In I Cor. 9:12, the fact that
Paul refuses to exercise his right to be supported by the Corinthians
(cf. 9:11) means, by contrast, that he "endures all things" (ἀλλὰ πάντα
στέγομεν)[105]. In the light of what Paul has just said in I Cor. 4:12,
where the fact that Paul "labors, working with his own hands" is listed
as part of his *Peristasenkatalog*[106], it is natural to understand the
πάντα of 9:12 to refer primarily to those hardships and sufferings
which resulted from Paul supporting himself[107]. This is confirmed by

---

103 This is also the conclusion of J.D.G. Dunn in his recent study, "The Responsible
Congregation (1 Cor. 14:26-40)", in *Charisma und Agape (1 Ko 12-14)*, 1983, pp.201-
236, pp.230f.: "At all events it is clear enough that at least a significant
section of the church in Corinth, presumably those converted during Paul's initial
visit and so the founding members of the church, were ready to acknowledge Paul's
authority as apostle (I Cor. 9:1-2). And the reference of the various issues to
him, which provided the occasions for I Corinthians, provides sufficient proof
that Paul's authority with respect to the Corinthian church was widely recognized by the Corinthian believers".
104 See Dautzenberg, "Verzicht", pp.222-224, where he also stresses that from Paul's
perspective his refusal to be paid was a sign of his love for the church.
105 So again, Dautzenberg, "Verzicht", pp.219-220 and 220n.1, who translates στέγομεν
"aushalten" or "ertragen" on the basis of the similar ideas in II Cor. 6:3f. and
I Cor. 4:12. This meaning is also clearly evidenced by its use in I Thess. 3:1
and 5; see F.F. Bruce, *1 and 2 Thessalonians*, p.60.
106 That Paul works to support himself in his preaching of the gospel is also listed
as part of his other catalogs of suffering in II Cor. 6:1-10 (see v.5) and II
Cor. 11:23-33 (see vv.23 and 27).
107 In addition, as Dautzenberg, "Verzicht", p.224 has once again insightfully
pointed out, the fact that Paul includes his work as part of those experiences
which comprise his "being condemned to death" in I Cor. 4:9ff. is not at all
strange given Paul's anthropology. In his words, "Die enge Zusammenschau von
Leiden und ständiger Arbeit ist gerade im Horizont des jüdischen Menschenbildes
möglich: in beiden Bereichen geht es um den Einsatz der ψυχή, des Lebens, um den
Verzicht auf Lebensgenuss und Lebensfreude und damit jüdisch-semitisch um Todes-
nähe" (this conclusion is based on his major work, *Sein Leben Bewahren*, 1966,
pp.114-123).

what we know about the actual experience of the itinerant, small-scale hand-worker or artisan in the ancient world. For as Hock has recently pointed out, many of the difficult sufferings and hardships listed by Paul in I Cor. 4:11-13 were the common lot of the traveling craftsmen of Paul's day[108]. Hence, Paul's statement in I Cor. 9:12 that his lack of support by the Corinthians necessitated that he "endure" the many hardships associated with trying to support oneself by working with one's hands would not have struck Paul's readers as strange. But that he would do so *voluntarily*, when he, more than anyone else, possessed the "right" or "authority" (ἐξουσία) to be supported by the Corinthians (cf. I Cor. 9:11-12a) would have been striking indeed. As such, the adversative relationship between Paul's right to support on the one hand (9:12a), and his decision to suffer instead of exercising this right on the other hand (9:12b), provides a powerful foundation for Paul's overall argument in I Cor. 8:1-11:1.

But, as indicated by the ἵνα-clause of I Cor. 9:12d itself, it also raises the question of Paul's personal purpose or motive for embracing such suffering. In Paul's words, he "endures all things", ἵνα μή τινα ἐγκοπὴν δῶμεν τῷ εὐαγγελίῳ τοῦ Χριστοῦ. The parallels between this statement and Paul's prior statements in I Cor. 8:9 and 13 (πρόσκομμα// σκανδαλίζω//ἐγκοπή) make it clear that by ἐγκοπή in 9:12d Paul is referring to those things, which, although legitimate in and of themselves, would nevertheless hinder the progress of the gospel and therefore ought to be avoided διὰ τὸ εὐαγγέλιον (9:23a). In the Corinthians' case, this meant not eating meat which had been offered to idols in the presence of those Christians whose consciences were still "weak" (8:10-12), and in front of those unbelievers for whom idol worship was still a reality (10:27-28)[109]. In Paul's case, this meant, among other things, offering the gospel "free of charge" (cf. ἀδάπανος, 9:18).

It cannot be emphasized too strongly, however, that for Paul, this conscious decision to adapt oneself to the weakness of others for the sake of the gospel was not merely a matter of pragmatic mission strategy[110], though it of course aims to facilitate the spreading of the gos-

---

108 *The Social Context of Paul's Ministry, Tentmaking and Apostleship*, 1980, pp.35-37,60,78n.17,84n.94 and cf. p.28 in reference to II Cor. 11:27.

109 Conversely, it must also be emphasized that the position of the "weak" did not involve, from Paul's perspective, "sin", and thus could be tolerated, in contrast to the problems cited in I Cor. 5:1-5; 6:15-20 and 11:17-22. Cf. W. Schrage, *Ethik des Neuen Testaments, Grundrisse zum NT, NTD Ergänzungsreihe, Bd. 4*, 1982, p.186: "Zunächst ist daran zu erinnern, daß es sich bei den Divergenzen in 1 Kor. 8-10 und Röm. 14-15 von keinen fundamentalen Fragen der Lebensführung handelt und Paulus eine Gewissensentscheidung, die etwa Gottes Gebot überspränge, kaum toleriert hätte".

110 G. Eichholz, *Die Theologie des Paulus im Umriß*, 1977², p.49 makes this same point and raises the important exegetical question: "Was bedeutet das, wenn es sich nicht im Sinn einer Technik verstehen läßt, wenn es über alles Technische weit

pel (cf. 9:19-22)[111]. Instead, as we have already pointed out above,
Paul's decision to support himself, like his admonitions to the "strong"
in Corinth, is grounded in the fact that do so is to walk in the way
that surpasses all other ways (καθ᾽ ὑπερβολὴν ὁδόν, I Cor. 12:31),
namely, that of Christian "love" (cf. 8:1). It is not simply a coincidence, therefore, that the same contrast between knowledge/arrogance
and love, with which Paul opens his discussion of the issue of meat offered to idols in 8:1, is also found in Paul's definition of love in I
Cor. 13:2 and 4; or that Paul uses the same formulation to describe
love in I Cor. 13:7 that he uses to describe his own practice of self-
support in I Cor. 9:12: love "endures all things" (πάντα στέγει). For
Paul intends his own example of self-support to be seen as an embodiment
of that same Christian principle of love which he is admonishing the Corinthians to follow. It thus becomes crucial for understanding Paul's
apostolic self-conception, as well as for an understanding of his ethical admonitions in general, to realize that Paul saw his own decision
to "become all things to all men" (I Cor. 9:22) to be an extension of
the basic ethical principle, "Let no one seek his own (good), but that
of his neighbor" (I Cor. 10:24). For inasmuch as this mode of behavior
was to be equated with love (cf. I Cor. 13:4f.: ἡ ἀγάπη ... οὐ ζητεῖ τὰ
ἑαυτῆς!), it was the only behavior appropriate to the gospel itself.
Hence, for Paul, the way to avoid causing a hindrance to the gospel
was to embody that gospel by following the ethic of love, as illustrated by his own refusal to exercise his right to support from the Corinthians. In other words, I Cor. 9:12, 19 (and its explication in 9:20-
21) and 22 all interpret one another. Paul's decision to support himself (i.e. to endure all things) is an *outworking* of his desire to
"make himself a slave to all", or "to become all things to all men";
while his purpose in doing so, i.e. that he might not place a hindrance

---

hinausgreift?" He answers this question in terms of Paul's commitment to do
everything for the sake of the gospel. For Eichholz's own specific definition of
what this means, cf. pp.50-55, in which for him the key concept also becomes
Paul's "Intention der Liebe", which he sees as "der Schlüssel zur Interpretation
des ganzen Kanons seines missionarischen Handelns" (p.55).

111 Despite the many insights which G. Theißen brings to this text, I remain uncon-
vinced concerning his central thesis that I Cor. 9 reflects a conflict between
two basic types of missionary practice, the "Wandercharismatiker" and the "Ge-
meindeorganisatoren", rooted in the Palestinian "Jesusbewegung" and the Hellenistic Gentile mission respectively. See his "Legitimation und Lebensunterhalt.
Ein Beitrag zur Soziologie urchristlicher Missionare", in his *Studien zur Soziologie des Urchristentums*, WUNT 19, 1979, pp.201-230, pp.202, 211, 213f. Theißen's
thesis cannot do justice to Paul's positive argument for his right to be paid
in 9:4-14, which Theißen can only describe as "merkwürdig" given his supposition
that Paul is being criticized in Corinth for his practice. In short, Theißen
seems to fall prey to the temptation to read opposition into Paul's argument
where it does not exist.

in the way of the gospel, is an expression of his goal "to win the more", or "save some", or as Paul summarizes it in 9:23a: to do all things διὰ τὸ εὐαγγέλιον:

Ground Clause	Purpose Clause
9:12: ἀλλὰ πάντα στέγομεν	ἵνα μή τινα ἐγκοπὴν δῶμεν τῷ εὐαγγελίῳ τοῦ Χριστοῦ
9:19: πᾶσιν ἐμαυτὸν ἐδούλωσα	ἵνα τοὺς πλείονας κερδήσω
9:22: τοῖς πᾶσιν γέγονα πάντα	ἵνα πάντως τινὰς σώσω

And the adversative relationship which exists between Paul's decision, expressed in the ground clauses of 9:12, 19 and 22 and his "apostolic" "rights", referred to in 9:4, 5, 12a and 19a, indicates that these purpose clauses are to be taken as an expression of Paul's love for the Corinthians[112]. Thus, although I agree with Ronald F. Hock that I Cor. 9:19 must be interpreted in the light of the preceding verses, I am not convinced that the main point of his article is correct, namely, that ἐμαυτὸν ἐδούλωσα ought to be viewed exclusively in the light of what precedes[113]. That is to say, for Hock, I Cor. 9:19 refers specifically to the fact that Paul worked with his hands in a trade and thus reflects "the snobbish and scornful attitude so typical of upper class Greeks and Romans"[114]. In Hock's view, in speaking of "enslaving himself", Paul is thus referring to the fact that his trade made him appear "slavish", since "by entering the workshop he had brought about a considerable loss of status ..."[115]. In his later study, *The Social Context of Paul's Ministry, Tentmaking and Apostleship*, Hock then goes on to argue that ἐλεύθερος in I Cor. 9:19 refers to the fact that Paul "was economically dependent on no one ..."[116]. Hence, Hock interprets 9:19 to mean, "He could be economically independent only by plying a slavish trade ..."[117]. The main problem with Hock's view is that Paul explicitly says that he has made himself a slave πᾶσιν. From the context it seems clear, therefore, that what Paul has in mind is his decision to become ὑπὸ νόμον, ἄνομος and ἀσθενής for the sake of the gospel (vv.20-22), in which the πᾶσιν of v. 19 is further defined. Furthermore, the question must be asked whether Paul's argument would be served by demeaning the very work in which the majority of the Corinthians themselves were probably engaged(!)[118], especially when this would only intensify the conflicts between the various

---

112 That Paul intended the Corinthians to understand his refusal to accept support to be an expression of his love for them is further confirmed by the parallel structure of Paul's argument in I Thess. 2:7-9. Here Paul's decision to support himself is also the visible sign or outworking of his love for his church (2:7c), since it was his love which motivated his willingness to do so (2:8a,c). And here too, Paul is able to argue that his suffering (cf. 2:2 with 2:8b and 9) is a sign of his love for the Thessalonians only because the hardships involved in supporting himself were endured *in spite of the fact* that, as an apostle of Christ, Paul had every right to be supported by them (2:7a). Hence, Paul's hardships were suffered as a result of his voluntary decision not to demand support for his preaching. Thus his working day and night can only be taken as an expression of Paul's love for his church.

113 "Paul's Tentmaking and the Problems of His Social Class", *JBL* 97(1978)555-564, p.558.

114 "Tentmaking", p.562.

115 "Tentmaking", pp.559f. See the evidence listed by Hock for this view. His key text is Cicero, *De off.* I.150.

116 *Social Context*, p.61.

117 *Social Context*, p.61.

118 See Wayne A. Meeks, *The First Urban Christians, The Social World of the Apostle Paul*, 1983, pp.51-73, who argues convincingly that "the 'typical' Christian ... the one who most often signals his presence in the letters by one or another small clue, is a free artisan or small trader" (p.73).

social levels which already existed in Corinth as it was[119]. Moreover, although in Paul's day artisans and small traders were often high in income, but low in occupational prestige, Paul's own very positive admonitions concerning working with one's hands in I Thess. 4:11f. (see too II Thess. 3:10-12 and Eph. 4:28) would seem to belie Hock's emphasis on Paul's "snobbish" attitude. In addition, M. Rostovtzeff has pointed out that in the Roman and Hellenistic periods, retail traders were, in fact, one step below the upper class, together with teachers, doctors, etc. and formed the "backbone of municipal life"[121]. To be a member of this working class (not *lower* class!) need not, therefore, necessarily carry negative connotations. It has also been questioned how representative this "snobbish" attitude of the upper class towards the working class actually was[122]. Hence, as MacMullen stresses, when we read statements such as that found in Cicero, *De off.* I.150, which demean those engaged in the trades and retail dealing, we must bear in mind that this is the judgment of the small, rich minority and that it was based on the conviction that poverty was vile, dishonorable and ugly, and that only the rich could afford to be honest[123], a presupposition certainly foreign to Paul. Finally, the "snobbish" attitude Hock attributes to Paul also seems to be out of place in the light of the positive Jewish view of labor reflected in Aboth 2:2. Hock objects that this source is late, but it is no more remote than the writings of Cicero. It seems best, therefore, to see Paul's decision to support himself to be an application of his more basic principle of becoming a slave "to (the consciences) of all" and to interpret his "freedom" in terms of the ἐξουσία in view in chapters 8-10 (cf. 8:9//10:29)[124].

c. *The Nature of Paul's Boast in I Cor. 9:15-18*

This brings us to our third and final point concerning Paul's argument in I Cor. 9, namely, the nature of Paul's καύχημα as outlined in I Cor. 9:15-18. For inasmuch as Paul's decision not to earn his living from the gospel is to be taken, from the perspective of the Corinthi-

---

119 This has been pointed out in the various works of G. Theißen. See in his collection *Studien zur Soziologie des Urchristentums*, "Legitimation", pp.226-229; his entire essay "Die Starken und Schwachen in Korinth. Soziologische Analyse eines theologischen Streites", pp.272-289 and his "Soziale Schichtung in der korinthischen Gemeinde. Ein Beitrag zur Soziologie des hellenistischen Urchristentums", pp.231-271, esp. pp.231, 267.

120 What is technically called "high status inconsistency (low status crystallization)", see Meeks, *Urban Christians*, p.73; see pp.61,65.

121 *The Social and Economic History of the Roman Empire, Vol. I*, 2nd. rev.ed. by P.M. Fraser, 1966, p.190.

122 See Ramsay MacMullen, *Roman Social Relations 50 B.C. to A.D. 284*, 1974, pp.88-91.

123 *Roman Social Relations*, pp.115-117 and 199-200nn.90 and 91, esp. his reference to the attitude of the slave Trimalchio, the custom of advertising one's occupation on one's tombstone and the quotation from Petronius, *Satyricon* 29. See too J.H.W.G. Liebeschuetz, *Antioch: City and Imperial Administration in the later Roman Empire*, 1972, pp.52f., who refers to Libanius' very positive view of shopkeepers. For the view that Cicero's judgment was representative, see besides Hock, M.I. Finely, *The Ancient Economy*, 1973, pp.45-54, 60, 122.

124 Meeks, *Urban Christians*, p.61, also accepts Hock's view that Paul's manner of talking about his work resembles that found among the higher social levels, but he expresses himself very cautiously in simply concluding that Paul's decision to do menial work was thus "something worthy of comment". He doesn't refer to I Cor. 9:19 at all. If Paul did share an upper class attitude towards work, this would naturally make his working even more striking to the Corinthians, but there does not seem to be a basis for concluding that Paul refers to his work as such as "slavish".

ans, as an indication and demonstration of Paul's love for them, it
also becomes, from Paul's perspective, an aspect of his apostolic ministry about which he can "boast" and for which he will be recompensed[125].
This becomes clear from the structure of Paul's argument in verses 15-
18. In 9:15a, Paul wants to eliminate the possibility that the Corinthians might take his extended defense of the legitimacy of being paid
as an apostle in 9:6-14 to be a hidden plea that he too now be paid by
the Corinthians for the preaching the gospel. For as the anacoluthon
in 9:15b makes clear, there is nothing more important to Paul, even his
very life, than the fact that he offers his gospel free of charge. The
reason for the almost inconceivable weight which Paul thus attaches to
his practice of self-support lies in his understanding of this practice
as his "boast" (καύχημα), which would be "nullified" or "invalidated"
(κενόω) should someone pay him for his ministry[126]. Hence, Paul would
rather die than lose this "boast", because, as verses 16 and 17 point
out (cf. the γάρ of v.16), the fact that Paul preaches *per se* cannot,
in Paul's case, be a ground for boasting in and of itself (9:16a: ἐὰν
γὰρ εὐαγγελίζωμαι, οὐκ ἔστιν μοι καύχημα).

The reason for this surprising, and by no means self-evident, statement lies in Paul's self-conception as an apostle[127], which in our context is expressed in terms of the "necessity" or "constraint" (ἀνάγκη)
laid upon Paul to preach (9:16b)[128]. For as often pointed out[129], in

---

125 The connection between Paul's argument concerning his ministry to the Corinthians
　　in the rest of ch. 9 and his own reward as an apostle in vv.15-18 becomes clear
　　once the former is recognized to be the basis for the latter. In fact, E. Käse-
　　mann, "Variation", p.224, questions "ob die Merkwürdigkeiten des Texts etwa
　　Indiz einer ungewöhnlich bedeutsamen Aussage und vielleicht sogar der Sachmitte
　　des ganzen Kapitels sind?" See too Dautzenberg, "Verzicht", p.213.
126 For this meaning of κενόω in I Cor. 1:17; 9:15; II Cor. 9:3 and Rom. 4:14 cf. A.
　　Oepke, art. κενός κ.τ.λ., *TDNT, Vol. III*, 1965, pp.659-662, pp.661f.
127 See Dautzenberg, "Verzicht", p.221, who entitles his discussion of I Cor. 9:15b-
　　18: "Der Verzicht auf das Unterhaltsrecht als konkrete Darstellung des paulinischen
　　Amtsverständnisses und als Kennzeichen der paulinischen Mission". On I Cor. 9:16
　　as a statement reflecting Paul's call and/or self-conception, cf. P. Stuhlmacher,
　　Das paulinische Evangelium, Bd. I, 1968, pp.87., 246; J.Chr. Beker, *Paul*, p.7;
　　G. Eichholz, *Theologie*, pp.39f.; J. Munck, *Paul*, pp.22, 40f.; and H. Conzelmann,
　　Erster Korintherbrief, p.194, 194n.6.
128 For the meaning of ἀνάγκη as "necessity" or "constraint" elsewhere in Paul, cf.
　　Rom. 13:5; I Cor. 7:37; II Cor. 9:7; Philem. 14; and in the rest of the NT, Mtt.
　　18:7; Lk. 14:18; Heb. 7:12; 7:27; 9:16; 9:23 and Jude 3. Cf. also II Macc. 6:7;
　　15:2 and III Macc. 4:9; 5:6. In the LXX it is usually used, however, in the sense
　　of the constraint laid upon one due to suffering or distress and thus comes to
　　mean simply "distress" or "tribulation", etc. See I Ki. 22:2; Job 5:19; 15:24;
　　Ps. 24(25):17; 106(107):6, 13; Jer. 9:15, etc. This meaning is also found in Paul
　　(I Cor. 7:26; II Cor. 6:4; 12:10; I Thess. 3:7) and in Luke 21:23.
129 As Käsemann, "Variation", p.234, points out, this analogy to the prophets is the
　　"nächste Parallele" (see p.234n.71 for other literature). For this understanding
　　of I Cor. 9:16 and the idea that Paul's understanding of his call and message
　　correspond to the OT call and message of the prophets in general, see now C.
　　Wolff, *Der erste Brief ... an die Korinther*, p.29 and most recently, P. Stuhl-
　　macher, "Das paulinische Evangelium", pp.160, 179. On Paul's prophetic self-

speaking of the "constraint" laid upon him, Paul is portraying his own
apostolic experience of preaching the gospel in terms of the experience
of those OT prophets who felt compelled to deliver the divine message
entrusted to them, regardless of their own desire, or lack of desire,
to do so[130]. As W. Grundmann put it, "In this office Paul has the same
experience as the prophets; he is under a divine constraint which he
cannot escape"[131]. The "ἀνάγκη" Paul refers to in 9:16 is not to be
equated, therefore, with the inescapable "necessity" of an impersonal
fate[132], but is rather the "necessity" or "constraint" which results
from the call of God itself[133]. The statement in I Cor. 9:16 thus reflects Paul's understanding of his "conversion-call" in which, according to Galatians 1:15f., the revelation of God's Son was inextricably
linked with Paul's call to *preach* Christ among the Gentiles (cf. the
ἵνα of Gal. 1:16b: ἵνα εὐαγγελίζωμαι αὐτὸν ἐν τοῖς ἔθνεσιν). Hence,
Paul understood his call to preach the gospel to be part and parcel of
his "conversion" to Christ[134]. In other words, Paul was not first call-

___

understanding in general, see already A.D. Nock, *St. Paul*, 1938, p.65; J. Munck,
Paul, pp.25f., 36; Otto Betz, "Die Vision des Paulus im Tempel von Jerusalem.
Apg. 22:17-21 als Beitrag zur Deutung des Damaskuserlebnisses", in *Verborum
Veritas, FS Gustav Stählin zum 70. Geburtstag*, 1970, pp.113-123, pp.117-119; J.
Chr. Beker, *Paul*, p.10 and his discussion of Paul's prophetic self-understanding
on pp.115-118 and finally the article by Traugott Holtz, "Zum Selbstverständnis
des Apostels Paulus", *ThLZ* 91(1966)322-330, esp. pp.323f.

130 The classic example of this is Jeremiah's lament in Jer. 20:9; but see also Jer.
4:19; Is. 21:3; Amos 3:8; Micah 3:8 and the "hand of God" motif in Is. 8:11;
10:1; 28:2; Jer. 15:17; Ez. 3:14, 24; 37:1, which, as Abraham J. Heschel, *The
Prophets*, 1962, p.444 points out, "is the name the prophet uses to describe the
urgency, pressure, and compulsion by which he is stunned and overwhelmed ...".
For Heschel's excellent summary of the prophetic compulsion, see p.444. That
this idea was also present elsewhere in the early church is shown by the parallel idea in Acts 4:20.

131 Art. ἀναγκάζω κ.τ.λ., *TDNT, Vol. I*, 1964, pp.344-347, p.346. For a good summary
of this constraint as it relates to Paul's call in general, see Seyoon Kim, *The
Origin of Paul's Gospel*, WUNT, 2. Reihe, Bd. 4, 1981, pp.65f.

132 Contra e.g. R. Hock, "Paul's Tentmaking", p.59, who suggests that the center of
Paul's argument in 9:16-18 is "the philosophical problem of fate and free will".

133 The most important contribution and main point of E. Käsemann's study of I Cor.
9:15-18 is his emphasis on the centrality of this ἀνάγκη-motif for Paul's argument and his corresponding polemic against all attempts to interpret it as
merely some sort of ethical "Berufspflicht" or psychological compulsion deriving
from Paul's gratitude to God; see "Variation", pp.232-234.

134 As already stressed almost 50 years ago by A.D. Nock, *St. Paul*, 1938, p.69, who
argued that Paul's "vocation and conversion were identical". More recently,
this point has been well made on the basis of Paul's use of καλέω in Gal. 1:15f.
(which in Paul usually refers to becoming a Christian, see Rom. 8:30; I Cor. 1:9;
7:15; I Thess. 2:12, etc.) by Akira Satake, "Apostolat und Gnade bei Paulus",
NTS 15(1968)96-107, see esp. pp.96f. See too U. Wilckens, "Die Bekehrung des
Paulus als religionsgeschichtliches Problem", *ZThK* 56(1959) 273-293, pp.274f.
The classic treatment of this point is now that of Krister Stendahl in his essay,
"Call Rather than Conversion", in his *Paul among Jews and Gentiles*, 1976, pp.
7-23. Although I agree with Stendahl's emphasis that Paul's Damascus road experience did not mean that Paul changed religions, it nevertheless seems better
to retain the language of conversion in the light of the drastic change which
took place in Paul's thinking as a result of the revelation of Christ which he

ed to follow Christ and then made an apostle; rather, Paul was called
to follow Christ *as an apostle*[135]. Paul's identity as a follower of
Christ was thus *identical* with his self-conception as an apostle. This
explains why, in our context, Paul is able to move directly from a discussion of his own apostolic practice in I Cor. 9:19-23 to a discussion
of the necessity of enduring in faith in 9:24-10:13. In addition, it
also explains why Paul cannot boast in the fact that he preaches the
gospel *per se*. For the compulsion he feels to preach is identical with
the compulsion or necessity which brought him to faith in Christ and
vice versa. As Käsemann put it so well,

> Denn ἀνάγκη in diesem Sinne ist mit dem Evangelium über sein Leben gekommen.
> Das Evangelium selber ist für ihn jene Gottesmacht, welche den Menschen der-
> art schicksalhaft überfällt, wie Paulus es tatsächlich bei Damaskus erfahren
> hat, und ihn so in ihren Dienst zwingt, daß die alte Existenz ins Sterben ge-
> rufen wird und von der neuen gilt: 'Ich lebe nicht mehr selber, Christus lebt
> in mir ....'[136]

Consequently, since his call to preach cannot be separated from his
call to Christ, any boasting which might be associated with the fact
that Paul preaches is eliminated on the basis of the principle of
grace established in I Cor. 1:26-31: God has chosen his people in spite
of their distinctives, in order that μὴ καυχήσηται πᾶσα σάρξ ἐνώπιον
τοῦ θεοῦ (I Cor. 1:29). The adversative relationship which stands at
the heart of Paul's statement about himself in I Cor. 15:8-10 demonstrates, moreover, that Paul viewed his own call in terms of precisely
this same grace, i.e. the grace which eliminates boasting.

Finally, the identity between Paul's conversion and his call also
explains Paul's somewhat surprising ability to support his assertion
that he is under constraint to preach the gospel by pointing out that
eschatological judgment awaits him if he fails to carry out his mandate
(cf. the γάρ of verse 16c). For in the light of this identification, not
to preach would be to deny Christ himself, the result of which is to
be ἀνάθεμα (cf. I Cor. 16:22)[137].

In verse 17 Paul then goes on to support his main point in verse 16,
i.e. that his preaching *per se* provides no ground for boasting, by es-

---

experienced. I have thus chosen to describe it as a twofold, though inseparable
experience, and have opted for the clumsy terminology of "conversion-call".

135 My switch in terminology from talking about Paul's call to preach the gospel to
his apostleship is intentional and is intended to reflect the fact that for Paul
the two were, in fact, synonymous. So too E. Käsemann, "Legitimität", p.31; P.
Stuhlmacher, *Das paulinische Evangelium*, pp.68f. and his "Ende des Gesetzes",
pp.25f.n.26; Otfried Hofius, "'Gott hat unter uns aufgerichtet das Wort der Versöhnung' (2Kor 5:19)", *ZNW* 71(1980)3-20, p.17 and 17n.66 (who speaks of their
"untrennbaren Zusammenhang") and Kim, *Origin*, pp.57-59.

136 "Variation", pp.234-235.

137 For a discussion of this eschatological threat of judgment which stands over Paul
because of the "*heilsgeschichtliche* Raum" in which he finds himself cf. P. Stuhlmacher, *Das paulinische Evangelium, Bd. I*, pp.87f.

tablishing a contrast between ἐκών/ἄκων[138] on the one hand, and
μισθός/οἰκονομία on the other hand[139]. Paul's call to preach is now
defined as that "stewardship" entrusted to him by God[140], which in
the light of I Cor. 4:1 certainly refers to the fact that Paul has
been entrusted with the "mysteries of God" (i.e. Paul considers himself to be an οἰκονόμος μυστηρίων θεοῦ)[141]. Thus, since this steward-

---

138 For the meaning of ἐκών and ἄκων as "voluntary" and "against one's will and intention" respectively, cf. F. Hauck, art. ἐκών κ.τ.λ., *TDNT*, *Vol. II*, 1964,
pp.469-470. Hauck points out that ἐκών is the antonym of βία and ἀνάγκη.

139 Based on the punctuation given in Nestle-Aland, *Novum Testamentum Graece*, 1979[26]
and taking the two conditional statements of v.17 to be unreal and real respectively. J. Reuman's attempt, "Οἰκονομία-Terms in Paul in comparison with Lukan
Heilsgeschichte", *NTS* 13(1966/1967)147-167 (abbr. as "Oikonomia"), p.159, to
interpret I Cor. 9:17b and 18a as one statement, so that εἰ δὲ ἄκων, οἰκονομίαν
πεπίστευμαι becomes the protasis of a conditional sentence, with τίς οὖν μοῦ
ἐστιν ὁ μισθός as its apodosis, although possible grammatically, fails to be
convincing for two reasons. First, he must interpret 9:16a: "For if I preach
the gospel *on the basis of remuneration that the others have*, then there is no
ground for glorying for me" (emphasis mine). But this addition to the protasis
(which I have emphasized in quoting his translation) is neither necessary nor
implied in the context. Second, and even more telling however, is the fact that
Reuman's interpretation demands that we understand Paul to be contradicting himself in 9:17-18. For in Reuman's reconstruction, the conditional statement in
9:17a is construed to be the "actual case", rather than an unreal condition -
i.e. Paul does preach ἐκών! But inasmuch as 9:17b is also "a statement of the
actual situation", Paul is asserting that he preaches ἐκών and ἄκων at the same
time! In Reuman's words, "Thus Paul sees himself as a free man, working voluntarily, with apostolic authority. But he cannot help stating also, in absolute
humility, that his very apostolic office involves the sort of compulsion and
necessity that is laid on an οἰκονόμος, one who fills the stewards role in a
Greek household - an office usually held by a slave". But such an interpretation
not only renders Paul's thought highly confusing, it also ignores the explicit
statement in 9:15, which defines Paul's boast as his voluntary decision not to
be supported, thus destroying the antithetical parallelism which seems to be
clearly established in the text. Reuman's view seems to be motivated by his
desire to deny the fact that Paul could be speaking of a reward in the real
sense of the term. As he asserts, " ... strictly speaking there is in 17 and
the following verses no reference to a future reward. The only reward he mentions
is one now in the present, involving a ground for boasting". But in the light of
I Cor. 3:8ff. the opposite seems to be the case. Cf. also Barrett, *The First
Epistle to the Corinthians*, pp.209f., who also tries to read v.17 and v.18 as
one statement because he cannot see a "good reason" why μισθός and οἰκονομία
should be construed as alternatives, i.e. he poses the question, "Why, if I am
entrusted with an office, should I not be rewarded for carrying it out?" (p.210).
But once the slave-status of the steward is given its due weight in the passage,
this objection falls away.

140 For the idea of an οἰκονομία being entrusted to someone by God, cf. Is. 22:21LXX;
and for the idea of an οἰκονομία being entrusted with a message to be delivered,
cf. Esther 8:9LXX. John Reumann, "Oikonomia = 'Covenant'; Terms for Heilsgeschichte in Early Christian Usage", *NovT* 3(1959)282-292, p.282, based on his
extensive study of this terminology in his doctoral thesis, interprets I Cor.
9:17 and Col. 1:25 as referring to Paul's "commission" or "stewardship" or the
"divine office granted to him in God's program". He refers to Lk. 16:2-4 as a
good example of the usual classical sense of the office of the οἰκονόμος (p.
282n.1).

141 Cf. Paul's parallel statements in Gal. 2:7 and Phil. 1:16, from which it becomes
clear that the "mysteries of God" refer to the gospel itself. Moreover, as
Reuman, "Oikonomia", p.161, points out, following Bornkamm and R. Brown (cf.
p.161n.1 for literature), these "mysteries" are to be interpreted against the

ship is received ἄκων, Paul's faithfulness in carrying it out cannot
be a ground for boasting since the corresponding slavery-status of
stewards[142] places their obedience in the realm of that "forced labor"
for which there is no μισθός[143]. In contrast, Paul can refer to the
fact that he offers the gospel free of charge as his καύχημα since,
by definition, the voluntary nature of this act means that it is a
work for which Paul expects to be recompensed, i.e. to receive a μισθός
in the eschaton[144]. As a result, it seems impossible to avoid the conclusion that in I Cor. 9:15-18 Paul makes an ontological distinction
between his preaching *per se*, in which he cannot boast (i.e. no μισθός
is expected for it), and his preaching free of charge, for which he
will be recompensed and in which, therefore, he does boast[145]. Paul
thus establishes two categories of conduct which may be represented
in the following chart:

---

background of the סוד/רז in the OT, i.e. they are God's revealed secrets as made
known to his servants the prophets. This becomes especially clear in Eph. 3:1-12,
esp. vv.2f.

142 Again, see Reuman, "Oikonomia", p.158. Reuman emphasizes that Paul's reference to
compulsion in I Cor. 9:16, as well as his statement in I Cor. 4:1f., represent
the same "mood", that is " ... all the servile connotations which οἰκονόμος
could have in the Greek world - slaves under orders, *who must be faithful in
executing their offices*". See too G. Theißen, *Psychologische Aspekte*, pp.67f.,
on the identity of the οἰκονόμος as a slave. Theißen points to the fact that
οἰκονόμος and δοῦλος are used synonymously in Lk. 12:41-46, in contrast to its
use in Lk. 16:1ff.; Paul's use of the ἀνάγκη-motif in I Cor. 9:16-18 (cf. Homer,
I.1, 6,458) and Paul's statements in I Cor. 9:19 and 4:1ff. as all supporting
this identification.

143 Cf. Rom. 8:20, where the passive nature of the subject of ἄκων, here expressed
as οὐχ ἑκοῦσα, is clearly evident. It is significant, moreover, that the application of this imagery to the creation in 8:20 leads Paul to picture the creation
in terms of "slavery" in 8:21. Hence, in Rom. 8:20f. we also encounter the same
association of unwillingness/slavery that we find in I Cor. 9:17. See too the
close parallel in Luke 17:7-10.

144 Contra e.g. G. Theißen, "Legitimation und Lebensunterhalt", pp.220f., who interprets Paul's decision to preach free of charge as part of Paul's "persönlich aus-
zeichnendes göttliches Geschick" because "Gott selbst hat ihn zum Verstoß gegen
die üblichen Normen urchristlichen Wandercharismatikertums genötigt. Er kann gar
nicht anders. Ein Zwang liegt auf ihm ... I Kor 9:15-18)". But Paul's point is
just the opposite. The compulsion he feels relates to his preaching, not to his
preaching *free of charge*.

145 Part of the problem in reading this text is that we are so conditioned by the
negative connotations which are associated with the idea of boasting elsewhere
in Paul's letters (cf. Rom. 3:27; I Cor. 1:29; 3:21; 4:7; 5:6; 13:4; II Cor.
11:16, 18) that it becomes almost impossible to recognize that "boasting" as such
is *not* a negative moral category for Paul. Rather, the issue for Paul is what
one boasts in, not whether one boasts or not. Paul can therefore speak positively
of his own boast and even encourage his readers to boast in him as well (cf. Rom.
15:17f.; I Cor. 15:31, cf. 15:10; II Cor, 1:14; 7:14; 8:24; 9:2f.; 10:8,13; 11:10;
12:5f.; I Thess.2:19; Phil.2:16; II Cor. 5:12; Phil. 1:26). For other positive
uses of the idea of "boasting" in something, cf. Rom. 4:2; 5:2,3,11. It is debat-
able whether the boast of the Jews referred to in Rom. 2:17,23 ought to be seen
as negative or positive.

Preaching *per se*	Preaching ἀδάπανος
result of ἀνάγκη	no ἀνάγκη to do so
done ἄκων	done ἑκών
οὐαί expected if not done	μισθός expected if done
classified as οἰκονομία	classified as καύχημα

Rather than expressing a Pauline paradox[146], or even a joke[147], Paul's summary statement in I Cor. 9:18 is therefore best interpreted as a re-statement of verse 15, with Paul's question in verse 18a taken to refer to that for which he expects to be "paid" in the last judgment[148]. More-over, Paul's criterion cited in I Cor. 3:14 that only the work which "remains" (μενεῖ) will receive a reward explains why Paul can be con-fident that his commitment to preach the gospel without charge will be recompensed in I Cor. 9:15ff. For as we have seen above, Paul's deci-sion to support himself is, in essence, an expression of his *love*, which, according to I Cor. 13:13, is the greatest of the three essential Chris-tian qualities that "remain" (cf. μένει in 13:13). Thus, rather than not having anything in common with one another as Käsemann maintained[149], Paul's refusal to be supported by the Corinthians was itself an

---

146 I.e. that Paul's "wage" existed in the fact that he has no wage, so Käsemann, "Variation", p.228 and H. Conzelmann, *Der erste Brief an die Korinther*, p.195.

147 So Dungan, *Sayings of Jesus*, p.23, who sees Paul's argument in I Cor. 9:16-18 to be a joke based on a pun. In his opinion, Paul turns "jocular" at this point, "facetiously asking, 'What are the wages of someone who is not entitled to any?' he answers, 'Why, to do the work for free!'" He then goes on to lament that Paul's joke "has largely been wasted on centuries of sober-sided Christian exegetes", myself included.

148 Following Käsemann, "Variation", p.223n.5, who translates καταχρήσασθαι in I Cor. 9:18 "intensiv gebrauchen", as in I Cor. 7:31, not "mißbrauchen"; contra Dungan, *Sayings of Jesus*, p.24, who argues that it means "abuse" rather than "usefully" as normally thought (cf. p.24n.1). In spite of the fact that Dungan admits that this translation cannot be proven (p.24), he nevertheless posits, on the basis of this unsupported view, an antithetical parallelism between 9:18 and 9:15 (i.e. between καταχρήσασθαι and κέχρημαι, cf. p.24n.1), which then becomes the basis of his overall view that Paul's argument in 9:4-18 is directed against the abuse of the Lord's command concerning support for the apostles (cf. pp.3, 14, 19). But this unfounded assumption concerning the meaning of καταχρήσασθαι will not bear the weight of his conclusions. Paul's boast in 9:12b is not that he does not "abuse" this regulation, but that he does not use it at all.

149 "Variation", p.228. Käsemann argued that "der Verzicht, der im Blick auf die himmlische Vergeltung und im eigenen Interesse geschieht, hat nichts mit dem Verzicht auf das persönliche gute Recht durch die Liebe gemeinsam", i.e. that if these two aspects did come together Paul would be guilty of "Trugschlüssen und Verwechselungen" (p.228). This objection derives, however, from the common assump-tion that that which is done for a reward cannot at the same time be an act of love. On the inappropriateness of this assumption for understanding NT ethics, cf. John Piper, *'Love your enemies'. Jesus' love command in the synoptic gospels and in the early Christian paraenesis. A history of the tradition and interpre-tation of its uses. SNTS Monograph Series 38*, 1979, p.166 and his convincing discussion of the role of rewards in the teaching of Jesus in Luke's Gospel on pp.162-170, and in general on pp.60f.

expression of his love, which, because it would *remain* through the
fire of God's judgment, would be recompensed. As such, Paul could boast
in it!

Paul's boast in I Cor. 9:15c thus brings us back to the first two
points concerning I Cor. 9 of significance for our study of II Cor.
2:17. As we have seen, Paul's commitment to support himself as portrayed in I Cor. 9 is to be understood as an expression of his *love*
for the Corinthian church which derives its significance for Paul's
larger argument from the generally, if not universally, accepted *authority* of the apostle itself. As such, Paul's practice of preaching the
gospel ἀδάπανος can still be looked to not only as an appropriate outworking of his apostolic calling which provides an authoritative example of the ethic of love worthy of emulation, but also as an essential part of Paul's own καύχημα as an apostle, precisely because it is
an outworking of that love. Moreover, the foundation upon which these
three interrelated motifs are built and the force which molds them into
an organic unity is Paul's self-conception as one to whom God has entrusted his "mysteries" and who, as God's οἰκονόμος, is consequently
constrained by that gospel to preach throughout the Gentile world. For
Paul's apostolic *authority* resides in his call to preach the gospel;
his *love* is defined as whatever serves to further its advance; and his
boast is found in the fact that he has given up his rights as an a-
postle in order not to place a hindrance in its way. With this in mind,
the startling nature of Paul's treatment of these same themes in II Corinthians becomes readily apparent.

2. II Cor. 11:7-15

Paul's reintroduction of the theme of his commitment to preach the
gospel without charge in II Cor. 11:7-11 is framed within two comparisons[150]. In 11:5f. Paul asserts that he considers himself not to be

---

150 Recently, Abraham J. Malherbe, "Antisthenes and Odysseus, and Paul at War", *HTR*
76(1983)143-173, pp.168, 172, has argued that Paul refers to his life-style of
self-support already in 10:1 (following Hock in taking ταπεινός in 10:1 to be a
reference to Paul's "voluntary self-humiliation" as a result of supporting himself
with manual labor) so that the issue in 10:1-6 is not that of an "intellectual
confrontation", but rather a matter of Paul's conduct. Malherbe therefore concludes concerning 10:1-6, as I will below concerning 11:7ff. and 12:12ff., that
Paul's "humble life, in which God's power is manifested, is the armament with
which he attacks his opponents. Thus he calls on his readers, not to listen to
him, but to look at what is right in front of their eyes (10:7)" (p.172). As a
result, Malherbe also suggests that the closest parallel to II Cor. 10:3-6 is
II Cor. 2:14-16! (p.166n.131). Similarly, but for entirely different reasons, G.
Theißen, "Legitimation und Lebensunterhalt", p.217, argued earlier that κατὰ
σάρκα in 10:2 refers to the fact that Paul "sorge sich durch seine Handwerks-
arbeit allzu sehr um irdische Dinge. Er vertraue zu wenig auf Christus". Hence,

inferior in any way to the "super apostles" (ὑπερλίαν ἀποστόλων), while
in 11:12-15 he refuses to allow the "false apostles" (ψευδαπόστολοι)
of 11:13a to be compared to himself. Thus, in the first case, the comparison is directed from Paul to the "super apostles" and is *positive*
in nature, while in the second case the comparison is *negative* in nature, being directed from the "false apostles" to Paul. Moreover, each
of the two comparisons functions to provide a ground or support for
Paul's statements in 11:1-4 and 11:7-11 respectively, while at the same
time providing a transition to the next unit of thought. Paul's positive
comparison in 11:5f. is intended to support (note the γάρ of 11:5)[151]
his concern that in accepting "another Jesus", "different spirit" and
"different gospel" from those who have come into Corinth than the one
they had received from Paul (cf. 11:4)[152], the Corinthians have, in
fact, been tricked by Satan into abandoning the truth (cf. 11:3). For
the unexpressed thought between verses 4 and 5 is the implied mistaken
rejection of the authority and legitimacy of Paul's own ministry and
gospel inherent in the Corinthians' willingness to accept the ὁ ἐρχόμενος (e.g. "And in so doing you have mistakenly rejected my authority
and gospel, for ...")[153]. The force of Paul's assertion that he is

---

the attack on Paul in II Cor., according to Theißen, is that "er denke zu viel
an seine materielle Existenz, anstatt sie ausschließlich von seiner Zugehörigkeit
zu Christus abhängig zu machen" (p.219). But I have decided to limit my discussion to the two explicit treatments of this theme in chs. 11 and 12.

151 Contra Josef Zmijewski, *Der Stil der paulinischen 'Narrenrede'. Analyse der Sprachgestaltung in 2 Kor 11:1-12:10 als Beitrag zur Methodik von Stiluntersuchungen
neutestamentlicher Texte, Bonner Biblische Beiträge, Bd. 52*, 1978, pp.114f. For
although he refers to v.5's "Art" as a "(begründender bzw. versichernder) Aussage-
satz" (p.114), he then goes on to reject this meaning in favor of understanding
the γάρ as a "Bekräftigungsformel ... im anknüpfenden oder weiterführenden Sinn"
(p.115). His main reason for doing so is that v.5 also functions to provide a
transition to what follows and is, as such, "einen gedanklichen Neueinsatz" (p.
115). But it is precisely the fact that v.5 introduces a new thought which
suggests that the γάρ retain its more usual function as a "Begründungspartikel"
(p.115). For v. 5 does not further define or extend the same thought found in v.4.

152 Reading ἀνέχεσθε rather than ἀνείχεσθε in 11:4b. See the various commentaries for
the arguments in favor of this reading and Käsemann, "Legitimität", pp.38f. for
a good critique of the opposing proposals of A. Hausrath and A. Schlatter.
Käsemann also argues that καλῶς ἀνέχεσθε in 11:4 parallels ἡδέως ἀνέχεσθε in 11:19
and that ὁ ἐρχόμενος in 11:4 parallels οἱ τοιοῦτοι in 11:13. He thus translates
11:4: "ihr läßt euch das ganz schön gefallen" (p.39).

153 Windisch, *Zweiter Korintherbrief*, p.329, also recognized the need for such a
"Zwischengedanke" and supplied, "'also bitte, läßt euch mein Auftreten dann
auch gefallen'". But this attempt finds no support in 11:1-4 and becomes, in
reality, the introduction to an independent section in Paul's argument since,
for Windisch, 11:5-15 is an "Abschweifung" in Paul's thought. It seems improbable,
however, that Paul's introductory thesis statement itself would remain unexpressed.
It seems more appropriate to treat 11:5-15 as an integral part of Paul's ongoing
argument and to anchor this unexpressed assertion as closely as possible to its
context. Against the idea that 11:5-15 is such an "Abschweifung", cf. J. Zmijewski,
Stil, pp.114ff. Bultmann's attempt, *Zweiter Korintherbrief*, p.205, to supply this
missing thought is therefore more helpful: "'haltet mich aus, so gut wie ihr jene
ertragt!'". Nevertheless, this too does not adequately explain the actual force
of the γάρ in v.5 as a support for Paul's concern in 11:4. This is also the weak-

equal to the "super apostles" is to make it clear to the Corinthians that in rejecting Paul's gospel they have abandoned the basic apostolic gospel common to both Paul and the Church as a whole, as represented and built upon the original "pillar apostles". As such, Paul's positive comparison in 11:5 recalls his prior statements in I Cor. 15:1-11, in which Paul identified the gospel which he preached and the Corinthians had received (note the parallels between I Cor. 15:1 and II Cor. 11:4)[154] with the tradition Paul himself had received (cf. παρέλαβον, I Cor. 15:3), both from Jerusalem as well as from the churches in Damascus and Antioch, as the tradition *common* to all the apostles (cf. Gal. 1:18f.; 2:2, 6-9)[155]. This explains why Paul can make the surprising statement in I Cor. 15:11 that it is of little significance whether the Corinthians originally heard the gospel from Paul or from one of the other "apostles" listed in 15:3-7, since they all represent the same message. That this is the backdrop to Paul's comparison in II Cor. 11:5 becomes evident in 11:6, when Paul makes explicit that his γνῶσις, here referring to the gospel[156], is in no way deficient, being on a par with the gospel delivered by the "pillar apostles" themselves, even if his delivery of that gospel was not couched in sophisticated rhetoric (εἰ δὲ καὶ ἰδιώτης τῷ λόγῳ; cf. I Cor. 2:1, 4; II Cor. 1:12). Thus, to stray from *Paul's* gospel is to stray from the gospel of the "pillar apostles", and hence from the gospel of the Church

---

ness in the attempts of those like Barrett, *Second Corinthians*, pp.277f. and his "Paul's Opponents in II Corinthians", *NTS* 17(1971)233-254, p.243; and Lietzmann, *An die Korinther*, p.146, who suggest that the γάρ of v.5 actually relates back to Paul's statement in vv.1 or 3. For the most natural reading is to take it as a support for what immediately precedes.

154 I Cor. 15:1a: τὸ εὐαγγέλιον ὃ εὐηγγελισάμην ὑμῖν
    II Cor. 11:4a: ἄλλον Ἰησοῦν κηρύσσει ὃν οὐκ ἐκηρύξαμεν
    I Cor. 15:1b: ὃ καὶ παρελάβετε
    II Cor. 11:4b: ἢ πνεῦμα ἕτερον λαμβάνετε ὃ οὐκ ἐλάβετε
                   ἢ εὐαγγέλιον ἕτερον ὃ οὐκ ἐδέξασθε

155 For a helpful discussion of the relationship between Paul's statement in I Cor. 15:3 that he had *received* the tradition cited in I Cor. 15:3ff. and his insistence in Gal. 1:1, 11f., 15f. that the origin and authority of his gospel was the call and revelation which he received *directly* from God, see P. Stuhlmacher, "Das paulinische Evangelium", pp.160-170. It is important to keep Stuhlmacher's emphasis in mind that "nicht erst in den Pastoralbriefen, sondern schon bei Paulus selbst erscheint das Evangelium als Heilsgut, das dem Apostel zur unverfälschten Verkündigung und Weitergabe anvertraut worden ist (vgl. 1.Kor. 9:16-18; Gal. 1:11; 2:2,7; 1.Thess. 2:4). Das Paulus geoffenbarte Evangelium hat auf diese Weise eine ganz natürliche Affinität zu Lehre und Tradition" (p.166). Stuhlmacher's point is that Paul's own experience on the road to Damascus functioned as a criterion for his acceptance and adaptation of the tradition he encountered in the Church as a whole (cf. pp.166f.).

156 The close connection between γνῶσις in II Cor. 2:14 and ὁ λόγος τοῦ θεοῦ in 2:17 makes this identification probable, as well as Paul's definition of this knowledge in II Cor. 4:6 as ἡ γνῶσις τῆς δόξης τοῦ θεοῦ ἐν προσώπῳ Χριστοῦ. Of course, "knowledge" in the Corinthian correspondence can have a much broader denotation and be both positive and negative in connotation; cf. I Cor. 1:5; 8:1,7,10,11; 12:8; 13:2,8; 14:6; II Cor. 6:6; 8:7 and 10:5.

as a whole. By implication, therefore, Paul's comparison isolates his opponents, represented in II Cor. 11:4 by the impersonal ὁ ἐρχόμενος, from the position and prestige of the "super apostles", thus denying them any possibility of claiming to be the true representatives of the genuine apostolic tradition and authority.

Perhaps the most fundamental exegetical decision to be made concerning Paul's argument in II Cor. 11-12 is whether the "super apostles" of 11:5 and 12:11 are to be identified with the "false apostles" (=deceitful workers = servants of Satan) in 11:13-15, who as Paul's opponents have recently arrived in Corinth and are represented collectively as ὁ ἐρχόμενος in 11:4; or whether the two designations represent two distinct groups, with the "false apostles" being closely related to and even claiming to represent, in some fashion, the "super apostles", but nevertheless remaining a distinguishable entity. In this latter position, which I share, the "super apostles" belong to the same circle of apostles as the "pillar apostles" of Gal. 2:9, though they need not be coterminous with it, and are associated, above all, with the "mother church" in Jerusalem. The two basic positions have already been set out in detail by E. Käsemann, who argued that the two designations represented two distinct fronts[157], and R. Bultmann, who attempted to respond to Käsemann's view[158]. The major supporter of Käsemann's basic position has been C.K. Barrett, although he disagrees with Käsemann's description of Paul's opponents in Corinth as "pneumatics"[160]. In Barrett's view, the opponents were Jewish Christian Judaizers from Palestine who claimed the pillar apostles as their source of legitimacy, so that the situation behind II Cor. essentially parallels that behind Galatians, except for the fact that in Corinth the Judaizing gospel has been mixed with certain Hellenistic elements (which Barrett calls the process of "Corinthianization") not found in the "'pure' Judaizing" at work in Galatia[161]. Although I find the arguments of Käsemann and Barrett compelling, especially the observation that Paul would hardly compare himself positively to those in 11:5f. whom he then later describes as "servants of Satan" in 11:14f., their view remains the minority position. For a recent attempt to bring the two basic positions together, see the essay by Margaret E. Thrall, "Super-Apostles, Servants of Christ, and Servants of Satan"[162]. She argues that although the term "super apostles" refers to the Jerusalem apostles, it is nevertheless used by Paul to refer to the missionaries now in Corinth because he thinks it possible that some of the Jerusalem apostles might be included among them[163]. Paul thus oscillates in his discussion, speaking alternately to the false apostles and the super apostles, since he is not sure whether both are present in Corinth or not[164]. But her attempts to explain Paul's sudden switch in subject matter from the one to the other in 11:12 and 11:18-23 remain unconvincing to me, as well as her attempt to argue that Paul could describe the servants of Christ in 11:23 as servants of Satan in 11:13-15 because of the twofold role of Peter in the Synoptic tradition[165]. Paul's point in 11:13-15 is not that true apostles can sometimes act in a way that

157 "Die Legitimität des Apostels, Eine Untersuchung zu II Korinther 10-13", *ZNW* 41(1942)33-71, esp. pp.38f.; 41-43; 45-49.
158 In *Exegetische Probleme des zweiten Korintherbriefes zu 2. Kor. 5:1-5; 5:11-6:10; 10-13; 12:21, Symbolae Biblical Upsalienses, Vol. 9*, 1947, esp. pp.20-30.
159 Cf. his "ΨΕΥΔΑΠΟΣΤΟΛΟΙ (2 Cor. 11:13)" (see above, n.84); his "Christianity at Corinth", *BJRL* 46(1964)269-297; the introduction to his commentary, pp.30-35 and his last major article on the subject, "Paul's Opponents in II Corinthians" (see above, n.84).
160 Cf. "Legitimität", pp.37f.
161 "Paul's Opponents", p.251.
162 *JSNT* 6(1980)42-57.
163 "Super-Apostles", pp.42,46,48.
164 "Super-Apostles", pp.48,50.
165 "Super-Apostles", pp.52-54.

is not appropriate to the gospel, but that the false apostles are deceitful
in disguising themselves as true apostles of Christ! Is it probable that Paul
would say this about Peter or James? Instead, the term "super-apostles" itself
seems best explained as Paul's attempt to emphasize that these apostles were
called before him (I Cor. 15:5ff.) and enjoyed undisputed recognition and
authority (Gal. 2:6)[166].

The point to be emphasized, therefore, is that in the light of Paul's
prior statements in I Cor. 15:3ff., the fact that Paul's opponents
preach an "εὐαγγέλιον ἕτερον" than the one Paul preached also means
that they no longer belong to the common apostolic tradition, regardless of their purported claim to be "apostles" themselves, or to represent the pillar apostles. Hence, from Paul's perspective, they are
"ψευδαπόστολοι, ἐργάται δόλιοι, μετασχηματιζόμενοι εἰς ἀποστόλους
Χριστοῦ...μετασχηματίζονται ὡς διάκονοι δικαιοσύνης" (11:13, 15). Hence,
given Paul's identification of his own gospel with the common apostolic
tradition in II Cor. 11:1-6 and his ability to characterize his opponents' teaching as an εὐαγγέλιον ἕτερον, it seems implausible simply
to maintain, as G. Theißen does, that "Seine Konkurrenten waren kaum
die 'Lügenapostel, trügerischen Arbeiter und Satansdiener' (II Kor
11:13), als die Paulus sie verunglimpft: Es waren normale urchristliche
Missionare, die sich mehr an die Regeln für Wandercharismatiker hielten
als Paulus"[167]. For regardless of whether one agrees with Theißen's
reconstruction of the two types of missionary practices among the early
Christians and their origins, there must have been substantial differences in doctrine between Paul and his opponents as well. This brings
us to Paul's insistence in 11:12 that these "false apostles" not be
classed together with him in their "boast" (cf. the ἵνα-clause of 11:
12b)[168], which is intended to be Paul's rationale for his continuing
decision not to accept financial support from the Corinthians (cf.
11:9)[169]. But in order to see how Paul's negative comparison in 11:12

---

166 As suggested to me by Dr. Stuhlmacher in a private conversation.
167 "Legitimation und Lebensunterhalt", p.221.
168 Following J. Zmijewski, *Stil*, p.146, 146n.273 and the majority of commentators in
    taking the second ἵνα-clause of 11:12b to be dependent upon τῶν θελόντων ἀφορμήν
    and thus representing the desire of Paul's opponents, though I would emphasize
    that this is given from Paul's perspective. It appears that Paul interpreted at
    least part of the motivation behind his opponents' criticism of his practice to
    be their desire to eliminate the obstacle to their own demand for support created
    by Paul's decision to support himself. Thus, Paul is determined to maintain his
    practice for the same reason that his opponents would like him to change it, i.e.
    because it is *different* than the norm. For an opposing view, cf. Hock, *Social
    Context*, p.100n.118, who argues that II Cor. 11 is a reversal of I Cor. 9 in that
    Paul now wants his opponents to conform to his practice. Hock correspondingly
    construes both ἵνα-clauses in v.12 to be dependent upon ὃ δὲ ποιῶ, καὶ ποιήσω.
    But Paul's purpose in II Cor. 11 seems to be to expose his opponents true iden-
    tity as servants of Satan, not to reform their behavior.
169 Again, see J. Zmijewski, *Stil*, p.144, although I find his attempt to take ὃ δὲ
    ποιῶ καὶ ποιήσω together as *one* relative clause modifying an unexpressed main
    clause unconvincing (cf. pp.145f.). It seems best to take καὶ ποιήσω as the main

actually accomplishes this purpose, it will first be necessary to trace
the logic of Paul's argument in II Cor. 11:6b-11 in the light of our
prior discussion of this same theme in I Cor. 9.

The first observation to be made in this regard is that Paul's argument in 11:6b-11, which leads to the negative comparison of verse 12,
is intended to perform the same function as the positive comparison established in verse 5, namely, to support the validity of Paul's gospel.
For in verse 6b Paul goes on to assert that he himself has demonstrated
or revealed *to the Corinthians* (φανερώσαντες ... εἰς ὑμᾶς), in an all
inclusive manner (ἐν παντὶ ... ἐν πᾶσιν), the genuine nature of his
γνῶσις (Χριστοῦ). That is, in verse 6b Paul argues that not only his
harmony with the common traditions of the Church, but also the nature
of his own ministry, provides evidence that his knowledge (= gospel)
is, in fact, the true and authoritative one. Paul's support for this
assertion is then introduced in verse 7 with a rhetorical question
introduced with ἤ, which in order to bring out its logical function in
the argument must be transported into a negative indicative statement
introduced with a grounding conjunction: "because I did not sin in
humbling myself in order that you might be exalted, in that (ὅτι) I
preached the gospel of God to you without charge (δωρεάν)[170]. Construed in this manner, Paul's rhetorical question in verse 7 supplies
the first support for his assertion in verse 6b that his own ministry
has made the genuine nature of his gospel evident by indicating that
Paul's ministry in Corinth was aimed at benefiting the *Corinthians*, i.e.
its purpose was that *they* be exalted (ἵνα ὑμεῖς ὑψωθῆτε). The second
half of the question reminds the Corinthians of the *way* in which this
purpose was accomplished, namely, by Paul's decision to support himself
during his ministry in Corinth. Verses 8 and 9 then explain how this
was possible, given the shaky financial circumstances which often sur-
rounded the itinerant craftsman in Paul's day and the assumption that
as the ministry grew in scope Paul's ability to work might have been
diminished, though not abrogated[171]. The main point of verses 8 and 9

___

clause, with ὃ δὲ ποιῶ as the subordinate relative clause, so that 11:12 parallels
Paul's emphasis on the future already found in vv.9c and 10. Zmijewski argues
against this view by suggesting that this makes v.12 "nur eine überflüssige
Wiederholung" and that it destroys the train of thought, since the question in
view ever since v.11 is Paul's motive, not his "Handlungsweise" itself. But
this distinction is precisely what Paul does *not* want to maintain - his behavior is a window to his motives.

170 For other examples of this same use of a rhetorical question introduced with
ἤ in Paul, see Rom. 2:4; 3:29; 6:3; 9:21; 11:2, 35 (from Job 41:3); I Cor. 1:13c;
6:2, 9, 16 (depending on the variant chosen), 19; 9:6, 8, 10; 11:22; 14:36; II
Cor. 1:17; 3:1; 6:15 and 13:5.

171 Cf. too W.A. Meeks, *Urban Christians*, p.66, who points out that Paul's refusal
of support from the Corinthians was not absolute (see above, p.238 and 238n.137).
On the precarious situation of the artisan in ancient society, cf. Hock, *Social*

is to assert further, however, that Paul's goal in supporting himself was, and continues to be (cf. ἐτήρησα καὶτηρήσω, v.9b), to keep from being a "burden" (ἀβαρής) to the Corinthians. Thus, on the one hand, the expected negative answer to the rhetorical question in verse 7 is supported both by Paul's reference to his purpose in doing so stated *within* the question (i.e. ἵνα ὑμεῖς ὑψωθῆτε) and by his further emphasis in verse 9 on the fact that in doing so he has never been, nor will ever become a burden to the church in Corinth. On the other hand, verses 7-9 also combine to support Paul's prior assertion in verse 6b that the nature of his ministry itself serves as evidence of the genuine nature of his gospel by pointing out to the Corinthians that there is no ground *in his behavior* for the accusation of his opponents that Paul was using the ministry of the gospel to serve his own ends (cf. 12:16-18)[172]. Quite the contrary, *as his decision to support himself demonstrates*, Paul humbled himself in order that the Corinthians might be exalted[173]. Moreover, from Paul's perspective, the fact that Paul has never become a burden to the Corinthians by relying on them to support him, provides *concrete evidence* that his motives in preaching the gospel were not duplicitous[174]. Finally, we know from Paul's prior argument in I Cor. 8-10 that Paul viewed his decision to preach the gospel free of charge to be an expression of that very gospel itself (cf. especially the concrete example in 8:13 of the principle stated in 9:19-22 and its summary in 10:33). Hence, Paul can point to the fact that he preached the gospel free of charge, i.e. to an essential aspect of his humiliation and *suffering*, as evidence not only of his sincerity and single-mindedness, but also of the genuine nature of his gospel, based on the presupposition that a genuine gospel produces a genuine apostolic life-style. For in addition to the passages from I Corinthians just referred to, Paul's statement in II Cor. 11:7a that he humbled *himself* in order that the *Corinthians* might be exalted also recalls Paul's prior principle in I Cor. 10:24 that one should not seek his own good,

---

Context, pp.35, 37-42, 65 and 93n2, who argues that προσαναπληροῦν in 11:9 refers to the fact that the Macedonian aid was intended only to compensate for the needs Paul could not meet with his own work and not to replace his need to work itself (cf. p.93n.2).

172 This is the common view of these verses. For regardless of how one understands the identity of Paul's opponents or their theology, it seems apparent that they accused Paul of somehow using his ministry in general, and most probably the collection in particular, to defraud the Corinthians. For a different, but in my view unconvincing, view of 12:16-18, cf. Derk William Oostendrop, *Another Jesus, A Gospel of Jewish Christian Superiority in II Corinthians*, 1967, pp.75-78.

173 On ἐμαυτὸν ταπεινῶν in 11:7 as a reference to Paul's humiliation in having to support himself, cf. Hock, "Paul's Tentmaking", pp.561f. and his *Social Context*, p.64. For a response to the implications Hock draws from this fact, see above, pp.234f.

174 So too G. Dautzenberg, "Verzicht", p.226.

but the good of his/her neighbor. That Paul is building his argument
in II Cor. 11 on the foundation he has already laid in I Cor. 9 is then
further confirmed in verse 10, which is simply a reiteration of what
he has already argued for in more detail in I Cor. 9:15-18, i.e. that
this decision to preach free of charge in Corinth is an essential part
of his "boast" and thus will not be (allowed to be) stifled (cf. the
passive construction in v.10: οὐ φραγήσεται εἰς ἐμέ). This statement
thus picks up Paul's prior allusion in verse 7 to the criticism he is
suffering in Corinth based on his decision to refuse their support and,
in doing so, forms a transition to his conclusion in verses 11-15. For
the fact that in verse 7 Paul chooses to describe his refusal to accept, or indeed, demand support from the Corinthians as a possible
ἁμαρτία reflects one of the accusations raised against Paul in the
polemical situation in which he now found himself in writing to the
Corinthians[175]. Moreover, although the precise nature of the "sin" Paul
was accused of committing remains unclear[176], it appears, in the light
of II Cor. 11:11 and 12:16-18, that Paul's practice was being construed
as an expression of the fact that he did not love the Corinthians, but
was engaged, instead, in working out an elaborate scheme to defraud
them. At any rate, Paul responds by reminding the church in Corinth that
what his opponents label ἁμαρτία is, in reality, an essential part of
the very καύχησις for which he fully expects to be *rewarded* by God in
the eschatological judgment (cf. II Cor. 11:10; I Cor. 9:16-18 and the
discussion of this latter text above)! Their criticism is Paul's boast!

Having said this, verse 11a then poses the question raised by Paul's
statement in verse 10, namely, what Paul's purpose in deciding to
preach the gospel free of charge actually was. The first answer to this
question, given in verse 11b, is the answer now being given by Paul's
opponents or the Corinthians themselves: Paul refuses the Corinthians'
support because he does not love them. But against the backdrop of
Paul's prior detailed exposition of the nature of his "boast" and the
reason for its reward in I Cor. 8-10, Paul can now simply dismiss this
suggestion with a reference to the divine sanction (ὁ θεὸς οἶδεν) which

---

175 So too Gerhard Friedrich, "Die Gegner des Paulus im II. Korintherbrief", in
Abraham unser Vater, *FS O. Michel*, ed. Otto Betz, et.al., 1963, pp.181-215,
p.188, who also concludes that 11:7 is not ironical as most commentators argue,
but comes from the reproach of Paul's opponents.

176 Given the fact that from Plato's day on the act of selling one's teaching was
often viewed as implying a positive claim concerning the worth of one's message
(see above), the fact that Paul refused to do so could have been presented by
his opponents as cheapening the value of the gospel (i.e. sinning against the
gospel), or as an indication that he was ashamed of what he did preach (cf. Rom.
1:16f.), since he knew it to be inferior to the true gospel of his opposition
(i.e. sinning against the Corinthians by preaching a false gospel). This latter
possibility seems more probable.

accompanies his decision, since this decision has already been shown
to be an expression of his love for the church, which, as such, carries
God's approval (cf. I Cor. 13:12f. and my discussion above). The new
element in Paul's argument in II Cor. 11 is his own answer to the question of 11a in verses 12-15. According to verse 12, Paul refused and
continues to refuse to accept support from the Corinthians in order to
establish a canon by which the true and false apostles may be distinguished from one another. Or in the words of the text, Paul refuses to
be supported by the Corinthians, which is his "καύχησις", in order that
(ἵνα) there will be no possibility for the "false apostles" to compare
their missionary practice, centered no doubt in a demand for support
as their "καύχησις", favorably with Paul's. The need for such a "canon
of true apostolicity" is then grounded (cf. the γάρ of 11:13) in the
deceptive nature of those who have disguised themselves as ἀποστόλοι
Χριστοῦ, but are, in reality, διάκονοι Σατανᾶ (cf. 11:13-15).

In establishing this negative comparison, Paul once again turns his
opponents' criticism on its head by making *his* behavior the criterion
of *their* actions, rather than attempting to follow his opponents' attempt to establish their behavior as the criterion for his practice.
Moreover, as we have just seen in Paul's statements in verse 11, the
decisive issue in determining who is, in fact, the true apostle is the
question of motive, i.e. whether Paul's missionary practice (and by
implication his gospel), or that of his opponents (with their "εὐαγγέλιον ἕτερον") is the one being motivated by love. Paul's argument is
clear. It is his practice which ought to function as the true canon
of authenticity since it results solely from his *voluntary* decision to
give up his legitimate rights as an apostle (cf. I Cor. 9:12, 17),
which can only be interpreted as an expression of love for the church.
In contrast, it is his opponents' insistence on their rights which reflects an attempt to take advantage of the Corinthians (cf. 11:20)!
Thus, Paul's accusation that his opponents are "enslaving" the Corinthians in 11:20 is intended to be read in stark contrast to his own
decision to become the "slave of all" as expressed in I Cor. 9:19 and
to his commitment to preach himself as the Corinthians' slave, stated
in II Cor. 4:5. The question raised by Paul's response to his opponents'
criticism in 11:7-11, therefore, is whether it is likely that Paul's
refusal to burden the Corinthians is an expression of a deceitful
motive, or whether it is more probable that his opponents' demand to
be supported reflects an attempt to use the Corinthians deceitfully.
In addition, Paul maintains that this outward behavior not only expresses a corresponding inner motive, but that it also reflects the
veracity or falsehood of the gospel with which it is bound together.

Hence, not only the determination of the "true apostle", but also the
preservation of the "true gospel" hangs in the balance. As a result,
the decision the Corinthians are now faced with in reading II Cor.
11:7ff. is whether Paul, together with his gospel, is to be the "canon
of authenticity" by which his opponents are to be evaluated, or whether
his opponents' claim to be the canon against which Paul is to be measured is, in fact, justified.

3. II Cor. 12:12-19

Paul's final discussion of the theme of his monetary self-support in
II Cor. 12:12-19 is once again introduced with a positive comparison of
his own apostolate with that of the "super apostles" (compare 12:11
with 11:5). This time, however, the fact that Paul is recalling his
prior discussion in I Cor. 15:1-11 becomes explicit in his adversative
conditional qualification εἰ καὶ οὐδέν εἰμι (12:11d), which, rather
than being an ironical allusion to the criticism of his opponents[177],
is best interpreted as Paul's own positive reference to his prior statements in I Cor. 15:8f. Thirdly, here too it is Paul's own activity in
Corinth which is adduced as evidence for the legitimacy of this comparison: the σημεῖα τοῦ ἀποστόλου which accompanied Paul's ministry in
Corinth indicate that his apostleship is in no way inferior to that of
the "super apostles" (compare 12:12 with 11:6b). And finally, the issue
in 12:12-19 is once again whether Paul's practice of preaching the gospel free of charge is a positive or negative indication of his motives
in Corinth (compare 12:15 with 11:11). For the opponents, it was an
indication that Paul considered the Corinthians "inferior" to his
other churches, since elsewhere he had been supported for his ministry
(cf. 12:13). For Paul, it was a concrete indication of his fatherly
love for the Corinthians, since it was his desire not to "burden" them
which had motivated his actions (cf. 12:13-16). Thus, as part of the
same "role reversal" which we saw in chapter 11, Paul again turns his
opponents' criticism into his own badge of honor by insisting that it

177 As is usually done; see Barrett, *Second Corinthians*, p.320, although Barrett also
   points out the parallel to I Cor. 15:8f.; Windisch, *Zweiter Korintherbrief*, p.
   396, who takes it to refer to Paul's weakness in parallel to II Cor. 11:6;
   Bultmann, *Zweiter Korintherbrief*, p.233, who withholds judgment concerning the
   two alternatives; and K. Prümm, *Diakonia Pneumatos*, Bd. *I*, 1967, pp.678f. and
   Bd. *II/2*, 1962, pp.107f., who sees this as another example of Paul's ironical
   comparison of his own ability and status with that of his opponents, in which
   Paul makes his point concerning his equality with them in the form of a "Be-
   scheidenheitsaussage". In contrast, my view is informed by my prior decision
   that the "super apostles" are to be equated with the pillar apostles of Gal. 2
   and I Cor. 15, so that there is no need to view this qualification in 12:11 as
   ironical, but rather as an expression of Paul's understanding of his call as
   the "last of the apostles" who had previously persecuted the Church and was
   therefore unfit to be an apostle apart from the grace of God.

is his own apostolic practice which, in fact, demonstrates what it
means to love the Corinthians; indeed, it indicates that he was the
one who loved the Corinthians *"more"* (cf. 12:15b). In the light of
Paul's behavior it is his opponents who are exposed as those who are
seeking what the Corinthians have, rather than the Corinthians themselves (12:14). The point of Paul's argument in 12:12-19 is seen most
clearly therefore in the summary statement of verse 16. For from Paul's
perspective, it seems absurd to maintain that he was somehow trying to
deceive the Corinthians financially, when he himself refused their support. His adversative statement in 12:16b is an ironical reaction to
the idea that his very refusal to take money from the Corinthians was
itself part of Paul's plan to deceive them. Verses 17 and 18 then extend Paul's self-defense to his co-workers in order to emphasize the
unity of their actions and, hence, of their motives as well[178].

The most significant aspect of Paul's argument in 12:12-19 for our
study, however, is Paul's own interpretation of the *nature* and *purpose*
of his argument in 12:19. For having presented what appears to be a
defense of his apostolic ministry before the scrutiny of the Corinthians
in 12:12-18, Paul then concludes this section, and perhaps 10:1-12:18
as a whole, by making the startling assertion that, in reality, he has
not been engaged in an apology before the Corinthians at all! Instead,
Paul is speaking κατέναντι θεοῦ ἐν Χριστῷ (12:19a). Furthermore, Paul's
purpose in doing so has not been to support *himself*, but to strengthen
the *Corinthians:* τὰ δὲ πάντα ... ὑπὲρ τῆς ὑμῶν οἰκοδομῆς (12:19b). The
key to understanding the first of these two statements is its parallel
to Paul's prior declaration in II Cor. 11:11 (ὁ θεὸς οἶδεν) and the
accompanying underlying assumption, explicitly expressed in I Cor. 4:4f.,
that since only God can reveal the motives of the heart, it is God
alone who is fit to examine or evaluate Paul's ministry (cf. Rom. 14:10-
12). Thus from Paul's perspective, it is senseless and unnecessary to
defend oneself before others, when one's only judge is the Lord. Paul's
"defense", therefore, is κατέναντι θεοῦ, not κατέναντι ὑμῶν[179]. Paul

---

178 Against those who have argued that Paul was using the good reputation of Titus
   to bolster his own image and authority (e.g. Plummer and Georgi). Cf. Oostendorp,
   Another Jesus, p.77n.4 for the relevant literature and the key argument against
   this view. In a word, Titus belongs to the sphere of Paul's authority and not
   vice versa. As Hughes, *Second Corinthians*, p.466 puts it, "there is no question
   of Paul's trying to 'spread' the responsibility in the matter of this collection.
   On the contrary, he stands squarely on his own feet. It was at *his* instigation
   that Titus had gone to Corinth, and it was he again who was responsible for
   sending 'the brother' with him. The character of Titus and 'the brother' in
   their conduct of affairs in Corinth reflected on the character of Paul who had
   sent them".

179 This understanding of 12:19 stands in contrast to that of those such as K.
   Prümm, *Diakonia Pneumatos*, Bd. I, pp.694f., who sees Paul's denial to be merely
   an attempt to avoid the terminology of "apology" since this is too easily asso-

does not deny that he has been engaged in an apology, but only that the
Corinthians are his judges[180]. As such, Paul's statement that he speaks
κατέναντι θεοῦ is intended to prohibit the Corinthians from drawing the
conclusion that the validity of Paul's ministry, though demonstrated
before the Corinthians, is somehow dependent upon the Corinthians' approval.

Paul's second statement in 12:19 is then intended, yet again, to use
his opponents' own criticisms against them, which we have seen to be
Paul's purpose throughout 11:7ff. and 12:12ff. Rather than defending
himself against the attacks of his opponents, Paul has been laying out
his case before God in order to give the Corinthians the opportunity,
as bystanders, to be strengthened in their faithfulness to Paul, which
given the identification between Paul and his message, is, at the same
time, an opportunity to recommit themselves to the true gospel. As a
result, Paul's statement that τὰ δὲ πάντα ... ὑπὲρ τῆς ὑμῶν οἰκοδομῆς
is, in reality, an implied *warning* to the Corinthians, since Paul is
already confident of God's judgment concerning his apostolic ministry
(cf. II Cor. 1:12; 10:7, 18; 11:11, 31). Hence, contrary to the supposition of the Corinthians, Paul is not the one who is presently on
trial before them; the Corinthians are on trial before Paul! This explains why Paul can switch so suddenly from his own "defense" to his
concern for the Corinthians in 12:21-13:10. For as he puts it in 13:6f.,
his hope is that the Corinthians will not make the mistake of thinking
that he has failed the test and thus reject him, since, in reality, they
are the ones who must test *themselves* to see if they are still in the
faith (13:5). The test, of course, is whether or not they reject Paul
and his gospel!

4. Conclusion

The essential difference between Paul's discussion of his decision
to support himself in I Cor. 9 and its counterpart in II Cor. 11 and
12 is the transformation in context which has taken place between the
two discussions. In I Cor. 9 Paul's apostolic authority is still basically intact in Corinth, although certainly already being challenged
elsewhere (cf. I Cor. 9:1f.). In II Corinthians Paul's apostolic au-

---

ciated with "Selbstverherrlichung" and "Fleischesgerühme". See e.g. Barrett,
Second Corinthians, p.328 and Windisch, *Zweiter Korintherbrief*, p.406. But cf.
Bultmann, *Zweiter Korintherbrief*, p.239 and Hughes, *Second Corinthians*, p.470,
who also point to I Cor. 4:3f. as the unexpressed background to 12:19.
180 Again, cf. Hughes, *Second Corinthians*, p.469n.156, who correctly emphasizes that
ὑμῖν in 12:19 is "emphatic by position" and translates it "Have you been thinking
all along that I have been defending myself before you?". So too Bultmann,
Zweiter Korintherbrief, p.239.

thority is no longer common ground between Paul and his church. But it
is also important to see the decisive influence of Paul's opponents on
his epistolary purpose in II Cor. 11 and 12. For whereas in I Cor. 9
Paul can use his distinctiveness over against the "pillar" or "super
apostles" in a *positive* way as the very foundation of his argument in
chapters 8 and 10 (i.e. the fact that he has *voluntarily* given up his
common right to financial support, which he shares with Peter, the
brothers of the Lord and the rest of the apostles, for the sake of the
gospel), in II Cor. 11 and 12 it is this distinctiveness itself which
now calls Paul's apostleship into question. For the comparison between
Paul and the "super apostles" which inaugurates both II Cor. 11:7ff.
(cf. 11:5) and 12:12ff. (cf. 12:11)[181] indicates that the "false a-
postles" were no doubt using this common apostolic right to financial
support as the basis not only for their own demands for such support,
but also as a basis for criticizing Paul. Paul is thus forced to respond in such a way that his opponents' claim to be the true representatives of the original apostolic tradition, as embodied in the pillar
apostles, is defused, while at the same time affirming his own continuity with these apostles since they too represent the common and true
apostolic tradition. As we have seen, he accomplishes this in two ways.
First, he reminds the Corinthians that his *difference* from the pillar
apostles, i.e. that he preached the gospel without seeking support from
the Corinthians, is his "boast", that is, it is part of his voluntary
response to the οἰκονομία entrusted to him by God, and not a negative
reflection of the quality of his gospel or ministry (cf. 11:5; 12:11),
an expression of his disdain for the Corinthians (cf. 12:13), an in-
trical part of an elaborate plan to defraud them (see 12:16-18), nor
in some other way a "sin" (11:7). Hence, although his practice regarding his financial support differed from the normal practice of the
"super apostles", this difference is nevertheless an outworking of their
common gospel. This is the reason Paul emphasizes in II Cor. 11:10 that
his "boast" will not be stopped ἐν τοῖς κλίμασιν τῆς Ἀχαΐας. For in
doing so he stresses that his practice of self-support is not intended
to be a critique of the super apostles, whose sphere of ministry lies
outside of Achaia. Rather, the specific circumstances at hand in Corinth
made this practice necessary in order to facilitate the spread of the
gospel (cf. I Cor. 9:12, 23)[182]. Paul's qualification in 11:10b enables

---

181 The importance of these two comparisons is also underscored by their structural
   function within chs. 10-13 as the markers delimiting the beginning and the end
   of the so-called "Narrenrede", thus forming an *inclusio*. Cf. J. Zmijewski,
   Stil, p.114n.2.
182 Unfortunately, we do not know what those circumstances were. For the common
   assumption that Paul refused such support in order to distance himself from

him to avoid a direct confrontation with Jerusalem, while at the same
time underscoring the fact that his decision to support himself means
not only that he loves the Corinthians, but that he loves them "more"
than his opponents (cf. 12:15). Second, Paul interprets his corresponding refusal to "burden" the Corinthians financially (cf. 11:9; 12:13f.,
16) to be the necessary result and outward expression of his love for
the Corinthians in preaching the gospel. By doing so he insinuates that
the outward similarity of his opponents' practice with the practice of
the "super apostles" actually masks the fact that it is they who are
attempting to take advantage of and deceive the Corinthians. By
responding in this way, Paul is able to "turn the tables" on his critics. Rather than calling his legitimacy as an apostle into question,
his apostolic practice now becomes the "canon of authenticity" for the
true apostolic practice in Corinth (cf. 11:12), as well as the "test
of genuine faith" for the Corinthians themselves (cf. 13:2-7). Finally,
Paul's response is made possible and supported by his underlying conviction that God alone is his judge, together with his corresponding
confidence that he enjoys this divine approval (cf. II Cor. 13:6f.).
Both this conviction and confidence are expressed in Paul's declaration
that he speaks κατέναντι θεοῦ ἐν Χριστῷ (12:19). He stands before God's
judgment (κατέναντι θεοῦ) in the confidence that comes from being "in
Christ" (cf. II Cor. 10:7). In turn, this conviction and confidence are
themselves built upon Paul's understanding of his call to be an apostle
as the one upon whom the prophetic compulsion (ἀνάγκη, I Cor. 9:16) has
been laid to preach the gospel to the Gentiles. Hence, Paul's discussion
of his decision to support himself in II Cor. 11 and 12 once again reveals that Paul understood his authority as an apostle to reside in his
call to preach, which resulted in a *concrete display of love* for the
Corinthians in which he could *boast* as that for which he would one day
be rewarded and to which he could point as *evidence* for the authentic-

---

the wandering Cynic philosophers of his day who also preached openly in the
markets and on the streets of the ancient cities was already seriously questioned
by A.D. Nock over 50 years ago in his classic study, *Conversion, The Old and the
New in Religion from Alexander the Great to Augustine of Hippo*, 1933, pp.191-192.
Nock's point was that this comparison suggested by modern scholars was irrelevant
inasmuch as Paul's locus of activity was the synagogue and home and not the
open air market. For this same point, see now Stanley Kent Stowers, "Social
Status, Public Speaking and Private Teaching: The Circumstances of Paul's
Preaching Activity", *NovT* 26(1984)59-82, who argues convincingly that such
public speaking required a kind of social status, reputation and recognized
social role not possessed by Paul and that from the NT accounts themselves it
is clear that the synagogue, workshop and, most importantly, the private home
provided the contexts for Paul's preaching and teaching (cf. p.81). Stowers thus
concludes, apparently independent of Nock's earlier emphasis, that "the widespread picture of Paul the public orator, sophist or street-corner preacher is
a false one" (p.81). Thus, the reason for Paul's refusal of financial support
remains unknown.

ity of his call itself[183]. Paul's "apology" in II Cor. 11 and 12 thus
picks up and is built solidly upon the same themes which we saw to be
at the heart of Paul's prior discussion in I Cor. 9. Having come this
far, and with this in mind, we are now in a position to understand the
meaning of Paul's statement in II Cor. 2:17 and its function within
Paul's argument in 2:14-3:3.

D. THE MEANING OF II COR. 2:17 AND ITS FUNCTION
WITHIN PAUL'S ARGUMENT IN 2:14-3:3

In the light of our previous investigations it now becomes clear
that Paul's negative comparison in II Cor. 2:17a, οὐ γάρ ἐσμεν ὡς οἱ
πολλοὶ καπηλεύοντες τὸν λόγον τοῦ θεοῦ, performs a twofold function.
On the one hand, Paul's use of καπηλεύειν in 2:17 to describe the practice of "the majority" or "the many" (οἱ πολλοί)[184] is intended to call
the genuineness of their ministry into question by depicting it in terms
of the retail dealer who sells his wares in the market. For as we have
seen above, although the precise nature of the negative nuance which
was associated with market trade in Paul's day was not uniform, so that
the use of καπηλεύειν alone cannot be used as the key to the *content*
of Paul's critique in 2:17[185], the imagery nevertheless does cast a

---

183 This conclusion is supported by G. Theißen's observation that "wo immer Paulus
   angegriffen wird, verweist er auf sein 'Werk'", "Legitimation und Lebensunterhalt", p.223. Theißen refers to this custom as Paul's "Funktionale Legitimation"
   and points out that Paul's use of this argument is based on the fact that
   "Paulus ist sich sehr wohl bewußt, daß er hinsichtlich seiner funktionalen Legitimation allen Konkurrenten überlegen ist ..." (p. 223).

184 On the use of πολλοί as a noun with the article to mean "the majority" or "the
   most", cf. J. Jeremias, art. πολλοί, *TDNT*, *Vol. VI*, 1968, pp.536-545, p.540. He
   refers to this as the "exclusive" meaning; i.e. "many, but not all" and points
   to Mtt. 24:12 as the other example of its use in the NT. For the "inclusive"
   meaning, i.e. "the totality which embraces many individuals", see Rom. 5:15b;
   5:19; 12:5; I Cor. 10:17,33; Mk. 9:26 (pp.541, 543). G. Delling, art. πλῆθος,
   TDNT, *Vol. VI.*, 1968, pp.274-283, p.278, thus sees its use in II Cor. 2:17 to
   be synonymous to πλῆθος. See too J.D.G. Dunn, *Unity and Diversity in the New
   Testament*, 1977, p.255, who therefore suggests that the majority of evangelists
   were opposed to Paul; N. Baumert, *Täglich Sterben*, p.31, who comments that it
   is "wahrscheinlich, daß er sich selbst als einzelnen den vielen gegenübergestellt
   und nicht eine kleinere Gruppe einer größeren". For a discussion of the textual
   variant λοιποί and the reasons for preferring πολλοί, see Barrett, *Second Corinthians*, p.96n.2; his article "Titus", p.9n.1 and his article, "ΨΕΥΔΑΠΟΣΤΟΛΟΙ",
   pp.384ff.

185 The tendency among those commentators who do argue that καπηλεύειν refers to
   selling in the market place is to read too much into Paul's use of this imagery.
   Cf. e.g. Bultmann, *Zweiter Korintherbrief*, pp.72f.; Georgi, *Die Gegner des
   Paulus*, pp.226f.; I.I. Friesen, *The Glory of the Ministry of Jesus Christ*, p.
   29; Hughes, *Second Corinthians*, p.38 and Hock, *Social Context*, p.63. A good
   recent example of this tendency is James I.H. McDonald, "Paul and the Preaching
   Ministry, A reconsideration of 2 Cor. 2:14-17 in its context", *JSNT* 17(1983)35-
   50, pp.42f., who rightly emphasizes that καπηλεύειν here means "to make a trade

serious doubt on the integrity of those so described. But the significant point is that this technical, transferred use of καπηλεύειν also
allowed Paul to call into question the practice of those he refers to
as οἱ πολλοί, *without calling into question the apostolic right of being paid for one's preaching in and of itself.* For the well established
tradition of using the marketplace metaphor in this way, which we have
seen attested from Plato and Isocrates to Lucian, Philostratus and the
Didache, as well as the general note of caution and negative connotations associated with the κάπηλος and retail trade in general in Sirach,
Philo and Josephus, provided Paul with a widespread linguistic conven-
tion which was admirably suited to his needs. Thus, in adopting this
polemical, metaphorical use of καπηλεύειν in II Cor. 2:17 Paul was able
to criticize the practice of the πολλοί, who were seeking support for
their ministry, without contradicting or rescinding his previous argument for the basic legitimacy of making one's living from the gospel in
I Cor. 9:7-14[186].

On the other hand, Paul's introduction of the καπηλεύειν-motif is
also intended to support the legitimacy of his own apostolic ministry.
In fact, Paul's *primary* concern in 2:17 is not to criticize his opponents. For Paul's criticism of the "majority" as those who "sell the
word of God as a retail dealer sells his wares in the market" is not
presented for its own sake, but instead forms the counterpart to Paul's

---

of the word of God", but who goes on to take this to mean "to reduce preaching
to a worldly occupation and so denude it of 'ultimate' or eschatological concern".
Paul's point thus becomes that "no ordinary preaching, with ordinary human
motivation, is sufficient here: no mere professional performance, nor well
turned rhetoric, nor evangelistic sideline ...". But καπηλεύειν alone cannot
bear this load. The point to be kept in mind is that this metaphorical use of
καπηλεύειν was used to represent a variety of different criticisms, not only
concerning the motives of those involved, but also concerning the quality of the
message sold as well. Moreover, as already indicated above, I am somewhat skep-
tical of Hock's suggestion that Paul's use of καπηλεύειν "further underscores
Paul's snobbish attitude toward work", "Paul's Tentmaking", p.562n.43.

186 This point has been missed by commentators in the past because the precise function of the καπηλεύειν-motif within the larger context of the writings of those
who used it was not clearly seen. Thus, e.g., Windisch, *Zweiter Korintherbrief*,
p.101, simply places Paul's statements in I Cor. 9:14 and II Cor. 2:17 side by
side without attempting to explain this seeming contradiction beyond attributing
it to the pressure Paul feels to defend himself because of his opponents, while
Dungen, *Sayings of Jesus*, pp.3,7 argues that I Cor. 9:4-6 must be read in the
light of II Cor., so that Paul is directly denouncing Peter and the brothers of
the Lord. Although more cautious, see too Barrett, "Titus", p.9n.1; *Second Corinthians*, p.104 and "ΨΕΥΔΑΠΟΣΤΟΛΟΙ", pp.384f. and G. Theißen, "Legitimation",
pp.215,219,223, for this common decision to equate the πολλοί of II Cor. 2:17
with the apostles of I Cor. 9, so that in both contexts Paul is criticizing the
Jewish Christian "pillar apostles", a solution suggested by the textual variant
λοιποί itself (cf. I Cor. 9:5). On the other hand, many commentators simply do
not attempt to explain the relationship between II Cor. 2:17 and I Cor.9 at all;
cf. e.g. Georgi, *Gegner*, pp.226-229, 234-236; A. Plummer, *Second Corinthians*,
pp.73-75 and P. Hughes, *Second Corinthians*, pp.82-84.

negative comparison. Paul's primary purpose in criticizing his opponents, therefore, is to make a positive assertion concerning the nature
of his own ministry, here presented as the ideal, and in so doing to
offer *evidence* (see the γάρ of 2:17a) for his sufficiency as an apostle.
For as already intimated, my point is that 2:17 is itself Paul's first
support for the unexpressed answer to 2:16b and not an interruption or
parenthesis in Paul's thought[187]. The implications of this comparison
and the nature of the evidence Paul adduces from it are then made explicit in the ἀλλά-constructions of 2:17b. Hence, in order to ascertain
the actual meaning of Paul's statement in 2:17, the identity of the
πολλοί and the nature of Paul's criticism signaled by his use of
καπηλεύειν must first be clarified.

1. The Identity of the πολλοί and the Point of Paul's Criticism

Paul's decision to contrast himself *negatively* to those he simply
identifies as the πολλοί in II Cor. 2:17, together with the nature of
the critique itself, indicate that Paul is not referring to the circle
of apostles listed in I Cor. 9:5 or their counterpart, i.e. the "super
apostles" in II Cor. 11:5 and 12:11. Rather, Paul is contrasting himself to those who have recently arrived in Corinth and are now questioning his authority and sufficiency as an apostle, i.e. the "false
apostles" of II Cor. 12:13-15[188]. For as we have seen, in both I Cor.
9 and II Cor. 11-12 Paul explicitly compares himself *positively* to the
λοιποί ἀπόστολοι, etc. and ὑπερλίαν ἀπόστολοι respectively, while at the
same time *distancing himself* from the "false apostles". Moreover, we
have also seen that Paul's criticism of his opponents in II Cor. 11 and
12 revolved around their motives, i.e. that their insistence on being
supported in Corinth did not derive from a love for the Corinthians, but
from a desire to take advantage of them (see II Cor. 11:20). In contrast, in I Cor. 9 Paul does not directly criticize either the legitimacy of "living from the gospel" as such, or the fact that the other
apostles were availing themselves of this right. Indeed, Paul himself
advances a detailed argument to support both its legitimacy and imple-
mentation in I Cor. 9:7-14. The idea that the common apostolic practice
of living from the gospel actually derived from a deceitful desire to

---

187 This point will be developed below. For an example of the view that Paul's evi-
    dence for his sufficiency is first given in 3:1-6, cf. R. Bultmann, *Zweiter
    Korintherbrief*, p.73. For the most recent example of this view, see J. Lambrecht,
    "Structure and Line of Thought in 2 Cor. 2:14-4:6", *Biblica* 64(1983)344-380, p.
    366.
188 See Georgi, *Gegner*, pp.219-220 for his list of the eight elements in common be-
    tween II Cor. 10-13 and 2:14-7:4, which support the supposition that the identity
    of Paul's opponents in these two sections is the same. Georgi, however, identi-
    fies these opponents with the "super apostles" of chs. 11 and 12 (see pp.39, 48).

take advantage of the Church is thus foreign to Paul's discussion in both I and II Corinthians. Hence, not only the negative comparison established in 2:17, but also the clearly negative imagery associated with καπηλεύειν when used in a transferred sense, necessitate that we identify the πολλοί with Paul's opponents currently in Corinth, in distinction to the "pillar apostles" in view in I Cor. 9, II Cor. 11:5 and 12:11.

It is not necessary at this point, however, to advance a theory concerning the precise identity of Paul's opponents in order to understand Paul's statement in 2:17 or his larger argument in 2:14-3:6. It is enough merely to keep in mind that the structure of Paul's argument in II Cor. 11 and 12 (see above) indicates that Paul's opponents were building their case for the legitimacy of their own apostolic authority and ministry on the similarity between their practice and that of the "pillar apotles" regarding the question of apostolic support and, in turn, criticizing Paul for his deviation from this norm[189]. This is confirmed by the fact that Paul's use of the marketplace imagery in 2:17 accomplishes the same dual purpose we saw to be at work in Paul's argument in chapters 11 and 12, namely, to cut his opponents off from the common apostolic tradition despite their *seemingly similar practice* and in so doing reassert his own unity with this tradition, in spite of his *obviously different practice*. For the point of Paul's criticism, as reflected in καπηλεύειν, is not that being paid for one's preaching is, in and of itself, morally wrong or inherently inferior to Paul's practice of supporting himself[190]. In fact, not only does Paul himself argue for its legitimacy in I Cor. 9, but we have also seen that within the development of the καπηλεύειν-motif from Plato on, the very act of selling one's teaching *per se* was often interpreted in the ancient world to be a positive claim concerning the value of the message being sold.

---

189 That Paul's opponents were being supported by the Corinthians has been generally recognized. See most recently G. Lüdemann, *Paulus, der Heidenapostel, Bd. II*, p.136.

190 Contra the basic position represented, for example, by Windisch, *Zweiter Korintherbrief*, p.101, who, because of his identification of the "false apostles" with the "super apostles", must conclude that in II Cor. 2:17 Paul is forced by the critique of his opponents to disdain a custom that is sanctioned by the Lord and otherwise highly thought of by Paul himself. See too Hock, *Social Context*, pp.49-59, 63, who argues that Paul's criticism is based on the fact that of the four possible means of support available to the philosopher of his day, Paul considered working the most suitable and honorable. Hock thus casts Paul's view in the light of that found in the Cynic epistle of Ps-Socrates, *ep.* 1.1-2, in which we read, "I generally do not regard it right to make money from philosophy, and that goes for me especially, since I have taken up philosophy on account of the command of God" (taken from Hock, p.49). But in I Cor. 9 Paul argues that one *should generally* be paid for preaching if one is called by God to be an apostle and that his practice is the *exception* which is *not* necessitated by his call!

Rather, as the argument in II Cor. 11 and 12 makes clear, his description of his opponents as those who are selling the word of God like a
retailer in the market is intended to raise the question of their
integrity in doing so, i.e. the question of their *motives*[191] and hence
of their practice as well. What is conveyed in II Cor. 11:13-15 with
the prefix ψευδο-, the adjective δόλιος, the verb μετασχηματίζω and the
comparison to Satan's strategy is thus also represented by his choice
of the marketplace metaphor in 2:17. Like *dishonest* merchants in the
market, Paul's opponents are attempting to deceive the Corinthians, or,
in terms of the metaphor itself, their ministry is best described as a
"shady business". For although Paul's opponents have assumed an outward
appearance of legitimacy by following the common apostolic custom regarding financial support represented by the "pillar apostles", from
which they are then able to mount an attack against Paul based on his
divergence from this practice[192], this appearance is a "sham". Their
purpose is simply to take advantage of the Corinthians. Paul's use of
καπηλεύειν in 2:17 therefore raises a general suspicion concerning the
motives of his opponents, although the specific nature of this suspicion is left undefined. But even in raising this general suspicion Paul
has already accomplished his goal of distinguishing their practice from
the true and genuine apostolic practice outlined in I Cor. 9 and exemplified by the "pillar apostles". For Paul's opponents could have used
his own strong arguments from I Cor. 9 for the legitimacy of seeking
one's living from the gospel to call his own apostolic claim into question. Thus, although it is not his primary purpose in II Cor. 2:17,
Paul's description of his critics as retail merchants dealing in the
word of God is designed to defuse this potentially explosive criti-

---

191 At this point Paul's use of the marketplace motif parallels its most classic
formulation as first seen in Plato's presentation of Socrates' critique of the
Sophists. In addition to my study above, see Hock, *Social Context*, p.53, who
comments that " ... Socrates, particularly in the Platonic writings, compared
Sophists to traders and merchants (κάπηλοι), the comparison being made to impute
to Sophists the motives of deceit and avarice. This criticism of Sophists became
traditional, but was also extended to philosophers too, if they charged fees or
otherwise were perceived as suspect" (cf. also p.95nn.23 and 24). Hock points to
Plato, *Apol.* 19D-E; 31B-C; 33A-B; *Prot.* 313C-D; *Men.* 92A; Xenophon, *Mem.* I.2.6-7,
61; 6.1-5, 11-14; *Apol.* 16.26; Diogernes Laentius 2.27 and Euthyd. 277B. But this
parallel by no means indicates dependence!
192 Although I have taken exception to certain aspects of his understanding of
καπηλεύειν, M. Rissi, *Studien*, p.18 has nevertheless captured the point of Paul's
negative comparison well: "Um nun Vers 17 zu verstehen, muß man beachten, daß
Paulus zunächst ironisch seinen Gegnern recht gibt. Wie sollen wir 'tüchtig' sein,
'denn wir sind ja nicht wie die vielen'. Aber an diesen Begründungssatz, der gegen
ihn zu sprechen scheint, hängt Paulus seine äußerst scharfe Kritik an, die eine
eindeutige Antwort auf die gegnerische Frage nicht vermissen läßt, indem er 'die
Vielen' charakterisiert als καπηλεύοντες τὸν λόγον τοῦ θεοῦ, 'die das Wort Gottes
verschachern'. Die partizipiale Apposition dreht die Anklage gegen Paulus um in
einen Angriff auf die Gegner".

cism without denying the legitimacy of seeking one's living from the
gospel in and of itself.

Paul's statement in 2:17 therefore occupies a mediating position between Paul's prior argument in I Cor. 9 and his direct criticism of his
opponents in II Cor. 11 and 12. For on the one hand, Paul's use of
καπηλεύειν refers back to and is built upon his contrasting practice of
supporting himself as outlined in I Cor. 9, while on the other hand
it also assumes and anticipates Paul's criticism of his opponents in
II Cor. 11 and 12. This becomes even more clear in the light of the
primary meaning of Paul's statement in 2:17, to which we now turn our
attention.

2. The Meaning and Significance of II Cor. 2:17

The point of Paul's negative comparison in 2:17 is made explicit by
two ἀλλ' ὡς-constructions, the second of which compliments the first
by further defining the nature of Paul's speaking ἐξ εἰλικρινείας, and
by two prepositional phrases:

$$\text{ἀλλ' ὡς ἐξ εἰλικρινείας, ἀλλ' ὡς ἐκ θεοῦ}$$
$$\text{κατέναντι θεοῦ ἐν Χριστῷ λαλοῦμεν.}$$

The second ἀλλ' ὡς-clause and the prepositional phrases which follow
do not introduce an additional contrast between Paul's ministry and the
practice of the πολλοί described in 2:17a, but instead serve to indicate
the larger context within which Paul's own practice of speaking ἐξ
εἰλικρινείας is to be understood. For the ἀλλ' ὡς-construction is repeated without an intervening coordinating conjunction and/or new verbal
idea. The impression thus given by the syntax of 2:17 is that after
having specified the nature of the contrast between himself and his
opponents, Paul then decided to expand this contrast by placing it
within the context of his apostolic self-understanding as the one who
speaks ἐκ θεοῦ κατέναντι θεοῦ ἐν Χριστῷ. Therefore, although the second
ἀλλ' ὡς-construction and the prepositional phrases which follow also
modify λαλοῦμεν, they nevertheless support, at the same time, Paul's
assertion that he speaks ἐξ εἰλικρινείας by emphasizing[193] the *source*
of Paul's preaching and the *motivation* behind his proclamation[194]. But
the precise meaning and significance of this densely formulated affirmation, which in and of itself remains opaque due to its brevity, only

---

193 See again Rissi, *Studien*, p.19, who interprets the second ἀλλ' ὡς to be an
   "emphatic repetition" of the first phrase, which is then supplemented by the
   prepositional phrases.
194 With J.H. Schütz, *Paul and the Anatomy of Apostolic Authority*, SNTSMS, Vol. 26,
   1975, p.211. But Schütz does not develop this point further. See as well,
   Bultmann, *Zweiter Korintherbrief*, p.73, who also understands the second ἀλλ' ὡς-
   construction to be describing the first.

becomes transparent in the light of Paul's negative comparison in
2:17a, upon which it is based, and Paul's other discussions of this and
related themes throughout his letters[195].

Paul's assertion that he speaks ἐξ εἰλικρινείας is stated in contrast
to the "many", whose *motives* (and hence activities) in preaching the
gospel are suspected to be deceitful, which indicates that Paul's point
in 2:17 is to stress that his own proclamation is *sincere*, being based
on *pure* intentions[196]. This interpretation, in distinction to that of
those who, due to their prior decision that καπηλεύειν means "to water
down" or "adulterate", have consequently taken 2:17b to refer to the
purity of Paul's message rather than his motives, is also supported by
the fact that the phrase ὡς ἐξ εἰλικρινείας is clearly adverbial, functioning to modify λαλοῦμεν, rather than adjectival in dependence on the
unexpressed object of λαλοῦμεν, τὸν λόγον τοῦ θεοῦ.

Moreover, the fact that Paul's positive statement in 2:17b does not
refer to the quality of his message *per se* is also confirmed by the
other two occurrences of εἰλικρίνεια in the Corinthian correspondence.
For in I Cor. 5:8 εἰλικρίνεια is paired together with ἀλήθεια as the
two qualities which ought to characterize the Corinthians *behavior*, as
indicated not only by their contrast to κακία and πονηρία in I Cor. 5:8
itself, but also by the larger context as a whole, in which the issue
in view is the association of the Corinthians with those guilty of
immorality of all sorts (cf. 5:1-5, 9-13). In addition, it is significant to note that although ἀλήθεια and εἰλικρίνεια in this context are
themselves inner qualities or attitudes, Paul is nevertheless able to
pit these inward dispositions *directly* against the immoral conduct of
those from whom the Corinthians are to separate themselves (compare I
Cor. 5:8 with 5:11). Paul's mode of expression in I Cor. 5:8ff. conse-

---

195 I.I. Friesen, *The Glory of the Ministry of Jesus Christ*, pp.29f., is a good representative of the common approach to this difficult passage. For like Friesen,
commentators have usually been content simply to interpret this text in a general
way as a reference to the fact that Paul's sincerity is witnessed to by his
refusal to accept money, the divine origin of his message, and from the fact
that Christ is the center from which Paul spoke. Although this interpretation
is certainly correct, it stops short of explaining how Paul's argument in 2:17
actually works both to support the legitimacy of his own apostleship and to offer
a defense against his opponents' claims.

196 The noun εἰλικρίνεια occurs only three times in the NT, all within the Corinthian
correspondence. For a discussion of the other two references in I Cor. 5:8 and
II Cor. 1:12, see below. The corresponding adjective, εἰλικρινής ("sincere") occurs in Phil. 1:10 and II Pet. 3:1. For its basic meaning "moral purity", cf. F.
Büchsel, art. εἰλικρινής κ.τ.λ., *TDNT*, *Vol. II*, 1964, pp.397-398. Cf. Philo's
use of the adjective in *De post.* 134; *De ebr.* 101; *De som.* II,20,74; *De spec.leg.*
I,99; *De Ab.* 129, etc. Of special interest is Philo's statement in *De vit.Mos.*
II,40 that the translators of the LXX are to be considered prophets and priests
"whose sincerity and singleness of thought has enabled them to go hand in hand
with the priest of spirits, the spirit of Moses" (οἷς ἐξεγένετο συνδραμεῖν
λογισμοῖς εἰλικρινέσι τῷ Μωυσέως καθαρωτάτῳ πνεύματι). Text and translation from
F.H. Colson, *Philo, LCL, Vol. VI*, 1959(1939).

quently reveals the same unexpressed presupposition we saw to be at
work in his argument in II Cor. 11:5ff. and 12:11ff., namely, the assumption that one's outward behavior is a direct expression of one's
inner motives or disposition[197]. For it is this identification which
enables Paul to move freely from the one category to the other, as he
does in I Cor. 5:8ff., or even to speak of "obeying" or "not obeying"
the truth in Gal. 5:7 and Rom. 2:8 respectively[198].

Moreover, it is Paul's understanding of humanity's plight which explains why in II Cor. 1:12 Paul describes his own behavior, both in the
world and towards the Corinthians, as being carried out ἐν ... εἰλικρινείᾳ τοῦ θεοῦ, which he then further clarifies as being done οὐκ ἐν
σοφίᾳ σαρκικῇ ἀλλ' ἐν χάριτι θεοῦ. In view of humanity's bankrupt nature, the sincerity which is the source or means of Paul's behavior can
only be a divine sincerity, i.e. a sincerity which belongs to God or
which finds its origin in God[199]. Hence, since the sincerity which
characterizes Paul's behavior originates in God, his conduct can also
be described as taking place ἐν χάριτι θεοῦ, rather than ἐν σοφίᾳ
σαρκικῇ. Furthermore, as the parallels between this contrast in II Cor.
1:12 and the contrast between the σοφία τοῦ κόσμου and the σοφία τοῦ

---

197 For the corresponding point, namely, the necessary unity in Paul's thought between the inner "Wollen" and the outer "Tun", see W. Schrage, *Ethik des Neuen
Testaments*, NTD Ergänzungsreihe, Bd. 4, 1982, p.177, Schrage points out that even
in II Cor. 8:10f., the text most likely to yield the impression that one's intentions are more important than the actual fulfillment of the ethical imperative,
"so gehört doch nach den folgenden Versen zum Wollen unabdingbar auch ein ent-
sprechendes Tun ...".

198 It is beyond the scope of this study to develop this point further. For this same
identification see Phil. 4:8f.; Col. 1:4-6 and Rom. 1:18ff. On this point see
the work of Roman Heiligenthal, *Werke als Zeichen, Untersuchungen zur Bedeutung
der menschlichen Taten im Frühjudentum, Neuen Testament und Frühchristentum*, WUNT
2. Reihe, Bd. 9, 1983.

199 Taking the genitive τοῦ θεοῦ to be a *genitivus auctoris*. See H.-J. Eckstein, *Der
Begriff Syneidesis bei Paulus, Eine neutestamentlich-exegetische Untersuchung zum
'Gewissensbegriff'*, WUNT 2. Reihe, Bd. 10, 1983, p.194, who says, "Im Fall des
genitivus auctoris würde Paulus nicht erst mit ἐν χάριτι θεοῦ den Ermöglichungsgrund und Ursprung seines Wandels, dessen er sich rühmt, angegeben, sondern schon
jetzt auf Gott als den verweisen, der die Befähigung dazu wirkt und schenkt". He
points to the commentaries of Schlatter and F.W. Grosheide as also representing
this view (cf. p.194n.71). Eckstein himself opts for a *genitivus obiectivus*,
interpreting Paul's meaning to be that he "bezeugt dann seine Lauterkeit 'vor
Gott'", thus taking Paul's statement to be a description of the nature of his
conduct, rather than in parallel to ἐν χάριτι θεοῦ (cf. pp.197f.). As such its
function corresponds to Paul's statement in II Cor. 12:19 that he speaks "vor
Gott in Christus" (p.194). But as I have argued, the two conceptions, though
related, are distinct, as the switch in prepositions itself from ἐκ to κατέναντι
in 2:17 indicates. Surprisingly, Eckstein does not bring 2:17 into his discussion
at all. Moreover, the similar structure throughout II Cor. 1:12 (ἐν ... οὐκ ἐν ...
ἀλλ' ἐν) indicates that Paul is attempting to make *one* point, not two, as necessitated by Eckstein's position. It is nevertheless important to emphasize that as
the source of Paul's activity, the sincerity of God also characterizes his activity, so that in pointing to its "Ermöglichungsgrund" Paul is also expressing
something about the nature of his activity itself.

θεοῦ = Χριστὸς ἐσταυρωμένος in I Cor. 1:20-24 (cf. 2:5) on the hand,
and Paul's statement in II Cor. 5:16f. that he no longer knows Christ
in a fleshly manner (κατὰ σάρκα)[200], being a "new creation", on the
other hand indicate, the contrast between ἐν σοφίᾳ σαρκικῇ/ἐν χάριτι
θεοῦ in II Cor. 1:12 is a contrast between his standing apart from
Christ and his standing as one called by Christ to be his apostle. For
in I Cor. 1:26-31, the decisive factor in recognizing the divine wisdom
in Christ is God's "call" or "election" (cf. vv.26, 27, 30), with its
concomitant gift of God's Spirit (2:12), though whom God reveals those
things which he has freely given in Christ (cf. 2:7-12, with 2:12 recalling 1:30). Similarly, in II Cor. 5:18 Paul's new creation, with its
new understanding of Christ, comes ἐκ τοῦ θεοῦ τοῦ καταλλάξαντος ἡμᾶς
ἑαυτῷ διὰ Χριστοῦ καὶ δόντος ἡμῖν τὴν διακονίαν τῆς καταλλαγῆς. Thus,
Paul is able to assert in I Cor. 2:13 that ἃ καὶ λαλοῦμεν οὐκ ἐν
διδακτοῖς ἀνθρωπίνης σοφίας λόγοις ἀλλ' ἐν διδακτοῖς πνεύματος, and in
II Cor. 5:20 that God makes his plea δι' ἡμῶν (cf. 6:1). Paul's affirmation in II Cor. 1:12 that his conduct is ἐν εἰλικρινείᾳ τοῦ θεοῦ/ἐν
χάριτι θεοῦ is at the same time, therefore, an affirmation concerning
his call to be a Christian apostle. Moreover, in II Cor. 1:12, as in I
Cor. 2:1-4 and II Cor. 6:3ff., Paul can point to his mode of *behavior*
as that which supports his legitimacy, since it is intended to be seen
as a direct result of the activity of God, i.e. God's sincerity, within
him. For although Paul's vacillation in his travel plans appears to be
a mode of behavior κατὰ σάρκα (1:17), in reality it corresponds to God's
own faithfulness in carrying out his promises in Christ (1:18-20).
Paul's purpose in not going through with his aforementioned plans was
"to spare" the Corinthians, i.e. like God's actions in Christ, Paul's
decision to change his plans was carried out for their sake as an expression of his love for them. In other words, Paul did so in order
that the Corinthians might be saved (cf. 1:23; 2:4; 7:9, 12). Hence,
rather than being an act of duplicity or deceitfulness which calls his
apostleship into question, Paul's change of plans, being an act of love
carried out ἐν ἁπλότητι καὶ εἰλικρινείᾳ τοῦ θεοῦ, becomes his καύχησις
(cf. I Cor. 9:14ff.!), confirmed by the μαρτύριον τῆς συνειδήσεως
αὐτοῦ[201].

---

200 Taking κατὰ σάρκα to modify οἴδαμεν. For the various positions which have been
suggested concerning this text and a good discussion of the view I accept, cf.
F.F. Bruce, *Paul and Jesus*, 1974, pp.15-22. Bruce argues that in II Cor. 5:16
"the contrast which Paul is making is one between his former attitude to Christ...
and his present attitude to Christ ..." (p.20). Paul's past understanding of and
attitude toward Christ, as well as his conception of the Messiah as such, have
now been fundamentally altered by his encounter with Christ himself (cf. pp. 20-
22).

201 The other example of Paul's use of his "conscience" as a witness to his own
integrity is Rom. 9:1, where once again this witness is linked to Paul's (poten-
tial) activity, which would be undertaken if it could save his fellow Jews (cf.

Consequently, in the light of I Cor. 5:8ff. and II Cor. 1:12, and against the background we have sketched out briefly above, Paul's assertion in II Cor. 2:17b also implies the claim that his practice of self-support, as an outworking of this "sincerity", is a true expression of the elective grace of God in his life. Conversely, Paul's description of his opponents as those who sell the Word of God like a pedlar in the market not only casts suspicion on their personal motives in preaching, but also calls into question, by implication, the very legitimacy of their call to be apostles, and with it the truth or validity of their gospel (cf. II Cor. 4:2)[202]. For if Paul's call as a result of the grace of God creates a sincerity within him that expresses itself in a self-supporting ministry in Corinth in conjunction with his proclamation of the gospel revealed by the Spirit (cf. I Cor. 2:10, 13 and the transition from καπηλεύειν to λαλεῖν in 2:17), then his opponents' insistence on being paid for preaching and their corresponding criticism of Paul's practice must result from what Paul calls in II Cor. 11:4 a πνεῦμα ἕτερον, while the content of their message is an ἄλλος 'Ιησοῦς, i.e. an εὐαγγέλιον ἕτερον. Paul's assertion that he is not like those who seek support from the Corinthians is thus an *evidential argument for the divine origin and nature of his apostolic ministry and gospel*, as well as an implicit criticism of his critics. For from Paul's perspective, one's outward behavior is a direct result and reflection of one's inner motives[203].

9:2f.). For an extended discussion of both of these texts, cf. Eckstein, *Syneidesis*, pp.179-199. My understanding of v.12b to be a further extension of 12a as a whole, instead of being taken to be in apposition to καύχησις, with the ὅτι-clause providing the content of the "boast", follows Eckstein's analysis of the various syntactical possibilities for II Cor. 1:12 on pp.191f. He argues that both in Rom. 9:1 and II Cor. 1:12 the "witness" is given by the conscience itself. He thus renders the genitive in 1:12 to be a *genitivus subiectivus* (cf. pp.195f.).

202 Cf. too II Cor. 6:7 where Paul lists the fact that his ministry is characterized by the "word of truth" as one of the factors which commends him as a διάκονος θεοῦ. For a good discussion of this point, see C.K. Barrett, "ΨΕΥΔΑΠΟΣΤΟΛΟΙ", pp. 383-389. Barrett argues for the inseparableness of genuine apostleship and right doctrine in Paul's thinking, pointing especially to Gal. 2:7f.. He then goes on to relate this basic conviction to Paul's criticism of the false apostles in II Cor. 2:17; 4:2; 5:12; 10:12-16; 11:3f., 13 and 26. Barrett's main point is that Paul's criticism of his opponents in these texts focuses on the fact that they are not just guilty of an innocent error in preaching, but instead, are engaged in an "intended deception", which leads to a "deliberate falsehood", for which Paul can have no tolerance (cf. pp.383, 386, 388f.). Concerning 2:17 he rightly points out that although καπηλεύειν need not necessarily include the intent to deceive, the parallel between II Cor. 2:17 and 4:2 indicates that Paul probably also meant to emphasize that his opponents falsified the word they preached (cf. p.384).

203 As *Test.Benj.* 6 illustrates, Paul's mode of argumentation represents a typically Jewish perspective, based as it is on the essential unity between one's "mind set" or "deliberations" and one's conduct. It is significant, moreover, that *Test.Benj.* 6 also represents the view that the good mind set is a direct result of the fact that "the Lord dwells in him", as well as the idea that the good

This evidential argument is then buttressed by the second ἀλλά-construction and the following two prepositional phrases in which the sincerity of Paul's proclamation is *explicitly* brought into the context of Paul's call to be an apostle (i.e. he speaks ἐκ θεοῦ)[204] and its corresponding motivation (i.e. he speaks κατέναντι θεοῦ ἐν Χριστῷ). The significance of Paul's assertion that he speaks "from God" only becomes clear, however, once it is recognized to be merely one part of the larger theme expressed by the ἐκ θεοῦ terminology running throughout the Corinthian correspondence, namely, that God is the one source of everything that exists (cf. I Cor. 8:6; 11:12), including the Christians' redemption and existence in Christ (cf. I Cor. 1:30; II Cor. 5:18) and the Spirit which Paul has received (cf. I Cor. 2:12). In I Cor. 7:7 this fundamental and common Christian conviction expresses itself in Paul's affirmation that ἕκαστος ἴδιον ἔχει χάρισμα ἐκ θεοῦ, which, in turn, demands that Paul refrain from insisting that his celibate life-style become the binding norm for all believers[205]. In the same way, although the ἐκ θεοῦ terminology is not present in I Cor. 12, Paul's statement in 12:4-6 nevertheless betrays this same conviction, which then undergirds his insistence in 12:7ff. on the organic unity and mutual interdependence of the individual members of the body of Christ, despite the *diversity* of their gifts. As a result, this conviction also underlies the admonition to maintain the unity of the church by accepting one another implicit throughout this chapter (cf. especially 12:7, 12, 14, 20f., 25). Thus the point in I Cor. 7:7 and chapter 12 is essentially the same. The recognition that God is the giver and source of all gifts within the Church necessitates that the validity of each person's gift(s) be recognized. Of special significance for our study, therefore, is the fact that I Cor. 12:28 makes explicit that this implied imperative also refers to the χάρισμα of apostleship as well. Against this backdrop, Paul's assertion in II Cor. 2:17 that he speaks ἐκ θεοῦ is not only a reminder to the Corinthians of the

---

"set of mind" does not know "deceit", "but it has one disposition, uncontaminated and pure, toward all men ... the works of Beliar are twofold, and have in them no integrity". (Trans. according to Charlesworth, *OT Pseudepigrapha*, pp.826f.). For one specific application of the basic conviction that one's inner desires inevitably lead to outward behavior, cf. *Test.Reub.* 5f. This identification between one's inner state and conduct is, of course, already found in the OT (see H.W. Wolff, *Anthropology of the Old Testament*, 1974, pp.51-58 for a discussion of this point) and is a common NT conviction (see e.g. Mtt. 12:33par.; Mk. 7:18-23par.; Lk. 6:43-46par.; Acts 5:3f.; Heb. 4:1-12; James 4:1f.; I Peter 1:14f.; 2:11f.).

204 So too J. Munck, *Paul and the Salvation of Mankind*, p.181, who translates ἐκ θεοῦ in 2:17: "as commissioned by God".
205 So too H. Conzelmann, *Erster Korintherbrief*, p.150; A. Schlatter, *Bote*, p.219 and C.K. Barrett, *First Corinthians*, p.158.

divine origin of his own calling[206], but also an implicit *warning* to
them not to usurp God's sovereignty by calling Paul's apostleship into
question[207].

Moreover, Paul's reference in II Cor. 4:5 to his commitment to become the "slave of all" and his corresponding insistence that he does
not preach himself, but Christ as the κύριος, makes it evident that
Paul's defense of his own authority and hence legitimacy as an apostle
in II Corinthians is intended to meet the twofold criterion[208] established for determining the genuine nature of spiritual gifts in I Cor.
12-13. For on the one hand, "no one speaking by the Spirit of God says,
'Jesus is accursed' and no one can say 'Jesus is Lord', except by the
Holy Spirit" (I Cor. 12:3, NASV). On the other hand, the purpose and
use of the genuine gift or calling is the common good of the Church
(12:7; cf. ch. 13 and 14:12), as Paul's own evaluation of the gift of
tongues and his regulation for its use in the Church in I Cor. 14 make
clear. The point of Paul's assertion in II Cor. 2:17 that he speaks
ἐκ θεοῦ is not, therefore, to "pull rank" on the Corinthians by relegating the question of his apostolic authority to the inaccessible realm
of divine judgment, thus removing his ministry from the possibility of
human scrutiny and ruling out the ability of the Corinthians to evaluate
his apostleship as a matter of principle[209]. Instead, Paul's statement
serves to caution the Corinthians that a rejection of his authority as
an apostle would, in effect, be a rejection of God's authority itself,
since both the *content of his message* (i.e. Paul stands in continuity
with the common apostolic tradition which preaches Christ as Lord, see
above, pp.145ff.) and the *nature of his practice* (i.e. Paul's decision
to support himself is an expression of his love for the Corinthians,

---

206 For the same assertion concerning the divine origin of Paul's apostleship, see
    Gal. 1:1; 2:7f.; Rom. 15:15f. and I Cor. 15:10. It is important to note, moreover,
    that in each case Paul's affirmation of his call carries within it an implied
    apologetic designed to underscore the legitimacy of his apostleship and/or gospel.
207 This implied *exhortative* function of Paul's statement in II Cor. 2:17b, which I
    will develop more below, brings to expression the implied apologetic force of
    Paul's entire discussion in II Cor. 2:14-3:6 and is a classic example of what
    Victor Furnish, *Theology and Ethics in Paul*, 1968, p.97, describes as Paul's
    "use of indicative statements in order to exhort", i.e. what he terms the "im-
    peratival indicative" (see his discussion on pp.97f. for other examples).
208 Similarly J.D.G. Dunn, "The Responsible Congregation (1 Cor 14:26-40)", pp.223-
    225, distinguishes three such criteria: 1) the confession 'Jesus is Lord', 2)
    love, and 3) the test of edification or community benefit. Since the act of
    edification is, by definition, love (see I Cor. 13:4-7), I have combined the
    last two into one category.
209 My point here is the corollary to E. Käsemann's emphasis in his essay, "Amt und
    Gemeinde im Neuen Testament", in his *Exegetische Versuche, Bd. I*, 1960², pp.
    109-134, p.121, on the fact that for Paul all Christians are considered to be
    "charismatics", so that "Der Apostel hat Ordnung eben nicht statisch auf Ämtern,
    Insitutionen, Ständen und Würden aufgebaut, sondern Autorität allein dem konkret
    geschehenden Dienst zuerkannt ..." (p.125). For this same point see too J.H.
    Schütz, *Anatomy of Apostolic Authority*, pp.6-8, 14, 183f.

being made for their good, see above, pp.133ff. and 149ff.) have *already*
demonstrated to the Corinthians the genuineness and divine origin of
his gift of apostleship, i.e. that he speaks ἐκ θεοῦ. Since Paul's a-
postleship has already passed this necessary test by meeting the twofold criterion of authenticity established in I Cor. 12-13[210], to reject his authority because his practice of supporting himself differed
from the usual apostolic "norm" is to usurp God's sovereignty in dele-
gating his gifts. Or in Paul's own words, it would mean committing the
sin of "judging the servant of another", namely, the servant of God
(Rom. 14:4). Once again it must be emphasized, therefore, that Paul's
positive declaration that he speaks ἐκ θεοῦ, like his prior assertion
that he speaks ἐξ εἰλικρινείας, is supported by visible proof, i.e. his
decision to support himself in Corinth. Moreover, since Paul has shown
himself to be *speaking* "from God", to reject his apostleship is to reject the true word of God with which he has been entrusted[211]. For in
affirming that he speaks "from God", Paul is affirming that his speech
is the speech of God[212].

Finally, Paul completes his densely formulated affirmation by asserting that he speaks κατέναντι θεοῦ ἐν Χριστῷ. Fortunately, we are
provided with an important insight into the meaning and function of
this last aspect of Paul's statement by its repetition in II Cor. 12:19
and the parallel thought found in II Cor. 4:2 and 5:9-11. For in view
of the former, it becomes clear that Paul's assertion that he speaks
"before God in Christ" in 2:17 is also intended to prevent the Corinthians from drawing the conclusion that Paul is on trial before them,
or that he is seeking their approval (see above, pp.154ff.)[213]. Unlike

---

210 By this I do not mean to imply that this "test" was a prerequisite to becoming
   an apostle, but that the nature of Paul's apostleship was a subsequent demonstration of the legitimacy of his call, which is the only "prerequisite" Paul
   considered valid (cf. I Cor. 15:8-10). See Bultmann, *Zweiter Korintherbrief*,
   p.73. But contra Bultmann, p.78, Paul's point is that he has given the Corinthians
   evidence of this "Berufung".
211 In this regard, Rom. 15:18 provides an important parallel to Paul's statement in
   2:17 that he speaks ἐκ θεοῦ. On Rom. 15:18 see esp. J. Roloff, *Apostolat*, p.95,
   who interprets the significance of the image of Paul as the priest of God in
   15:16 to be Paul's statement in 15:18.
212 For this identification see I Cor. 14:37. V. Bartling, "God's Triumphant Captive,
   Christ's Aroma for God (2 Cor 2:12-17)", *Concordia Theological Monthly* 22(1951)
   883-894, p.894n.16 therefore goes so far as to translate Paul's statement that
   he speaks ἐκ θεοῦ, "inspired by God", pointing to II Pet. 1:21 as the key parallel. For a similar view, cf. Windisch, *Zweiter Korintherbrief*, p.101, who understands it to mean, "in Gottes Auftrag nach göttlicher Eingebung reden, Gottes
   Worte sprechen". Besides II Pet. 1:21, Windisch points to Mtt. 10:20 par.; I
   Thess. 2:13; I Pet. 4:11a; Odes Sol. 26:10 and John 3:31 as parallels.
213 Similarly, F. Hahn, "Bibelarbeit über 2.Korinther 3:4-18", in *Erneuerung aus der
   Bibel, Die Bibel in der Welt, Bd. 19*, ed. S. Meurer, 1982, pp.82-92, p.84: "aus
   Gott vor Gott in Christus, d.h. er redet in Gottes Auftrag, er redet in steter
   Verantwortung vor Gott und er redet in der Zugehörigkeit zu Christus".

12:19, however, the "speaking" referred to in II Cor. 2:17 is not *primarily* Paul's prior discussion, but rather his proclamation of the Word
of God, taking τὸν λόγον τοῦ θεοῦ in 2:17a to be the unexpressed object of λαλοῦμεν in 2:17b. Paul's main point, therefore, is that his
proclamation of the gospel, being characterized by the sincerity which
he possesses as a result of the work of God's grace in his life (ἀλλ᾽
ὡς ἐξ εἰλικρινείας, ἀλλ᾽ ὡς ἐκ θεοῦ), is not dependent upon *their* approval for its authority and legitimacy, since Paul carries it out before the judgment of God himself[214]. At the same time, Paul is also
confident that he does enjoy God's approval inasmuch as he speaks before God "ἐν Χριστῷ", i.e. from his position or status as a Christian
(cf. II Cor. 4:2; 5:11b)[215]. And, although it is not the primary referent of 2:17, it seems appropriate to assume, given the polemical tone
of 2:14ff., the identification of the message with its messenger which
we have seen to be such an integral part of Paul's thinking in 2:14-16a
and the conclusion which Paul himself draws from 2:17 in 3:1 (see below), that Paul also intends to include his prior discussion of his
own apostolic ministry of suffering (2:14-16a) as an essential part of
his ministry of the λόγος τοῦ θεοῦ which Paul preaches "before God in
Christ". Thus, having completed his affirmation concerning the nature
(2:14-16a) and source (2:17b) of his apostolic ministry, Paul is quick
to point out, as he also does in II Cor. 3:1 and 12:19, that this affirmation ought not to be misconstrued as an attempt on Paul's part to
seek his approval from the Corinthians. For the fact that Paul has indeed demonstrated the legitimacy of his apostolic calling *to* the Corinthians should not be taken to mean that he also derives his authority
from the Corinthians. God is Paul's only judge, being the one before
whom Paul speaks[216]. This is also brought out in the close parallel to
2:17 found in II Cor. 4:2, in which Paul again asserts that the purity
of his motives, i.e. the fact that he has renounced τὰ κρυπτὰ τῆς
αἰσχύνης, results in a standard of behavior which recommends him πρὸς
πᾶσαν συνείδησιν ἀνθρώπων ἐνώπιον τοῦ θεοῦ. Here too Paul's conduct is
portrayed as a demonstration of his legitimacy to the Corinthians,
though being carried out "before God".

---

214 Again, H. Windisch, *Zweiter Korintherbrief*, p.102: "κατέναντι θεοῦ ... ist eine
    Berufung auf Gottes prüfendes und bestätigendes Urteil und Zeugnis (vgl. 1:23),
    subjectiv die Versicherung des Gefühls der Verantwortung".
215 For the corresponding motif that there is no righteousness or ground for boasting
    "before God" apart from Christ, even in the "works of the law", see Rom. 3:9,20;
    I Cor. 1:29; Gal. 3:11, etc. Conversely, for the one who is "in Christ", his/her
    praise comes "from God" (Rom. 2:29), while his/her boast is in the Lord (I Cor.
    1:31; II Cor. 10:17f.; cf. Rom. 15:18).
216 Although it cannot be developed here, this forensic interpretation of κατέναντι
    θεοῦ ἐν Χριστῷ λαλοῦμεν in II Cor. 2:17 is also supported by the corresponding
    motif of standing "before God" found elsewhere within II Cor. See II Cor. 7:9-12
    and 8:16-21.

Finally, the parallel in thought between Paul's assertion that he speaks "before God in Christ" in 2:17, so interpreted, and Paul's statement in II Cor. 5:9-11 makes it clear that in the former case, the fact that Paul speaks before the judgment of God also functions to express the source of Paul's *motivation* in his ministry[217]. For rather than seeking to please the Corinthians, as if his authority and legitimacy derived from their approval, Paul's consciousness of Christ's coming judgment is the mainspring of his apostolic activity. As he puts it in II Cor. 5:11: εἰδότες οὖν τὸν φόβον τοῦ κυρίου ἀνθρώπους πείθομεν. Hence, Paul's assertion that he speaks "before God in Christ" provides additional support for his statement that he speaks "from sincerity". For since Paul is aware that his motives and actions as an apostle will one day be revealed and judged (II Cor. 5:10; cf. I Cor. 3:12-14; 4:1-4 and Rom. 14:10), this affirmation, like his ministry as a whole, must be able to endure the scrutiny of Christ. As a result, Paul's insistence that he is free from the judgment of the Corinthians does not mean that he is free from judgment[218].

The meaning of Paul's statement in II Cor. 2:17 can now be *summarized* as follows. Paul's refusal to seek financial support from the Corinthians is evidence of the purity of his motives[219], as well as the divine legitimacy of his ministry, in contrast to the πολλοί, whose motives in preaching are clouded with the suspicion of deceit[220] as those who are misusing[221] the apostolic custom of living from the gospel in order to take advantage of the Corinthians. For as Paul's prior argument in I Cor. 9 makes clear, Paul's decision to support himself in Corinth was occasioned by his call to be an apostle and was thus a direct result of the grace of God in his life. Hence, Paul's call con-

---

217 Again see the parallel in *Test.Benj.* 6, where it is said concerning the "good set of mind" that "whatever it does, or speaks, or perceives, it knows that the Lord is watching over its life, for he cleanses his mind in order that he will not be suspected of wrongdoing either by men or by God".

218 For the relevant literature on II Cor. 5:9-11 contributing to the consensus among scholars that this passage also contains a polemical thrust, and a summary of this view, see Calvin J. Roetzel, *Judgment in the Community, A Study of the Relationship between Eschatology and Ecclesiology in Paul*, 1972, pp.173-175.

219 As such, 2:17 finds an exact parallel in II Cor. 7:2, where Paul simply states what he here provides evidence for, namely, that he "wronged no one, corrupted no one, took advantage of no one", as well as making explicit the admonition which is implied in 2:17, i.e. "make room for us".

220 So too Hock, *Social Context*, p.63; Bultmann, *Zweiter Korintherbrief*, pp.72f. and Wendland, *An die Korinther*, p.177. See Georgi, *Gegner*, pp.108-111, 114, 188 for documentation of the critique in the ancient world of those who sold their teaching that emphasized their deceit, etc.

221 As Georgi, *Gegner*, p.234, also correctly emphasizes. Georgi also suggests that Paul reproached his opponents for the fact that this reception of money was used by them as an endorsement of their self-confidence (p.235), which corresponds to Georgi's idea that Paul primarily criticizes his opponents in 2:17 for pushing their own personalities and abilities forward and boasting in themselves rather than in the gospel (see pp.226f.).

sequently brought with it a twofold realization: first, that his proclamation of the gospel found its source in the divine sincerity created within him by the grace of God (i.e. he speaks ἐξ εἰλικρινείας)
since he preaches the gospel as God's appointed spokesman (i.e. he
speaks ἐκ θεοῦ); second, that as God's apostle Paul's motivation was the
fact that his ministry was being carried out before the appraisal and
judgment of God himself (i.e. he speaks κατέναντι θεοῦ ἐν Χριστῷ). It
is for this reason that Paul's decision to support himself in Corinth
can be seen to be an expression of the sincerity of his love for the
church and an outworking of his desire to please God (i.e. to secure
a "boast", in the positive sense, before him). As such, rather than
calling his sufficiency as an apostle into question, Paul's decision
to support himself can be adduced by Paul as evidence for the fact that
he is the one who is, in reality, sufficient for the apostolic ministry
since it is a result of the sincerity of God within him and hence an
attestation of the grace of God in his life. II Cor. 2:17 thus provides the same argument for Paul's sufficiency as that found in I Cor.
15:9f., namely, that Paul's sufficiency derives from the grace of God
which he has received, a grace which can be seen in the fact that he
labored in the work of the gospel more than all of the rest of the
apostles!

This interpretation of Paul's affirmation in 2:17 is confirmed by
Paul's earlier, more detailed statement in I Thess. 2:3-10, in which
we encounter the same constellation of motifs present in 2:17, but without the metaphorical clothing and densely packed formulations which make
2:17 so hard to penetrate. I Thess. 2:3-10 thus provides a running commentary on II Cor. 2:17, not only confirming our exegesis of this difficult passage, but also indicating that both the structure and content
of Paul's "apology" in II Cor. 2:17 represent a common piece of Pauline
catechesis, which in turn reflects that important aspect of Paul's self-
understanding as an apostle which set him apart so dramatically from
his opponents. The parallels between these two texts become immediately
evident once the elements of the two passages are isolated and compared
with one another:

	II Cor. 2:17	I Thess. 2:3-10
Negative comparison as evidence for Paul's sufficiency or legitimacy	οὐ γάρ ἐσμεν ὡς οἱ πολλοὶ	οὔτε γὰρ ... ἐγενή- θημεν ... ἀλλὰ ἐγε- νήθημεν νήπιοι ... (2:5, 7-10)
The question of deceitful motives	καπηλεύοντες τὸν λόγον τοῦ θεοῦ	ἐν λόγῳ κολακείας ... οὔτε ἐν προφάσει πλεονεξίας ... οὔτε ζητοῦντες ἐξ ἀνθρώ- πων δόξαν (2:5f.)

Positive affirma- tion of Paul's motives	ἀλλ' ὡς ἐξ εἰ- λικρινείας ... λαλοῦμεν	ἡ γὰρ παράκλησις ἡμῶν οὐκ ἐκ πλάνης οὐδὲ ἐξ ἀκαθαρσίας οὐδὲ ἐν δόλῳ (2:3)
Divine source of motives	ἀλλ' ὡς ἐκ θε- οῦ λαλοῦμεν	ἀλλὰ καθὼς δεδοκιμάσ- μεθα ὑπὸ τοῦ θεοῦ πισ- τευθῆναι τὸ εὐαγγέλιον οὕτως λαλοῦμεν (2:4a)
Divine judgement of ministry	κατέναντι θεοῦ ἐν Χριστῷ λαλοῦ- μεν	(λαλοῦμεν), οὐχ ὡς ἀν- θρώποις ἀρέσκοντες ἀλ- λὰ θεῷ τῷ δοκιμάζοντι τὰς καρδίας ἡμῶν (2:4b)

Finally, the fact that Paul's statement in 2:17 is once again concerned
fundamentally with Paul's apostolic self-conception provides an important insight into the meaning and function of Paul's argument as it continues in 3:1-6. Thus, before turning our attention to 3:1-3, it will be
helpful to conclude this chapter by summarizing the role of 2:17 within
the argument of 2:14-3:3 as a whole.

3. The Place of 2:17 within the Argument of 2:14-3:3

Paul's thesis-like presentation of the revelatory function of his
apostolic ministry of suffering in II Cor. 2:14-16a naturally led to
the question of Paul's "sufficiency" in 2:16b not only because Paul's
"weakness" as an apostle was the central point of contention in the dis-
pute between Paul and his opponents in Corinth (see II Cor. 4:7ff.;
6:3ff.; 10:7-10; 11:6f., 21-23; 12:9f.; 13:4,9), but also because of
the life and death significance which Paul himself attached to his ministry in 2:15. However, Paul's answer to the question καὶ πρὸς ταῦτα τίς
ἱκανός; in 2:16b, though unexpressed, was not so self-evident. For in
spite of his opponents' insistence that Paul's weakness and suffering
called his apostleship into question (cf. especially II Cor. 10:10;
11:21), and in the face of the magnitude of the apostolic task itself,
Paul nevertheless asserts that he is, in fact, sufficient for the apostolic ministry! This is the clear implication of the γάρ in 2:17a. At
the same time, this γάρ also indicates that Paul's negative comparison
in 2:17 is intended to supply the reason or ground for this bold assertion. As we have seen above, it does this by adducing Paul's commitment
to support himself as *evidence* of the genuine nature of his apostolic
commission, including the gospel he preached. For as Paul had argued
earlier in I Cor. 9, his practice of self-support in Corinth was a visible demonstration of his love for the Corinthians in response to and
in conformity with his prophetic call to preach the gospel, while the
εἰλικρίνεια-motif in 2:17 itself also attributes Paul's practice to the
sovereign work of God's grace in his life (cf. I Cor. 15:9f.).

Furthermore, our investigation has also demonstrated that there is
an internal, organic unity between Paul's apostolic ministry of suffering (2:14-16a), his claim to be sufficient for this ministry (2:16b) and
his refusal to accept payment for it (2:17). For an essential part of
his suffering or weakness as an apostle was his voluntary decision to
support himself and the tribulations which accompanied this practice
(cf. I Cor. 4:11f.; II Cor. 6:4f.; 11:26f.). Hence, given the fact that
the subject matter remains the same, the transition in thought from
2:14-16a to 2:17 is a natural one. Paul simply moves from a statement
concerning the nature and function of his apostolic ministry of suffering in general, to a specific aspect of that suffering. The rationale
for this move becomes apparent in the light of Paul's discussion in
chapters 10-13. For there it is evident that Paul's practice of self-
support was one of the central bones of contention between Paul and his
opponents in Corinth (cf. 11:7-15; 12:13-19). Against this background,
Paul's support for his sufficiency in 2:17 also functions as an apologetic rebuttal to the criticisms of his critics. Indeed, the very form
of 2:17 itself, i.e. the negative comparison, serves not only to defend Paul from those who criticized him on the basis of his practice
of self-support, but also to return the volley of criticism back into the
court of his opponents. For in 2:17 Paul adduces as evidence for his
sufficiency to be an apostle the very weakness and suffering which his
critics argued called that sufficiency into question. As a result, Paul's
negative comparison defends his own sufficiency by casting suspicion on
the practice and hence sufficiency of his opponents. Paul's argument
in 2:17 thus completes the train of thought introduced in 2:14 by meeting the two needs created as a result of Paul's description of his apostolic ministry in 2:14-16a. On the one hand, it provides the evidence
necessary to support Paul's own unexpressed assertion of his sufficiency in response to the natural question of 2:16b. On the other hand, it
also serves to refute those who would question or deny that assertion,
while at the same time casting doubt on any counter-assertion of sufficiency based on a demand for support from the Corinthians.

But having come this far in his argument, Paul realized that the
evidential support for his sufficiency adduced in 2:17 could be misconstrued to be merely a "self-recommendation" since it was, in the
final analysis, still dependent upon Paul's own interpretation, i.e.
that his practice of supporting himself was, in fact, done ἐξ εἰλικρινείας and ἐκ θεοῦ[222]. Paul's evidence in 2:17 thus raises the question
of 3:1a, which Paul then immediately extends by a second, related question in 3:1b. Hence, Paul's statement in 2:17 not only ends one discussion, it creates another, and in so doing occupies the pivotal posi-

tion upon which Paul's argument in 2:14-3:3 turns. For just as Paul's
assertions in 2:14-16a lead to the question of 2:16b, whose answer is
left unexpressed but then supported in 2:17, so Paul's assertion in
2:17 leads to the questions of 3:1, whose answers are also left unexpressed but then supported in 3:2f. And in repeating the structure of
2:14-17, the support for the unanswered questions in 3:1 found in 3:2f.
provides the second pillar in Paul's defense of his apostolic calling,
i.e. his ministry of the Spirit.

---

222 It is important to emphasize that the questions of 3:1 relate to what Paul has
    just said in 2:17, not to what he has said previously in 2:14-16a, thus jumping
    over this crucial intermediary statement, as Plummer, *Second Corinthians*, p.76,
    does. For the view that 3:1 is occasioned by the fact that 2:17 could be inter-
    preted as "self-praise" or as an inappropriate self-recommendation, see Barrett,
    Second Corinthians, p.106; Windisch, *Zweiter Korintherbrief*, p.102; Lietzmann,
    An die Korinther, pp.109f and most recently, J. Lambrecht, "Structure and Line
    of Thought", p.351. The most extreme statement of this relationship to my knowl-
    edge is that of Schoeps, *Paul*, p.79, who takes 3:1 to be a reflection of Paul's
    opponents' reproach that he had become mad with "overwhelming conceit" and
    "crazy with boasting", since Paul "appears to derive his vocation to the apostol-
    ic office from his own intrinsic strength". But we will see below that the issue
    involved is not Paul's pride, but the competing modes of recommendation employed
    by Paul and his opponents.

Chapter Five

PAUL'S MINISTRY OF THE SPIRIT AS CORROBATORY EVIDENCE
OF HIS SUFFICIENCY (II COR. 3:1-3)

In II Cor. 3:1 Paul responds to his evidential argument in 2:17 by
positing two interrelated questions, which in turn lead to the affirmations of 3:2f. The key to Paul's argument in 3:1-3, as well as its place
within 2:14-3:6 as a whole, thus lies in understanding the significance
of these two questions and their relationship to one another[1].

A. THE MEANING OF II COR. 3:1

The first thing to be taken into account in determining the meaning
of Paul's questions in 3:1a is that their form and function correspond
to one of the central rhetorical features of the "diatribe", the "false
conclusion", though their *Sitz im Leben* and literary context are not
diatribal. For rather than being part of an extended diatribal discourse,
constructed to be used in a philosophical school or pedagogical situation in general, II Cor. 2:14-3:6 is "polemical", i.e. it is bound to
the specific situation at hand in which Paul must defend the legitimacy
of his apostolic ministry. As such, the use of the common diatribal
device of the "false conclusion" in 3:1 is another example of the widespread use of diatribal elements in nondiatribal literature[2]. Moreover,

---

1 The crucial importance of determining the relationship between the two questions
  in 3:1 for an understanding of Paul's argument has been emphasized above all by D.
  Georgi, *Die Gegner des Paulus im 2. Korintherbrief*, WMANT Bd. 11, 1964, pp.241f.
  and J.H. Schütz, *Paul and the Anatomy of Apostolic Authority*, SNTSMS Nr. 26, 1975,
  p.172, though with different results.
2 For an analysis of the diatribe as a style of discourse and argumentation used in
  the philosophical schools and an examination of the seven or eight (depending on
  whether Philo ought to be included) examples of this type or genre of literature
  from antiquity, see Stanley Kent Stowers, *The Diatribe and Paul's Letter to the
  Romans*, SBL Dissertation Series, Nr. 57, 1981, pp.7-78. II Cor. 3:1 seems to be an
  example of what Stowers says are those "few texts in some of the apostle's other
  letters (i.e. other than Romans) where he employs the style of the diatribe, but
  these are isolated within the larger context of the letter where he is dealing with
  the specific problems of the churches, as in I and II Corinthians" (p.179). I have
  taken 3:1 to be diatribal in style since, unlike II Cor. 10:10, Paul is not directly
  quoting his opponents, but anticipating their response (cf. Stowers' distinction on
  p.179).

as Stowers has demonstrated in his recent study of the diatribe, the
pedagogical device of the "false conclusion" is "usually stated rhetori-
cally and usually (implies) an objection"[3]. Furthermore, "false conclusions are predominantly found as questions"[4]. But most important for
our purposes is the fact that

> when objections and false conclusions appear at the beginning of a new
> section[5] in the diatribe they are not usually the result simply of some
> necessary internal logic of the preceding argumentation. Instead, they
> appear as the result of two factors: First, they are connected with the
> previous line of argument and come as a reaction to it. Second, they are
> the result of the author's perception of his intended audience, their needs
> and responses. Objections and false conclusions usually appear at a point
> where the author anticipates a certain understanding or reaction from his
> audience and wants to effect or guard against certain types of behavior or
> philosophical-ethical teachings. At a point where the author sees the need
> to effect or guard against a certain tendency an objection or false conclu-
> sion is thrown out and the discourse shifts in another direction. In the
> diatribe objections and false conclusions are an artificial and rhetorical
> replacement for the input of the students into the discussion[6]. Except, of
> course, on those occasions when actual objections have been recorded[7].

II Cor. 3:1 is an example of precisely this kind of rhetorical "false
conclusion", based, however, on the existence of a real objection. For
as the presence of the adverb πάλιν in 3:1a indicates, Paul is concerned
that his assertion in 2:17 will once again be misconstrued by his opponents and the Corinthians under their influence as another "self-recommendation"[8]. Thus, anticipating his opponents' accusation[9], Paul

---

3 *Diatribe*, p.119. Cf. pp.119-122 where Stowers lists the objections and false conclusions in Romans and outlines their formal characteristics.
4 Stowers, *Diatribe*, p.127.
5 As here in II Cor. 3:1.
6 Stowers, *Diatribe*, pp.140-141.
7 Stowers, *Diatribe*, p.233n.139 to the statement just quoted.
8 This force of πάλιν has often been pointed out. Cf. e.g. Windisch, *Zweiter Korintherbrief*, p.102; Wendland, *An die Korinther*, p.177; Lietzmann, *An die Korinther*, p.
109; Barrett, *Second Corinthians*, p.106; Hughes, *Second Corinthians*, p.85; Plummer,
Second Corinthians, pp.76f.; Schlatter, *Bote*, pp.500f.; J. Munck, *Paul and the Salvation of Mankind*, 1977(1959), p.183 and G. Barth, "Die Eignung des Verkündigers in
2 Kor 2:14-3:6", in *Kirche, FS Günther Bornkamm zum 75. Geburtstag*, ed. D. Lührmann
and G. Strecker, 1980, pp.257-270, pp.263f. Moreover, Plummer, Hughes, Schlatter
and Barrett all offer suggestions as to what could have given rise to this accusation in the past. This latter point need not be speculated upon for the purposes
of this study.
9 M. Rissi, *Studien zum Zweiten Korintherbrief: Der alte Bund - Der Prediger - Der
Tod, AThANT 56*, 1969, p.19 asserts that this accusation of "Selbstempfehlung" first
originated with Paul against his opponents, as reflected in II Cor. 4:5; though he
then admits that the πάλιν in 3:1 shows that the opponents addressed the charge
back to Paul (cf. p.19n.27). On the basis of the evidence available to us, however,
it is simply impossible to determine with certainty who first raised the accusations
in 3:1. For the force of Rissi's argument is unclear to me when he states that this
accusation must have originated with Paul, "sonst hätte ja das die zweite Frage in
3:1 einleitende ἢ μή keinen Sinn" (p.19). For even if 3:1b does originate with Paul
as an accusation against his opponents, this does not necessarily mean that 3:1a
does as well. For as I will argue below, the connection between the two questions
is their common "mode" of recommendation, not their common origin. Thus Paul could
easily have combined an accusation originally from his opponents with an accusation

himself raises this "false conclusion" at the beginning of this new section in the form of *two* rhetorical questions in order to deny it.

That the two questions in II Cor. 3:1 both refer to the same problem
of Paul's apparent "self-recommendation", rather than being a reference
to two distinct objections (i.e. that Paul recommended himself *and* that
he lacked letters of recommendation from others)[10] is indicated by the
structure of Paul's argument in 3:1 itself. For unlike Paul's use of the
diatribal false conclusion in Romans, where it is always immediately and
explicitly denied, usually with μἡ γένοιτο[11], *before* a new section or
false conclusion is introduced, Paul's response to his first question
in II Cor. 3:1 is not to express its denial, either within the question
itself by use of the negative particle μή, or by an additional external
assertion. Instead, like the objection in Romans 3:1, which also implies a false conclusion based on what Paul has said in 2:17-29[12], Paul
immediately follows his first question with a second rhetorical question introduced with ἤ, before supplying the necessary negative answer
still lacking for 3:1a by means of the negative particle μή in the question of 3:1b[13]. Thus, the two questions of II Cor. 3:1 are to be taken

---

against his opponents, or vice versa; contra e.g. also Georgi, *Gegner*, p.241. The
point to be emphasized is that 3:1 actually anticipates an accusation which will
be made, rather than trying to answer one that is still lingering from the past and
that, as I will also argue below, the two questions are meant to be seen as essentially one. Moreover, as Georgi, *Gegner*, p.242; Schütz, *Anatomy*, p.172; Prümm,
Diakonia, 1967, pp.100f; Lietzmann, *An die Korinther*, p.110; Wendland, *An die Korinther*, p.177 and Rissi himself, p.19, have all pointed out, within the polemical
situation in which it stands, 3:1 is best understood as a "mutual rebuke", i.e. an
accusation which Paul has received and expects to receive again and which he also
turns back on his opponents. My burden below is to show how Paul in fact accomplishes this.

10 As implied by those who treat the two issues separately. See e.g. Schlatter, *Bote*,
pp.500-503; Barrett, *Second Corinthians*, pp.105-107; Bultmann, *Zweiter Korintherbrief*, p.74 and Windisch, *Zweiter Korintherbrief*, pp.102f. On the other hand,
Georgi, *Gegner*, pp.242f.; cf. p.245, correctly sees that the letters of recommendation were "eine Erweiterung dieser Art der Selbstempfehlung ..." (i.e. referred
to in 3:1a), although he nevertheless misses the precise nature of the "Art der
Selbstempfehlung" which unites them. For according to Georgi, both 3:1a and b are
to be taken as an expression of the opponents' demonstration of their possession
of the Spirit (cf. p.243). But although this is true in and of itself, i.e. Paul's
opponents probably did point to their spiritual gifts and attainments in order to
support their claims in Corinth (if II Cor. 12:2 can be taken as a reflection of
the claims of Paul's opponents, which is by no means certain, as Georgi, pp.231,
244; Schütz, *Anatomy*, p.173 and E. Käsemann, "Die Legitimität des Apostels, Eine
Untersuchung zu II Korinther 10-13", *ZNW* 41(1942)33-71, pp.61ff. seem to assume),
I will argue below that the issue in 3:1 is quite different, namely, that of the
proper criterion as such.
11 Cf. Rom. 3:9 (here we find the answer οὐ πάντως); 6:2; 6:15; 7:7; 7:13; 9:14; 11:1;
11:11 (following Stowers' analysis, *Diatribe*, pp.119-122).
12 See Stowers, *Diatribe*, p.119.
13 Cf. Rom. 3:1, where the two questions, taken together, are then explicitly answered
in 3:2. Among recent commentaries, only that of Windisch, p.103, has emphasized
that the negative answer expected for the second question is also intended to refer back to the first. But even Windisch says that this negation only "indirekt
auch der ersten Frage gilt ...".

together as Paul's *single* response to the anticipated objection that
his statement in 2:17 was merely a "self-recommendation".

Paul's initial denial of this charge in 3:1a derives, once again,
from his ability in 2:17 to point to his own practice of self-support
in Corinth as the evidence needed to establish his claim to be sufficient for the apostolic ministry. For it became clear in chapter four
that Paul's statement in 2:17, far from being an exercise in "self-recommendation", was based upon his *divine call* to be an apostle on the
one hand, and upon the *nature of his ministry in Corinth itself* on the
other hand. Paul need not, and is not recommending himself - his work
as an apostle speaks for him (cf. I Cor. 15:10)[14].

But from Paul's perspective, it is precisely *because* this first accusation, i.e. Paul is simply recommending himself, cannot be maintained
that his need for letters of recommendation is also eliminated. For if
Paul were *not* in the position to point to such evidence as he does in
2:17[15], then he too would need such letters in order to provide the external witness or corroboratory evidence for his claims otherwise lacking in his own apostolic ministry. That is to say, in Paul's view, whatever their origin might have been[16], these letters of recommendation

---

14 It would take us too far afield for our present purposes to develop the closely related motif of συνίστημι (συνιστάνω) + reflexive pronoun in the sense of "to demonstrate oneself" within II Cor. as a whole (see 4:2; 5:12; 6:4; 7:11; 10:12; 10:18;
12:11). Suffice it to say that Paul's reference to his own accomplishments as his
recommendation in 3:1 conforms to his use of the συνίστημι-theme throughout II Cor.
To be recommended by the Lord (10:18) is to be able to point to what one has accomplished "in the Lord" as Paul does in 4:2; 6:4ff.; 12:11f. and as the Corinthians
can do in 7:11; while to "recommend oneself" in the negative sense is to lay claim
to something for which one has no such evidence (see 3:1; 5:12; 10:12).

15 Besides the evidence we have discussed in chapter four, see Paul's statement in II
Cor. 12:11b. It seems impossible to dismiss or reinterpret the fact that Paul too
buttressed his claim to authority by referring to his pneumatic accomplishments
and gifts, as Bultmann, *Probleme*, p.21 and Käsemann, "Legitimität", pp.70f. attempt
to do. For a good discussion of this point, see Bengt Holmberg, *Paul and Power*,
1978, pp.77-79. Holmberg correctly concludes that the problem in Corinth was that
"both (Paul's) power and his sickness were conspicuous and the latter tended to
throw discredit on the former ... But he did not interpret it as a paradoxical
identification of strength and weakness, as if only his weakness were visible, God's
power through him being invisible" (p.78).

16 This issue need not, and probably cannot be decided with any degree of convincing
probability on the basis of the evidence now available to us. For as J.B. Lightfoot,
Saint Paul's Epistle to the Galatians, 1876⁵, p.373, concluded over a century ago
in his essay "St. Paul and the Three", "It is wisest to confess plainly that the
facts are too scanty to supply an answer". For an example of those who argue that
the letters came from the authorities in Jerusalem, cf. Windisch, *Zweiter Korintherbrief*, pp.102f.; Käsemann, "Legitimität", pp.44-47; and Schoeps, *Paul*, pp.74f., 79,
82; while for the position that they came from other churches in the Hellenistic
world because of the stress on ἐξ ὑμῶν in 3:1, cf. J. Roloff, *Apostolat - Verkündigung - Kirche, Ursprung, Inhalt und Funktion des kirchlichen Apostelamtes nach
Paulus, Lukas und den Pastoralbriefen*, 1965, p.78; Georgi, *Gegner*, pp.230n.3, 243-
245; G. Barth, "Eignung", pp.233f. and Bultmann, *Probleme*, pp.22f. See Acts 15:23-
29 for an example of a letter of recommendation sent out from the church in Jerusalem and Acts 18:27 for a letter sent from one mission congregation to another. It

function as a *substitute* for the ability to boast in one's own work,
i.e. for the ability to demonstrate one's own legitimacy (cf. 4:2;
6:4ff.; 12:11f.). This understanding of letters of recommendation as a
"substitutional" source of authority or credibility, which allows Paul
to bring the two questions in 3:1 together, is not idiosyncratic to
Paul. It is the common function of such letters in the ancient world
in general, as evidenced not only by the letters of recommendation
written by Paul himself[17], but also in the other extant non-Pauline
letters of recommendation known to us from antiquity[18]. To need such
letters is to admit that one lacks that evidential accreditation from
his/her own life which is already evident or available to those whose
acceptance is being sought. That is to say, since someone in this situation can only recommend him/herself, the need consequently exists for
someone *else* to speak on one's behalf in order to substantiate the claim
being made. Hence, although a valid and at times necessary means of attestation in and of themselves, the very need for letters of recommendation points to a "credibility-deficiency" among those being addressed
in the one carrying such letters[19].

Paul's second question in II Cor. 3:1 is best understood therefore
as a further explication or interpretive restatement of the first. Just

is enough to say that the individuals or communities who wrote these letters had to
have been influential, or to have had some sort of readily recognizable credibility
with the Corinthians, as Lietzmann, *An die Korinther*, p.110, points out.

17 Cf. Philemon; Rom. 16:1f; I Cor. 16:10f.; II Cor. 8:16-24 and Col. 4:7-9. In each
case, Paul writes on behalf of someone who cannot recommend him/herself and offers
one or more *reasons* why the person being recommended ought to be readily accepted
(this is also true of the letters listed by Keyes, see next note). Of special interest in this regard is the report in Acts 18:27f. that Apollos was sent to Corinth from Ephesus with just such a letter of recommendation from the church there.
Thus Schlatter, *Bote*, p.502, was correct in pointing out that "es geschah nichts
Ungewöhnliches, wenn auch die, die nach Korinth zogen, solche Briefe besaßen ...".

18 As listed and reproduced in part by Clinton W. Keyes, "The Greek Letter of Introduction", *The American Journal of Philology* 56(1935)28-44, pp.32-38. Keyes lists
only Rom. 16:1f. from the Pauline corpus. There are no doubt more examples now
available. Unfortunately, I was not able to consult the treatment of "recommendation" as a common social practice intended to initiate a reciprocal friendship
based on πίστις or the letter of recommendation practice itself by Peter Marshall
in his *Enmity and Other Social Conventions in Paul's Relations with the Corinthians*, unpublished Ph.D. dissertation, Macquarie University, 1980, pp.141-202, 398-
426 (referred to in his article, "Social Shame" (see note n.21), pp.309n.40 and
313n.52).

19 To say more than this concerning the function of these letters or to speculate
about their content would be to overstep the limits of our evidence. For this caution, see C.J.A. Hickling, "The Sequence of Thought in II Corinthians, Chapter
Three", *NTS* 21(1975)380-395, pp.381f. For the suggestion that the letters actually
recounted the pneumatic deeds of those who carried them, Cf. J.S. Vos, *Traditionsgeschichtliche Untersuchungen zur Paulinischen Pneumatologie*, 1973, p.133 and
Georgi, *Gegner*, p.245; for the less likely supposition that they carried a declaration of an obligatory institutional authority, cf. Käsemann, "Legitimität", p.
45. The most that can be said is that they probably pointed to some quality or accomplishment which was intended to support the opponents' claim to authority in
Corinth.

as Rom. 3:1b defines more closely what is meant by 3:1a, so II Cor.
3:1b also defines what is meant by 3:1a, so that to ask the former
question *is* to ask the latter one and vice versa. Taken together, the
two questions in II Cor. 3:1 thus raise the issue of whether or not
Paul must adduce, like his opponents, any outside corroboratory evidence (i.e. letters of recommendation) in order to support his claim
to sufficiency and interpretation of his primary evidence pointed to
in 2:17. Paul's answer is an unqualified no[20]. For if he were to capit-
ulate to such a demand, he would at the same time be denying the significance of his assertion in 2:17 that his own work in Corinth commends
him[21]. Or in the terms of 3:1 itself, he would be drawing the false conclusion that his argument in 2:17 was, in fact, an exercise in "self-
recommendation".

In addition, Paul's insistence that he is in no need of letters of
recommendation *from* the Corinthians is the counterpart to his statement
in II Cor. 5:12 that he is not commending himself *to* the Corinthians.
For as we have seen in chapter four, Paul does not seek or need the
approval of the Corinthians in order to give credibility to his ministry, as if he were on trial before them, since Paul's only judge is
God himself. Rather, from Paul's perspective, it is the Corinthians'
faith and genuineness which is now being tested by their response to
those who are presently challenging Paul's authority in Corinth (see
II Cor. 13:3-9)[22]. For Paul is confident of his own calling from and
standing before God (cf. II Cor. 2:17; 5:11; 10:7; 13:2,6,10).

Paul's argument in II Cor. 3:1 can now be summarized. In anticipation of the charge that his argument for his sufficiency in 2:17 is
merely an exercise in "self-recommendation", so that what Paul really
needs in order to demonstrate his sufficiency is letters of recommendation to confirm and verify his claim, Paul reminds the Corinthians,
by denying this false conclusion, that it is his divine call and ministry in Corinth which resulted from it (also publicly recognized by
Jerusalem (!), see Gal. 2:7-9) that supports his claim. II Cor. 2:17

---

20 Contra Bultmann, *Zweiter Korintherbrief*, p.74, who suggests that "Die rhetorische
   Frage will natürlich den Vorwurf als unberechtigt hinstellen; aber die zweite
   Frage läßt ihn als in gewissem Sinn richtig erscheinen! Denn wenn Paulus weiter-
   fragt ..., so will er ja sagen: er hat keine Empfehlungsbriefe von anderer Seite
   nötig, da er sich selbst empfehlen kann - wie freilich, das sagt dann V.2f. und
   vgl. 4:2!" Such a view is not possible, however, given the logical relationship
   between 3:1a and b.
21 Paul's present argument in II Cor. 2:17-3:1 thus makes the idea improbable that
   πάλιν in 3:1 indicates that Paul had indeed recommended himself in the past, but
   now refused to do so again, as Peter Marshall, "A Metaphor of Social Shame:
   ΘPIAMBEYEIN in 2 Cor. 2:14", *NovT* 25(1983)302-317, p.314, suggests.
22 See C.K. Barrett, "Paul's Opponents in II Corinthians", *NTS* 17(1971) 233-254, pp.
   248f. Barrett comes to a similar conclusion, namely, that in accepting Paul's
   opponents, the Corinthians have been using the wrong criterion for evaluation.

itself is all the "recommendation" Paul needs to commend himself. For
this "primary evidence", being the "divine attestation" of his calling
and ministry presented to the Corinthians themselves, is adequate to
support his claim to sufficiency[23]. The rhetorical questions of 3:1 can
thus be transported into two indicative statements in the following way:

3:1a: My argument in 2:17 is not an exercise in "self-recommendation";

3:1b: in other words, I do not need, as some do, letters of recommendation
to you or from you to speak on my behalf.

"Self-recommendation" in the negative sense and "letters of recommendation", from Paul's point of view, are not two different modes of recommendation, both of which are denied, but rather two aspects of the
same type of recommendation, i.e. a recommendation necessitated by a
lack of evidence from one's own work which is already present and known
among those to whom one is recommended.

B. THE LETTER OF PAUL AS THE LETTER OF CHRIST:
II COR. 3:2f.

1. The Transitional Function of 3:1

It is the identification in Paul's thinking between "self-recommendation" and "letters of recommendation" in II Cor. 3:1 that provides the
point of transition and connecting link in Paul's argument between what
first appears to be two unrelated themes, namely, between Paul's reference to his practice of self-support in 2:17 and his reference to his
role as the founder of the Corinthian church in 3:2f[24]. This is also reflected in II Cor. 10-12, where Paul moves from a discussion of his
authority over the Corinthians, with its corresponding "canon" of one's
"founding function" in 10:12-18, to a discussion of the genuineness of
his apostleship as such, with its "canon" of "weakness" in chapters 11-
12. For as 10:1-11 illustrates, Paul's opponents were using his weakness
as an apostle to call into question his authority over the Corinthians,

---

23 One thing that cannot be said on the basis of II Cor. 2:17-3:1, therefore, is that
Paul is "without personal concern ... for the establishment of his reputation ..."
(!), as W. Kasch, *TDNT*, *Vol. VII*, p.898, maintains.

24 C.J.A. Hickling, "Sequence", pp.382f. regards the transition from the "relatively
trivial starting point" in 3:1 to the "intensely theological" issue of the relationship between Christ, the Corinthians and Paul in 3:2f. to be so great as to
be a "μετάβασις εἰς ἄλλο γένος". But given Paul's view of his own suffering as
stated in 2:14-16a and the connection between the divine attestation in 2:17 and
the argument in 3:1 discussed above, Paul's argument does not appear to be such
"a sudden leap from the relatively trivial to the heights" (p.383). Cf. K. Prümm,
Diakonia, 1967, p.99: "Die plötzliche Art der Einführung ist nur Zeichen einer
engen inneren Verknüpfung mit dem Voraufgehenden".

thus bringing the two aspects together (cf. especially 10:8-11). In II
Cor. 2:14-3:3 the order is reversed. Paul moves from a discussion of his
"weakness" as *the* characteristic and proof, i.e. "canon", of his apostolic calling and his sufficiency for it in 2:14-17 to a discussion of
his relationship to the church in Corinth as its founder in 3:2-3. But
the concept which binds these two distinct aspects of Paul's ministry
as an apostle together is once again his opponents' criticism as anticipated and reflected in 3:1. Moreover, here too Paul argues that on
both fronts it is his ministry in Corinth itself which recommends him,
whether it be his decision to support himself on the one hand (2:17),
or his role as the church's spiritual father on the other hand (3:2f.).
Therefore, although the subject matter in 3:2f. is different than that
of 2:17, the basic issue nevertheless remains the same, i.e. the nature
of Paul's recommendation. II Cor. 3:1 thus functions as the transition
between these two themes by presenting the negative counterparts to
Paul's recommendations. This transitional function can best be seen
when it is diagrammed in the following manner:[25]

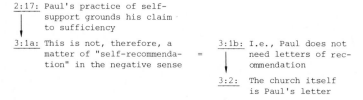

2:17: Paul's practice of self-
      support grounds his claim
      to sufficiency

3:1a: This is not, therefore, a   3:1b: I.e., Paul does not
      matter of "self-recommenda-   =   need letters of rec-
      tion" in the negative sense   ommendation

                                          3:2:   The church itself
                                                 is Paul's letter

2. The Corinthians as Paul's Letter of Recommendation

The meaning and function of Paul's basic affirmation in II Cor. 3:2f.,
ἡ ἐπιστολὴ ἡμῶν ὑμεῖς ἐστε, is thus readily apparent. Paul is in no
need of letters of recommendation in order to corroborate his primary
evidence in support of his claim to sufficiency for the apostolic ministry in general, or for his authority in Corinth in particular (3:1),
because the Corinthians themselves fulfill this function. As the result
of Paul's apostolic work, the church in Corinth *is* Paul's letter of rec-

---

25 Since having come to this conclusion concerning the transitional function of 3:1,
   I am pleased to have discovered that my understanding of the nature of this transition, even to the point of suggesting a similar form of diagram to represent it,
   has also been presented by H. Van Dyke Parunak, "Transitional Techniques in the
   Bible", *JBL* 102(1983)525-548, pp.540-542. Parunak refers to this type of transition
   as a "direct hinge" and offers Ez. 44-46 and I John 2:3-11 as examples. He defines such a "direct hinge" as "a transitional unit of text, independent to some
   degree from the larger units on either side, which has affinities with each of
   them and does not add significant information to that presented by its neighbors.
   The two larger units (in our case 2:14-17 and 3:2-3) are joined together, not directly, but because each is joined to the hinge" (pp.541f.). For his diagram, cf.
   p.541.

ommendation. The argument implicit in II Cor. 3:2 is therefore the same
as we have already seen in I Corinthians 9:1f.[26] (cf. II Cor. 10:14): it
is Paul's own missionary work as the founder of the church in Corinth
which recommends his authority as an apostle over the Corinthians. Moreover, given the polemical situation behind II Corinthians, Paul's assertion that the Corinthians are his "letter of recommendation" also
carries a very distinct implication for his readers. For inasmuch as the
church in Corinth is a direct result of Paul's ministry, to deny Paul's
apostleship would be tantamount to a denial of their own existence as
Christians[27]. As a result, Paul's basic assertion in II Cor. 3:2 not
only grounds 3:1b, and in so doing furthers Paul's apologetic on behalf
of his sufficiency for the apostolic ministry, it also makes clear to
the Corinthians the implication of their willingness to side with those
who call Paul's sufficiency into question. Morna Hooker is therefore
fully justified in declaring that II Cor. 3:2 is a "brilliant metaphor"[28].

Having made his basic point, Paul then goes on to develop it by means
of a series of participial phrases which, upon closer examination, fall
into two distinct groups syntactically, and as I will argue below, logically as well. The demarcation is indicated syntactically by the switch
in number and gender from the feminine singular participles ἐγγεγραμμένη,
γινωσκομένη and ἀναγινωσκομένη modifying ἐπιστολή in 3:2 to the mascu-
line plural participle φανερούμενοι with its subordinate finite proposition ὅτι ἐστε ἐπιστολή Χριστοῦ in 3:3a, which is dependent upon the
initial finite predicate ὑμεῖς ἐστε. The remaining feminine singular
participles in 3:3b then relate to the predicate nominative ἐπιστολή
Χριστοῦ. From the syntax it is clear, therefore, that Paul intends to
make *two* distinct statements concerning the Corinthians:

1) ἡ ἐπιστολὴ ἡμῶν ὑμεῖς ἐστε and
2) (ὑμεῖς) ἐστὲ ἐπιστολὴ Χριστοῦ,

with the second assertion being syntactically dependent upon the first.
Each assertion is then further defined by its own set of participial
modifiers. Hence, although φανερούμενοι is dependent upon the initial

---

26 Contra Oostendorp, *Another Jesus*, p.34, who argues that it is misleading to interpret II Cor. 3:2 as a parallel to I Cor. 9:2 because of the distinction between
Paul's attempt to prove that he was called by Christ in I Cor. 9:2 and his defense
of his upright performance of the ministry in 3:2. Nevertheless, even though this
distinction is a valid one, the structure of the argument is the same in both
texts.
27 This has often been pointed out; cf. recently, Dunn, *Jesus and the Spirit*, p.276;
M.D. Hooker, "Beyond the Things that are written? St. Paul's Use of Scripture",
NTS 27(1981)295-309, p.296 and T. Provence, "'Who is Sufficient for these Things?'
An Exegesis of 2 Corinthians 2:15-3:18", *NovT* 24(1982)54-81, p.61.
28 "St. Paul's Use of Scripture", p.296.

proposition ἡ ἐπιστολὴ ἡμῶν ὑμεῖς ἐστε, so that 3:2f. comprises only
one sentence grammatically, the versification preserved in our text,
which makes a break beginning with φανερούμενοι, faithfully reproduces
Paul's intention. We will return to the significance of these observations below. For the moment it is enough to point out that on the basis
of the syntax alone we are justified in considering the two assertions
separately before trying to relate them together. For only in this way
can the question of the interconnection between these two statements,
which presents such a problem to exegetes, be resolved.

In turning our attention to Paul's initial development of his basic
assertion in II Cor. 3:2 that the Corinthians are *his* ἐπιστολή, we are
confronted with two exegetical difficulties. The first surrounds the
question of the textual variant ἡμῶν/ὑμῶν, while the second, though not
unrelated problem is the apparent internal contradiction which many
commentators have suggested is inherent in the conception of a letter
written on the "heart" which is nevertheless, at the same time, "known
and read ὑπὸ πάντων ἀνθρώπων". In other words, on whose heart is Paul's
letter of recommendation actually written and how can it be known to all
in spite of its internal character?

In answer to the first question it must be emphasized that those recent commentators who argue that ὑμῶν is the better reading are able to
do so *only* on internal grounds, since, as C.K. Barrett himself admits,
this reading is "weakly attested"[29] externally. Indeed, as Bruce Metzger
points out, the "overwhelming textual support"[30] is in favor of ἡμῶν,
so much so that the editors of the 26th edition of the Nestle-Aland
Novum Testamentum Graece chose to omit altogether the evidence in its
favor[31]. The burden of proof clearly lies, therefore, with those who
would deny this reading. It is thus surprising that the internal reasons
adduced for doing so actually argue strongly for the very position they
are said to disprove, namely, that ἡμῶν is the better reading. For on
the one hand, Bultmann and Barrett both suggest that ὑμῶν is to be preferred because it makes more sense in the context. In Bultmann's view,
because the idea of a letter written in Paul's heart

ist im Zusammenhang doch ganz unmotiviert. Ein ins Herz des Paulus geschrie-
bener Brief kann doch nicht als Empfehlungsbrief gelten, und γινωσκομένη καὶ

---

29 *Second Corinthians*, p.96n.3. Barrett nevertheless opts for this reading.
30 *A Textual Commentary on the Greek New Testament*, 1975, p.577.
31 See their explanation of this policy on p.47(ET): "The evidence for the text is
   not given in full only when the variants have such poor support that they can *in
   no way be considered as alternatives for the text*, but are of interest only for
   the history of the text" (emphasis mine).

ἀναγινωσκομένη kann von ihm nicht gesagt werden, und die V.3 gegebene Exegese
φανερούμενοι ὅτι paßt nicht[32].

In Barrett's view because, on the one hand,

your both gives the required sense, that the Corinthians themselves are -
even though unwillingly - Paul's commendation, and leads to the next stage
in the argument[33],

while on the other hand,

if 'our' is accepted instead of your the plural hearts becomes difficult,
though not impossibly so...[34].

But it is for precisely these very reasons that ἡμῶν is to be considered the more difficult, and therefore preferred reading internally as
well! For given the contextual difficulties which ἡμῶν poses for understanding Paul's argument, it is easier to imagine a scribe looking to
v.3b and altering ἡμῶν to ὑμῶν for the sake of clarity in the argument,
than to posit a textual emendation which makes Paul's thought even more
difficult to follow[35].

On the other hand, it has been argued that ἡμῶν is a later assimila-
tion, either to II Cor. 7:3 (ἐν ταῖς καρδίαις ἡμῶν ἐστε)[36], or to the
immediately preceding phrase, ἡ ἐπιστολή ἡμῶν[37]. These parallels, however, can just as easily be used to support the authenticity of ἡμῶν[38],
not to mention the fact that some commentators have maintained that it
is questionable to assume that II Cor. 7:3 is determinative one way or
the other for our present context[39].

This same ambiguity also surrounds the attempt to argue on a theo-
retical level for one of the respective alternatives. For example,
Oostendorp proposes that ὑμῶν is to be preferred because Paul must be
able to provide proof to the Corinthians in Corinth[40]. But given the

---

32 Zweiter Korintherbrief, pp.74f.
33 Second Corinthians, p.96n.3.
34 Second Corinthians, p.107. Provence, "Sufficient", p.60, follows Bultmann and
   Barrett, arguing that "It is the mixture of the two metaphors (i.e. between 3:2
   and 3) which supplies the strongest argument for understanding the proper reading
   of the disputed text in v.2 to be ὑμῶν. The epistle is written upon the hearts of
   the Corinthian Christians 'by the Spirit of the living God'".
35 So too Georgi, Gegner, p.246n.3; Windisch, Zweiter Korintherbrief, p.105 and W.
   Baird, "Letters of Recommendation. A Study of II Cor. 3:1-3", JBL 80(1961)166-172,
   p.167. This same point also extends to Weiss's suggestion that the entire phrase
   ἐγγεγραμμένη ... ἡμῶν be struck as a gloss (cf. Bultmann, Zweiter Korintherbrief,
   p.75n.18), for which there is no textual support.
36 Barrett, Second Corinthians, p.96n.3.
37 So Rissi, Studien, p.20 and Hickling, "Sequence", p.382n.2.
38 Especially 7:3, as pointed to to support ἡμῶν by e.g. A. Schlatter, Bote, p.502;
   Lietzmann, An die Korinther, p.110; Baird, "Letters", p.170; J. Lambrecht, "Structure and Line of Thought in 2 Cor. 2:14-4:6", Biblica 64(1983)344-380, p.351n.18
   and I. Friesen, The Glory of the Ministry of Jesus Christ, 1971, p.35. Cf. K. Prümm,
   Diakonia, 1967, p.101 for an interpretation based on ἡμῶν which takes ἐπιστολή
   ἡμῶν as its starting point.
39 As emphasized by both Bultmann, Zweiter Korintherbrief, p.75 and Rissi, Studien,
   p.20n.30.
40 Another Jesus, p.34.

nature of a letter of recommendation itself, it can just as easily be argued, *theoretically*, that Paul himself must be the one to carry this letter, since he is the one being recommended[41]. Thus, in the light of the inconclusive nature of the internal evidence[42], and the fact that ἡμῶν is commonly agreed to be the *lectio difficilior*, there is no compelling reason to decide against the vast majority of the textual witnesses.

This brings us to the question of the logical relationship, or lack thereof, between a letter of recommendation which has been engraved (cf. the perfect passive ἐγγεγραμμένη)[43] on Paul's heart[44], and his corresponding assertion that this letter is γινωσκομένη καὶ ἀναγινωσκομένη ὑπὸ πάντων ἀνθρώπων. The apparent tension between these two statements, as already seen above in Bultmann's comments, lies in the assumption that a letter written on Paul's heart, being internally concealed, cannot be publicly known and read, let alone "by all men". The problem has been put most pointedly by Hans Windisch:

> Die Anschauung, daß die kor. Gemeinde wie ein 'katholischer Brief' in der ganzen Welt umgeht, wird freilich empfindlich gestört durch V.2b ... Denn dieser Wendung fehlt jede direkte Beziehung auf die Außenwelt ... Solch eine 'Schrift' kann aber höchstens die nächste Umgebung lesen, wenn der Träger sie ihr eröffnet. Wenn P. so geschrieben hat, dann hat er diese Schwierigkeit nicht gesehen, oder er hat es unterlassen, das wichtige Moment 'und aus unserem Herzen hervorleuchtend, wenn wir euren Ruhm verkünden' zum Ausdruck zu bringen[45].

In reality, however, this problem probably owes its origin more to commentators' convictions concerning the "non-objective" and "non-verifiable" nature of Paul's apologetic elsewhere in II Corinthians[46], than

---

41 This is one of Baird's main points in his attempt to argue for the authenticity of ἡμῶν; cf. "Letters", pp.169-171.

42 The twosided nature of the internal arguments can readily be seen in that Barrett, *Second Corinthians*, pp.96,107 uses the same two arguments to support his decision for ὑμῶν that Lietzmann, *An die Korinther*, p.110 uses to support ἡμῶν!

43 Following the translation suggested by G. Schrenk, art. γράφω κ.τ.λ., *TDNT, Vol. I*, 1964, pp.742,773, p.770: "the word ἐγγράφω is used in the sense of 'engrave', which is the original meaning of γράφω, γραφή, γράμμα". For the justification of this translation see below.

44 Taking the plural καρδίαις ἡμῶν to be a reference to Paul himself as a continuation of the "apostolic plural" begun in 2:14; see above, pp.12ff. and Kümmel, add. to Lietzmann, *An die Korinther*, p.199 and Wendland, *An die Korinther*, pp.177f. As such, the plural presents no difficulty for the reading ἡμῶν, contra Barrett, *Second Corinthians*, p.107.

45 *Zweiter Korintherbrief*, pp.104f. In Windisch's opinion, this problem is caused by Paul's anticipation of Prov. 7:3, which he explicitly quotes in v.3 (p.104). On the question of OT allusions in II Cor. 3:2, see below.

46 See above, p.56 for Käsemann's view, which is the classic representation of this position in our day. Käsemann's position is supported by his fundamental understanding of the non-objective nature of faith and the gospel, as distinctly formulated in the concluding paragraphs to his two essays, "Begründet der neutestamentliche Kanon die Einheit der Kirche?" and "Zum Thema der Nichtobjektivierbarkeit", both in *Exegetische Versuche und Besinnungen, Erster Band*, 1970[6], pp. 223 and 236 respectively. For a more recent presentation of this view, cf. Walter

to the impossibility of understanding the inner connection between
these two statements. For if II Cor. 3:2 is approached without this assumption and analyzed in the light of what Paul says in the Corinthian
correspondence concerning his relationship to the Corinthians as their
"father", the inner connection becomes transparent. For as we have already seen, Paul's basic assertion in 3:2a (ἡ ἐπιστολὴ ἡμῶν ὑμεῖς ἐστε)
is based on his self-understanding as the founder of the Corinthian
community. Thus, when Paul goes on to assert that this letter of recommendation, i.e. the Corinthians, *has been written* on his heart, the
use of the perfect tense of the participle (ἐγγεγραμμένη) is best explained as a reference to this very fact. In other words, the Corinthians were written on Paul's heart at the point in time at which the church
was founded and have continued to be in his heart ever since[47]. As such,
the relationship between Paul and his church indicated by the perfect
participle ἐγγεγραμμένη in 3:2 corresponds to Paul's understanding of
himself as the Corinthians' "father" developed throughout I and II Corinthians[48].

The significance of this correspondence for understanding Paul's train
of thought in II Cor. 3:2 is brought to the fore as soon as the implications of Paul's "fatherhood" for his ministry in regard to the Corinthians are outlined. For on the one hand, it is precisely because Paul
is their "father" that he refuses, out of his fatherly love for the Co-
rintians (cf. 12:14f.), to burden them with his support since, in his
words, "children are not responsible to save up for their parents, but
parents for their children" (II Cor. 12:14). Moreover, as we have pointed out above, Paul's decision to support himself in Corinth is merely

---

Klaiber, *Rechtfertigung und Gemeinde, Eine Untersuchung zum paulinischen Kirchenverständnis, FRLANT 127*, 1982, pp.162f. Klaiber too supports his position that
there is no "aufweisbare Kriterion" for the validity of Paul's message by pointing
to, among other things, the doctrine of justification by faith (cf. p.163) understood against the traditional Lutheran view of the law/gospel constrast, cf. pp.
185-187.

47 This is my attempt to express the basic significance of the κοινή perfect tense
in this instance. Cf. Blass-Debrunner-Funk, *A Greek Grammar of the New Testament*,
1961, §340 and A.T. Robertson, *A Grammar of the Greek New Testament*, 1934, pp.893,
895.

48 Paul's portrayal of himself as the Corinthians' "father" in I and II Cor. corresponds to his ability to portray himself as a result of this same "founding function" as the "mother" of the Christians in Galatia in Gal. 4:19, while in I Thess.
2:7f. and 11 Paul reflects this same self-understanding by referring to himself
in the same context as the Thessalonians' mother *and* father. It is significant to
note, in addition, that in this latter passage Paul's use of this corresponding
parental image is introduced in order to convey what we will see below is also
the main thrust of Paul's "fatherhood" image in the Cor. correspondence, namely,
that his parental relationship to his churches implies a love for his church which
expresses itself openly in his commitment to suffer on her behalf (cf. I Thess.
2:8) which, in turn, testifies to the legitimacy of his gospel and the genuine
nature of his apostolic ministry (cf. I Thess. 2:10f.).

one specific aspect of his suffering as an apostle on behalf of the Corinthians (cf. I Cor. 4:11f.; II Cor. 11:7ff.). Thus, in II Cor. 6:4ff.,
Paul can list his "catalogue of sufferings" not only as that which commends his ministry as such (cf. 6:3), but also as that which provides
evidence of his fatherly love for the Corinthians, specifically that
of his acceptance of them as his children. For in II Cor. 6:11, the
second conclusion[49] which Paul draws from his suffering is that his
"heart" is "opened wide" toward the Corinthians. That by this expression
Paul is once again conceiving of his suffering as an outworking of his
love for the Corinthians is evident by the further development of this
theme in 6:12f[50] (see my discussion of I Cor. 9 above). For in 6:12-13
Paul appeals to the Corinthians that they reciprocate his *feelings* for
them (cf. σπλάγχνοις in 6:12). The basis of this appeal, as the paren-
thetical statement ὡς τέκνοις λέγω in 6:13 makes clear, is Paul's conception of his relationship to the Corinthians as that of a parent to
his children. In other words, the unexpressed premise for Paul's argument in 6:11-13 is that children are obligated to return the affection
of their parents - an affection which Paul has amply demonstrated[51].
On the other hand, Paul attributes his *continuing concern* for the Corinthians itself to his parental role as their "father". For in I Cor.
4:15 the fact that Paul is their "father" ἐν Χριστῷ 'Ιησοῦ διὰ τοῦ
εὐαγγελίου is the motivation Paul expresses for his decision to write
the Corinthians concerning his suffering in I Cor. 4:7-13, albeit not
"to shame" them, but "to admonish" them ὡς τέκνα ... ἀγαπητά (I Cor.
4:14; cf. 4:16). In the same way, Paul's ζῆλος θεοῦ on behalf of the
Corinthians in II Cor. 11:2 is based on the fact that he was the one
who "betrothed" them to Christ, a clear reference to his "founding function" as their apostolic father. For since Paul was the one who initiated this relationship, he feels responsible to preserve the Corinthians' purity until their marriage to Christ can be consumated (11:2). It
is this concern, therefore, which motivates Paul's "foolishness" in II
Cor. 10-13 (cf. 11:1), since the Corinthians are now in danger of being
led astray from Christ (cf. 11:3f.). Paul's expression of concern for
the Corinthians in I Cor. 4:14f. and II Cor. 11:2-4, derived from his
parental relationship to them and occasioned by the danger of sin which

---

49 Following Bultmann, *Zweiter Korintherbrief*, p.177 and Plummer, *Second Corinthians*,
   p.203 in seeing 6:11 to be relating back to Paul's previous discourse.
50 Taking 6:11b to be more than merely a synonymous repetition of 11a, as Bultmann,
   Zweiter Korintherbrief, p.177 does. Instead, I follow Barrett, *Second Corinthians*,
   p.191; Plummer, *Second Corinthians*, p.201; Kümmel, add. to Lietzmann, *An die Korinther*, p.206 and Schlatter, *Bote*, p.575 in seeing in this important second phrase
   a reference to Paul's affection for the Corinthians.
51 So too Schlatter, *Bote*, pp.575f.: "Er stützt sich dabei auf sein Vaterrecht; vgl.
   I 4:14". Contra e.g. Barrett, *Second Corinthians*, p.192, who takes Paul's appeal
   to mean that "there is no apostolic authority by which he can compel it".

besets them, is thus another specific example of *suffering* Paul undergoes for their sake, i.e. of the "daily pressure upon (him) of concern
for all the churches" explicitly identified as one of Paul's tribulations in II Cor. 11:28. It is this "anxiety" over the Corinthians which
has determined his behavior toward them in the past, whether that en-
tailed writing the "sorrowful letter" mentioned in II Cor. 2:4 and
7:8ff. as an expression of his love for them, changing his travel plans
in order "to spare" them his wrath (cf. II Cor. 1:15f., 23 in the light
of 13:2f.,10), or even giving up other possibilities for ministry because of his overbearing concern and fear for their welfare (cf. II Cor.
2:12f.; 7:5). Thus, no matter how severe and threatening Paul's letters
are, the Corinthians need only consider Paul's *concern* and *suffering* on
their behalf, specifically his decision to support himself in Corinth
and the results of his concern for their spiritual well-being, to be
assured that his attitudes and actions, even when he must "test" their
faith and obedience (see II Cor. 2:9; 7:12; 13:5, 7), are grounded in
his fatherly love and concern for his children. For as Paul himself summarizes it in II Cor. 7:3,

> I do not speak to condemn you; for I have said before that you are in our
> hearts to die together and to live together.

Thus, when Paul says in II Cor. 3:2 that the Corinthians, as his letter of recommendation, have been written on his heart, this reference
to his parental role in regard to the Corinthians carries a very concrete connotation, namely, of his continuing concern and commitment to
suffer on their behalf. Once this is realized, Paul's further assertion
that this letter of recommendation, i.e. that he is the founding "father"
of the Corinthian church, is "known and read by all men" follows logically from his previous affirmation[52]. For the suffering which Paul
undergoes as an apostle, precisely because he was the one who was called to establish the church in Corinth, can be readily seen by all. In
fact, as Paul himself put it in I Cor. 4:9, in his suffering he has become "a spectacle to the world". Or, in our own context, Paul's being
"led to death" is said to manifest the knowledge of God ἐν παντὶ τόπῳ
(2:14). One need only look at Paul's activities to see that the Corinthians are on his heart! Once again, therefore, the "internality" of
Paul's corroboratory evidence in II Cor. 3:2 is not to be equated with
an inability to be known, so that an inherent contradiction must be
posited to exist in Paul's thinking, either consciously or unconsciously.
Rather, what is "written on Paul's heart" is manifest for all to see,

---

52 Even the use of ἀναγινώσκειν itself in 3:2 is an attempt on Paul's part to continue
   the logic of his metaphor. Cf. Bultmann, art. ἀναγινώσκω κ.τ.λ., *TDNT*, *Vol. I*, 1964,
   p.343 and K. Prümm, *Diakonia*, 1967, p.102.

since the suffering in view is a direct result of his apostolic calling
to be the founder of the Corinthian church.

The structure of Paul's argument in II Cor. 3:2 thus parallels the
structure of his prior argument in 2:17, both of which are based upon
Paul's understanding of his suffering as an apostle. What can be known
and read by all men in Paul's suffering on behalf of the Corinthians is
that he is their "father through the gospel" (cf. I Cor. 4:15). As such,
his decision to support himself, his change in travel plans and his
"weighty letters", rather than being those aspects of his ministry in
Corinth which call his apostleship into question[53], are in reality at-
testations of that very apostleship, since they are a direct result of
Paul's incontrovertible parental relationship to the Corinthians. Far
from being part of an attempt to use the Corinthians for his own ends,
Paul's suffering testifies not only to the divine sincerity of Paul's
ministry (2:17; cf. 1:12), but also to his genuine fatherly affection
for the Corinthians (3:2; 7:3), which in the light of II Cor. 10:13 and
Paul's parallel statement concerning Titus in II Cor. 8:16 is equally
God-given.

Moreover, understood in this way, Paul's positive statement concerning his own ministry in II Cor. 3:2 contains the same critique of his
opponents that we saw implied in 2:17. This becomes especially apparent
when Paul's assertion concerning himself in II Cor. 7:2 is compared
with his accusation against his opponents in II Cor. 11:20. Paul's refusal to "recommend himself" in II Cor. 3:1f. therefore fulfils the
same purpose as that stated in his corresponding denial of II Cor. 5:12.
By pointing to the Christian existence of the Corinthians themselves as
his corroborating evidence, which can be known and read by all men in
his *suffering* on their behalf (cf. II Cor. 4:12), Paul is attempting to
give the Corinthians the ἀφορμή they need to be proud of their apostle,
and from which they can respond to those who are questioning his a-
postleship because of this very suffering. Ἐν καρδίᾳ in II Cor. 5:12
does not refer to that which cannot be seen *per se*[54], but to the mode
of Paul's ministry, i.e. to the fact that as an apostle he suffers (cf.
4:7ff.) because of his "heart", which in the context refers to that behavior motivated and determined by the love of Christ controlling Paul
(5:13f.). In contrast, ἐν προσώπῳ refers to that outward strength in
which those false apostles boast whose ministry is not controlled and
shaped by the cross = love of Christ.

---

53 Based on Paul's explicit references to these criticisms in II Cor. 1:17; 10:1f.,
   9f.; 11:7 and 12:12f., 17; 13:3.
54 Contra e.g. U. Luz, *Das Geschichtsverständnis des Apostels Paulus*, BevTh 49,
   1968, p.127.

Finally, this interpretation of II Cor. 3:2 makes it unnecessary to posit an allusion either to Proverbs 7:3, as Windisch and C. Wolff have suggested[55], or to Jeremiah 38:33(LXX), as suggested most recently by Earl Richard[56], in order to explain Paul's thinking at this point. For the "heart"-motif, as we have seen, is part of the larger theme of Paul's "fatherhood" running throughout the Corinthian correspondence. As such, its introduction at this point is a natural development of the "self-recommendation"-theme in 3:1f. Moreover, the use of the verb ἐγγράφειν in conjunction with this motif is also a natural one, given Paul's desire to express the fact that the letter of recommendation is located in his heart. For the use of ἐγγράφειν to refer to something placed in the heart or soul is a common idiom in the ancient world, being attested in a variety of contexts and periods, both Jewish and non-Jewish[57]. Thus, although by the first century ἐγγράφειν can simply mean "to write" or "to put into writing" as a semantic equivalent for γράφειν[58], when associated with the heart (or soul), as in our context, it is best to give it its distinctive sense of "to engrave" or "inscribe", which entails the appropriate idea of having to embed what is being written into the substance being written upon, as suggested by the prefix ἐγ-γράφειν[59]. Given the existence of this common idiom, together with the internal logic of Paul's argument, there is no reason to suppose, therefore, that Paul is deriving his thought *specifically* from

---

55 See above, n.45 and Christian Wolff, *Jeremia im Frühjudentum und Urchristentum, TU 118*, 1976, p.135.

56 "Polemics, Old Testament, and Theology. A Study of II Cor. 3:1-4:6", *Revue Biblique* 88(1981)340-367, pp.345f. He points to Kümmel and Jewett as further representatives of this view, see p.346n.20, though he notes that Kümmel refers to both Jer. and Prov. as the backdrop.

57 Cf. besides Jer. 38:33(LXX) and Prov. 7:3, Plutarch, *Moralia* 779B (with ψυχαῖς) and the references from Philo, Josephus, Aeschylus, Xenophon and the Test.Jud. listed by G. Schrenk, *TDNT, Vol. I*, p.770.

58 Cf. e.g. Lucian, *The Lover of Lies* 38; Plutarch, *Aristides* VII.5; Sophocles, *Trachiniai* 157; Josephus, *Ant.* XVI.324; the example from Moultan-Milligan, *The Vocabulary of the Greek Testament, Part III*, 1921, p.178 and the use of ἐγγράφειν to refer to that which is written in a letter in Josephus, *Ant.* XI.271; XVII.137 and Thucydides I.132; in books in Josephus, *Ant.* X.35, in the "book of God" in Philo, *Quod.det.* 139; and in a petition in *Oxyr.Pap.* 3273.5(1st cent.). Schrenk, *TDNT, Vol. I*, p.770 also lists examples of the complimentary situation, i.e. where γράφειν can be used to mean "to inscribe in the heart or soul" as an equivalent to ἐγγράφειν.

59 For this meaning, "inscribe" or "engrave", cf. Philo, *Leg.all.* I.19; Josephus, *Ant.* I.70-71; III.166; IV.308; VIII.261; XI.331; XII.416; XIV.188; XIX.291; XII.89 (on leather books, hence the need to be "inscribed"); Epictetus III.16,9 (for writing notes on wax tablets); Herodotus I.203; II.102; IV.91; VIII.82; VIII.23; Plutarch, *Moralia* 873B. The other well-attested meaning for ἐγγράφειν is the technical sense of "to enroll in", "register", "enlist", etc. in an official list or document such as a will, contract, public register for military service or citizenship, etc. Cf. e.g. in the NT Lk. 10:20 and elsewhere in Philo, *De opif.* 143; *Leg.all.* III.244; *De agr.* 81; *De vit. Mos.* II.274; *De spec.Leg.* III.72 (and often); Josephus, *Ant.* XVI.225; Demosthenes 44:35; 53:14; Lucian, *Herm.* 23; *Zeus Pants* 26; Plutarch, *Antony* LXXI.2; *Publicola* XI.2; *Moralia* 37E; 182D; 671C; 761B, etc. and *Oxyr. Pap.* 485.25; 486.26; 494.27, etc.

Prov. 7:3 or Jer. 38:33(LXX), especially when in both OT contexts, that which is written on the heart is the law, which up until now has not been introduced into our context. Hence, if Paul were already alluding to either of these texts in particular in verse 2, which is of course possible, the indications are too slight to detect from our distance. The question must also be posed concerning the rationale behind choosing one of these passages over the other, as Windisch, Wolff and Richard all do, since II Cor. 3:2 itself offers no such indication and the allusions in II Cor. 3:3 indicate that the closest parallel to the heart-motif there is Ezekiel 11:19 and 36:26f. rather than either Jer. 38:33 or Prov. 3:3 and 7:3[60]. Hence, rather than importing the OT allusions from II Cor. 3:3 back into 3:2, it seems more appropriate to suppose that once Paul was compelled by the polemical situation in Corinth to respond to the possible "false conclusion" that he was in need of letters of recommendation, the motifs in 3:2 developed organically by making use of a common idiom, of which Jer. 17:1; 38:33: Prov. 3:3 and 7:3 are *all* examples. Paul could then fill this idiom with his own particular content. H. Räisänen's statement that the "somewhat odd image" in 3:2 "is used by Paul ... without any OT reminiscences" is therefore too radical[61]. The point is that there are OT examples of this idiom, but they are not determinative for Paul's thought in 3:2. Instead, the natural development of Paul's argument in 3:2, which resulted in the association of motifs "engraved in the heart", then led to Paul's further assertions in 3:3, where Paul develops his second major point concerning his "letter of recommendation". That is to say, it is Paul's statement that his letter of recommendation has been engraved in his heart which provides the transition to the OT imagery in 3:3, rather than the other way around as Windisch has suggested[62]. The important, but difficult, question of the intrinsic relationship between the motifs of 3:2 and 3, as well as that of the meaning of 3:3 itself, still remain, however, to be considered. In order to do so, it will be necessary to take up the latter question first.

---

60 Neither Windisch nor Richard present an argument for their preference for one of these texts above the other. Wolff's view is part of his extensive study of the history of the interpretation of Jer. 31:31ff., to which we will return in Volume Two of this study.
61 *Paul and the Law, WUNT 29*, 1983, p.243.
62 *Zweiter Korintherbrief*, p.104.

3. The Corinthians as the "Letter of Christ" (II Cor. 3:3)

a. The Meaning of 3:3 and Its Function within Paul's Argument

The meaning of Paul's second assertion concerning the Corinthians in
II Cor. 3:1-3, ἐστὲ ἐπιστολὴ Χριστοῦ (3:3), as well as its relationship to Paul's prior assertion in 3:2, ἡ ἐπιστολὴ ἡμῶν ὑμεῖς ἐστε, are
both dependent upon one fundamental exegetical decision, namely, the
meaning to be ascribed to the participial phrase διακονηθεῖσα ὑφ' ἡμῶν.
Does Paul intend to say by this that he is the author, in some sense,
of this letter of Christ; or does he merely intend to express the fact
that he is the one who delivers this letter as, in J.D.G. Dunn's words,
"Christ's postman"[63]? On the other hand, in order to understand the
force of Paul's argument, i.e. that which makes it work and renders it
compelling to his audience, the point of the twofold description of
this letter expressed in the antitheses of 3:3b needs to be determined.
This entails not only discerning the meaning of the antitheses themselves, but also their relationship to one another. But once again, the
answer to this question depends upon whether one perceives Paul to be
the writer or deliverer of the letter so described. If the former, then
we are faced with a bold assertion on Paul's part concerning the nature
of his own apostolic ministry; if the latter is the case, then we are
forced to understand Paul's argument in 3:3 to be a reference to some
sort of "Himmelsbrief" sent by Christ, which is only tangentially related to Paul himself[64] and which, correspondingly, can only be evaluated by divine criteria[65].

The strongest presentation of the view that διακονηθεῖσα ὑφ' ἡμῶν
refers to Paul's role as a "courier" of the letter written by Christ
is that of W. Baird in his important article "Letters of Recommendation.
A Study of II Cor. 3:1-3"[66]. Baird's argument for this interpretation
is based on his premise that one must begin with the "primary metaphor"
of 3:1-3 as the key to its coherence, i.e. the figure of the letter of
recommendation introduced in 3:1. For as Baird points out, "the primary

---

63 *Baptism in the Holy Spirit, A Re-examination of the New Testament Teaching on the
   Gift of the Spirit in relation to Pentecostalism Today*, 1970, p.137.
64 For the idea of a letter written by God to man, i.e. a "Himmelsbrief", see the
   sources and literature listed by Bultmann, *Zweiter Korintherbrief*, p.75 (who himself rejects its relevance for this context); the rabbinic references listed by
   A. Marmorstein, "The Holy Spirit in Rabbinic Legend", in *Studies in Jewish Theology, The Arthur Marmorstein Memorial Volume*, ed. J. Rabbinowitz and M.S. Lew,
   1950, pp.122-144, pp.143f. and the related notes; and finally, the article "Himmelsbrief" by L. Röhrich, *RGG³, Bd. 3*, 1959, pp.338f. For examples of commentators
   holding this view, cf. Windisch, p.105; Lietzmann, p.110 and Wendland, p.178; see
   too Georgi, *Gegner*, p.246. For another rejection of this view, cf. Rissi, *Studien*,
   p.21. Rissi's argument, however, is weak, based as it is solely on the fact that
   Paul does not use the precise terminology of a "letter from heaven".
65 As concluded by J.S. Vos, *Traditionsgeschichtliche*, p.136.
66 *JBL* 80(1961)166-172, pp.168-171.

figure of speech in the passage represents the Corinthian community as an epistle of recommendation"[67]. He then argues that this metaphor is maintained at least through verse 3a, including the participial phrase διακονηθεῖσα ὑφ' ἡμῶν, because of the use of ἐστὲ ἐπιστολή[68]. Since Paul is still developing the idea of the Corinthians as a letter of recommendation in 3:3a, it is this metaphor which provides the interpretive key for understanding Paul's role. It follows, therefore, that since 3:3a is *also* taken to mean "you are a letter of recommendation", Paul must, in Baird's view, be the courier and not the amanuensis of the letter[69]. For in the ancient world the epistle of recommendation was carried by the one being recommended[70]. Baird thus concludes that by referring to this courier-function, διακονηθεῖσα ὑφ' ἡμῶν "is not changing the figure to make it refer to his ministry of the gospel, but is still employing the metaphor of the epistle of recommendation"[71]. Baird then supports this conclusion by arguing that the interpretation "deliver" or "carry"[72] accords with the probable meaning of the verb διακονέω itself, as attested elsewhere in Paul and in Josephus. In his words,

> The change (in metaphor), of course, might seem to be suggested by Paul's use of διακονέω. But although he often uses διακονία for his ministry of the gospel, he never uses the verb διακονέω in that way; it is, however, employed for Paul's collection and delivery of the offering for the saints in Jerusalem (Rom.15:25; II Cor. 8:19-20). The verb διακονέω is found in Josephus (*Antt.* vi,298) with the meaning "to deliver" a message, and, as the RSV indicates, this is the meaning which it probably should have in II Cor. 3:3.[73]

As a result, "Paul is not to be understood as either the writer or the ultimate recipient of the letter"[74]. In the same way, Paul's prior statement in 3:2 that the letter of recommendation has been engraved on his heart "is not referring to the receiving of the letter but the carrying of it ... to be revealed to all men when with open heart (II Cor. 6:11) he declares to them the Corinthians' faith (cf. I Thess. 1:8)"[75]. Finally, in order to be consistent with this interpretation, Baird interprets ἐπιστολὴ Χριστοῦ to mean "letter *from* Christ", suggesting that Paul has introduced this idea in order to clarify the letter's authorship and thus prevent the Corinthians from falsely concluding that they had written it (cf. 3:1: "from you")[76]. Baird summarizes his position by saying,

---

67 "Letters", p.169.
68 "Letters", p.169.
69 "Letters", p.169.
70 Baird bases this point on Keyes; see above, n.18 and "Letters", p.169.
71 "Letters", p.169.
72 "Letters", p.170.
73 "Letters", p.169.
74 "Letters", p.170.
75 "Letters", p.170.
76 "Letters", p.170.

It seems evident that in II Cor. 3:1-3a, Paul is employing the figure of the
Greek epistle of introduction with a high degree of accuracy and consistency.
He needs no literal letter of recommendation to or from any church. He has
a figurative epistle whose content is the Christian of Corinth. That letter
is written by Christ. It recommends its courier, Paul, to all men as an authorized minister of the gospel of God.[77]

But although Baird correctly emphasizes the primary role of the motif of the letter of recommendation and the coherence of Paul's thought
in 3:1-3, his attempt, as well as that of others, to construe διακονέω
in 3:3 to mean merely "deliver" or "carry"[78], quite apart from any
analogy to letters of recommendation, does not do justice to its Pauline
usage elsewhere, nor to the present context. For in the light of the
fact that Paul also refers to the collection as a διακονία in II Cor.
8:4; 9:1, 12, 13 and Rom. 15:31, which not only meets the financial
needs of the saints, but also itself serves to glorify God (see II Cor.
8:19; 9:12f.!), we ought to be careful not to draw a hard distinction
between Paul's "ministry of the gospel to the Gentiles", i.e. his
διακονία in this sense (cf. Rom. 11:13; II Cor. 5:18; 6:3; 11:8), and
his role in arranging the collection for Jerusalem, which is also a
διακονία to others and to God[79]. That this distinction is a false one
becomes especially apparent when we keep in mind that according to Gal.
2:10 Paul's mandate to remember the poor[80] was an integral part of his
larger mandate to take the gospel to the Gentiles (see Gal. 2:7, 9),
and that in II Cor. 8:7-9 Paul grounds his admonition to the Corinthians
concerning the collection by an appeal to that same gospel (cf. v.9)[81].
It should also be kept in mind that in II Cor. 4:15 Paul can say exactly the same thing concerning the spread of the gospel, i.e. the χάρις
which has come to the Corinthians, that he says concerning the collection in II Cor. 9:12f., i.e. the χάρις τοῦ θεοῦ (cf. 8:1). Surely then,
when Paul uses the verb διακονέω in II Cor. 8:19f. and Rom. 15:25 to
refer to his activity on behalf of the collection, the terminology he
employs itself (διακονία/διακονέω) indicates that he regarded his role
in the collection as much more than merely being the one responsible
for delivering the money. The collection is designated a διακονία and

---

77 "Letters", pp.170-171.
78 So too, e.g. Lietzmann, *An die Korinther*, p.11; Wendland, *An die Korinther*, p.178;
   E. Richard, "Polemics", p.347 and H. Räisänen, *Paul*, p.243.
79 See Georgi, *Gegner*, pp.31-38, esp. p.34 for διακονία etc. in the NT.
80 It is beyond the scope of our present purpose to enter the discussion concerning
   the significance of the collection itself or whether the "poor" in view refers
   specifically to the Jewish Christians in Jerusalem or not. For the relevant literature and a discussion of the issues, see U. Wilckens, *Der Brief an die Römer*,
   3. Teilband Röm 12-16, EKK VI/3, 1982, pp.125-127.
81 See G. Eichholz, *Die Theologie des Paulus im Umriß*, 1977², p.134 on II Cor. 8:9:
   "Von der Summe der Christologie bis zur Empfehlung der Kollekte ist nur ein Schritt:
   ja das Christusgeschehen wird in für uns vielleicht ungewohnter Direktheit zum
   Grund für den Appell des Paulus".

is said to be "ministered" (διακονέω) by Paul and his co-workers precisely because it is part of Paul's lager διακονία of the gospel. It is
only appropriate, therefore, that Paul see the collection to be a result
of the grace of God at work in the various churches (cf. II Cor. 8:1,
6f., 19) and that he equate the Corinthians' participation in this ministry with obedience to their confession εἰς τὸ εὐαγγέλιον τοῦ Χριστοῦ
(II Cor. 9:13)[82]. Thus, there is no reason to doubt on the basis of
Pauline usage elsewhere that in our present context διακονέω refers to
Paul's gospel ministry as an apostle, especially when to do so would
destroy the seemingly obvious correspondence between Paul's use of
διακονέω in 3:3 and Paul's description of himself in 3:6 as a διάκονος
καινῆς διαθήκης on the one hand, and the designation of his corresponding apostolic ministry as a διακονία τοῦ πνεύματος/τῆς δικαιοσύνης in
3:8f. (cf. 4:1). Although only of secondary importance, Baird's reference to Josephus, Ant. VI.298 also does not confirm his interpretation,
since the use of the verb in this context carries a much more general
meaning than "to deliver a message". In the context the messengers do
deliver a message as commanded. But the meaning of διακονέω itself is
more appropriately rendered in the general sense of "fulfilling the task
entrusted to them", as frequently found in Josephus' writings[83].

Second, Baird's view fails to account for the use of the perfect tense
ἐγγεγραμμένη in 3:2 and the aorist διακονηθεῖσα in 3:3. For in spite of
his insightful observation that these two verbs refer to the same thing,
their common punctilliar nature, as well as their shared subject matter
is best explained as a reference to the founding of the Corinthian church.
We have already seen above how this sense fits the context and serves
to explain the logic of Paul's argument in 3:1f. If, in turn, our decision to take διακονέω to be a reference to Paul's ministry as an a-
postle is warranted, then the most natural reference for the aorist
διακονηθεῖσα is Paul's ministry of bringing the gospel to Corinth and
the resulting conversion of those Corinthians now in Paul's church.[84]
In other words, what Paul *implies* in 3:2 in his emphasis on the fact

---

82 Cf. D. Georgi, *Die Geschichte der Kollekte des Paulus für Jerusalem, Theologische
   Forschung 38*, 1965, p.76n.302 for an analysis of the syntactical structure of
   this verse. He demonstrates on the basis of the parallel structure between 9:13b
   and c that εἰς τὸ εὐαγγέλιον must relate back to ὁμολογία, rather than directly
   to ὑποταγή; hence my attempt to bring this out.
83 See *Ant.* IX.25; X.177; XIV.358; XVII.140; XVIII.77,125,193,262,269,277,280,283,293,
   304; XIX.41,194. For the use of διακονέω for ministering to God, see *Ant.* VII.365;
   and for priestly service to the people, *Ant.* X.72.
84 So too Barrett, *Second Corinthians*, p.108; Prümm, *Diakonia*, 1967, p.110 and similarly Kümmel, additions to Lietzmann, *An die Korinther*, p.199 and Schlatter, *Bote*,
   p.103, both of whom attribute the letter to the work of Christ and Paul. Windisch,
   Zweiter Korintherbrief, p.105 sees the aorist tense to be a reference to the founding of the church, but still maintains that Paul is merely the deliverer of the
   letter.

that this letter has been engraved in his heart is now expressed *direct-ly* with the participial phrase διακονηθεῖσα ὑφ' ἡμῶν. In addition, as Baird too points out, the recognition of the parallel between these two statements further supports the propriety of reading ἡμῶν in 3:2[85]. Moreover, once διακονηθεῖσα ὑφ' ἡμῶν is understood to be a reference to Paul's apostolic ministry of establishing the church in Corinth, the grounding function[86] of the participle φανερούμενοι becomes apparent and the compelling nature of Paul's argument for his audience can be appreciated. For if those who argue, like Baird, that in 3:3 Paul is merely the courier of the letter written by Christ are right, then Paul's apology, based as it is on the existence of the Corinthians as Christians in 3:2, loses this evidential force in 3:3. For in this view, Paul's assertion in 3:2 that the Corinthians are his letter of recommendation which can be known by all is supported only by the additional assertion that this letter has been written by Christ, which, of course, his opponents would immediately deny with their counter-assertion that they were, in reality, the true servants of Christ (cf. II Cor. 11:23)[87]. Hence, the third reason for rejecting the position presented by Baird is its failure to correspond to the manner of Paul's apostolic self-defense consistently employed thus far in 2:14-3:2 and confirmed by Paul's "apology" elsewhere in II Corinthians. Or put differently, it cannot adequately explain the meaning and function of 3:3 in relation-ship to 3:2 as expressed in the participle φανερούμενοι in 3:3a. The best way to illustrate this point is to present my own summary of the meaning and function of this complex statement.

In II Cor. 3:3 Paul extends the preceding metaphor of the Corinthi-ans as Paul's "letter of recommendation" by stressing that the Corin-thians owe their existence as Christians to *Christ* as he was made known to them *by the Spirit in the gospel ministry of Paul* (cf. I Cor. 2:1-16; 4:15; II Cor. 10:13f.). Hence, if not the sole author of this "letter of recommendation", Paul is at least its "co-author" (cf. I Cor. 15:10b; Gal. 2:20). For as the participial phrase διακονηθεῖσα ὑφ' ἡμῶν indi-cates, the Corinthians owe their existence as Christians to Paul's ministry in Corinth. As the "letter of Christ", the Corinthians are part of what Christ has accomplished through Paul and therefore can become Paul's letter of recommendation which, at the same time, is a recommen-dation from the Lord (see II Cor. 10:18 and above, p.180n.14). Paul's

---

85 "Letters", p.171.
86 So too, e.g. Bultmann, *Zweiter Korintherbrief*, p.75; Windisch, *Zweiter Korinther-brief*, p.105 and Barrett, *Second Corinthians*, p.108.
87 Baird's own attempt to alleviate this problem by arguing that ἐν πλαξὶν καρδίαις σαρκίναις in 3:3b is a reference to Paul's heart and thus an allusion to his com-mission to the apostolic ministry also fails to be convincing once his understand-ing of διακονηθεῖσα ... is rejected. See "Letters", pp.171f.

initial two assertions in 3:3a (φανερούμενοι ὅτι ἐστὲ ἐπιστολὴ Χριστοῦ
διακονηθεῖσα ὑφ' ἡμῶν) simply make *explicit* the premises which we have
already seen were *implicit* in his first two assertions in 3:2, thus providing the support needed for his prior argument:

1) ἡ ἐπιστολὴ ἡμῶν ὑμεῖς ἐστε *because* ὑμεῖς ἐστὲ ἐπιστολὴ Χριστοῦ
2) ἐγγεγραμμένη ἐν ταῖς καρδίαις ἡμῶν *because* διακονηθεῖσα ὑφ' ἡμῶν.

The new factor in 3:3, and that which extends Paul's argument beyond
what he has already asserted, is then introduced in the two following
participial phrases. It is at this point, however, that Paul's development of the second letter-motif initiated in 3:3 seems to break down.
For it appears to be the universal opinion of recent commentators, even
among those who wish to stress the coherence of Paul's basic thought in
this passage as a whole, that in introducing the ideas of 3:3b Paul
mixes his metaphors to the point of divergence[88]. In fact, for some
scholars, the mixed metaphor of 3:3b even renders Paul's thought "a
mess"[89]. The reason for this astounding consensus is that the two images of 3:3b are understood to be *parallel* to one another, with the
first image taken to refer to the second. As a result, Paul ends up
drawing a contrast between that which is written with ink on the stone
tablets of the law and writing with the Spirit on tablets of fleshly
hearts. For the sake of the second aspect of the comparison, said to
be Paul's controlling interest, the first aspect thus becomes absurd.
But this apparent confusion of categories, i.e. ink on the stone tablets
of the law, is eliminated once Paul's twofold thought in 3:3b is seen
to develop not in parallel categories, so that Paul's *two* statements in
3:3 are taken to represent merely *one* contrast, but in *succession* to
one another, so that Paul's two statements are taken *independently* of
one another, thus producing *two* separate comparisons.

In the first contrast, ἐγγεγραμμένη οὐ μέλανι ἀλλὰ πνεύματι θεοῦ
ζῶντος, Paul intends to stress the *means* by which this letter belonging
to Christ has been written, namely, not by means of human instrumentality, but by the living God himself through his Spirit, or in Bultmann's
words, "die wunderbare wirkende Kraft Gottes"[90]. For as I. Hermann has
correctly emphasized,

---

88 Cf. e.g. Baird, "Letters", p.171; Lietzmann, *An die Korinther*, pp.110f., Prümm,
   Diakonia, 1967, p.104; Wendland, *An die Korinther*, p.178; Barrett, *Second Corinthians*, pp.81f. This consensus has been well summarized by T. Provence, "Sufficient", p.60.
89 This is the judgment of M.D. Hooker, "Beyond", p.296. See too Bultmann, *Zweiter
   Korintherbrief*, p.77.
90 *Zweiter Korintherbrief*, p.75.

Das οὐ μέλανι ἀλλὰ πνεύματι deutet darauf hin, daß Pneuma im gleichen Sinn
verstanden werden will wie μέλαν: als Mittel, durch das und mit dessen Hilfe
etwas ausgeführt wird. *Damit wird Pneuma zum Funktionsbegriff*[91].

As a statement about the nature of Paul's ministry in Corinth, this
contrast is thus best understood as a summary of Paul's prior description of his apostolic ministry of the Spirit in I Cor. 2:1-5, where the
contrast between human instrumentality (cf. 2:1) and the power of the
Spirit (cf. 2:4) is said to have determined both the method and content
of Paul's missionary preaching in Corinth.

In the second contrast, (ἐγγεγραμμένη) οὐκ ἐν πλαξὶν λιθίναις ἀλλ'
ἐν πλαξὶν καρδίαις σαρκίναις, Paul indicates the *locality* of this
"writing", i.e. that the letter of Christ has not been written on stone
tablets, but "on tablets composed of fleshly hearts"[92]. Understood in
this way, this second contrast, in describing the "material" used for
the writing of the letter, does not relate to both elements of the preceding comparison, but only to its main point that the letter has been
written with God's Spirit. For having said this, Paul then goes on to
describe the sphere in which the Spirit has been active. In other words,
the second contrast functions to amplify the first. Without its metaphorical dress, Paul's thought in 3:3 can therefore be represented as
follows:

1. The Corinthians are now Christians

2. as a result of Paul's apostolic ministry of the gospel in Corinth.

3. For as Christians they owe their existence to the work of the Spirit
   of God

4. which has worked in their hearts (through Paul's gospel).

Paul's statement in 3:3 furthers his argument not only by making explicit the implicit grounds for his assertions in 3:2, but also by reminding the Corinthians of that which they absolutely cannot deny: they
owe their existence as Christians to the work of the Spirit which they
received *through Paul's ministry*[93]. Hence, as recipients of the Spirit

---

91 *Kyrios und Pneuma*, p.28. For the reasons already listed above, however, Hermann's
corresponding view of Christ as the "Begründer" of the church in 3:3 must be rejected, though his observation that the Spirit is "das Mittel, durch das Christus
in seiner Kirche tätig ist ..." is certainly right (cf. pp.27f.).

92 This is my attempt to render the difficult phrase ἐν πλαξὶν καρδίαις σαρκίναις.
Because of its strong textual support and the fact that it is obviously the most
difficult reading, it appears unwarranted to opt for one of the various emendations
often suggested by commentators. Moreover, as Barrett, *Second Corinthians*, p.96n.4
has pointed out, the text "is probably due to the O.T. allusion" - which explains
its awkwardness. For a good discussion of this textual problem, cf. Hughes, *Second
Corinthians*, pp.89f.n.10.

93 So already E. Sokolowski, *Die Begriffe Geist und Leben bei Paulus in ihren Beziehungen zu einander*, 1903, p.73, who points to I Cor. 2:5 and 3:5 as the key
parallels and concludes, "Ist nun die Gemeinde mittels des Geistes ein Empfehlungsbrief für P. geworden, so kann es sich P. nicht anders vorgestellt haben, als dass
ihr Glaube durch Wirken des Geistes zustande gekommen sei".

in their hearts, their own, visible pneumatic existence makes it manifest that they are Christians and that Paul's ministry, through which
they received the Spirit, is genuinely apostolic. It is the very existence of the Spirit in the Corinthian church which supports Paul's claim
to apostolic authority in Corinth, since he was the one through whom the
Spirit came. This explains Paul's choice of the verb φανερόω to introduce this assertion as a continuation of the theme of the open manifestation initiated in 2:14 and then continued as an essential element in
Paul's "self-recommendation" in 4:2 and 5:11[94]. For the fact that the
Spirit was present in the hearts of the Corinthians, far from being
hidden and indiscernible, was publicly recognizable, open and evident
to any who joined their worship, as I Cor. 12 and 14 make abundantly
clear. By pointing to the Spirit as his supporting proof for his apostolic ministry, Paul was offering an argument which the Corinthians could
not deny without denying their own faith and pneumatic experience[95].

II Cor. 3:2 and 3:3 are thus built upon two different images, each
with its own internal logic. The point of connection between the two
is the Corinthians themselves (cf. ἐστέ/ἐστέ in 3:2 and 3)[96]. For it is
as a letter of Christ, written by the Spirit on their hearts, that the
Corinthians function as Paul's letter of recommendation. In addition,
the force of Paul's argument in 3:3 lies in the fact that he can point
to the visible work of the Spirit in the Corinthians' midst as undeniable evidence for the assertions of 3:1f. As a result, Paul's suffering,
presented in 2:14-17 and pointed to in 3:2, and the charismatic work
of the Spirit introduced in 3:3, are not in tension with one another.
Rather than being at odds with each other as the *loci* of two contrasting
theologies, i.e. a theology of the cross vs. a theology of glory (=Spir-
it)[97], Paul's suffering and the work of the Spirit are brought together

---

94 The centrality of this theme in 2:14-7:4 has been emphasized above all by Norbert
Baumert, *Täglich Sterben und Auferstehen. Der Literalsinn von 2 Kor 4:12-5:10*,
SANT 34, 1973, p.95, who also links it up with the παρρησία of Paul in 3:7-18.

95 Paul's argument in II Cor. 3:3 thus parallels his argument in Gal. 3:1-5, the
force of which has been surprisingly overlooked in previous studies of Galatians,
It appears, however, that Gal. 3:1-5 is, in fact, the very heart of Paul's argument in Galatians. rather than a parenthesis as often assumed. Cf. J. Jervell,
"Das Volk des Geistes", in *God's Christ and His People*, *FS Nils Alstrup Dahl*, ed.
J. Jervell and W.A. Meeks, 1977, pp.87-106, p.88: "Es wird oft übersehen oder nur
notdürftig bemerkt, daß (Paul) in erster Linie mit sehr handgreiflichen Argumenten
operiert: Die Geisterfahrungen der Gemeinde. Es ist überall bei Paulus so, dass er
nie Rechtfertigung sagt, ohne Geist zu sagen: Gal. 1-5; Röm. 3-7 und 8:1; 1 Kor.
6:11; 2; 2 Kor 3:4ff.; bes. V.8-9; Fil. 3:9 ... In Gal. weist Paulus die Gemeinde
auf die ursprünglichen Geisterfahrungen der Gemeinde hin, 3:1-5, was nicht als ein
zweitrangiges Argument im Verhältnis zur Schriftexegese abgewertet werden darf".

96 Contra those who see the link to be the letter of recommendation. See most recently, E. Richard, "Polemics", p.349 and following him, J. Lambrecht, "Structure",
p.351n.19.

97 For a good representative of this common view of Paul's theology, see J.Chr. Beker,
Paul the Apostle, pp.291,294,301. Beker suggests that the precise relationship

in our text as two complementary aspects of Paul's apostolic ministry, both of which provide empirical proof for the genuine nature of his ministry, the former known and read by all men, the latter clearly manifest (φανερόω). For it must be kept in mind that for Paul it is God's power/glory which is revealed through Paul's suffering (cf. II Cor. 4:6f. and see above, pp.98ff.) and that this power/glory is not a hidden theological assumption or postulat, but an ontological reality experienced by the believer which results in the conversion and transformation of those encountered by it, i.e. in their being created anew, ontologically understood (cf. I Cor. 1:26ff.; 2:5, 12-16; 3:16; 5:4f.; 6:19; II Cor. 3:17f.; 4:6; 5:17)[98]. J.D.G. Dunn is therefore certainly right when he emphasizes that "the Spirit, and particularly the gift of the Spirit, was a *fact* of experience in the lives of the earliest Christians", a statement which he says is "too obvious to require elaboration"[99]!

At the same time, it is not without significance that Paul chooses to make his point in 3:3 by establishing a contrast between the tablets of the heart and the tablets of stone, two important OT images, the latter of which can only be a reference to the law[100]. For in doing so, it becomes evident that Paul not only intends to make a statement about the locality of his ministry of the Spirit, but that he also wishes to remind the Corinthians of the *nature* of this letter so written, and thus, by implication, to express an important point about the nature of his own ministry. The significance of Paul's argument from the Spirit, as well as its implications for Paul's self-understanding as an apostle, will only become clear, therefore, after we have examined the OT allusions in II Cor. 3:3 and have placed them within Paul's view of the Spirit in general.

---

between these two aspects remains "unclear" in Paul's thinking (p.291) since "Paul often speaks of the Spirit in an inherently triumphant manner that prevents its integral relation with the weakness and suffering of the crucified Christ" (p.294). Thus, as is often the case, Beker suggests that the two aspects are in a "dialectical" relationship (cf. p.301). But cf. pp.17,34, where Beker also emphasizes that the truth of the gospel is verified by its power as an "effective word", though again he sees a "dialectical tension" between the truth and power of the gospel.

98 This point has been well made by P. Stuhlmacher, "Erwägungen zum ontologischen Charakter der καινή κτίσις bei Paulus", *EvTh* 27(1967)1-35, pp.27,28,29,33,35 and most recently by Udo Schnelle, *Gerechtigkeit und Christusgegenwart, Vorpaulinische und paulinische Tauftheologie, Göttinger theologische Arbeiten 24*, 1983, esp. his conclusions on pp.161-166 ("Paulus als Pneumatiker"), though I see no reason to distinguish Paul's view of the Spirit, with its "ontologisch-soterialogisch orientierten Denken", from Paul's doctrine of justification as "ein späteres Stadium paulinischer Theologie" as Schnelle does (cf. p.165).

99 *Baptism in the Holy Spirit*, p.225. See the 21 references from the NT which he provides as support. Dunn is probably also right when he attributes current attempts to deny this fact by "automatically" relegating the Spirit in the NT to the realm of the sacraments or by psychologizing the Spirit "out of existence" to "the poverty of our own immediate experience of the Spirit" (p.226)

100 See the LXX of Ex. 24:12; 31:18; 32:15; 34:1 and Dt. 9:10.

b. The Significance of 3:3 in the Light of Its OT Background

Scholars are divided over the precise identity of Paul's OT allusions in II Cor. 3:3b. The prevailing view has been that Paul's twofold contrast in 3:3b is a collage of those interrelated prophetic
texts from the LXX which focus on the promise of the new heart/new
covenant, over against the LXX version of the giving of the law on
Mount Sinai. The reference to the πλάκες λίθιναι is thus said to recall texts such as Exodus 24:12; 31:18; 32:15; 34:1 and Deuteronomy
9:10, while its counterpart, together with its association with the
Spirit, reflect Jeremiah 38:33; Ezekiel 11:19 and 36:26f. The repetition of the tablet-motif in this second element is said to be due to
Paul's desire to continue the parallel to the stone tablets of the
law[101]. Within this fusion of texts, the only question has been which
of these two prophetic texts, i.e. Jer. 38:33 or the two passages from
Ezekiel, actually occupied the *determinative* role in Paul's thinking
by providing the dominant image, which is then elaborated by the other[102]. In contrast, although all seem to agree that the "stone tablet"-
imagery refers to the tablets of the law, Schlatter, and more recently
H. Räisänen, have argued that Paul's contrasting thought in II Cor.
3:3b does not derive in any substantial way, if at all, from Jer. 38:33
(LXX), but instead refers exclusively to the two parallel passages from
Ezekiel[103], while Christian Wolff has maintained that neither Jer.38:33
nor Ez. 11:19; 36:26f. are in view, but rather Proverbs 3:3 and 7:3[104].

The first thing to be emphasized is that the determination of allusions is by no means easily carried out especially when biblical
terminology becomes an essential part of an author's own vocabulary,
as it certainly has with Paul. In our text, therefore, it is virtually

---

101 For various examples of this view, cf. Wendland, *An die Korinther*, p.178; Bultmann,
   Zweiter Korintherbrief, p.76; Prümm, *Diakonia*, 1967, pp.104, 202; Lietzmann, *An
   die Korinther*, p.110; Dunn, *Baptism*, p.48 and Lambrecht, "Structure", p.367.
102 For an example of those who argue that Jer. 38:33(LXX) is dominant, cf. Richard,
   "Polemics", pp.347-349; Hooker, "Beyond", p.296; Hughes, *Second Corinthians*, pp.
   89-91; Vos, *Traditionsgeschichtliche*, p.137; for the primacy of Ezek. cf. Richardson, "Spirit and Letter: A Foundation for Hermeneutics", *Evangelical Quarterly*
   45(1973)208-218, p.210; Hickling, "Sequence", pp.388f. and Provence, "Sufficient",
   pp.60f.
103 Schlatter, *Bote*, p.503 and H. Räisänen, *Paul and the Law*, pp.242-245.
104 *Jeremia*, p.135. Wolff's point concerning II Cor. 3:3 is part of his larger thesis
   that Jeremiah's prophecy of a "new covenant" in Jer. 31:31 is not referred to in
   Paul's writings *at all*, including II Cor. 3:6 and the "Abendmahl" tradition of I
   Cor. 11:25 (cf. pp.131-133,136), and that "Ferner fand sich in den paulinischen
   Briefen kein Anhalt dafür, daß das Jeremia-Buch überhaupt benutzt wurde" (pp.141f.).
   This conclusion is part of his larger point that Jeremiah's prophecy of the "new
   covenant" played no role in early Judaism as a whole (cf. pp.117-119,122-124),
   including the Qumran writings (cf. pp.125-130), and is found in the NT only in
   Hebrews 8:8-12 and 10:16f. (cf. pp.145f.). Now see H. Räisänen, *Paul and the Law*,
   pp.242f.,245, who follows Wolff in his judgment concerning II Cor. 3:6ff.

impossible to decide with certainty whether the terminology of the
"tablet of the heart" found in Prov. 3:3 and 7:3 and Jer. 17:1 also
plays a conscious role in Paul's thinking at this point as part of the
origin of his terminology in 3:3b[105], or whether, as is usually suggested,
the tablet-motif is a carry-over from Paul's reference to the law. But
it does seem impossible to maintain, as Wolff does, that the passages
from Proverbs are the sole and determinative source of Paul's contrast,
since in Proverbs 3:3 and 7:3 alone we find no reference either to the
idea of a "fleshly" heart, or to the main point of Paul's contrast
that the Spirit is now active in these hearts. For as has often been
pointed out, both of these motifs are too closely paralleled in Ezekiel
11 and 36 for these passages to be excluded[106]. The only question to
be determined is whether or not Jer. 38:33 ought to be included as part
of Paul's conceptual field at this point. The strongest reason for doing so is the reference to the new covenant of Jer. 38:31(LXX) in
3:6[107], which is understood to be parallel in some way to 3:3, so that
already in 3:3 Paul is said to be alluding in general to this passage,
or to have it "in mind"[108] when he speaks of the letter ἐγγεγραμμένη...
ἐν πλαξὶν καρδίαις σαρκίναις (cf. Jer. 38:33: ἐπὶ καρδίας αὐτῶν γράψω
αὐτούς = God's laws). But there are several good reasons for exercising
caution at this point. On the one hand, the motif of "engraving" in
3:3, being a carry-over from 3:2[109], is first used in reference to that
which has been "engraved" on the stone tablets of the law. Hence, if
it refers specifically to an OT text at all, it probably picks up the
use of the motif of "writing" or "engraving" (γράφειν) on the tablets
of stone found in the LXX of Ex. 24:12; 31:18; 32:15f.; 34:1 and Dt.
9:10, rather than that of writing in the heart found in Jer. 38:33,
though it is assuming too much to single out Ex. 31:18 as *the* text in
view, as R. Bultmann and E. Richard do[110]. On the other hand, the

---

105 Cf. Windisch, *Zweiter Korintherbrief*, pp.104,106 and Bultmann, *Zweiter Korinther-
    brief*, p.76, both of whom suggest Prov. 7:3 (Windisch 3:3 as well), though not
    exclusively.
106 Most recently H. Räisänen, *Paul and the Law*, pp.243f.: "It is noteworthy that the
    OT passage Paul undoubtedly alludes to is the promise of a new heart in *Ezekiel*"
    (p.244). Räisänen then correctly concludes. "Wolff, op.cit. 135, is not justified
    in glossing over this reference" (p.244n.86).
107 The position of Wolff and Räisänen concerning 3:6 is in my opinion not convincing,
    though a detailed discussion of this point must be left for volume two of this
    study.
108 Cf. e.g. I. Hermann, *Kyrios und Pneuma*, p.27, who maintains "daß Paulus über das
    Vordergründige des 'nicht mit Tinte geschriebenen Briefes' (die Gemeinde) hinaus
    bereits jetzt den gesamten Status des Neuen Bundes im Auge hat, wie er ihn in den
    folgenden Versen (4ff.) zu umschreiben gedenkt".
109 Contra Richard, "Polemics", pp.347f., who argues that ἐγγεγραμμένη in v.2 derives
    from Jer. 38:33, while its use in v.3 comes from Ex. 31:18.
110 Cf. Bultmann, *Zweiter Korintherbrief*, p.76 and E. Richard, "Polemics", p.348. The
    grammatical and stylistic parallels between Ex. 31:18 and II Cor. 3:3 which Richard

"fleshly heart"-motif found in 3:3 explicitly occurs in both Ez. 11:19
and 36:26, thus providing a more appropriate explanation for this syntactically awkward expression in 3:3 than to suggest that the "heart"-
motif is taken from Jer. 38:33 quite apart from its modification as
found in our context[111]. In addition, the motif of the Spirit, which
is so central to Paul's thought in 3:3, is missing altogether in Jer.
38:33ff., while the characteristic idea of the law written in the heart
from Jeremiah does not occur in II Cor. 3:3[112]. Here it is the letter
of Christ which is written on the heart[113]. Finally, as a matter of
exegetical principle, Paul's thought ought to be followed as he himself
unfolds it before bringing similar Pauline themes together. Thus, even
if the traditions from Jer. 38:33 and Ez. 11:19; 36:26 (cf. 37:26ff.)
were closely associated, or even collapsed together for Paul[114] in what
has now become known as his "rabbinic way of thinking", we nevertheless
do an injustice to his *explicit* train of thought in any particular
passage when we read his mind by maintaining that everything he said
about a specific point, including his OT support, is always in view.
Thus, in our context, although I disagree with Wolff and Räisänen that
an allusion to Jer. 38:33 is also lacking in II Cor. 3:6, this does not
mean that we are justified in reading this allusion in 3:6 back into
3:3, when no *explicit* reference to either the "law written on the heart"
or the "new covenant" has yet been introduced, though the characteristic
content of the old covenant/new covenant is now certainly in view
(tablets of stone/tablets of fleshly hearts)[115]. To do so would be to
"jump the gun" on Paul's thinking and to run the risk as a result of
diminishing the distinctives of Paul's argument in 3:3. For as Paul
himself indicates, albeit negatively, his concern in 3:3 is not with
the new covenant in relationship to the law, as in 3:6ff., but with a
contrast between the two "materials" of God's activity as "writer": the

---

points out may simply derive from standard linguistic conventions on the one hand,
and from Paul's desire to continue the parallel between the two tablets on the
other.

111 Räisänen is therefore correct in concluding that "there is at least no clear
linguistic connection" between II Cor. 3:3 and Jer. 38:33; *Paul and the Law*, p.
244.

112 For this latter point, see again Räisänen, *Paul*, p.245. But although Räisänen is
correct in stressing that "it is clear that it is *not* the *law* in any sense that
has been written in the Corinthians' hearts according to verse 3", his following
statement, as I will argue in volume two of this study, does not reflect Paul's
thought in 3:6: "The tablets of stone stand for the γράμμα which is the *opposite*
of πνεῦμα (v.6)" (p.245).

113 Contra those who read the law into this text. Cf. e.g. I. Hermann, *Kyrios*, p.27
and Hughes, *Second Corinthians*, pp.89f.

114 Cf. Lars Hartman, "Bundesideologie in und hinter einigen paulinischen Texten", in
Die Paulinische Literatur und Theologie, Teologiske Studier 7, ed. S. Pedersen,
1980, pp.103-118, pp.108, 112.

115 For the strongest proponent of the need to read 3:3 from the perspective of 3:6,
see Bultmann, *Zweiter Korintherbrief*, pp.76f. For the opposite view, see esp.
Hickling, "Sequence", p.386 and Hughes, *Second Corinthians*, p.89.

stone tablets (of the law) and the fleshly tablets of the heart as the
recipient of the Spirit. It is crucial, therefore, that we do not read
the tablet of stone/tablet of fleshly heart contrast in 3:3 in terms
of the letter/Spirit contrast of 3:6. For although closely related,
Paul's point in these two contrasts is nevertheless not identical[116].
In approaching the significance of Paul's contrast in 3:3, we must content ourselves with looking to the texts of Exodus (par. Dt. 9:10) and
Ezekiel for help in understanding the nature of Paul's contrast before
we turn our attention to his further development of this theme in 3:6[117].
In this way, both the distinctiveness of the two contrasts, with their
respective OT backgrounds, as well as their commonality will come to
light.

What then is the significance of Paul's contrast in II Cor. 3:3b when
viewed against the background of Exodus and Ezekiel? Unfortunately, the
predominant answer to this question has not taken its starting point
from the OT texts in view, except to point out the source of Paul's
terminology, but has rather seized upon the contrast between "ink" vs.
"Spirit" and "stone" vs. "heart" as abstract indications of two contrasting qualities. Thus, Paul's contrast in II Cor. 3:3b is taken to
be a contrast between the outward and the inward or externality and
internality[118], which can then be associated with death vs. life[119],
conscious vs. unconscious[120], that which cannot be enjoyed vs. that
which can[121], ritualism vs. the Spirit which is equated with a "rule
book mentality" vs. spontaneity[122], stiffness vs. suppleness[123], external compliance vs. harmony of thought and action[124], etc. The common
denominator which runs through this perspective, regardless of its vari-
ations, is that "stone tablets", being made out of *stone*, are therefore
negative; while the "*fleshly* heart" is their positive counterpart. Understood in this way, II Cor. 3:3b becomes another from of the traditional
law/gospel antithesis: that which is written on stone tablets, i.e. the

116 Though not because, as often suggested, Paul switches from the letter of recommendation theme in 3:3 to the law/gospel contrast in 3:6. For a representative
presentation of this view, cf. Lietzmann, *An die Korinther*, pp.110f.
117 In this regard it is also interesting to note that in the 25th. ed. of Nestle-
Aland's *Novum Testamentum Graece*, 1975(1927), p.461, Jer. 31:33 was included as
one of the parallels to 3:3 in the margin, while in the 26th. ed., 1979, p.476,
it is omitted.
118 E.g. Ridderbos, *Paul*, pp.218-219; Bultmann, *Theologie*, pp.222f.; Vos, *Traditionsgeschichtliche*, pp.137f. and E. Schweitzer, et.al., art. σάρξ κ.τ.λ., *TDNT*, *Vol.
VIII*, 1971, pp.98-151, pp.143f.
119 Bultmann, *Zweiter Korintherbrief*, pp.76f.
120 So G. Theißen, *Psychologische Aspekte paulinischer Theologie*, *FRLANT 131*, 1983,
pp.146-156.
121 J. Jeremias, art. λίθος, *TDNT*, *Vol. IV*, 1967, pp.268-280, p.269.
122 J.D.G. Dunn, *Jesus and the Spirit*, pp.201,223 and similarly in *Baptism*, pp.137,
146f.
123 Prümm, *Diakonia*, 1967, pp.105,107-109.
124 Roy A. Harrisville, *The Concept of Newness in the New Testament*, 1960, p.58.

law, being insufficient because of its nature, is replaced by the work
of the Spirit as an expression of the gospel[125].

At first, this interpretation appears to be supported by the stone-
imagery used in Ezekiel 11:19 and 36:26 to represent the hard, incor-
rigible heart which refuses to, indeed cannot, keep God's commandments;
in contrast to the heart of flesh which, filled with God's Spirit, is
enabled, even compelled, by God to keep his law (cf. Ez. 11:20 and
36:27). But it is precisely this contrast between the two conditions
of the heart which Paul does *not* introduce in II Cor. 3:3[126]. Moreover,
there is no such corresponding negative nuance associated with the fact
that the law was written on stone, either in Ezekiel, where the new
heart of flesh is given in order that God's law might be kept, not done
away with (!)[127], or elsewhere in the Old Testament[128]. On the contrary,
the very fact that God gave Moses the law on stone tablets seems to be
one of the hallmarks of its *glory*, as intimated by the repetition of
this motif in connection with the first giving of the law in Ex. 24:12
and 31:18 (cf. Dt. 9:10), the explicit designation of these tablets as
the ἔργον θεοῦ in Ex. 32:16, having been written with "the finger of God"
(Ex. 31:18; Dt. 9:10) and God's demand that they be replaced after the
sin with the golden calf in Ex. 34:1.

Furthermore, that the law was written specifically upon stone tablets
did not carry a negative connotation, but instead was understood to be
one of its positive attributes, is confirmed by the development of this
theme throughout early Jewish literature. Thus, in Jubilees (2nd cent.
B.C.E.), the tablets of stone which Moses receives on the Mountain of
God (cf. Jub. 1:1) can be identified, as their earthly reproduction,
with the "heavenly tablets" from which the angel dictates God's words
(cf. 1:26f.; 2:1); so much so in fact, that the designation "heavenly
tablets" becomes a customary way of referring to the law itself throughout the Jubilean commentary on and expansion of Gen. 1:1-Ex. 12:50[129].

---

125 To give just one example, see E. Käsemann, "Geist und Buchstabe", pp.255-257.
   Käsemann's view is combined with his conviction that Paul's use of Scripture in
   II Cor. 3:3 is an example of his "Manipulation" of the OT, i.e. an example of
   what Vielhauer calls the "bewußter Umdeutung des alttestamentlichen Textes" (see
   p.255 and 255n.31). I will argue below that the nature of the contrast in 3:3b
   corresponds both to the texts from Exodus and Ezekiel themselves and to common
   Jewish understanding.
126 This contrast, though not expressed in the text, is nevertheless often assumed to
   be there; cf. e.g. T. Provence, "Sufficient", pp.60f.; Hickling, "Sequence", pp.
   388f.; and Bultmann, *Zweiter Korintherbrief*, p.76.
127 Cf. W. Zimmerli, *Ezechiel, 1. Teilband*, BKAT XIII/1, 1969, pp.250f.and *2. Teilband*,
   BKAT XIII/2, 1969, pp.879f.; F. Hahn, "Die alttestamentlichen Motive in der urchristlichen Abendmahlsüberlieferung", *EvTh* 27(1967)337-374, p.369 and most recently H. Räisänen, *Paul and the Law*, p.244.
128 Besides the texts already mentioned from Ex. and Dt., cf. Ex. 32:19; 34:4,28f.;
   Dt. 4:13; 5:22; 9:9,11,15,17; 10:1-5; I Kgs. 8:9 and II Chron. 5:10 for the other
   OT references to the tablets of the law.
129 Cf. Jub. 3:10,31; 4:5,32; 6:17 in comparison with 6:11f. and 22; 16:3,9; 18:19;
   19:9; 23:32; 24:33; 28:6; 30:9; 31:32 and 33:10.

The "heavenly tablets" are, of course, also conceived to be the
source of information for Jubilees itself as the "second law" revealed
to Moses (cf. Jub. 6:22). But the complicated question of the relationship between the Mosaic law and Jubilees from the perspective of Jubilees need not detain us here. The important point for our purposes is
the unmistakable positive development of the tablet-motif encountered
in Jubilees in which the OT tradition of the tablets of stone has now
been extended into the idea of a heavenly set of tablets as the locus
of revelation. In this regard it is also important to point out that
the "heavenly tablets" in Jubilees contain more than just the revelation
recorded in the OT law and Jubilees since they can be pointed to as the
depository for recording the divine judgment of all living creatures
(cf. 5:13f.; 30:20)[130], and that the tablet-motif itself can be used
to represent other divine messages as well (cf. 32:21f.). The purpose
of this positive development of the stone tablet-motif in Jubilees is
to underscore not only the divine origin of the law (and Jubilees), but
also its everlasting permanence and certainty as testified to by its
written and engraven nature (cf. Jub. 6:23; 16:30; 32:10f.,15; 49:8)[131].
Hence, in Jub. 15:25f. we read concerning the importance of being cir-
cumcised on the eighth day that

> this law is for all the generations for ever, and there is no circumcision
> of the days, and no omission of one day out of the eight days; for it is an
> eternal ordinance, ordained and written on the heavenly tablets.[132]

Indeed, it is the very fact that the laws have been written on such
tablets, both heavenly and earthly, which ensures that the righteousness
of God, and especially the calender advocated in Jubilees, can still be
seen and retained in spite of its perversion through the forgetfulness
and unrighteousness of Israel[133]. To be written on stone tablets, therefore, far from being a negative sign of its inadequacy, is, for the
author of Jubilees, an essential aspect of the law's value, since it
indicates the permanent nature of the law's testimony and commands[134].
It is this conviction which no doubt led to the corresponding picture
of the existence of "heavenly tablets" from which the law was dictated
and upon which the permanent record of God's ordinances, the status of

---

130 For a parallel tradition, cf. I Enoch 98:7f.; 104:7f.
131 For a similar emphasis, this time on the eternality of that which has been "written
by the finger of God" in the "book of the most high", cf. Joseph and Asenath, Ap-
pendix III, found on p.80 of E.W. Brooks' edition, *Joseph and Asenath*, 1918.
132 Translation from R.H. Charles, *The Apocrypha and Pseudepigrapha of the Old Testament, Vol. II*, 1977(1913), p.36.
133 See Jub. 1:5-7,9f.,14; 6:34-38; 16:29-31; 33:15-18; 50:13.
134 Cf. J. Jeremias, *TDNT, Vol. IV*, p.269, who also observes that the emphasis on the
stone tablets reflects the fact that "stone was regarded as the most enduring
writing material, hence the stone tables of the Mosaic law ...". He nevertheless ·
reads a pejorative connotation into 3:3; see above, n.121.

his creatures and his plans for the future of the world are recorded.

As an illustration of this same conviction, we read in I Enoch 81:1f.
(2nd. cent. B.C.E. - 1st cent. C.E.) that Enoch was commanded to

> look at the stone tablets[135] of heaven; read what is written upon them and
> understand (each element on them) one by one. So I looked at the tablet(s)
> of heaven, read all the writing (on them), and came to understand every-
> thing. I read that book and all the deeds of humanity and all the children
> of the flesh upon the earth for all the generations of the world[136].

Moreover, in I Enoch 103:2-4 the fact that the future blessings intended for the righteous are inscribed on the same "tablets of heaven" is
once again given as an indication of their surety and permanence, and
can thus be pointed to as a source of encouragement for the faithful
(cf. 108:7-10).

A third important witness to this positive nature of the tables of
the law is found in the Testament of Levi 5:4 and 7:5 (2nd cent. B.C.E.),
where according to the better textual tradition, the law itself is referred to as the "tablets of heaven" (πλάκες τῶν οὐρανῶν)[137]. Here the
implicit connection found in Jubilees and I Enoch is now made explicit.

But the esteem accorded to the tablets of the law is also reflected
in the tradition in a variety of other ways as well. For example, in
II Baruch 6:7-9 (early 2nd cent. C.E.) the two tablets are one of the
precious things hidden in the earth by an angel at the time of the
destruction of Jerusalem in 587 B.C.E., only to be revealed again at
the consumation of the age. This point is also made in *The Lives of the
Prophets*, Jer. 14 (1st cent. C.E.), where we are told that the glory of
God abides over the buried tablets since the glory of God will never
cease from his law (cf. Jer. 9,11,12)[138]. Although not clear in and of
itself, a similar esteem could be reflected in IV Ezra 14:22-26 (late
1st cent. C.E.), where in response to Ezra's plea that God inspire him
to rewrite the law for his people yet to be born, God once again requires that Ezra, like Moses, prepare tablets (*buxos*) for this purpose
(cf. IV Ezra 14:24; Ex. 34:1). At least it is evident that an essential
aspect of the giving of the law in the tradition consisted in its having

---

135 Translation from E. Isaac, "1 (Ethiopic Apocalypse of) Enoch", *Old Testament
   Pseudepigrapha*, *Vol. I*, ed. J.H. Charlesworth, 1983, p.59. At this point I am
   following the literal translation found in footnote 81b.
136 For this same tradition cf. I En. 93:2; 106:19.
137 I.e. the so-called "β" text group. The other tradition, i.e. the "α" text group
   reads πατέρων. For the evidence cf. R. H. Charles, *The Greek Versions of the
   Testaments of the Twelve Patriarchs*, 1960² (1908), p.38. My preference for this
   reading is based on the evaluation of the textual evidence in M. DeJonge, *Testamenta XII Patriarcharum, Pseudepigrapha Veteris Testamenti Graece*, *Vol. I*, ed.
   A.M. Denis and M. DeJonge, 1964, pp.XIII-XV. For a reference to the tablets of
   the commandments, cf. Test.Asher 2:10.
138 For this same tradition of the buried tablets, cf. Ps.-Philo, LAB (Hebrew Fragments) 26:12-13.

been engraven on such tablets, since this is one of the two motifs employed by the author of IV Ezra to indicate his intended parallel between Ezra's writing of the law and its original reception by Moses[139].
In yet another graphic example of this tendency to glorify the tablets
of the law, the targum Ps-Jon. to Ex. 31:18 describes the "tablets of
stone" written with the finger of God in the MT text as "tablets of
sapphirestone from the throne of glory, weighing forty seïn"[140]. This
same tradition is also found in the late midrashic compilations of Ex.R.
46.2; Lev.R. 32.2 and Song of Songs R. 5.14, §3 and in b.Ned. 38a, in
which the sapphire nature of the stone tablets is taken to be the reason
why Moses became rich from the chippings (פסולת) left over from making
the second set of tablets (cf. פסל, Ex. 34:1). This miraculous nature
of the stone is also emphasized in the rabbinic tradition that although
made of such hard stone, the tablets could nevertheless be rolled up
like a scroll, thus explaining why they can be referred to as such in
Numbers 5:23 (cf. Num.R. 9.48; S.S.R. 5.14, §1)[141]. Thus, given the
holy nature of the tablets themselves, even the remains of the broken
set are said to be kept in the ark in Num.R. 4.20, while in Lev.R. 8.3
the tablets become a canon for that which is "beloved" by God. In Ex.R.
46.3 it is the presence of the tablets, since they are of the utmost
holiness, which renders it impossible for the alien to eat of the paschal lamb (cf. Ex. 12:43): for "shall those who serve idols have any
connection with the Tables which are the work of God?"[142]. It is this
same conviction concerning the holiness of the tablets which also appears to be behind the earlier mishnaic teaching that the tablets were
one of the ten things created on the eve of the Sabbath in the week of
creation, found in Aboth 5.9, while it is certainly reflected in the
midrash on Ex. 34:29 which attributes the glory on Moses' face not to
his encounter with God, but to his contact with the tablets (cf. Ex.R.
47.6; Dt.R. 3.12)! This glorification of the tablets in later rabbinic
tradition reaches its apex in Pirke de Rabbi Eliezer, chapter 45, where
the tablets take on a life of their own. For now the tablets themselves
are able to see Israel's sin with the golden calf, upon which their
letters not only fly off, but once the letters vanish, their weight in-
creases to such a degree that Moses is forced to cast them to the

---

139 The other is the fact that Ezra is commanded to come away for 40 days, as was
   Moses; cf. Ex. 24:18; 34:28; Dt. 9:9,18 and IV Ezra 14:23.
140 Translation from J.W. Etheridge, *The Targums of Onkelos and Jonathan ben Uzziel on
   the Pentateuch*, 1968(1862), p.549. Cf. also A. Diez Macho, *Neophyti 1, Tomo II
   Exodo*, 1970, p.503n.8.
141 In S.S.R. 5.14, §1 it is even asserted that the tablets were "hewn from the orb
   of the sun"; cf. Maurice Simon, *Song of Songs, Midrash Rabbah, Vol. IX*, 1951, p.
   245.
142 Translation from S.M. Lehrman, *Exodus, Midrash Rabbah, Vol. III*, 1951, p.530.

ground[143]. Finally, Ex.R. 41.6 offers us an entirely different reflection on the significance of the fact that the tablets were made of stone by presenting three explanations for the choice of this particular material:

1) because most of the penalties for disobeying the Torah were stoning;

2) because the law was given for Jacob's sake, who is referred to as the "stone of Israel" in Gen. 49:24; and

3) because "unless one hardens his cheeks like stone, he will not acquire the Torah", which in b. Er. 54a is interpreted to mean either that one must receive one's reproaches stoically, or that one must never grow tired of studying the law.[144]

But once again, there is no intimation that the stone quality of the tablets is seen to be an indication of a negative quality to be associated with the law. If anything, the first and third reasons represent the seriousness with which the law is to be taken as the revelation of God's will *par excellence* and the center of Israel's existence as God's people. Nowhere is this last point more graphically illustrated than in the fact that the ark of the covenant, which was placed within the holy of holies as the focal point of Israel's worship, contained only the two stone tablets[145]. Thus, as this representative sample shows[146], there is, to my knowledge, no indication at any period in Jewish-tradition that the stone-nature of the tablets of the law ever carried a negative connotation similar to the heart of stone imagery in Ezekiel 11:19 and 36:26[147]. Moreover, since there is no indication in the context[148] that Paul himself is making this unique association in II Cor.

---

143 For this same tradition of the writing flying away from the tablets in response to the golden calf incident, cf. Num.R. 9.48.

144 Translation and reference to b. Er. 54a are both from S.M. Lehrman, *Exodus, Midrash Rabbah, Vol. III*, p.476 and 476n.2.

145 Cf. Dt. 10:1-5; I Kgs 8:9; II Chron. 5:10 and Josephus, *Ant.* VIII.104.

146 For a convenient listing of the numerous midrashic traditions concerning the tablets, cf. Louis Ginzberg, *The Legends of the Jews, Vol. V*, 1955(1925), p.109 n.99 and *Vol. VI*, 1946(1928), pp.49f.nn.258-260; 59f.nn.302-307.

147 H. Räisänen's assertion, *Paul and the Law*, p.244, that "it is a well-known Rabbinic association to establish a connection between the stone heart of the book of Ezekiel and the stone tablets of Exodus: it is proper that stone should watch over stone (the law over the stone heart, identified with the evil inclination)" must therefore be carefully interpreted. For this association is not made to denigrate the law in any way, but to explicate its function. In fact, as Lev.R. 35.5 makes clear, the link between the stone tablets and Ez. 36:26 is made in order to show that the law exercises a positive function of safeguarding and protecting one from the evil inclination. This is also the point made by S. Schechter, *Aspects of Rabbinic Theology*, 1961 (1909),pp.274f. (also pointed to by Räisänen, cf. p.244n.85).

148 To read 3:6 as such an indication assumes what must be demonstrated, while to bring a more general conception of "Paul's view of the law" from elsewhere to this text is to prejudice the exegesis, as for example H. Räisänen does, *Paul and the Law*, pp.241f.,244f., when he concludes on the basis of his view of Paul's understanding of the law that since "there is no basis for a theology of an abrogation of the law in Jer. 31 or the related texts (he points to Ez. 11:20; 36: 27, cf. p.242n.71)", that "Paul could not seize on Jer. 31 if he understood the

3:3, the common attempt to read into his reference to the stone tablets
any such pejorative connotation or negative nuance is completely without support. Consequently, there is also no reason to interpret the contrast between the stone tablets and the tablets of the heart as a contrast between something negative and something positive, as has been
done in the past. The reference to the law as "stone tablets" in II Cor.
3:3b, if not honorific, as it is elsewhere in both pre- and post-Pauline
Jewish tradition, is at least a normal designation of the revelation
given to Moses which derives from the biblical account of the giving of
the law itself[149]. As such, it is safe to say that the reference to the
law as "stone tablets" in 3:3b in no way contradicts Paul's assumption
in 3:7-11 that the law ἐγενήθη ἐν δόξῃ (cf. 3:7, 9, 11). In fact, it is
an essential aspect of this very glory. On the other hand, the reference
to the "hearts of flesh", deriving as it does from Ezekiel 11:19 and
36:26, also picks up a biblical tradition with many parallels in extra-
biblical Jewish literature. For in view of Israel's history of disobe-
dience, it became common to emphasize the nation's "hard heart", while
at the same time expressing hope in God's corresponding eschatological
promise to replace this "heart of stone" with a *new* heart of flesh and
a new spirit/Holy Spirit in order that his people might keep the law
and thus remain faithful to the covenant[150]. Paul's statement in 3:3
that the Corinthians' existence as Christians is a result of the work
of the Spirit in their hearts of flesh is thus an expression of his confidence that this very eschatological promise from Ezekiel is now being
fulfilled[151]!

---

passage in its original meaning or in consonance with contemporary Jewish understanding" (p.242). He thus concludes concerning v.3 that "it is clear that it is
not the *law* in any sense that has been written in the Corinthians' hearts according to verse 3", reading 3:3 in terms of 3:6, the latter taken to an example of
this "abrogation of the law". But this question is not in view at all in v.3, hence
it is neither confirmed nor denied! Moreover, it is not at all clear that 3:6 intends to argue that the law is replaced by the Spirit!

149 Cf. Baumann, art. לוח, *ThWAT*, IV, *Lieferung 3/4*, 1982, pp.495-499,p.496, who
points out concerning לוח "wie sehr im AT die Bedeutung 'Gesetzestafeln' im Vorder-
grund steht ...".

150 For various adaptations of this perspective, here formulated in terms of Ezekiel,
cf. e.g. IV Ezra 3:19-23,36; 7:23f.,45-49,72; 8:6f.; 9:29-37 in comparison with
6:26; Jub. 1:7,10,21-23 (cf. 15:33f.); Apoc.Mosis 13:3-5; Test.Levi 18:10-11;
Test.Judah 24:2f.; Odes of Sol. 4:3; Test.Job. 48:2,4; 49:1; 50:1;Life of Adam and
Eve 29:8f.; I En. 108:2; Sib.Or. III,703,719; Ps-Philo, LAB 30:6; Baruch 1:17-21
(cf. 2:8); Ex.R. 41:7.

151 I see no reason to make a distinction between Ezekiel's antithesis as "moral" and
Jeremiah's in 31:31ff. as "heilsgeschichtlich" as Hickling, "Sequence", p.389
does, since in both passages the context is precisely the same, i.e. the eschatological restoration of Israel after the Exile (cf. Ez. 11:13-18; 36:19-25 and Jer.
31:23-28, 38-40). And all three texts refer to the future keeping of the law,
which is certainly moral (cf. Ez. 11:20; 36:27; Jer. 31:32f.). Thus, in both cases,
the hope is eschatological and moral. See most recently, Werner E. Lemke, "Jeremiah
31:31-34", *Interpretation* 37(1983)183-187, p.186: "both Jer and Ez envisaged a
similar restoration and internalization of the relationship between Yahweh and his
people ...".

c. The Meaning of II Cor. 3:3b

In II Cor. 3:3b Paul wishes to affirm that the Corinthians' relationship to Christ has not been established by the Spirit's work in conjunction with the law, but by the Spirit's work in their hearts, pictured in terms of the promise from Ezekiel. Against the background of
Ezekiel, the contrast between the two spheres of God's revelatory-sal-
vific activity, i.e. the "law" and the "heart", is best understood,
therefore, as a contrast between the two basic ages in the history of
salvation, which are represented by these two fundamental rubrics. For
while in the "old age" the locus of God's activity and revelation was
the law, in the "new age", according to Ezekiel, God will be at work in
the heart. Again at this point, however, we must be careful not to read
more into this statement than is there. For the question of the nature
of the law, the "problem" with the law, the function of the law in the
history of redemption, or the relationship between the law and the gospel,
though important for Paul and treated by him elsewhere (including 3:6ff.),
are not the point or focus of Paul's assertion here. Moreover, it should
be kept in mind that in Ezekiel itself, the hope for the future work of
God in the heart in no way alters the validity of the law. And Paul himself, as is well-known, can speak positively of the law in and of itself (see II Cor. 3:7, 9, 11; Rom. 7:10, 12f., 14, 16). Hence, if anything is to be assumed as implicit in Paul's contrast in regard to the
law, it is that the law is now being kept by those who have received
the Spirit, as Ezekiel prophesied! When forced to speak of a relationship between these two realms of God's activity, we should not, therefore, transpose the negative/positive (οὐκ/ἀλλά) contrast which exists
between the two *affirmations* in 3:3b, i.e. Paul's negative denial that
the Spirit at work in the Corinthians is related to the law = old age
and his corresponding positive affirmation that the Spirit is at work
in their hearts = new age, into a contrast between the *nature* of the
law and the heart themselves. Nor should we transpose the contrast between the law and the heart into a contrast between the law and the
Spirit[152], thus creating a contrast either between two conflicting
qualities or two diverse ways of salvation. Rather, if in view at all,
the relationship between these two realms of God's activity is best
understood in terms of the same *qal wahomer / a minori ad maius* (πολλῷ
μᾶλλον) relationship expressed in II Cor. 3:7-11, i.e. from something

---

152 Contra Kümmel, additions to Lietzmann, *An die Korinther*, p.199; Bultmann, *Zweiter
    Korinterbrief*, p.76; Räisänen, *Paul and the Law*, p.245; I. Hermann, *Kyrios*, pp.
    108f. and E. Käsemann, "Geist und Buchstabe", pp.255f., to give just a few ex-
    amples of this widespread view.

glorious to something even more glorious[153]. Although it cannot be argued here, the external/internal contrast which is implicit between the
stone tablets and the *fleshly* heart in 3:3, or explicit in 3:6 between
the letter and the Spirit, is not, therefore, a contrast between two
qualities or ways of salvation (see above, p.207). Rather, it is a contrast between the law as it usually functioned in the old covenant in
its impotency to change one's heart, being merely the external declaration of God's will, and the potency of the Spirit in its work in the
heart, the result of which is that the law itself is now able to be
kept[154].

In saying this, however, the clear and startling significance of
Paul's statement in 3:3b should not be overlooked. For in establishing
this contrast, Paul is not merely pointing to the fact that the eschatological promise of Ezekiel is now being fulfilled. He is also asserting
that it is being fulfilled through his *own* ministry, since Paul is the
one through whom the Spirit came to the Corinthians (cf. διακονηθεῖσα
ὑφ' ἡμῶν). Hence, the significance of Paul's contrast in II Cor. 3:3b,
when viewed against the background of Exodus and Ezekiel, is twofold.
On the one hand, Paul affirms that the age characterized by the law as
the locus of God's revelatory activity is over. In contrast, the Corinthians owe their relationship to Christ not to the revelation of God
in the law, but to God's work in changing their hearts through his
Spirit. As such, the conversion and new life of the Corinthians are evidence that the new age has arrived[155], i.e. the age of the "fleshly
heart" prophesied by Ezekiel[156]. This also means, however, that any attempt to argue that since the death and resurrection of Jesus the eschatological coming of the Spirit is still bound together with the old covenant in the law must be rejected[157]. Paul's positive affirmation in II

153 Cf. the same view of the relationship between the Mosaic law and the law which
will be written on the heart in the eschatological age found in the rabbinic
tradition concerning Jer. 31:31ff. as exemplified in the examples listed in
Billerbeck, *Kommentar, Bd. III*, pp.89f.
154 This will be developed in volume two of this study on the basis of II Cor. 3:6-18
and the parallels in Rom. 2:27-29; 7:5f. and 8:2-4. See my theses in the conclusion to this study below.
155 So too Peter R. Jones, *The Apostle Paul: A Second Moses according to II Corinthians 2:14-4:7*, unpublished Ph.D. diss., Princeton Theological Seminary, 1973, p.
33n.2: "The Corinthian Christian Gentiles are demonstrable proof of the gospel
of the new covenant".
156 Apart from the implications he draws from this concerning the nature of the law
and the old covenant, Ridderbos, *Paul*, p.215, is right in emphasizing that the
letter/Spirit contrast in 3:6 is a "redemptive-historical contrast, namely, as
the two dominating principles of the two aeons marked off by the appearance of
Christ"; or as he puts it on p.216, "two regimes" (cf. pp.221-223). See too Dunn,
Baptism, pp.48,135 (minus his earlier negative conclusions concerning the law,
cf. pp.48,146f., etc.) and U. Luz, *Das Geschichtsverständnis des Apostels Paulus*,
BEvTh 49, 1968, pp.127,130.
157 See e.g. Is. 63:11 where God is said to have put the Holy Spirit in the midst of
his people through Moses (cf. Num. 11:17,25,29; Hag. 2:5)!

Cor. 3:3 thus provides the foundational premise and unexpressed presupposition for his argument in Galatians 3:1-4: in the new covenant God bestows his Spirit directly in the hearts of his people in response to their faith in the gospel. Hence, to replace or supplement this gospel as the medium of the Spirit with the law as the center of the old covenant becomes a denial of the gospel itself (cf. Gal. 2:18, 21). It thus seems probable that the position of the opponents who attempted to do this in Galatia was also present in Corinth, though no doubt modified to fit the Corinthian situation. This would explain why Paul develops his apologetic for his sufficiency as an apostle in contrast to the law in 3:3b and then goes on to extend it in 3:6ff. In affirming that the Spirit comes through the gospel, he denies that the old covenant is still in force and hence robs his opponents of their footing.

On the other hand, the Corinthians are also evidence for the fact that Paul now occupies a crucial role in the coming of the new age as its apostle. For as the Corinthians themselves could testify, the Spirit at work in their midst and in their hearts was mediated to them through Paul. Thus, just as the authority of Moses was identified with and supported by the law which he mediated to Israel, Paul's authority is identified with and supported by the changed hearts which come about as he mediates the Spirit to those who hear the gospel and are baptized as *the* eschatological gift bar none[158].

Although it seems misleading to describe Paul as a "second Moses", since Paul's allusion in 2:16b and 3:4-6 is not to the expectation of such a figure but to the call of Moses and its development in the OT prophetic tradition (see above, chapter three), Paul's *role* is nevertheless similar to that of Moses in that he too functions as the one through whom God's revelation is brought to his people. For if my exegesis of 2:14-3:3 is correct, Paul views himself as an eschatological agent of revelation through whom the Spirit is now being poured out in the gospel. Consequently, Paul's authority, like the authority of Moses, also finds its source of validity precisely in the revelation which he brings as a result of his call[159]. Hence, Paul's authority derives from and is best

---

158 It is not necessary for our purposes to develop Paul's view of the Spirit or its work beyond this basic point. For this point as well as a development of its implications for Paul's theology in general which corresponds basically to the direction I am taking, cf. Ridderbos, *Paul*, pp.67f., 215-217, 221f.; Stuhlmacher, "καινὴ κτίσις", pp.27-29; L. Goppelt, *Theologie des Neuen Testaments*, 1978³, pp. 447-453; W. Klaiber, *Rechtfertigung und Gemeinde*, pp.122-129,174-190 (minus his emphasis on the non-verifiable nature of the Spirit); W.D. Davies, *Paul and Rabbinic Judaism, Some Rabbinic Elements in Pauline Theology*, 1980⁴, pp.184f., 202f., 207-216; R. Harrisville, *Concept of Newness*, pp.60f. and the massive, but overlooked work by Kurt Stalder, *Das Werk des Geistes in der Heiligung bei Paulus*, 1962.

159 See again, P.R. Jones, *Second Moses*, p.34: "just as the Law, i.e. the tables of stone, was Moses' letter of recommendation to Israel for his role as their law-

supported by the gospel which he received from Christ and now embodies
in his suffering. For the effect of that gospel, as the *power* of God
now being manifested in the lives of the Gentiles through the Spirit of
God which has been poured out in their hearts[160], is clearly evident
for all to see. As Nils Dahl put it so well,

> The preaching of the gospel is not simply a report about the new covenant,
> as performative speech it effectively mediates the covenant promises. The
> existence of the church at Corinth not only testifies to the success of
> Paul's work, like a letter of recommendation; it even certifies the valid-
> ity of the new covenant, *as the stone tablets of the law confirmed the va-*
> *lidity of the old.* The Spirit of the living God is the inscription on the
> Corinthians' hearts[161].

If it is appropriate to refer to Moses in his ministry as the "lawgiver", it is certainly appropriate, therefore, to summarize Paul's
apostolic role in the ministry of the *gospel* as the "Spirit-giver".
For the emphasis throughout 3:1-3 lies on the Spirit of God now present in Corinth[162]. And it is precisely for this reason that Paul's
reception and execution of his ministry must take place in the "earthen
vessel" of his suffering (cf. II Cor. 4:7ff.). Not because he wishes
to combat a "theology of glory" with his own personally embodied "theology of the cross" as an I Cor. 4:6ff., but in order that the glory and
power which he himself reveals, i.e. the very Spirit of God, might in
no way be associated with his own person and/or talent (II Cor. 12:7ff.).
As we have seen, therefore, when Paul must defend his authority as an
apostle he need only point to his suffering *and* the work of the Spirit
as the concrete, verifiable evidence for his claims which are shocking
in their magnitude, since they place him on a par with the central
figure, apart of course from Christ, in the history of redemption,
namely Moses.

---

giver and prophet, so the Corinthian community of believing Gentiles is Paul's
authentication for his apostolic role".

160 For a development of the theme of the Spirit as the power of God effecting obedience to God and submission to the law over against the power of sin, see P.W.
Meyer, "The Holy Spirit in the Pauline Letters. A Contextual Explanation", *Interpretation* 33(1979)3-18, esp. pp.8f., though I do not see how he can bring this
emphasis together with his corresponding attempt to argue that "there is no suggestion that this power 'makes Christians new creatures'. Its transforming force
is promissory ..." (p.9, cf. pp.12-16). For if, as Meyer emphasizes, the Spirit
is the "presence of God's liberating power vis-à-vis the power of sin" (p.12),
what is this new life in the Spirit if not a "new creation", albeit one not yet
perfected nor exempt from suffering. For my point see the early work of R.B.
Hoyle, *The Holy Spirit in St. Paul*, 1927, pp.97,99,101,106 and the literature
cited above, p.203n.98.

161 "Promise and Fulfillment", in his *Studies in Paul, Theology for the Early Christian Mission*, 1977, pp.121-136, p.126. Unfortunately, Dahl does not develop this
crucial insight further except to place it within his overall emphasis on the
Spirit as a sign of the fulfillment of God's promises, cf. pp.126f.

162 So too K.H. Rengstorf, art. στέλλω κ.τ.λ., *TDNT, Vol. VII*, 1971, pp.594-595.

Although strictly speaking Paul probably did not conceive of himself as a "second Moses", he certainly did understand his ministry to the "Israel of God" (Gal. 6:16) to be the eschatological counterpart to the giving of the law. This is evident not only in his conception of his ministry of suffering as an embodiment of the cross of Christ (II Cor. 2:14-17), but also in his conviction that his ministry of the Spirit was a fulfillment of Ezekiel 11:19 and 36:26 (II Cor. 3:1-3). For in both cases, Paul's argument for his sufficiency to be an apostle of the new covenant is based on a comparison to Moses, the mediator of the old covenant; in the first instance to the call of Moses, in the second to his ministry of the law (cf. 2:16b; 3:3b)[163].

---

163 The emphasis of my study on the importance of the Spirit in Paul's self-under-standing thus goes against that of I. Hermann's important work, *Kyrios und Pneuma*, pp.20f.,23-25,108,110,123,140,etc. in which he places the emphasis on the risen Christ who is to be identified with the Spirit. For in doing so, Hermann loses the importance of the Spirit itself. As a result, he is able to take into account only half of Paul's argumentation, i.e. the apologetic value of Paul's suffering, but cannot do justice to Paul's ministry of the Spirit.

CONCLUSION

SUFFERING AND THE SPIRIT AS THE TWIN-PILLARS OF PAUL'S
APOSTOLIC SELF-DEFENSE

A. PAUL: THE SPIRIT-GIVER WHO SUFFERS

As we have seen, Paul's argument in II Cor. 2:14-3:3 unfolds in three
stages. Having occasion to refer to his anxiety over Titus in 2:12f.,
Paul is forced by the polemical situation in which he now finds himself to remind the Corinthians of the role his suffering, including his
anxiety over his churches (cf. II Cor. 11:28 with 2:12f.), plays within his apostolic ministry. He does so by introducing the imagery of a
triumphal procession (θριαμβεύειν), with himself as the captive slave
of God who is constantly being led to death. With this image Paul graphically portrays that it is through his daily experience of death = suffering that the glory and power of God are being revealed. In 2:15-16a
Paul then links this imagery to his understanding of the cross of Christ
as the wisdom of God, here pictured as an acceptable sacrifice. II Corinthians 2:15-16a thus supports Paul's statement in 2:14 by asserting
that *his own* suffering is now also a vehicle for this same "sacrificial
aroma" to God. Rather than calling his apostolic ministry into question,
it is precisely Paul's suffering which therefore commends him to the
Corinthians within the church, as well as defending him from the attacks
of his opponents from outside the church.

Paul's portrayal of his apostolic ministry in 2:14-16a, with its
corresponding twofold effect among mankind, then leads to the second
stage in his argument in which he raises and answers the question of
his own sufficiency for such a high calling. Though left unexpressed,
Paul's answer to this question is clear. He not only "asserts" that he
is sufficient for this life and death producing ministry, but he also
offers as evidence in support of this assertion the fact that he supported himself financially while in Corinth rather than exercising his
right as an apostle to earn his living directly from his preaching of
the gospel (2:17)[1]. Once again, therefore, it is Paul's ministry of
suffering, outlined in 2:14-16a and defined in terms of his practice of

---

1 In order to see how his argument works, see above, chapter four.

self-support in 2:17 (cf. I Cor. 4:12; II Cor. 11:27), which functions
to ground the validity of his apostleship.

Finally, in the third stage of Paul's argument, he buttresses his
apologetic based on the evidence afforded by his suffering by presenting in 3:1-3 a second piece of incontrovertible evidence, i.e. the Corinthians themselves. For as their "father in the gospel" (cf. I Cor.
4:15), the Corinthians cannot deny that they owe their very existence
as Christians to Paul. Moreover, the strength of his argument lies in
the undeniable fact that the Corinthians have received the Spirit which
now dwells in their hearts and is active in their midst through Paul's
ministry. As a result, it becomes impossible to pit Paul's suffering
against his possession of the Spirit or to argue, as his opponents apparently did, that "weakness" and the power and glory of the gospel in
the Spirit, i.e. "strength", cannot co-exist in the apostolic ministry.
Paul is weak and suffers as an embodiment of the cross of Christ, but
he is also a pneumatic through whom the power and Spirit of God are being manifested and poured out.

In the course of this three-stage argument Paul thus develops two
basic assertions concerning his apostolic ministry. On the one hand,
his suffering makes it evident that, as an apostle of the new covenant,
Paul stands between the death and resurrection of Christ, i.e. the
glory of God, and the "life" of his church (or the death of those who
reject his ministry of suffering), in the intermediary role of a revelatory agent. On the other hand, the essential content of his mediation
between God in Christ and the church is the Spirit. Thus, as the "Spirit-
giver" with the gospel, Paul's role is parallel to that of Moses', the
mediator *par excellence* between YHWH and Israel[2], whose task it was to
give the law. That Paul had this parallel in view in our passage is indicated in two ways: first, by his introduction of the sufficiency theme
in 2:16b as an allusion to the call of Moses in Ex. 4:10(LXX), and second, by the introduction of a contrast between his ministry of the
Spirit and the law in 3:3b. Paul's argument in II Cor. 2:14-3:3 thus
finds its most fundamental support in what for the Corinthians was the
empirically verifiable fact that they had received the Spirit. In turn,
as the "Spirit-giver", Paul is the intermediary agent of the eschatological reality of the new age characterized by the work of the Spirit
in the hearts of flesh prophesied by Ezekiel. It thus seems almost impossible to over exaggerate the significance which Paul attributed to
his apostolic ministry in II Cor. 2:14-3:3.

---

2 This statement hardly needs substantiation. See Lothar Perlitt, "Moses als Prophet", *EvTh* 31(1971)588-608, p.607: "In der israelitischen Religion der Distanz
 zwischen Gott und Mensch überschritt nur einer diese Grenze: Mose".

For if Paul's suffering and his ministry of the Spirit are, in fact, convincing evidence for the validity of his apostolic authority and ministry, a ministry which he attributes directly to God (cf. 2:14; 2:17b; 3:5f.), then the Corinthians' decision to reject that ministry becomes, from Paul's perspective, a rejection of God as well. It is for this reason that Paul ends his second canonical letter to the Corinthians, of which 2:14-3:6 is the "theological heart", with the severe warning to the Corinthians to test themselves in order to make sure that they are still "in the faith". For upon his arrival, Paul will be forced to use his power, revealed in his weakness, to tear down all those who have failed this test by rejecting his apostleship (cf. 13:5,10).

B. A HYPOTHESIS FOR FURTHER RESEARCH

This brings us to the end of our study. It does not, however, bring us to a final conclusion, either in regard to Paul's self-understanding as an apostle in general, or in regard to his corresponding apologetic for his apostolic ministry in II Corinthians. For in emphasizing his call by God to be a revelatory agent of the Spirit in the role of a Moses-like intermediary between God and his people in 2:14-3:3, Paul naturally raises the question of the relationship between his ministry of the Spirit and suffering and Moses' ministry of the law[3]. It is to this question that Paul thus turns his attention in 3:4-18, under the general rubric of the γράμμα/πνεῦμα contrast introduced in 3:6. For in picking up his prior reference to the call of Moses in 2:17 in 3:4f. and to his ministry of the Spirit in 3:3 in 3:6, Paul develops these basic assertions in terms of his call to be a διάκονος καινῆς διαθήκης, which he then further defines as a ministry which consists not of the "letter", but of the "Spirit". Finally, he then offers the reason for the spiritual nature of this ministry of the "new covenant": τὸ γὰρ γράμμα ἀποκτέννει, τὸ δὲ πνεῦμα ζῳοποιεῖ. Paul's following discussion in 3:7-18 is devoted to explaining the meaning of this saying, which, in and of itself, remains so cryptic. The task which still lies ahead, therefore, is to complete Paul's argument concerning the nature of his apostolic ministry established in 2:14-3:3 by examining how Paul understood this ministry in relationship to the ministry of Moses as presented in 3:4-18. But given the results of our study thus far, it is al-

---

3 On this fundamental point, cf. W.D. Davies, "Paul and the People of Israel", *NTS* 24(1978)4-39, p.11: "It is important to recognize that in II Cor. 3 Paul is concerned essentially with the contrast between two ministries, not with that between two covenants on which two distinct religions were founded".

ready possible to present a number of working-hypotheses concerning the
basic meaning of the letter/Spirit contrast and its relationship to
Paul's self-understanding as an apostle, which for the sake of conven-
ience can be presented in the following six theses:

*1. Jeremiah 31:31-34 is the context within which the letter/Spirit
contrast is to be understood.*

The introduction of the "new covenant" terminology in II Cor. 3:6 to
define Paul's διακονία not only repeats the emphasis from Ezekiel 11:19
and 36:26 in 3:3, but also provides the necessary transition to what
follows by calling to mind the unique emphasis from Jer. 31:31-34 on
the law written on the heart as the foundation for the universal knowledge of YHWH among his people. Against the background of Ez. 11:19 and
36:26, Jeremiah 31:31ff. thus provides the starting point and frame of
reference for understanding Paul's letter/Spirit contrast in 3:6ff. For
as a servant of the "new covenant" pictured in Jeremiah's prophecy,
Paul understands himself as having been commissioned to be an "apostle
of the Spirit".

*2. Paul's statement that the "letter kills" is not a negative state-
ment concerning the law per se.*

Taking Jer. 31:31ff. as our starting point, it thus becomes clear
that Paul's statement that the letter kills is, in this context, his
attempt to describe the law as it functioned in the "old covenant"
whenever it encountered Israel's "heart of stone" referred to by
Ezekiel, or the unfaithfulness pictured by Jeremiah. As such, II Cor.
3:6b is not a negative statement concerning the structure or nature of
the law itself, but a restatement of the problem inherent in the old
covenant from its beginning (cf. Jer. 31:32), i.e. that the hard hearts
of the people remained unchanged by the revelation of the law. This
point, stated programmatically in 3:6, is then underscored in two ways
in 3:7-18. On the one hand, the *a minori ad maius* argument for the glory
of the διακονία τοῦ πνεύματος in 3:7-11 presupposes and is based upon
the unquestionable glory of the διακονία τοῦ θανάτου = law. For in all
such arguments, the force of the comparison stands or falls on the truth
of the premise, taken to be common ground between the parties in the
discussion. In our case, this common-ground assumption is expressed in
3:7a. There is no hint in our text, therefore, that Paul wishes to denigrate the law in any way, despite the fact that its function in Israel's
history was to effect death and condemnation (cf. 3:7,9). On the other
hand, in 3:12-15 Paul explicitly develops the point made in both Ezekiel
and Jeremiah concerning the problem with the old covenant by turning to
the actual account of the establishment of that covenant in Exodus, especially as it reaches its climax in the golden calf incident and second

giving of the law in Exodus 32-34. For in this way he is able to adduce the biblical account itself as support for his assertion in 3:14 that ἐπωρώθη τὰ νοήματα αὐτῶν and his corresponding understanding of the killing-function of the law as a διακονία τοῦ θανάτου. At this point it will also be argued, against the prevailing consensus, that Paul's understanding of the veil of Moses in relationship to both the hardened minds of the sons of Israel (cf. 3:13f.) and the glory of the covenant itself, described as καταργουμένη in 3:7,11,13, corresponds to what the Exodus narrative as it now stands originally intended to teach. Hence, Paul's point throughout 3:6-18 is to follow Ezekiel, Jeremiah and Exodus 32-34 (cf. Ex. 32:9f.; 33:3-5) in assigning the problem with the old covenant not to the law as such, but to the fact that the hearts of the people remained hardened to God's will. As a result, the glory of God could not dwell in their midst without utterly destroying them (cf. Is. 63:10).

3. *The "Spirit" which "makes alive" represents and refers to the activity of God in changing the heart by means of his Spirit in order that God might dwell in the midst of his people in such a way that his glory is once again manifest for all to see.*

This conclusion derives from Paul's argument concerning the nature of his παρρησία, in contrast to the necessity Moses felt to veil himself. Paul's "boldness" is based on the present work of the Lord = Spirit inasmuch as the work of the Spirit in removing the veil over the heart is to make it possible for his people to see God's glory. Although not explicitly stated in our context, this understanding of the work of the Spirit in the new covenant also implies that Paul conceived of the work of the Spirit as enabling those whose hearts are changed to keep the law which was broken under the old covenant. For only those who keep God's commandments may enjoy God's presence. This point must be established, of course, in comparison with Paul's teaching concerning the law elsewhere, especially in conjunction with his view of the role of the Spirit in Romans 7-8 and his understanding of the "new creation" in Christ reflected in I Cor. 7:19; 8:6; 10:23f.; II Cor. 5:17; Gal. 5 and 6:15 and Rom. 14:6-14.

4. *But the "Spirit" which "makes alive" also represents the activity of God in changing the heart by means of his Spirit in order that the law itself might now be properly understood; and by implication, the Old Testament as a whole.*

According to 3:14, the veil which still exists over the heart (cf. 3:15) also exists ἐπὶ τῇ ἀναγνώσει τῆς παλαιᾶς διαθήκης. Thus, the work of the Spirit also carries a corresponding hermeneutical implication

based on the important OT unity between the moral and the theoretical/
practical spheres of life, epitomized in the maxim that "the fear of
the Lord is the beginning of wisdom" (cf. Prov. 1:7; 9:10; 15:33; Job
28:28 and Ps. 111:10). This means, in turn, that the barrier to a proper understanding of the law removed "in Christ" is not intellectual,
but moral. The importance of this point for Paul's immediate argument
is found in the fact that according to 3:7-11, a proper understanding
of the glory inherent in the law is an essential prerequisite for an
understanding of the exceedingly glorious nature of the gospel. Again,
therefore, the relationship between the law and the gospel is not one
of discontinuity, but of a continuous progression from glory to glory.
To remove the barrier to a proper understanding of the law is to remove the barrier to the "glory of God in the face of Christ" (II Cor.
4:6), which, again, is the work of the Spirit as presented in I Cor.
1:18-2:16. It remains to be investigated precisely how this proper understanding of the law is achieved, i.e. how this veil is removed which
lies over the reading of the "old covenant". But given the fact that
the barrier to be removed is a moral one and the example of Paul's own
reading of the OT in II Cor. 3:7-18 itself, the distinctively Christian
OT hermeneutic cannot be said to consist in a new esoteric way of reading the OT, much less in a set of predetermined exegetical presuppositions which are only available to those already within the new covenant
relationship to God.

5. *The result of this renewed access to the glory of God is the actual transformation of those who are able to perceive it (II Cor.
   3:18).*

At this point in Paul's argument the theme encountered in 3:2f. is
once again picked up as evidence for the validity of Paul's ministry.
This explains why Paul's emphasis on the glory of the ministry of the
Spirit in 3:7-11 and 3:18 both lead to expressions of confidence in 3:12
and 4:1 respectively. For the fact that the glory of. God is present in
Paul's ministry is evident for all to see in the transformation of those
encountered by it.

6. *Finally, as Paul's own statement in 4:1 illustrates, we have never
   left the apologetic level of argumentation in 3:4-18, despite its
   seemingly abstract, "theological" character, nor have we departed
   from a presentation of Paul's self-understanding as an apostle or
   "διάκονος" of the "new covenant".*

The parallel between II Cor. 4:2 and 2:17, as well as the criticism
of Paul's gospel in 4:3, demonstrate that the issue still at stake
throughout 3:4-18 is whether or not Paul's ministry of suffering can
be brought together with his ministry of the Spirit. Moreover, Paul's

proof that they can be, and indeed are, is also still the same, namely, the Christian existence of the Corinthians themselves as a result of their own perception of the glory of God in Paul's ministry. This means, therefore, that Paul's interpretation of the law also finds its support in the effects it is producing among the Corinthians and that the Christian hermeneutic as such is to be tested against the criterion of its results. Paul's view of the law is built upon his ministry of the Spirit, both of which are part of his apostolic ministry of suffering as the embodiment of the cross of Christ.

These theses remain to be demonstrated. But if they prove to be correct, then we must begin not only to revise our understanding of the nature of Paul's ministry and source of apostolic authority, as suggested by the study now at hand, but also to rethink the law/gospel contrast in a fundamental way only now beginning to take place in Pauline studies.

ABBREVIATIONS

Abbreviations follow the customary practice as shown, e.g. in the *Journal of Biblical Literature* 95(1976)339-344, or when modified are easily recognizable. For the sake of uniformity, all biblical quotations have been given according to the American pattern (i.e. 10:10), though when referred to in secondary literature the name of the biblical book has been retained in the language of the quotation.

The first time a work is referred to in each chapter, its complete title, etc. has been given. Thereafter an abbreviated form has been used.

Finally, unless otherwise noted, articles from the *Theologisches Wörterbuch zum Neuen Testament*, ed. G. Kittel and G. Friedrich, have been cited according to the English translation, *Theological Dictionary of the New Testament*, trans. G.W. Bromiley (Grand Rapids: Eerdmans), abbreviated as *TDNT*. The commentaries have almost always been given in a shortened form.

BIBLIOGRAPHY OF WORKS CITED

Only those works explicitly cited appear in the bibliography.

COMMENTARIES ON II CORINTHIANS

BARRETT, C.K.: *A Commentary on the Second Epistle to the Corinthians*. Harper's New Testament Commentaries. New York: Harper and Row, 1973.

BERNARD, J.H.: *The Second Epistle to the Corinthians*. The Expositor's Greek Testament, Vol. 3. Grand Rapids: Eerdmans, 1979(1903).

BULTMANN, Rudolf: *Der zweite Brief an die Korinther*. Kritisch-exegetischer Kommentar über das Neue Testament, Sonderband. Göttingen: Vandenhoeck & Ruprecht, 1976.

CALVIN, J.: *The Second Epistle of Paul the Apostle to the Corinthians and the Epistles to Timothy, Titus and Philemon*. Calvin's Commentaries, Vol. 10. Trans. T.A. Smail. Grand Rapids: Eerdmans, 1964.

HEINRICI, C.F. Georg. *Das zweite Sendschreiben des Apostel Paulus an die Korinther*. Berlin: Wilhelm Hertz, 1887.

HÉRING, Jean: *The Second Epistle of Saint Paul to the Corinthians*. London: The Epworth Press, 1967.

HODGE, Charles: *An Exposition of the Second Epistle to the Corinthians*. Thornapple Commentaries. Grand Rapids: Baker Book House, 1980(1859).

HUGHES, Philip E.: *Paul's Second Epistle to the Corinthians*. The New International Commentary on the New Testament. Grand Rapids: Eerdmans, 1962.

LIETZMANN, Hans: *An die Korinther I - II*. Handbuch zum Neuen Testament, Bd. 9. Ergänzt von W.G. Kümmel. Tübingen: J.C.B. Mohr (Paul Siebeck), 1969[5].

MEYER, H.A.W.: *Critical and Exegetical Hand-book to the Epistles to the Corinthians*, Translated from the fifth German ed., 1869. Winona Lake: Alpha Publications, 1979(1883).

MOULE, H.C.G.: *The Second Epistle to the Corinthians*. London: Pickering and Inglis LTD, 1976(1962).

PLUMMER, Alfred: *A Critical and Exegetical Commentary on the Second Epistle of St. Paul to the Corinthians*. The International Critical Commentary. Edinburgh: T. & T. Clark, 1978(1925).

PRÜMM, K.: *Diakonia Pneumatos. Der zweite Korintherbrief als Zugang zur Apostolischen Botschaft. Bd. I: Theologische Auslegung des zweiten Korintherbriefes.* Rome/Freiburg/Wien: Herder, 1967.

— : *Diakonia Pneumatos. Bd. II/Teil 1: Theologie des zweiten Korintherbriefes, Apostolat und christliche Wirklichkeit.* Rome/Freiburg/Wien: Herder, 1960.

— : *Diakonia Pneumatos. Bd. II/Teil 2: Die apostolische Macht.* Rome/Freiburg/Wien: Herder, 1962.

SCHELKLE, Karl Hermann: *Der zweite Brief an die Korinther.* Geistliche Schriftlesung, Bd. 18. Düsseldorf: Patmos-Verlag, 1964.

SCHLATTER, Adolf: *Paulus Der Bote Jesus. Eine Deutung seiner Briefe an die Korinther.* Stuttgart: Calwer Verlag, 1969[4].

STRACHAN, R.H.: *The Second Epistle of Paul to the Corinthians.* The Moffatt New Testament Commentary, Vol. 8. London: Hodder and Stoughton, 1948[5].

TASKER, R.V.G.: *The Second Epistle of Paul to the Corinthians. An Introduction and Commentary.* The Tyndale New Testament Commentaries. London: The Tyndale Press, 1969(1958).

WENDLAND, Heinz-Dietrich: *Die Briefe an die Korinther.* Das Neue Testament Deutsch, Bd. 7. Göttingen: Vandenhoeck & Ruprecht, 1972[13].

WINDISCH, Hans: *Der zweite Korintherbrief.* Kritisch-exegetischer Kommentar über das Neue Testament, Bd. 6. Göttingen: Vandenhoeck & Ruprecht, 1970[9].

TEXTS AND TRANSLATIONS

Only those texts and/or translations are given which have been quoted. Primary sources which have been referred to, but not quoted have been omitted. In the bibliography below, LCL refers to The Loeb Classical Library (Cambridge: Harvard University Press).

Ägyptische Urkunden aus den königlichen Museen zu Berlin. Teil I, Bd. 4: Griechische Urkunden. Berlin: Staatliche Museen, 1912.

BROOKS, E.W.: *Joseph and Asenath. The Confession and Prayer of Asenath, daughter of Pentephres the priest.* Translations of Early Documents 2/7. London: Society for Promoting Christian Knowledge and New York: MacMillan and Co., 1918.

BURY, R.G.: *Plato.* LCL, Vol. IX, 1952(1926).

CARY, Earnest: *The Roman Antiquities of Dionysius of Halicarnassus.* LCL, Vols. I-VII, 1947-1956.

CHARLES, R.H.: *The Apocrypha and Pseudepigrapha of the Old Testament in English. Volume I: Apocrypha.* Oxford: At the Clarendon Press, 1978(1913).

— : *The Apocrypha and Pseudepigrapha of the Old Testament in English. Volume II: Pseudepigrapha.* Oxford: At the Clarendon Press, 1977(1913).

— : *The Greek Versions of the Testaments of the Twelve Patriarchs.* Darmstadt: Wissenschaftliche Buchgesellschaft, 1960[2].

CHARLESWORTH, James H.: *The Old Testament Pseudepigrapha. Volume 1: Apocalyptic Literature and Testaments.* Garden City: Doubleday & Company, Inc., 1983.

COLSON, F.H. and WHITAKER, G.H.: *Philo.* LCL, Vols. I-X, 1958-1962.

CONYBEARE, F.C.: *Philostratus. The Life of Apollonius of Tyana.* LCL, Vol. I, 1948 (1912).

DEJONGE, M.: *Testamenta XII Patriarcharum, edited according to Cambridge University Library MS Ff. I.24 fol.203a-262b with short notes.* Pseudepigrapha Veteris Testamenti Graece, Vol. 1. Leiden: E.J. Brill, 1964.

DODDS, E.R.: *Plato: Gorgias. A Revised Text with Introduction and Commentary*. Oxford: At the Clarendon Press, 1959.

ETHERIDGE, J.W.: *The Targums of Onkelos and Jonathan ben Uzziel on the Pentateuch with the Fragments of the Jerusalem Targum from the Chaldee*. New Ypork: KTAV Publishing House, Inc., 1968(1862).

FOWLER, Harold North: *Plato*. LCL, Vol. II, 1952(1921).

FRIEDLANDER, Gerald: *Pirke de Rabbi Eliezer (The Chapters of Rabbi Eliezer the Great). According to the Text of the Manuskript belonging to Abraham Epstein of Vienna*. London/New York: Bloch, 1916.

HARMON, A.M.: *Lucian*, LCL, Vol. IV, 1953.

KILBURN, K.: *Lucian*. LCL, Vol. VI, 1959.

LAKE, Kirsopp: *The Apostolic Fathers*. LCL, Vol. I, 1977(1912).

LAMB, W.R.M.: *Plato*. LCL, Vol. IV, 1952(1924).

LEHRMAN, S.M.: *Exodus, Midrash Rabbah, Vol. III*. London and Bournemouth: Soncino Press, 1951.

MACHO, Alejandro Diez: *Neophyti 1. Targum Palestinense Ms de la Biblioteca Vaticana. Vol. II: Exodo*. Madrid/Barcelona: Consejo Superior de Investigaciones Cientificas, 1970.

MARCUS, Ralph and Allen WIKGREN: *Josephus. Jewish Antiquities*. LCL, Vol. VIII, 1963.

NORLIN, George: *Isocrates*. LCL, Vols. I and II, 1954(1928) and 1956(1929).

Novum Testamentum Graece. Ed. E. NESTLE and K. ALAND et al. Stuttgart: Deutsche Bibelstiftung, 1975[25] and 1979[26].

PATON, W.R.: *Polybius. The Histories*. LCL, Vols. I-VI, 1979(1922)-1980(1927).

PERRIN, Bernadotte: *Plutarch's Lives*. LCL, Vols. I-XI, 1961-1971.

RAHLFS, Alfred: *Septuaginta, Vols. 1 and 2*. Stuttgart: Deutsche Bibelstiftung, 1935.

ROBSON, E. Iliff: *Arrian*. LCL, Vol. II, 1958(1933).

The Septuagint Version of the Old Testament. Zondervan Edition. Grand Rapids: Zondervan, 1970.

SIMON, Maurice: *Esther and the Song of Songs, Midrash Rabbah, Vol. IX*. London and Bournemouth: Soncino Press, 1951.

THACKERAY, H.St.J.: *Josephus. The Jewish War*. LCL, Vols. II and III, 1961(1928).

VERRALL, A.W.: *The 'Seven Against Thebes' of Aeschylus, with an Introduction, Commentary and Translation*. London/New York: MacMillan and Co., 1887.

WHITE, Horace: *Appian's Roman History*. LCL, Vols. I-IV, 1958(1912)-1955(1913).

SECONDARY LITERATURE

ANDERSON, Graham: "Lucian: a Sophist's Sophist". In *Yale Classical Studies, Vol. 27: Later Greek Literature*. Ed. John J. Winkler and Gordon Williams. Cambridge: Cambridge University Press, 1982, pp.61-92.

AST, Fridrich: *Lexicon Platonicum Sive Vocum Platonicarum Index, Vols. 1-3*. Darmstadt: Wissenschaftliche Buchgesellschaft, 1956(1835-1838).

BAILEY, Kenneth: "The Structure of 1 Corinthians and Paul's Theological Method with Special Reference to 4:17", *NovT* 25(1983)152-181.

BAIRD, William: "Letters of Recommendation. A Study of II Cor. 3:1-3", *JBL* 80(1961)166-172.

BARRETT, C.K.: "Titus". In *Neotestamentica et Semitica, Studies in Honour of Matthew Black*. Ed. E.E. Ellis and Max Wilcox. Edinburgh: T. & T. Clark, 1969, pp.1-14.

— : "Cephas and Corinth". In *Abraham unser Vater. Juden und Christen im Gespräch über die Bibel. Festschrift für Otto Michel zum 60. Geburtstag.* Ed. Otto Betz, M. Hengel and P. Schmidt. Leiden: E.J. Brill, 1963, pp. 1-12.

— : "Paul's Opponents in II Corinthians", *NTS* 17(1970/1971)233-254.

— : "Christianity at Corinth", *BJRL* 46(1964)269-297.

— : "ΨΕΥΔΑΠΟΣΤΟΛΟΙ (2 Cor 11:13)". In *Mélanges Bibliques en hommage au R.P. Béda Rigaux*. Ed. A. Descamps and A. de Halleux. Gembloux: J. Duculot, 1970, pp.377-396.

— : *A Commentary on the First Epistle to the Corinthians.* Harper's New Testament Commentaries. New York: Harper and Row, 1968.

BARTH, Gerhard: "Die Eignung des Verkündigers in 2 Kor 2:14-3:6". In *Kirche, Festschrift für Günther Bornkamm zum 75. Geburtstag.* Ed. Dieter Lührmann and Georg Strecker. Tübingen: J.C.B. Mohr (Paul Siebeck), 1980, pp.257-270.

BARTLING, Victor: "God's Triumphant Captive, Christ's Aroma for God (2 Cor 2:12-17)", *Concordia Theological Monthly* 22(1951)883-894.

BATES, W.H.: "The Integrity of II Corinthians", *NTS* 12(1965/1966)56-69.

BATEY, Richard: "Paul's Interaction with the Corinthians", *JBL* 84(1965)139-146.

BAUER, Walter: *A Greek-English Lexicon of the New Testament and Other Early Christian Literature.* Trans. and adapted by William F. Arndt and F. Wilbur Gingrich. Chicago: The University of Chicago Press, 1957.

BAUER, Walter: *A Greek-English Lexicon of the New Testament and Other Early Christian Literature.* Revised and augmented by F.W. Gingrich and F.W. Danker. Chicago: The University of Chicago Press, 1979².

BAUMANN, G.: art ליב, *Theologisches Wörterbuch zum Alten Testament, Bd. IV, Lieferung 3/4.* Ed. G.J. Botterweck and H. Ringgren. Stuttgart: Kohlhammer, 1982, pp.495-499.

BAUMERT, Norbert: *Täglich Sterben und Auferstehen. Der Literalsinn von 2 Kor 4:12-5:10.* Studien zum Alten und Neuen Testament, Bd. 34. München: Kösel Verlag, 1973.

BEKER, J. Christiaan: *Paul the Apostle. The Triumph of God in Life and Thought.* Philadelphia: Fortress Press, 1980.

BERGER, Klaus: "Die impliziten Gegner. Zur Methode des Erschließens von "Gegnern' in neutestamentlichen Texten". In *Kirche, Festschrift für Günther Bornkamm zum 75. Geburtstag.* Ed. Dieter Lührmann and Georg Strecker. Tübingen: J.C.B. Mohr (Paul Siebeck), 1980, pp.373-400.

BETZ, Otto: "Die Vision des Paulus im Tempel von Jerusalem. Apg. 22:17-21 als Beitrag zur Deutung des Damaskuserlebnisses". In *Verborum Veritas. Festschrift für Gustav Stählin zum 70. Geburtstag.* Ed. Otto Böcher and Klaus Haacker. Wuppertal: Theologischer Verlag Rolf Brockhaus, 1970, pp.113-123.

— : "Fleischliche und 'geistliche' Christuserkenntnis nach 2. Korinther 5:16", *ThB* 14(1983)167-179.

BIEDER, W.: "Paulus und seine Gegner in Korinth", *ThZ* 17(1961)319-333.

BLASS, F. and A. DEBRUNNER: *A Greek Grammar of the New Testament and Other Early Christian Literature.* Trans. and rev. Robert Funk. Chicago: The University of Chicago Press, 1961.

BORNKAMM, Günther: *Paul.* New York: Harper and Row, 1971.

BOWIE, E.L.: "The Importance of Sophists". In *Yale Classical Studies, Vol. 27: Later Greek Literature.* Ed. John J. Winkler and Gordon Williams. Cambridge: Cambridge University Press, 1982, pp.29-59.

BROWN, Francis, S.R. DRIVER and Charles A. BRIGGS: *A Hebrew and English Lexicon of the Old Testament.* Oxford: At the Clarendon Press, 1976(1972).

BRUCE, F.F.: *1 and 2 Thessalonians.* Word Biblical Commentary, Vol. 45. Waco, TX: Word, 1982.

— : *Paul and Jesus.* London: SPCK, 1977.

BRUN, Lyder: "Zur Auslegung von II Kor 5:1-10", *ZNW* 28(1929)207-229.

BÜCHSEL, F.: art. εἰλικρινής κ.τ.λ., *TDNT Vol. II*, 1964, pp.397-398.

BULTMANN, R.: art. ἀναγινώσκω κ.τ.λ., *TDNT, Vol. I*, 1964, pp.343-344.

— : *Exegetische Probleme des zweiten Korintherbriefes zu 2. Kor. 5:1-5; 5:11-6:10; 10-13; 12:21*. Symbolae Biblical Upsalienses Vol. 9. Uppsala: Wretmans Boktryckerei A.-B., 1947.

— : *Theologie des Neuen Testaments*. Ed. Otto Merk. UTB 630. Tübingen: J.C.B. Mohr (Paul Siebeck), 1980[8].

CAMPENHAUSEN, H. Frhr. von: *Kirchliches Amt und geistliche Vollmacht in den ersten drei Jahrhunderten*. Beiträge zur historischen Theologie, Bd. 14. Tübingen: J.C.B. Mohr (Paul Siebeck), 1963[2].

CANTOR, Norman F.: *Medieval History, The Life and Death of a Civilization*. New York: MacMillan Publishing Co., 1969[2].

CONZELMANN, Hans: *Der erste Brief an die Korinther*. Kritisch-exegetischer Kommentar über das Neue Testament, Bd. 5. Göttingen: Vandenhoeck & Ruprecht, 1981[12].

— : art. χάρις κ.τ.λ., *TDNT, Vol. IX*, 1974, pp.372-415.

CRANFIELD, C.E.B.: "Changes of Person and Number in Paul's Epistles". In *Paul and Paulinism. Essays in honour of C.K. Barrett*. Ed. M.D. Hooker and S.G. Wilson. London: SPCK, 1982, pp.280-289.

CULLMANN, Oscar: *Christ and Time. The Primitive Christian Conception of Time and History*. Philadelphia: Westminster Press, 1975 (rev. ed.).

DAHL, Nils Alstrup: "Promise and Fulfillment". In his *Studies in Paul. Theology for the Early Christian Mission*. Minneapolis: Augsburg Publishing House, 1977, pp.121-136.

— : "Paul and the Church at Corinth According to 1 Corinthians 1:10-4:21". In *Christian History and Interpretation: Studies Presented to John Knox*. Ed. W.R. Farmer, C.F.D. Moule and R.R. Niebuhr. Cambridge: At the University Press, 1967, pp.313-335.

DAHN, K. and H.-G. LINK: art. θριαμβεύω. *The New International Dictionary of New Testament Theology, Vol. I*. Ed. Colin Brown (ET with additions and revisions of *Theologisches Begriffslexicon zum Neuen Testament)*. Grand Rapids: Zondervan, 1975, pp. 649-650.

DAUTZENBERG, G.: "Der Verzicht auf das apostolische Unterhaltsrecht. Eine exegetische Untersuchung zu 1 Kor 9", *Biblica* 50(1969)212-232.

DAVIES, W.D.: "Paul and the People of Israel", *NTS* 24(1978)4-39.

— : *Paul and Rabbinic Judaism. Some Rabbinic Elements in Pauline Theology*. Philadelphia: Fortress Press, 1980[4].

DELLING, Gerhard: art. ὀσμή, *TDNT, Vol. V*, 1967, pp.493-495.

— : art. πλῆθος, *TDNT, Vol. VI*, 1968, pp.274-283.

DEMANN, Paul: "Moses und das Gesetz bei Paulus". In *Moses in Schrift und Überlieferung*. Düsseldorf: Patmos-Verlag, 1963, pp.205-264.

DICK, Karl: *Der Schriftstellerische Plural bei Paulus*. Halle a.S.: Niemeyer, 1900.

DILL, Samuel: *Roman Society from Nero to Marcus Aurelius*. New York: Meridian Books, 1964(1956).

DINKLER, Erich: art. Korintherbriefe. In *Die Religion in Geschichte und Gegenwart: Handwörterbuch für Theologie und Religionswissenschaft, Bd. 4*. Ed. Kurt Galling et al. Tübingen: J.C.B. Mohr (Paul Siebeck), 1960[3], pp.17-23.

DODD, C.H.: "New Testament Translation Problems II", *The Bible Translator* 28(1977) 110-112.

DUDLEY, Donald R.: *The Civilization of Rome*. New York: The New American Library, 1962[2].

DUNGAN, David L.: *The Sayings of Jesus in the Churches of Paul. The Use of the Synoptic Tradition in the Regulation of Early Church Life.* Philadelphia: Fortress Press,
1971.

DUNN, J.D.G.: *Baptism in the Holy Spirit. A Re-examination of the New Testament Teaching on the Gift of the Spirit in relation to Pentecostalism Today.* Philadelphia:
Westminster Press, 1970.

— : *Jesus and the Spirit: A Study of the Religious and Charismatic Experience of
Jesus and the First Christians as reflected in the New Testament.* London: SCM
Press, 1975.

— : *Unity and Diversity in the New Testament. An Inquiry into the Character of
Earliest Christianity.* London: SCM Press, 1977.

— : "The Responsible Congregation (1 Cor. 14:26-40)". In *Charisma und Agape (1 Ko 12-
14).* Rome: St. Paul's Abbey, 1983, pp.201-236.

ECKSTEIN, Hans-Joachim: *Der Begriff Syneidesis bei Paulus. Eine neutestamentlich-
exegetische Untersuchung zum 'Gewissensbegriff'.* Wissenschaftliche Untersuchungen
zum Neuen Testament 2. Reihe, Bd. 10. Tübingen: J.C.B. Mohr (Paul Siebeck), 1983.

EGAN, Rory B.: "Lexical Evidence on Two Pauline Passages", *NovT* 19(1977)34-62.

EICHHOLZ, Georg: *Die Theologie des Paulus im Umriss.* Neukirchen-Vluyn: Neukirchener
Verlag, 1977^2.

ELLIS, E.E.: "II Corinthians 5:1-10 in Pauline Eschatology", *NTS* 6(1959/1960) 211-224.

— : "Christ Crucified". In *Reconciliation and Hope. New Testament Essays on Atonement
and Eschatology presented to L.L. Morris on his 60th Birthday.* Ed. Robert Banks.
Grand Rapids: Eerdmans, 1974, pp.69-75.

— : "Paul and His Opponents. Trends in Research". In his *Prophecy and Hermeneutic in
Early Christianity, New Testament Essays.* Wissenschaftliche Untersuchungen zum
Neuen Testament, Bd. 18. Tübingen: J.C.B. Mohr (Paul Siebeck), 1978, pp.80-115.

FARRER, Austin M.: "The Ministry in the New Testament", in *The Apostolic Ministry,
Essays on the History and the Doctrine of Episcopacy.* Ed. K.E. Kirk. London: Hodder
and Stoughton, 1946, pp.115-182.

FINDLAY, George G.: "St. Paul's Use of ΘPIAMBEYΩ", *The Expositor* 10(1879) 403-421.

FINKELSTEIN, Moses I.: ""Ἔμπορος, Ναύκληρος and Κάπηλος: A Prolegomena to the Study
of Athenian Trade", *Classical Philology* 30(1935)320-336.

FINLEY, M.I.: *The Ancient Economy.* London: Chatto & Windus, 1973.

— : "Aristotle and Economic Analysis". In *Studies in Ancient Society: Past and
Present Series.* Ed. M.I. Finley. London/Boston: Routledge and Kegan Paul, 1974,
pp.26-52.

— : *Die Griechen, Eine Einführung in ihre Geschichte und Zivilization.* München:
Beck, 1976.

FRIEDRICH, Gerhard: "Die Gegner des Paulus im 2. Korintherbrief". In *Abraham unser
Vater. Juden und Christen im Gespräch über die Bibel. Festschrift für Otto Michel
zum 60. Geburtstag.* Ed. Otto Betz, M. Hengel and P. Schmidt. Leiden: E.J. Brill,
1963, pp.181-215.

FRIESEN, Isaac I.: *The Glory of the Ministry of Jesus Christ, Illustrated by a Study
of 2 Cor. 2:14-3:18.* Basel Theologische Dissertationen VII. Basel: Friedrich
Reinhard Kommissionsverlag, 1971.

FURNISH, Victor Paul: *Theology and Ethics in Paul.* Nashville: Abingdon Press, 1968.

GAUSS, Hermann: *Philosophischer Handkommentar zu den Dialogen Platos, 3. Teil, Erste
Hälfte.* Bern: Lang, 1960.

GEORGI, Dieter: *Die Gegner des Paulus im 2. Korintherbrief. Studien zur Religiösen
Propaganda in der Spätantike.* Wissenschaftliche Monographien zum Alten und Neuen
Testament 11. Neukirchen-Vluyn: Neukirchener Verlag, 1964.

— : art. Corinthians, Second Letter to the. *The Interpreter's Dictionary of the Bible,*
Supplementary Volume. Ed. Keith Crim. Nashville: Abingdon, 1976, pp.183-186.

— : *Die Geschichte der Kollekte des Paulus für Jerusalem.* Theologische Forschung 38.
Hamburg-Bergstedt: Reich, 1965.

GINZBERG, L.: *The Legends of the Jews, Vols. II, III, V and VI.* Philadelphia: The
Jewish Publication Society of America, 1954(1910), 1954(1911), 1946(1928) and
1955(1925).

GOPPELT, Leonhard: *Theologie des Neuen Testaments, Bd. 2.* UTB 850. Ed. Jürgen Roloff.
Göttingen: Vandenhoeck & Ruprecht, 1978³.

GRUNDMANN, W.: art. ἀναγκάζω κ.τ.λ., *TDNT, Vol. I,* 1964, pp.344-347.

GUNTHER, J.J.: *St. Paul's Opponents and Their Background. A Study of Apocalyptic and*
Jewish Sectarian Teachings. Supplements to Novum Testamentum, Vol. XXX. Leiden:
E.J. Brill, 1973.

GÜTTGEMANNS, Erhardt: Review of D. Georgi, *Die Gegner des Paulus im 2.Korintherbrief,*
Zeitschrift für Kirchengeschichte 77(1966)126-131.

— : *Der leidende Apostel und sein Herr. Studien zur paulinischen Christologie.* Forschungen zur Religion und Literatur des Alten und Neuen Testaments 90. Göttingen:
Vandenhoeck & Ruprecht, 1966.

HAHN, Ferdinand: "Die alttestamentlichen Motive in der urchristlichen Abendmahlsüberlieferung", *EvTh* 27(1967)337-374.

— : "Bibelarbeit über 2. Korinther 3:4-18". In *Erneuerung aus der Bibel.* Die Bibel
in der Welt, Bd. 19. Ed. Siegfried Meurer. Stuttgart: Deutsche Bibelstiftung,
1982, pp.82-92.

HANSON, A.: "1 Corinthians 4:13b and Lamentations 3:45", *ExpTimes* 93(1982)214-215.

HARRISVILLE, Roy A.: *The Concept of Newness in the New Testament.* Minneapolis:
Augsburg Publishing House, 1960.

HARTMANN, Lars: "Bundesideologie in und hinter einigen paulinischen Texten". In *Die*
Paulinische Literatur und Theologie. Teologiske Studier 7. Ed. Sigfred Pedersen.
Arhus: Forlaget Aros and Göttingen: Vandenhoeck & Ruprecht, 1980, pp.103-118.

HAUCK, F. art. εἰκών κ.τ.λ., *TDNT, Vol. II,* 1964, pp.469-470.

HEILIGENTHAL, Roman: *Werke als Zeichen. Untersuchungen zur Bedeutung der menschlichen*
Taten im Frühjudentum, Neuen Testament und Frühchristentum. Wissenschaftliche
Untersuchungen zum Neuen Testament 2. Reihe, Bd. 9. Tübingen: J.C.B. Mohr (Paul
Siebeck), 1983.

HENGEL, Martin: "Leiden in der Nachfolge Jesus". In *Der leidende Mensch, Beiträge zum*
unbewältigten Thema. Ed. Hans Schulze. Neukirchen-Vluyn: Neukirchener Verlag,
1974, pp.85-94.

HERMANN, Ingo: *Kyrios und Pneuma. Studien zur Christologie der paulinischen Haupt-*
briefe. Studien zum Alten und Neuen Testament, Bd. 2. München: Kösel, 1961.

HESCHEL, Abraham J.: *The Prophets.* New York and Evanston: Harper and Row, 1962.

HICKLING, C.J.A.: "The Sequence of Thought in II Corinthians, Chapter Three", *NTS*
21(1975)380-395.

— : "Centre and Periphery in the Thought of Paul". In *Studia Biblica 1978: III.*
Papers on Paul and Other New Testament Authors. Ed. E.A. Livingstone. JSNT Supplement Series 3. Sheffield: Dept. of Biblical Studies, University of Sheffield,
1980, pp.199-214.

HOCK, Ronald F.: "Paul's Tentmaking and the Problem of His Social Class", *JBL* 97
(1978)555-564.

— : *The Social Context of Paul's Ministry, Tentmaking and Apostleship.* Philadelphia:
Fortress Press, 1980.

HODGSON, Robert: "Paul the Apostle and First Century Tribulation Lists", *ZNW* 74
(1983)59-80.

HOFIUS, Otfried: "'Gott hat unter uns aufgerichtet das Wort von der Versöhnung' (2 Kor 5:19)", *ZNW* 71(1980)3-20.

HOLMBERG, Bengt: *Paul and Power. The Structure of Authority in the Primitive Church as Reflected in the Pauline Epistles*. Coniectanea Biblica, NT Series 11. Lund: CWK Gleerup, 1978.

HOLTZ, Traugott: "Zum Selbstverständnis des Apostels Paulus", *ThLZ* 91(1966)322-330.

HOOKER, Morna D.: "Beyond the Things that are written? St. Paul's Use of Scripture", *NTS* 27(1981)295-309.

HOYLE, R. Birch: *The Holy Spirit in St. Paul*. London: Hodder and Stoughton, 1927.

IACOBITZ, Caroli: *Lucianus, Accedunt scholia auctiora et emendatiora, index et rerum et verborum*. Leipzig: Koehler, 1966(1841).

JASTROW, Marcus: *A Dictionary of the Talmud Babli and Yerushalmi, and the Midrashic Literature, Vol. I*. London: Luzac & Co. and New York: G.P. Putnam's Sons, 1903.

JEREMIAS, Joachim: art. πολλοί, *TDNT, Vol. VI*, 1968, pp.536-545.

— : art. λίθος, *TDNT, Vol. IV*, 1967, pp.268-280.

JERVELL, J.: "Das Volk des Geistes". In *God's Christ and His People. Studies in honour of Nils Alstrup Dahl*. Ed. J. Jervell and W.A. Meeks. Oslo: Universitetsforlaget, 1977, pp.87-106.

JONES, Peter Ronald: *The Apostle Paul: A Second Moses according to II Corinthians 2:14-4:7*. Unpublished Ph.D. diss. Princeton Theological Seminary, 1973.

— : "The Apostle Paul: Second Moses to the New Covenant Community, A Study in Pauline Apostolic Authority". In *God's Inerrant Word: An International Symposium on the Trustworthiness of Scripture*. Ed. J.W. Montgomery. Minneapolis: Bethany Fellowship, Inc. 1974, pp.219-241.

KAMLAH, E.: "Wie beurteilt Paulus sein Leiden?", *ZNW* 54(1963)217-232.

KASCH, W.: art. συνίστημι κ.τ.λ., *TDNT, Vol. VII*, 1971, pp.896-898.

KÄSEMANN, E.: "Amt und Gemeinde im Neuen Testament". In his *Exegetische Versuche und Besinnungen, Erster Band*. Göttingen: Vandenhoeck & Ruprecht, 1970[6], pp.109-134.

— : "Begründet der neutestamentliche Kanon die Einheit der Kirche?". In his *Exegetische Versuche und Besinnungen, Erster Band*, 1970[6], pp.214-223.

— : "Zum Thema der Nichtobjektivierbarkeit". In his *Exegetische Versuche und Besinnungen, Erster Band*, 1970[6], pp.224-236.

— : "Eine paulinische Variation des 'amor fati'". In his *Exegetische Versuche und Besinnungen, Zweiter Band*. Göttingen: Vandenhoeck & Ruprecht, 1970[3], pp.223-239.

— : "Geist und Buchstabe". In his *Paulinische Perspektiven*. Tübingen: J.C.B. Mohr (Paul Siebeck), 1972[2], pp.237-285.

— : "Die Heilsbedeutung des Todes Jesu bei Paulus". In his *Paulinische Perspektiven*, 1972[2], pp.61-107.

— : "Die Legitimität des Apostels. Eine Untersuchung zu II Korinther 10-13", *ZNW* 41(1942)33-71.

KENT, H.A. Jr.: "The Glory of the Christian Ministry. An Analysis of 2 Corinthians 2:14-4:18", *Grace Theological Journal* 2(1981)171-189.

KEYES, Clinton W.: "The Greek Letter of Introduction", *The American Journal of Philology* 56(1935)28-44.

KIM, Seyoon: *The Origin of Paul's Gospel*. Wissenschaftliche Untersuchungen zum Neuen Testament 2. Reihe, Bd. 4. Tübingen: J.C.B. Mohr (Paul Siebeck), 1981.

KLAIBER, Walter: *Rechtfertigung und Gemeinde. Eine Untersuchung zum paulinischen Kirchenverständnis*. Forschungen zur Religion und Literatur des Alten und Neuen Testaments 127. Göttingen: Vandenhoeck & Ruprecht, 1982.

KLEINKNECHT, Karl Theodor: *Der leidende Gerechtfertigte. Die alttestamentlich-jüdische Tradition vom 'leidenden Gerechten' und ihre Rezeption bei Paulus.* Wissenschaftliche Untersuchungen zum Neuen Testament, 2. Reihe 13. Tübingen: J.C.B. Mohr (Paul Siebeck), 1984.

KLINZING, Georg: *Die Umdeutung des Kultus in der Qumrangemeinde und im Neuen Testament.* Studien zur Umwelt des Neuen Testaments 7. Göttingen: Vandenhoeck & Ruprecht, 1971.

KREMER, Jacob: "'Denn der Buchstabe tötet, der Geist aber macht lebendig'. Methodologische und hermeneutische Erwägungen zu 2Kor 3:6b". In *Begegnung mit dem Wort. Festschrift für Heinrich Zimmermann.* Ed. J. Zmijewski and E. Nellessen. Bonner Biblische Beiträge 53. Bonn: Peter Hanstein Verlag, 1980, pp.219-250.

KÜMMEL, W.G.: *Introduction to the New Testament.* Nashville: Abingdon Press, 1975 (rev. ed.).

LADD, G.E.: *The Presence of the Future. The Eschatology of Biblical Realism.* Grand Rapids: Eerdmans, 1974.

LAMBRECHT, J.: "Structure and Line of Thought in 2 Cor 2:14-4:6", *Biblica* 64(1983) 344-380.

LANG, Friedrich: "Die Gruppen in Korinth nach 1. Korinther 1-4", *ThB* 14(1983)68-79.

LEMKE, Werner E.: "Jeremiah 31:31-34", *Interpretation* 37(1983)183-187.

LIDDELL, Henry George and Robert SCOTT: *A Greek-English Lexicon, with a Supplement.* Rev. and augmented by Henry Stuart Jones. Oxford: At the Clarendon Press, 1978 (1940[9]).

LIEBESCHUETZ, J.H.W.G.: *Antioch: City and Imperial Administration in the Later Roman Empire.* Oxford: At the Clarendon Press, 1972.

LIGHTFOOT, J.B.: *Saint Paul's Epistles to the Colossians and to Philemon.* London: MacMillan and Co., 1879[3].

— : *Saint Paul's Epistle to the Galatians.* London: MacMillan and Co., 1876[5].

LÜDEMANN, Gerd: *Paulus, der Heidenapostel. Bd. II: Antipaulinismus im frühen Christentum.* Forschungen zur Religion und Literatur des Alten und Neuen Testaments 130. Göttingen: Vandenhoeck & Ruprecht, 1983.

LUZ, Ulrich: "Theologia crucis als Mitte der Theologie im Neuen Testament", *EvTh* 34 (1974)116-141.

— : *Das Geschichtsverständnis des Apostels Paulus.* Beiträge zur evangelischen Theologie 49. München: Chr. Kaiser Verlag, 1968.

MACHALET, Christian: "Paulus und seine Gegner. Eine Untersuchung zu den Korintherbriefen". In *Theokratia. Jahrbuch des Institutum Judaicum Delitzschianum, II. Festgabe für Karl Heinrich Rengstorf zum 70. Geburtstag.* Ed. Wolfgang Dietrich, P. Freimark and H. Schreckenberg. Leiden: E.J. Brill. 1973, pp.183-203.

MACMULLEN, Ramsay: *Roman Social Relations 50 B.C. to A.D. 284.* New Haven/London: Yale University Press, 1974.

MALHERBE, Abraham J.: "Antisthenes and Odysseus, and Paul at War", *HTR* 76(1983)143-173.

MANSON, T.W. "2 Cor 2:14-17: Suggestions towards an Exegesis". In *Studia Paulina. In Honorem Johannis de Zwaan Septuagenarii.* Ed. J.N. Sevenster and W.C. van Unnik. Haarlem: De erven F. Bohn W.V., 1953, pp.155-162.

MARMORSTEIN, A: "The Holy Spirit in Rabbinic Legend". In *Studies in Jewish Theology, The Arthur Marmorstein Memorial Volume.* Ed. J. Rabbinowitz and M.S. Lew. London/New York/Toronto: Oxford University Press, 1950, pp.122-144.

MARSHALL, Peter: "A Metaphor of Social Shame: ΘΡΙΑΜΒΕΥΕΙΝ in 2 Cor 2:14", *NovT* 25 (1983)302-317.

MAURER, Ch: art. σκεῦος, *TDNT, Vol. VII*, 1971, pp.358-367.

MCDONALD, James I.H.: "Paul and the Preaching Ministry, A reconsideration of 2 Cor
2:14-17 in its context", *JSNT* 17(1983)35-50.

MCEVENUE, Sean E.: *The Narrative Style of the Priestly Writer*. Analecta Biblica 50.
Rome: Biblical Institute Press, 1971.

MEEKS, Wayne A.: *The First Urban Christians, The Social World of the Apostle Paul*.
New Haven/London: Yale University Press, 1983.

METZGER, Bruce: *A Textual Commentary on the Greek New Testament*. London/New York:
United Bible Societies, 1975 (corrected ed.).

MEYER, P.W.: "The Holy Spirit in the Pauline Letters. A Contextual Explanation",
Interpretation 33(1979)3-18.

MOORE, G.F.: "Conjectanea Talmudica: Notes on Rev. 13:18; Matt. 23:35f.; 28:1; 2 Cor
2:14-16; Jubilees 34:4,7; 7:4", *Journal of the American Oriental Society* 26(1905)
315-333.

MOULTON, J.H. and G. MILLIGAN: *The Vocabulary of the Greek New Testament Illustrated
from the Papyri and other non-literary sources*. London: Hodder and Stoughton,
1915-1929.

MOXNES, Halvor: *Theology in Conflict. Studies in Paul's Understanding of God in
Romans*. Supplements to Novum Testamentum, Vol. LIII. Leiden: E.J. Brill, 1980.

MUNCK, Johannes: *Paul and the Salvation of Mankind*. Atlanta: John Knox Press, 1977
(1959).

NESTLE, Wilhelm: *Platon. Ausgewählte Schriften IV: Protagoras*. Leipzig/Berlin: de
Gruyter, 1931[7].

NOCK, A.D.: *St. Paul*. London: Butterworth Ltd., 1938.

— : *Conversion. The Old and the New in Religion from Alexander the Great to Augustine
of Hippo*. Oxford: At the Clarendon Press, 1933.

OBRIEN, Peter Thomas: *Introductory Thanksgivings in the Letters of Paul*. Supplements
to Novum Testamentum, Vol. XLIX. Leiden: E.J. Brill, 1977.

O'COLLINS, Gerald G.: "Power Made Perfect in Weakness: 2 Cor 12:9-10", *CBQ* 33(1971)
528-537.

OEPKE, A.: art. κενός κ.τ.λ., *TDNT*, *Vol. III*, 1965, pp.659-662.

OOSTENDORP, Derk William: *Another Jesus. A Gospel of Jewish Christian Superiority in
II Corinthians*. Kampen: J.H. KOK N.V., 1967.

PARUNAK, H. Van Dyke. "Transitional Techniques in the Bible", *JBL* 102(1983)525-548.

PERLITT, Lothar: "Mose als Prophet", *EvTh* 31(1971)588-608.

PIPER, John: *'Love your enemies'. Jesus' love command in the synoptic gospels and in
the early Christian paraenesis. A history of the tradition and interpretation of
its uses*. SNTS Monograph Series 38. Cambridge: Cambridge University Press, 1979.

POPE, R. Martin: "Studies in Pauline Vocabulary: 1. of the Triumph-Joy", *ExpTimes*
(1909/1910)19-21.

PRICE, James L.: "Aspects of Paul's Theology and their Bearing on Literary Problems
of Second Corinthians". In *Studies in the History of the Text of the New Testament.
In Honor of Kenneth Willis Clark*. Ed. B.L. Daniels and M. Jack Suggs. Salt Lake
City: University of Utah Press, 1967, pp.95-106.

PROVENCE, Thomas E.: "'Who is Sufficient for these Things?' An Exegesis of 2 Corinthians 2:15-3:18", *NovT* 24(1982)54-81.

RÄISÄNEN, Heikki: *Paul and the Law*. Wissenschaftliche Untersuchungen zum Neuen Testament 29. Tübingen: J.C.B. Mohr (Paul Siebeck), 1983.

RENGSTORF, K.H.: *Apostolat und Predigtamt. Ein Beitrag zur neutestamentlichen Grund-
legung einer Lehre vom Amt der Kirche*. Stuttgart/Köln: Kohlhammer, 1954.

— : art. ἱκανός κ.τ.λ., *TDNT*, *Vol. III*, 1965, pp.293-296.

— : art. στέλλω κ.τ.λ., *TDNT*, *Vol. VII*, 1971, pp.594-595.

REUMANN, John: "Oikonomia = 'Covenant'; Terms for Heilsgeschichte in Early Christian Usage", *NovT* 3(1959)282-292.

—— : "Οἰκονομία-Terms in Paul in comparison with Lukan Heilsgeschichte", *NTS* 13 (1966/1967)147-167.

RICHARD, Earl: "Polemics, Old Testament, and Theology. A Study of II Cor. 3:1-4:6", *Revue Biblique* 88(1981)340-367.

RICHARDSON, P: "Spirit and Letter: A Foundation for Hermeneutics", *Evangelical Quarterly* 45(1973)208-218.

RIDDERBOS, Herman: *Paul, An Outline of His Theology*. Grand Rapids: Eerdmans, 1975.

RISSI, Mathias: *Studien zum zweiten Korintherbrief: Der alte Bund - Der Prediger - Der Tod*. Abhandlungen zur Theologie des Alten und Neuen Testaments 56. Zürich: Zwingli, 1969.

ROBERTSON, A.T.: *A Grammar of the Greek New Testament in the Light of Historical Research*. Nashville: Broadman Press, 1934.

ROBINSON, D.W.B.: "The Priesthood of Paul in the Gospel of Hope". In *Reconciliation and Hope. New Testament Essays on Atonement and Eschatology presented to L.L. Morris on his 60th Birthday*. Ed. Robert Banks. Grand Rapids: Eerdmans, 1974, pp. 231-245.

ROETZEL, Calvin J.: *Judgment in the Community. A Study of the Relationship between Eschatology and Ecclesiology in Paul*. Leiden: E.J. Brill, 1972.

RÖHRICH, L.: art. Himmelsbrief. In *Die Religion in Geschichte und Gegenwart: Handwörterbuch für Theologie und Religionswissenschaft, Bd. 3*. Ed. Kurt Galling et al. Tübingen: J.C.B. Mohr (Paul Siebeck), 1959, pp.338-339.

ROLOFF, Jürgen: *Apostolat - Verkündigung - Kirche. Ursprung, Inhalt und Funktion des kirchlichen Apostelamtes nach Paulus, Lukas und den Pastoralbriefen*. Gütersloh: Mohn, 1965.

ROSTOVTZEFF, M: *The Social and Economic History of the Hellenistic World, Vols. II and III*. Oxford: At the Clarendon Press, 1953(1941) and 1959(1941).

—— : *The Social and Economic History of the Roman Empire, Vol. I*. Second revised ed. by P.M. Fraser. Oxford: At the Clarendon Press, 1966.

SATAKE, Akira: "Apostolat und Gnade bei Paulus", *NTS* 15(1968)96-107.

SCHECHTER, Solomon: *Aspects of Rabbinic Theology*. New York: Schocken Books, 1961(1909).

SCHNACKENBURG, R.: "Apostles Before and During Paul's Time". In *Apostolic History and the Gospel. Biblical and Historical Essays presented to F.F. Bruce on his 60th Birthday*. Ed. W.W. Gasque and R.P. Martin. Grand Rapids: Eerdmans, 1970, pp.287-303.

SCHNELLE, Udo: *Gerechtigkeit und Christusgegenwart. Vorpaulinische und paulinische Tauftheologie*. Göttinger theologische Arbeiten 24. Göttingen: Vandenhoeck & Ruprecht, 1983.

SCHOEPS, H.J.: *Paul: The Theology of the Apostle in the Light of Jewish Religious History*. Philadelphia: Westminster Press, 1961.

SCHRAGE, Wolfgang: "Leid, Kreuz und Eschaton. Die Peristasenkataloge als Merkmale paulinischer theologia crucis und Eschatologie", *EvTh* 34(1974)141-175.

—— : *Ethik des Neuen Testaments*. Grundrisse zum NT. Das Neue Testament Deutsch Ergänzungsreihe, Bd. 4. Göttingen: Vandenhoeck & Ruprecht, 1982.

SCHRENK, G.: art. γράφω κ.τ.λ., *TDNT, Vol. I*, 1964, pp.742-773.

SCHÜRMANN, Heinz: "Die Apostolische Existenz im Bilde, Meditation über 2 Kor 2:14-16a". In *Ursprung und Gestalt, Erörterungen und Besinnungen zum Neuen Testament*. Kommentare und Beiträge zum Alten und Neuen Testament. Düsseldorf: Patmos-Verlag, 1970, pp.229-235.

SCHÜTZ, John Howard: *Paul and the Anatomy of Apostolic Authority*. SNTS Monograph Series 26. Cambridge: Cambridge University Press, 1975.

SCHWEITZER, E.: et al. art. σάρξ κ.τ.λ., *TDNT, Vol. VII*, 1971, pp.98-151.

SOKOLOWSKI, Emil: *Die Begriffe Geist und Leben bei Paulus in ihren Beziehungen zu einander. Eine exegetisch-religionsgeschichtliche Untersuchung*. Göttingen: Vandenhoeck & Ruprecht, 1903.

STALDER, Kurt: *Das Werk des Geistes in der Heiligung bei Paulus*. Zürich: EVZ-Verlag, 1962.

STENDAHL, Krister: "Call Rather than Conversion". In his *Paul among Jews and Gentiles and Other Essays*. Philadelphia: Fortress Press, 1976, pp.7-23.

STOWERS, Stanley Kent: *The Diatribe and Paul's Letter to the Romans*. SBL Dissertation Series 57. Chico, CA: Scholars Press, 1981.

— : "Social Status, Public Speaking and Private Teaching: The Circumstances of Paul's Preaching Activity", *NovT* 26(1984)59-82.

STRACK, Hermann and Paul BILLERBECK: *Kommentar zum Neuen Testament aus Talmud und Midrasch. Bd. I und III*. München: C.H. Beck'sche Verlagsbuchhandlung, 1956² and 1926.

STUHLMACHER, Peter: "Erwägungen zum ontologischen Charakter der καινὴ κτίσις bei Paulus", *EvTh* 27(1967)1-35.

— : "'Das Ende des Gesetzes'. Über Ursprung und Ansatz der paulinischen Theologie", *ZThK* 67(1970)14-39 (now in his *Versöhnung, Gesetz und Gerechtigkeit. Aufsätze zur biblischen Theologie*. Göttingen: Vandenhoeck & Ruprecht, 1981, pp.166-191).

— : "Achtzehn Thesen zur paulinischen Kreuzestheologie". In *Rechtfertigung, Festschrift für Ernst Käsemann zum 70. Geburtstag*. Ed. J. Friedrich, W. Pöhlmann and P. Stuhlmacher. Tübingen: J.C.B. Mohr (Paul Siebeck), 1976, pp.509-525 (= *Versöhnung*, pp.192-208).

— : "Theologische Probleme des Römerbriefpräskripts", *EvTh* 27(1967)374-389.

— : *Das paulinische Evangelium. I. Vorgeschichte*. Forschungen zur Religion und Literatur des Alten und Neuen Testaments 95. Göttingen: Vandenhoeck & Ruprecht, 1968.

— : "Das paulinische Evangelium". In *Das Evangelium und die Evangelien. Vorträge vom Tübinger Symposium 1982*. Ed. P. Stuhlmacher. Wissenschaftliche Untersuchungen zum Neuen Testament 28. Tübingen: J.C.B. Mohr (Paul Siebeck), 1983, pp.157-182.

STUMPFF, Albrecht: art. εὐωδία, *TDNT, Vol. II*, 1964, pp.808-810.

TANNEHILL, Robert C.: *Dying and Rising with Christ. A Study in Pauline Theology*. Beiheft zur Zeitschrift für die neutestamentliche Wissenschaft und die Kunde der älteren Kirche 32. Berlin: Töpelmann, 1967.

THEISSEN, Gerd: "Legitimation und Lebensunterhalt. Ein Beitrag zur Soziologie urchristlicher Missionare". In his *Studien zur Soziologie des Urchristentums*. Wissenschaftliche Untersuchungen zum Neuen Testament 19. Tübingen, J.C.B. Mohr (Paul Siebeck), 1979, pp.201-230.

— : "Die Starken und Schwachen in Korinth. Soziologische Analyse eines theologischen Streites". In his *Studien zur Soziologie des Urchristentums*, 1979, pp.272-289.

— : "Soziale Schichtung in der korinthischen Gemeinde. Ein Beitrag zur Soziologie des hellenistischen Urchristentums". In his *Studien zur Soziologie des Urchristentums*, 1979, pp.231-271.

— : *Psychologische Aspekte paulinischer Theologie*. Forschungen zur Religion und Literatur des Alten und Neuen Testaments 131. Göttingen: Vandenhoeck & Ruprecht, 1983.

THRALL, Margaret E.: "Super-Apostles, Servants of Christ, and Servants of Satan", *JSNT* 6(1980)42-57.

— : "A Second Thanksgiving Period in II Corinthians", *JSNT* 16(1982)101-124.

TRENCH, R.CH.: *Synonyma des Neuen Testaments*. Tübingen: J.C.B. Mohr (Paul Siebeck), 1907.

art. "TRIUMPH". In *The Oxford Classical Dictionary*. Ed. N.G.C. Hammond and H.H. Scullard. London: Oxford University Press, 1970², p.1095.

art. "TRIUMPHUS", by W. Ehlers. In *Paulys Real-Encyclopädie der Classischen Altertums-wissenschaft, II. Reihe, Bd. 7,1.* Ed. G. Wissowa, W. Kroll and K. Mittelhaus. Stuttgart: J.B. Metzlersche Verlagsbuchhandlung, 1939, pp.493-511.

VERSNEL, Hendrik Simon: *Triumphus. An Inquiry into the Origin, Development and Meaning of the Roman Triumph.* Leiden: E.J. Brill, 1970.

VIELHAUER, Philipp: "Paulus und die Kephaspartei in Korinth". In *Oikodome, Aufsätze zum Neuen Testament, Bd. 2.* Ed. Günter Klein. Theologische Bücherei 65. München: Kaiser, 1979, pp.169-182.

VOS, Johannes Sijko: *Traditionsgeschichtliche Untersuchungen zur Paulinischen Pneumatologie.* Van Gorcum's Theologische Bibliotheek, Nr. 47. Assen: Van Gorcum, 1973.

WALLISCH, E.: "Name und Herkunft des römischen Triumphes", *Philologus* 99(1954/1955) 245-258.

WEBSTER'S Seventh New Collegiate Dictionary. Springfield: G. & C. Merriam Co., 1972.

WEISS, Konrad: "Paulus - Priester der christlichen Kultgemeinde", *THLZ* 79(1954)355-364.

WENSCHKEWITZ, Hans: "Die Spiritualisierung der Kultusbegriffe Tempel, Priester und Opfer im Neuen Testament", ΑΓΓΕΛΟΣ, Archiv für neutestamentliche Zeitgeschichte und Kulturkunde 4(1932)70-230.

WETTSTEIN, Jacobus J.: *Novum Testamentum Graecum, Tomus II.* Graz, Austria: Akademische Druck und Verlagsanstalt, 1962(1752).

WILCKENS, U.: "Die Bekehrung des Paulus als religionsgeschichtliches Problem", *ZThK* 56(1959)273-293.

— : *Der Brief an die Römer. 3. Teilband Röm 12-16.* Evangelisch-katholischer Kommentar zum Neuen Testament. Zürich/Neukirchen-Vluyn: Benziger/Neukirchener Verlag, 1982.

WILLIAMSON, Lamar Jr.: "Led in Triumph, Paul's Use of Triambeuō", *Interpretation* 22(1968)317-332.

WINDISCH, Hans: art. καπηλεύω. In *Theologisches Wörterbuch zum Neuen Testament, Bd. 3.* Ed. G. Kittel. Stuttgart: Kohlhammer, 1938, pp.606-609.

WOLFF, Christian: *Jeremia im Frühjudentum und Urchristentum.* Texte und Untersuchungen zur Geschichte der altchristlichen Literatur 118. Leipzig: Hinrich, 1976.

— : *Der erste Brief des Paulus an die Korinther, Zweiter Teil: Auslegung der Kapitel 8-16.* Theologischer Handkommentar zum Neuen Testament 7/II. Berlin: Evangelische Verlagsanstalt, 1982.

WOLFF, Hans Walter: *Anthropology of the Old Testament.* Philadelphia: Fortress Press, 1974.

ZAHN, Theodor: *Introduction to the New Testament, Vol. 1.* Minneapolis: Klock & Klock Christian Publishers, 1977(1909).

ZERWICK, Maximilian: *Biblical Greek Illustrated with Examples.* Scripta Pontificii Instituti Biblici, Nr. 114. Rome: Pontificial Biblical Institute, 1977(1963).

ZIMMERLI, Walther: *Ezechiel, 1. and 2. Teilband.* Biblischer Kommentar: Altes Testament, Bde. XIII/1,2. Neukirchen-Vluyn: Neukirchner Verlag, 1979[2] and 1969.

ZMIJEWSKI, Josef: *Der Stil der paulinischen 'Narrenrede'. Analyse der Sprachgestaltung in 2 Kor 11:1-12:10 als Beitrag zur Methodik von Stiluntersuchungen neutestament-licher Texte.* Bonner Biblische Beiträge 52. Köln/Bonn: Peter Hanstein Verlag, 1978.

(IV Ezra)

7:72	213
8:6f.	213
9:29-37	213
14:22-26	210
14:23	211
14:24	210

Jubilees

1:1	208
1:5-7	209
1:7	213
1:9f.	209
1:10	213
1:14	209
1:21-23	213
1:26f.	208
2:1	208
3:10	208
3:31	208
4:5	208
4:32	208
5:13f.	209
6:11f.	208
6:17	208
6:22	208f.
6:23	209
6:34-38	209
15:25f.	209
15:33f.	213
16:3	208
16:9	208
16:29-31	209
16:30	209
18:19	208
19:9	208
23:32	208
24:33	208
28:6	208
30:9	208
30:20	209
31:32	208
32:10f.	209
32:15	209
32:21f.	209
33:10	208
33:15-18	209
34:4	46
34:7	46
49:8	209
50:13	209

Liber Antiquitatum Biblicarum (Ps-Philo)

26:12-13	210
30:6	213

Life of Adam and Eve

29:8f.	213

Lives of the Prophets

Jer.9	210
Jer.11	210
Jer.12	210
Jer.14	210

III Maccabees

4:9	138
5:6	138

Odes of Solomon

4:3	213
26:10	170

Sibylline Oracles

III,703	213
III,719	213

Testament of Job

48:2	213
48:4	213
49:1	213
50:1	213

Testaments of the Twelve Patriarchs

T.Benj. 6	167,172
T.Judah 24:2f.	213
T. Levi 5:4	210
T. Levi 7:5	210
T. Levi 18:10f.	213
T. Reub. 5f.	168

IV. NEW TESTAMENT

Matthew

7:13	106
10:20par.	170
12:33par.	168
17:22	72
18:7	138
20:18	72
23:35f.	46
24:12	158
28:1	46

Mark

7:18-23par.	168
9:26	158
9:31	72
10:26	90,98
10:33	72
14:12	52

INDEX OF SUBJECTS

In compiling this index, only subjects which do not appear explicitly in the
table of contents have been listed. References to page numbers include the
footnotes on that page.

Wissenschaftliche Untersuchungen zum Neuen Testament

Begründet von Joachim Jeremias und Otto Michel

Herausgegeben von
Martin Hengel und Otfried Hofius

22
Otto Bauernfeind
*Kommentar und Studien zur
Apostelgeschichte*
1980. XVIII, 492 Seiten. Ln.

21
August Strobel
Die Stunde der Wahrheit
1980. VII, 150 Seiten. Br.

20
Drei hellenistisch-jüdische Predigten
Erl. von F. Siegert
1980. 109 Seiten. Br.

19
Gerd Theißen
*Studien zur Soziologie des
Urchristentums*
2. Aufl. 1983. VI, 364 Seiten. Br. Ln.

18
E. Earle Ellis
*Prophecy and Hermeneutic in Early
Christianity*
1978. XVII, 289 Seiten. Ln.

16
Karlmann Beyschlag
Simon Magus und die christliche Gnosis
1974. VII, 249 Seiten. Ln.

15
Andreas Nissen
*Gott und der Nächste im antiken
Judentum*
1974. IX, 587 Seiten. Ln.

14
Otfried Hofius
Der Vorhang vor dem Thron Gottes
1972. VIII, 122 Seiten. Br.

13
Helmut Merkel
*Die Widersprüche zwischen den
Evangelien*
1971. VI, 295 Seiten. Br. Ln.

12
Gerhard Maier
Mensch und freier Wille
1971. VII, 426 Seiten. Br. Ln.

11
Otfried Hofius
Katapausis
1970. IX, 281 Seiten. Br. Ln.

10
Martin Hengel
Judentum und Hellenismus
2. Aufl. 1973. XI, 693 Seiten. Ln.

8
Christoph Burchard
Untersuchungen zu Joseph und Aseneth
1965. VIII, 180 Seiten. Br. Ln.

7
Ehrhard Kamlah
*Die Form der katalogischen Paränese
im Neuen Testament*
1964. VIII, 245 Seiten. Br. Ln.

5
Friedrich Rehkopf
Die lukanische Sonderquelle
1959. VIII, 106 Seiten. Br.

1
Karl G. Kuhn
*Achtzehngebet und Vaterunser und
der Reim*
1950. III, 51 Seiten. Br.

2. Reihe

17
Gottfried Schimanowski
Weisheit und Messias
1985. XII, 410 Seiten. Br.

16
Eckhard J. Schnabel
Law and Wisdom from Ben Sira to Paul
1985. XVI, 428 Seiten. Br.

15
Terence V. Smith
Petrine Controversies in Early Christianity
1985. X, 249 Seiten. Br.

14
Uwe Wegner
Der Hauptmann von Kafarnaum
1985. VIII, 522 Seiten. Br.

13
Karl Th. Kleinknecht
Der leidende Gerechtfertigte
1984. X, 422 Seiten. Br.

12
Alfred F. Zimmermann
Die urchristlichen Lehrer
1984. IX, 258 Seiten. Br.

11
Marius Reiser
Syntax und Stil des Markusevangeliums
1984. XIV, 219 Seiten. Br.

10
Hans-Joachim Eckstein
Der Begriff Syneidesis bei Paulus
1983. VII, 340 Seiten. Br.

9
Roman Heiligenthal
Werke als Zeichen
1983. XIV, 374 Seiten. Br.

8
Berthold Mengel
Studien zum Philipperbrief
1982. X, 343 Seiten. Br.

7
Rainer Riesner
Jesus als Lehrer
2. Aufl. 1984. XII, 615 Seiten. Br.

6
Helge Stadelmann
Ben Sira als Schriftgelehrter
1980. XIV, 346 Seiten. Br.

5
Dieter Sänger
Antikes Judentum und die Mysterien.
1980. VIII, 274 Seiten. Br.

4
Seyoon Kim
The Origin of Paul's Gospel
2nd ed. 1984. XII, 413 Seiten. Br.

3
Paul Garnet
Salvation and Atonement in the Qumran Scrolls
1977. VIII, 152 Seiten. Br.

2
Jan A. Bühner
Der Gesandte und sein Weg im 4. Evangelium
1977. VIII, 486 Seiten. Br.

1
Mark L. Appold
The Oneness Motif in the Fourth Gospel
1976. IX, 313 Seiten. Br.

J.C.B. Mohr (Paul Siebeck)
Tübingen